REILLY Robin
Josiah Wedgwood
1730-1795

B/WED/738.3.092/WED

Please renew/return this item by the last date shown.

So that your telephone call is charged at local rate,
please call the numbers as set out below:

	From Area codes 01923 or 0208:	From the rest of Herts:
Renewals:	01923 471373	01438 737373
Enquiries:	01923 471333	01438 737333
Minicom:	01923 471599	01438 737599

L32b

9 JAN 2001

31 JAN 2002

−2 NOV 2001

−5 MAY 2007

27 NOV 2001   30-5-07

21 DEC 2001

12 JAN 2002   −8 OCT 2008

31 AUG 2010   7/12

L33

JOSIAH WEDGWOOD

BOOKS BY THE SAME AUTHOR

HISTORY AND BIOGRAPHY
The Rest to Fortune: The Life of Major-General James Wolfe
The Sixth Floor
The British at the Gates: the New Orleans Campaign in the 1812 War
William Pitt the Younger

ART AND CERAMICS
British Watercolours
Wedgwood (2 volumes)
Wedgwood Jasper
Wedgwood Portrait Medallions: An Introduction
The Collector's Wedgwood

WITH GEORGE SAVAGE
Wedgwood: The Portrait Medallions
The Dictionary of Wedgwood

ROBIN REILLY

JOSIAH WEDGWOOD 1730–1795

M

MACMILLAN

LONDON

First published 1992 by Macmillan London Limited

a division of Pan Macmillan Publishers Limited
Cavaye Place London SW10 9PG
and Basingstoke

Associated companies throughout the world

ISBN 0–333–51041–0

1 3 5 7 9 8 6 4 2

A CIP catalogue record for this book is available from
the British Library

Phototypeset by Intype, London
Printed and bound in Great Britain by
Mackays of Chatham PLC, Chatham, Kent

Be it so, my dear friend, even so be it, let us begin, proceed, & finish our future schemes, our days & years, in the pursuit of *Fortune, Fame* & the *Public good*.

JOSIAH WEDGWOOD TO THOMAS BENTLEY
1 October 1769

The decline & weakness's of old age afford but a melancholly prospect, since it is, & will be so, let us, my dear friend enjoy, & diffuse among our friends every real happiness within our reach & not torment ourselves with needless anxieties, nor waste an hour of the very small portion of time alotted to us here.

JOSIAH WEDGWOOD TO THOMAS BENTLEY
Easter Sunday 1778

CONTENTS

INTRODUCTION

More has been written about Wedgwood than about any other pottery or porcelain factory. Great collections have been formed, particularly in the United States of America, societies have been founded to study the subject, and collectors' clubs devoted to the acquisition of old and modern Wedgwood have sprung up all over the world. It is the more remarkable that, amidst all this enthusiasm for the wares, so much less attention has been paid to the man who invented or developed them and laid the foundations of the firm which still produces them.

In October 1862, Godfrey Wedgwood wrote to Eliza Meteyard in response to her enquiry: 'I am fully satisfied that there are not materials for a really satisfactory life of my great-grandfather. I am sorry that such a man should have left so little to chronicle behind him. He appears to have been a man of deeds having little time to leave any memorandum of them.' It is probable that Godfrey suspected his great-grandfather of semi-literacy, and he was evidently unaware of the startling discovery, by Joseph Mayer of Liverpool some eleven years earlier, of a huge quantity of Wedgwood manuscript material. This find, which included most of Josiah Wedgwood's letters to his partner Thomas Bentley, reveals Josiah Wedgwood not only as a fluent, candid and lively correspondent, a tireless inventor, a surprisingly capable chemist and an industrial manager greatly in advance of his time, but also as a radical thinker who was as much a product of the Enlightenment as of the prolonged period of invention and development loosely described as the Industrial Revolution.

Miss Meteyard gained access to this great hoard and set about the task of writing a biography of Josiah Wedgwood that would also encompass a definitive description of his work as a potter. Her labour was enormous and her achievement astonishing, and she laid the foundations for all later studies of Wedgwood. Her biography was published in two volumes in 1865–6 and was followed almost immediately by a less ambitious one by the ceramic historian Llewellyn Jewitt. Samuel Smiles, who had included a brief narrative of Josiah's exemplary career in *Self-Help*, produced a short biography in 1895, following an even shorter one by Sir Arthur Church the previous year. The ceramic chemist William Burton wrote an account of the Wedgwood wares with some biographical material, misleadingly titled *Josiah Wedgwood and his Pottery*, in 1922. Julia Wedgwood's *The Personal Life of Josiah Wedgwood*, published in 1915, came closer to providing a human portrait than any earlier work. Only one biography of Josiah Wedgwood has been published in the later twentieth century: a slim volume, even slimmer in primary-source research, repeating old errors without adding anything material to modern knowledge of the subject. Lady Farrer's three volumes of Josiah Wedgwood's letters (1903 and 1906) are unfortunately too incomplete, and too erratic and personal in the editing, to provide a satisfactory basis for a biography.

The only academic historian to study Wedgwood's work in recent years, Dr Neil McKendrick, has concentrated on Josiah's business methods and factory management. His carefully researched articles, however, lack evidence of a knowledge and understanding of pottery history and techniques. His 'major life' of Josiah Wedgwood, announced as 'virtually complete' in 1978 and formally announced again in 1982 under the title *Josiah Wedgwood and the Industrial Revolution*, effectively denied the field to other biographers for more than a decade but remains unpublished.

Miss Meteyard's biography suffers from two serious defects: she was neither an experienced historian nor a ceramist; and she was, or became, so deeply admiring of her subject that she was unwilling to use any material that showed him as less than perfect by the exacting Victorian standards of public virtue. Her research was painstaking and thorough, and her contribution to the understanding of Wedgwood's early wares unrivalled for more than a century, but her portrait of Josiah Wedgwood is hagiographic and anaemic.

Josiah Wedgwood was neither saintly nor bloodless. Apart from his importance as one of the leading industrial figures of his period, and his activities in connection with contemporary politics and movements for reform, the construction of trunk roads and canals and patronage of the arts, there is much of human interest in his character: his physical courage; his perseverance in the face of apparently insurmountable difficulties; his warmth and loyalty in friendship; his dry wit and occasionally bawdy humour. There is much to be understood in his hypochondria, his ruthlessness and the consuming energy that allowed him so little respite. No rounded portrait, taking account of his frailties and acknowledging his fallibility, has ever been published.

When Josiah Wedgwood died in 1795, his name was as familiar in the courts of Europe and Scandinavia as those of Meissen and Sèvres, his Queen's ware had been in use at the Russian court for a quarter of a century, and vases presented by Lord Macartney to the Chinese Emperor Ch'ien Lung had been so greatly admired that they had been copied in porcelain at the Imperial factory. No single pottery has been so influential as Wedgwood's, and this influence was achieved without any of the massive subsidies given to Continental porcelain factories.

It was not only in the manufacture of ceramics that Wedgwood was an innovator. His letters, and particularly those written almost daily to Bentley during the period of their partnership, provide the most complete and illuminating history of industrial and business management to have survived from the eighteenth century. They record Wedgwood's introduction of cost accounting, among the first in any industry; his opening of a London warehouse and showrooms and his attention to display; his marketing methods, experimental employment of travelling salesmen and daring investment in the development of export business; the exploitation of patronage and the use of advertising; the study of taste and fashion; the forging of the first successful links between art and industry by the commissioning of painters and sculptors to create designs and models for reproduction; the design and organisation of his factory, his management of industrial relations and his care for his workers. The letters, which number more than 2000, are a crucial primary source for the industrial history of Britain.

The use of the convenient but imprecise label 'Industrial Revolution' to describe this period is no longer acceptable among historians, but there is a strong case for arguing that the inventions and developments in English pottery techniques, style and quality between 1730 and 1775 were revolutionary in their impact, not only because they made industrial mass production attainable but also because they altered the household furnishings, and thus the living standards, of much of the Western world. Wedgwood played an essential part in the creation of the 'consumer society' as he did also in laying the foundations for 'industrial design'. Although neither term would have been known to him, both would have been comprehensible.

His reputation as the man who 'converted a rude and inconsiderable Manufactory into an elegant Art' has had the dual effect of encouraging approving biographers to attribute even more to him than is his due and of obscuring his significance in the wider context of the birth and development of industry in Britain. More critical writers have blamed him for the debasement of a craft into a manufacturing industry.

This book is an attempt objectively to reassess Josiah Wedgwood's character and his achievements, and to construct a fair portrait from verifiable evidence. Nothing so truthfully illustrates a man's character as his own writings, especially when he has no thought that they may ever be published, and I make no apology for the length or frequency of the quotations from Josiah's letters and memoranda. Original orthography and punctuation have been retained, except for super-scribed abbreviations which have been expanded. I have relied largely upon the Wedgwood manuscript archives, desposited at Keele University and still in the process of being professionally catalogued. These archives comprise some 75,000 items and only a tiny fraction of them has ever been published. My thanks are due to the Trustees of the Wedgwood Museum for allowing me unrestricted access to this enormous accumulation of manuscripts over a period of nearly thirty years and for permission to quote extensively from it.

Permission to reproduce paintings and engravings, or to use copyright photographs, was kindly granted by Mrs R. D. Chellis, the Trustees of the British Museum, the Iveagh Bequest, Manchester City Art Gallery, Manchester Museum, the National Portrait Gallery, the Science Museum, London, the City Museum and Art Gallery, Stoke-on-Trent, and the Trustees of the Wedgwood Museum.

Last, I offer my grateful thanks to the many friends who have contributed to this book by generous cooperation, patient discussion and constructive advice: in particular Gaye Blake-Roberts, FMA, Curator of the Wedgwood Museum; Dr Ian Fraser, Christine Fyfe and Martin Phillips, successively archivists at Keele University; Mr and Mrs Frederick de Costobadie; Dr David Williams; and the late George Savage.

Robin Reilly
Somerset, 1991

CHAPTER ONE

An Uncertain
Start in Life

In 1802, a marble tablet was erected in the parish church of Stoke-on-Trent. It commemorated, some seven years after his death, the life of Josiah Wedgwood, the greatest manufacturing potter in ceramic history. It was commissioned and installed by Josiah's sons and is the work of a close friend of Wedgwood's, the celebrated neoclassical sculptor, John Flaxman; and yet it is chiefly remarkable for the fact that it bears the wrong date of Josiah's birth. The simple inscription 'August 1730' suggests that present-day ignorance of the details of his early life was shared by his family.

The Parish Register of St John's Church, Burslem, in Staffordshire, records the baptism of Josiah Wedgwood, son of Thomas Wedgwood and his wife Mary of the Churchyard Pottery, on 12 July 1730, and the same date was later noted by Tom Byerley, his nephew and partner, as the date of Josiah's birth.[1] In the eighteenth century, newly born babies had a precarious grasp on life and it was common practice to have them baptised without unnecessary delay, but such a precipitate rush to Christianity was reserved for infants who were not expected to live more than a few hours. It may be inferred, then, that Josiah was a sickly baby, and the loss in infancy or early childhood of four older brothers and sisters would not have encouraged expectations of his survival.

Josiah was the thirteenth[2] and youngest child in a Staffordshire family whose ancestry may be traced back to the fourteenth century. His great-great-grandfather, Gilbert Wedgwood, worked a small pottery in Burslem towards the end of the seventeenth century. Gilbert's second son, Thomas, successively worked four potteries, two of which he inherited from his mother's family. One, which he built for himself, is believed to have been the Churchyard Works inherited in turn by Josiah's grandfather and father, both of whom were named Thomas.

1

No evidence has been preserved of anything that they made and it may be assumed that what they produced was little different from the work of any other small potwork of the period: simple domestic earthenware objects made from local red or brown clays. It is likely, though not certain, that the Churchyard Wedgwoods augmented their small income from pottery by farming a smallholding on the same land.

Although they could not be considered as prosperous or even well-to-do, it is clear that the Wedgwoods were not uncomfortably poor. Gilbert's wife had been the heiress Margaret Burslem, and one of his grandsons had inherited the estate of William Colclough, who had married Margaret's sister. This substantial property, which included the Overhouse pottery and about 120 acres of land, appears to have been kept intact through succeeding generations, leaving little for any but the eldest son, but even Josiah's father, the third Thomas Wedgwood of the Churchyard Works, nevertheless thought himself of sufficient substance to buy for his family a pew in the parish church for the considerable price of £7.[3] At about the same period, the cost of wheat was 4s. a bushel, a calf could be bought for between 6 and 9s. and beef cost 1d. or 2d. a pound.[4]

Scarcely anything is known of Josiah Wedgwood's childhood and there is no primary evidence to sustain any of the imaginative accounts given in his biographies. In the absence of contemporary testimony,[5] we are obliged to rely on three secondary sources, each early enough for its author to be able to claim information acquired at one remove. The first is an account by Simeon Shaw of the history of the North Staffordshire potteries, published in 1823. It was for many years considered too inaccurate to merit serious consideration, but modern research has shown an unexpectedly large proportion of it to be factual. Shaw undoubtedly knew a number of Staffordshire people, including Enoch Wood, who had either met or been employed by Wedgwood, but he has little to say about Josiah's childhood.

Josiah's earliest biographers, Eliza Meteyard and Llewellyn Jewitt, were writing more than sixty years after his death. By then all his children had died and there were no grandchildren who remembered him. There were, however, still living in Staffordshire, the children and grandchildren of local people who had known and worked with him, and their recollections, however unreliable, should not be ignored.

In spite of the social pretensions indicated by his purchase of a pew, Josiah Wedgwood's father seems not to have been especially gifted or successful as a potter. He died in June 1739 at the age of fifty-two, having made no reputation and leaving little enough to maintain his large family. After provision for his widow, the greatest part of his estate, including the potworks, was left to his eldest son, also Thomas, with instructions to care for the younger children and pay to each of his brothers and sisters, with the single exception of Anne, the sum of £20 on reaching the age of twenty. It seems likely that Anne, the eldest daughter, had already received her share of the inheritance as a dowry when she married Philip Clarke. At least two of these legacies appear to have been ignored until they were paid by Josiah in 1776, three years after his brother Thomas's death.[6]

Josiah's mother was the daughter of the Unitarian minister at Newcastle-under-Lyme and she brought up her children in the same faith. They lived at first in a small pottery, probably rented, in Burslem, but moved in 1717 to the thatched Churchyard house and pottery after the death of the elder Thomas Wedgwood. His widow died two years later and in the same year Thomas and Mary lost their fourth child in infancy. Their second had already died at the age of two. During the following ten years, Mary Wedgwood bore eight more children, of whom two died in early childhood. The Wedgwood household, like all others of the period, rich and poor, was accustomed to grief.

The young Josiah had his first experience of bereavement shortly before his ninth birthday, when his father died. By then he had started school, walking the 7-mile round journey to and from a small establishment in the market-place of Newcastle-under-Lyme kept by one John or Thomas Blunt and his wife.[7] There he is said to have learned the rudiments of reading, writing and arithmetic before the death of his father and the straitened circumstances of his family required his removal to work in the family pottery then inherited by his brother.

This story, first published by Miss Meteyard and uncritically repeated by every subsequent biographer, is not supported by the testimony of Josiah's writings later in life. The earliest surviving evidence of his employment is in his formal Indenture of Apprenticeship which bound him to his brother for a period of five years from 11 November* 1744. By the terms of this document Josiah undertook not to 'imbezil or waste' or lend his master's goods. Other conditions were even more stringent: 'at Cards Dice or any other unlawful Gamees he shall not Play, Taverns or Ale Houses he shall not haunt or frequent, Fornication he shall not Commit – Matrimony he shall not Contract.' For any boy in his fifteenth year, it was going to be a long five years.

In return, Thomas contracted to 'learn his Apprentice the said Art of Throwing and Handleing' and to allow him 'Meat drink Washing

---

*Martinmas or Martlemas, the feast of St Martin of Tours and a traditional hiring date.

and lodging and Apparell of all kinds both linen and Woollen and all other Necessaries both in Sickness and in Health'. The particular significance of this part of the contract lies in the inclusion of the 'Art of Throwing'. In England, the system of formal apprenticeship had declined steadily from the end of the seventeenth century until, by about 1740, such undertakings had become exceptional. Only twenty-nine apprentices were registered in the potteries between 1710 and 1760, and, of the twenty-eight that have been traced, nine – including Josiah Wedgwood, Josiah Spode, John Turner and Enoch Booth – became master potters.[8] The difficult art of throwing on the wheel was the most highly rated of all the potter's skills and only those who were expected to become master craftsmen served such an apprenticeship.

The specific inclusion of throwing in Josiah Wedgwood's indenture has a second significance. It has been firmly established by earlier biographers that he suffered, at about the age of eleven or twelve, a virulent attack of smallpox which left his right knee so weak that he was temporarily obliged to use crutches and never recovered the full use of it. Meteyard, indeed, gives a detailed, moving but transparently invented account of the disease sweeping through the family: 'all lay very ill, Josiah more than the rest, as the small-pox took him in a confluent form, covering him from head to foot'. She adds: 'It has been stated that the effects of the small-pox were neglected, but of this there is no evidence.'[9] In fact there is no evidence for any of it, although some confirmation of the story may be found in the portrait of Josiah modelled by William Hackwood in 1782, which faithfully records the scars of smallpox, commonly seen among all ranks of the population at that period but seldom visible in contemporary portraits, and in the well-documented difficulties that Josiah later experienced with his right leg until it was amputated above the knee.

The potter's throwing-wheel required the use of one foot to provide the motive power to the 'kick-wheel' while the other provided purchase. This would not have been possible with severely restricted flexion, as the result of a weakened knee, and on a later occasion, when Josiah chose to throw some important commemorative vases, the wheel was turned by his partner. No such help would have been available to a young apprentice and it is therefore almost inconceivable that the 'Art of Throwing' should have been included in the indenture of one who was so handicapped. The conclusion must be that the smallpox attack occurred some time after the indenture was signed, probably around 1745–6.

There is some slight evidence of Josiah's early training as a thrower. Enoch Wood, himself a respected pottery manufacturer, whose elder brother William worked for Josiah Wedgwood for forty-one years, wrote in 1809: 'Fletcher says he used to work at the Churchyard Works and made balls of clay for two of the throwers at the same time – viz. Richard Wedgwood and Josiah Wedgwood.'[10] Although there is no surviving evidence to show that Richard was formally apprenticed to his eldest brother, there is no sound reason to reject this story and it is unfortunate that no date is attached to it.

The tradition that Josiah was removed from Mr Blunt's school at the age of nine to work for his brother is less easily accepted. Unless he was still at school or too ill to work, it is not obvious why his apprenticeship should have been delayed until he was well into his fifteenth year. Nor is it clear, if his formal education lasted for only two years, how or when he acquired either the basic skills in arithmetic, the ability to write fluent and legible English or his capacity, through reading, to broaden his education into literature, art and chemistry. Such achievements require some firmer foundation than two years at a local school, completed at the age of nine.

Whatever the truth, it is plain that Josiah was able to acquire considerable skill as a thrower before he became too lame to work the wheel, and his disability may even have accounted, in some measure, for his remarkable versatility as a potter. As he was later to prove, few tasks were performed by craftsmen in his factories which he was not able to carry out himself, often rather better than those he employed. His inability to take part in more strenuous activities may also have encouraged his interest in further learning.

He grew up in a country at war with Spain for trade in the New World, and later involved in the rush for possession of the Hapsburg dominions following the death of the Emperor Charles VI, but the population in general was little affected by foreign policy or military engagements. Recruitment to the army was by voluntary enlistment and conditions were such that none who could earn a living in any other way was likely to join, which is why it is all the more surprising to learn that Josiah's brother Richard left the pottery business to become a soldier. In Staffordshire, the young Josiah Wedgwood certainly saw pottery commemorating the brilliant capture of Portobello by Captain Edward Vernon in 1740, some of it perhaps at the factory belonging to his kinsmen, John and Thomas Wedgwood of the Big House, Burslem, and this early lesson in the exploitation of public events and popular heroes was not forgotten. The disaster of the Cartagena expedition the following year made no such impression, although the name of the British commander, Lord Cathcart, was later to be familiar to Wedgwood.

Troops were sent to the Low Countries in support of Maria Theresa's threatened claim to succeed to the Hapsburg possessions, guaranteed since 1713, and Frederick of Prussia was persuaded to protect King George II's homeland, the Electorate of Hanover, against the unwelcome attentions of the French, but there was little action for the army before the surprise victory over the French at Dettingen in 1743. Defeated the following year at Fontenoy, the British army was withdrawn in August 1745 to face an urgent threat at home. The 'Young Pretender', Prince Charles Edward Stuart, had landed in Scotland.

Little as the Hanoverian dynasty was loved, the return of the Stuarts would mean a return to the Catholic faith, a change that would not be welcomed by the majority of the British people. Since the 1715 rising the term 'Jacobite' had been a convenient label to attach to the Tory opposition in Parliament. If not formally Whig, Unitarians and other Dissenters were generally Whiggish and the sympathies of the Wedgwood family would not be in doubt. Such sympathies did not have much to do with loyalty to the Hanoverian King George II, who spoke little English, or to a government which had reimposed a tax on salt, an essential component of most Staffordshire pottery.

Prince Charles arrived on Scottish soil with seven companions on 25 July 1745 and by 16 September, having gathered an army of 1600, was in Edinburgh. On the morning of the 21st, in less than ten minutes' fighting, the British army sent against him was destroyed at Prestonpans. The Prince's army advanced south, evading a strong force sent against him, and slipped past the Duke of Cumberland and his 8000 troops at Lichfield in Staffordshire. The road to London was open. There was panic in the capital, where shops closed, business was suspended and the banks paid out in sixpences to gain time. But, although London seemed to be within his grasp, the Young Pretender's reception in the south was uncertain, his communications were dangerously stretched, and two hostile armies threatened to block his retreat. On the advice of his officers, he withdrew to Scotland.

The histories of Staffordshire contain many stories of the brutal behaviour of the troops on both sides.[11] The young Josiah Wedgwood, the first year of his apprenticeship completed, could not have escaped the excitement and apprehension that gripped the local population as the Young Pretender's highlanders stormed through the neighbourhood, and he would surely have taken the opportunity to cheer Cumberland's redcoats as they marched through Newcastle-under-Lyme. It was probably at this time that Josiah's brother Richard, five years his senior, with whom he had shared his first lessons in throwing, enlisted in the army. Nothing is known of Richard's military career, though he would have had plenty of opportunity for active service during the following thirty years. He died in 1777, distinguished in Josiah's letters only by a brief reference to his partiality for alcohol.[12]

The Stuart rebellion was not over and invasion was threatened from France. A strong force sent north to make short work of the rebels was routed at Falkirk on 16 January 1746, but two weeks later Cumberland resumed command of the King's army in Scotland and, reinforced by 5000 Hessian troops, began a lengthy and attritional campaign which ended in conclusive victory at Culloden on 15 April. The last hope of a Stuart restoration was crushed and with it the fear of invasion from France.

The war in Europe dragged on with increasing complication and futility. Only at sea, where a series of victories by squadrons under Anson, Hawke, Pocock and Fox swept the French navy from the seas, paralysed her trade and opened the way for attacks on her possessions overseas, were the British victorious. France could not afford to prolong the war. At best, she could hope to use her armies to dictate the terms of an early peace, the preliminaries of which were signed on 19 April 1748. Six months later, these were expanded into the treaty of Aix-la-Chapelle.

The peace, which lasted for seven years, was in reality no more than an uneasy truce. Little could be expected of a settlement which failed to determine the principal issues in dispute between England and France: their conflicting ambitions in America, India and the West Indies. It was nevertheless celebrated with public expressions of rejoicing. A 'jubilee masquerade in the Venetian manner' was held at Ranelagh, followed next day by a great firework display. An enduring legacy from these junketings, Handel's *Music for the Royal Fireworks*, was performed at Vauxhall and Green Park.

This period of peace coincided with Josiah Wedgwood's development from trained apprentice to partner in a respected pottery. For about three years after the end of his apprenticeship Josiah was employed by his brother but in 1752 he entered into partnership with John Harrison, a tradesman of Newcastle-under-Lyme, and Thomas Alders, who owned a potwork at Cliff Bank, near Stoke-on-Trent. It has been assumed that his reason for leaving the Churchyard pottery was discontent with his brother's lack of ambition. Thomas Wedgwood, we are told,

> had not the least sympathy with his young brother's ardent love for
> their joint art, but, on the contrary, was constantly reproving him for
> giving way to what he considered an idle and unprofitable curiosity

in making experiments and trying new processes, and earnestly counselled him not to risk his future prosperity by indulging his imagination
in forming new schemes and endless illusive projects.

Thomas is said to have feared the diminution of his own authority and
summarily rejected his brother's suggestion that they might become
partners. 'Thus driven from home', the young Wedgwood gladly
accepted the overtures of Harrison & Alders.[13]

This long-established account appears to be fictional. Thomas
Wedgwood inherited the Churchyard pottery from his father and, seventeen years later, the much larger Overhouse Works from a distant
cousin, Catherine Egerton, but he failed to make much of either. He
was no businessman but he supported his younger brothers and sisters
until they were either married or able to fend for themselves and, rather
less successfully, brought up his own children by two wives. There is
no evidence of any bitterness between him and his youngest brother,
such as there might have been had Josiah been 'driven from home'.

None of Josiah's brothers had joined the family business and it is
reasonable to conclude that before 1756, when Thomas received his
substantial Egerton legacy, its profits were barely enough to sustain
those who were still too young to earn a living elsewhere. Josiah would
readily have understood the limitations of the Churchyard Works and
the necessity of making his own way. There is no evidence that his
relations with his brother were ever less than friendly. It may, however,
be significant that Josiah's partnership with Harrison & Alders and his
removal from home to lodge with the family of Daniel Mayer, a draper
and tailor in Stoke-on-Trent, dated from the time of his brother's second
marriage.*

Josiah's first choice of partners was evidently not a happy one, for
the partnership lasted only two years. Little is known about the business, which continued, under the direction of Harrison's son, until
1802, when he was declared bankrupt. Thomas Alders died in 1781 and
John Harrison senior in 1798.

In 1754 Josiah was taken into partnership by Thomas Whieldon,
one of the most creative potters in Britain. Aside from his Wedgwood
kinsmen at the Big House, there was probably no one who could have
taught him so much about the innovative techniques that were already
changing an ancient craft into a substantial industry.

---

*His first wife, Isabel (Beech), died in childbirth in 1750. He married Jane
Richards in 1752.

CHAPTER TWO

The Search for White Gold

In Europe, the eighteenth century was a period of unprecedented advance in the manufacture of ceramics, and many of the most significant technical changes had already occurred by the time Josiah Wedgwood began his apprenticeship. By far the most notable development was the discovery in 1708 of the secret of Chinese porcelain, a formula successfully guarded for about 1000 years. Hardly less important was the development of pottery of such quality – in materials, manufacture and design – that it could compete with porcelain and satisfy the demands of the widening market for a fine but less costly product. Wedgwood appears to have been alone in appreciating the extraordinary opportunities offered by such a development. He was certainly the first to exploit them.

Specimens of Chinese porcelain had arrived in Europe in the twelfth century, more than 100 years before the return of Marco Polo from his travels with examples acquired in India. From about the middle of the sixteenth century supplies arrived regularly and, during the reign of the Emperor K'ang Hsi (1662–1722), in substantial quantities, along with such other exotic goods as lacquered furniture, silks and tea, brought to the West by the East India Companies.

Among the earliest pieces of Chinese porcelain to reach England was a Yuan dynasty bowl mounted in silver gilt, which was presented to New College, Oxford, by William Warham, Archbishop of Canterbury, in 1516. Henry VIII owned a single porcelain cup set in jewelled silver gilt, and a Ming bowl and vase,* similarly mounted, belonged to Queen Elizabeth I.

At this time porcelain was so rare as to be held in some awe and even endowed with magical properties. No one in Europe knew how

---

*Now in the Metropolitan Museum of Art, New York.

it was made and Marco Polo's explanation that the clay was left exposed to the air for thirty or forty years before use was embroidered into a romantic theory that the finished objects themselves must be buried for a century to acquire strength. Others believed that porcelain was not made from clay at all but from crushed shells.

Blue-and-white porcelain was especially popular in the West and great quantities were imported by the Portuguese until the capture of large cargoes of it encouraged the Dutch to take over the monopoly of the trade. Demand was greatly enhanced by the discovery that the Chinese would faithfully copy European silver, pewter and stoneware shapes from drawings sent from Holland. The style of Chinese porcelain for export changed. While the shapes were those of objects in everyday use in Europe and thus comfortably familiar, the decoration remained essentially Chinese and, to Western eyes, agreeably exotic. With the fall of the Ming dynasty in 1644 the monopoly was returned to Portugal and it was not until the middle of the eighteenth century, when the port of Canton had been open to European ships for some fifty years, that British merchants began to dominate the trade from Canton as they already dominated trade from India.

Chinese porcelain remained mysterious and precious, and possession of it was confined to the rich. Queen Mary II led the fashion in England, forming at Hampton Court what Macaulay disapprovingly described as 'a vast collection of hideous images, and of vases on which houses, trees, bridges, and mandarins were depicted in outrageous defiance of all the laws of perspective'. His jaundiced opinion was not shared by the ruling class, for this 'frivolous and inelegant' fashion 'spread fast and wide. In a few years almost every great house in the kingdom contained a museum of these grotesque baubles. Even statesmen and generals were not ashamed to be renowned as judges of teapots and dragons . . .'[1]

Japanese porcelain was less well known in Europe and much of it was wrongly identified as Chinese. No porcelain is known to have been made in Japan before about 1616 and the country was closed to all foreign commerce from 1637, except for a few authorised Chinese traders who were able to re-export goods through China, and those supplies permitted to Dutch merchants in a confined settlement at Nagasaki. Only one ship ever sailed with cargo from Japan to England before 1857.

In spite of these severe restrictions, a surprisingly large quantity of Japanese porcelain found its way to Europe. Examples are recorded in the earliest surviving list of porcelain in an English private house: the inventory drawn up by Culpepper Tanner, secretary to the 5th Earl of

Exeter, in 1688.[2] Although it was often incorrectly identified, blue-and-white painted porcelain from the Arita district was popular in Europe and the superb quality of the polychrome painting by Sakaida Kakiemon and his family in the second half of the seventeenth century was as highly regarded as any from China.

Supplies of oriental porcelain were never sufficient to satisfy European demand and, although the imported wares were largely in shapes intended for domestic purposes, much of the porcelain was kept for display or reserved for use on the grandest occasions. But the same, or similar, styles were wanted for daily use and the bluish-white tin-glazed earthenwares made in Europe were both cheap and suitable for painted decoration.

The first to produce substantial quantities of pottery painted in this style were the Dutch, particularly from their factories at Delft, but potteries in Germany and France soon followed. In England, the largest factories were at Bristol, Liverpool, Lambeth and Southwark, and good blue-and-white was also made in Dublin. Staffordshire did not become the home of blue-and-white earthenware until later in the century, when printing superseded handpainting.

All of this 'Chinese' decoration was, of course, *chinoiserie*: an invented style, an expression of the European 'Vision of Cathay', and based on an incomplete knowledge and little understanding of Chinese art. It is as Chinese to Europeans as it is evidently European to the Chinese.

Attempts to imitate Chinese porcelain were made by European potters at least as early as the middle of the sixteenth century, but all failed for lack of understanding of the two essential ingredients – a white china clay (*kaolin*) and feldspathic rock (*pai-tun-tzu* or 'petuntse') – the secret of which was rigorously guarded from Western merchants and travellers. The first accurate information on Chinese porcelain to be received in Europe was contained in the letters written between 1712 and 1722 by a French Jesuit, Père d'Entrecolles, to the Baron de Réaumur. D'Entrecolles was resident near Ching-tê-Chîu, where the Imperial kilns had been founded about 350 years earlier in the reign of the Emperor Hung-wu. By the early eighteenth century it had grown to a town of more than a million people, with at least 3000 kilns for the manufacture of porcelain.

These letters contain a full description of the art of porcelain production, including a form of 'assembly-line' decoration in which each workman was a specialist responsible for a part of the design; but the samples of materials that arrived in France could not be analysed and were not described in sufficient detail to be identifiable.

A second Jesuit missionary, P. J. B. du Halde, wrote an account of the composition and manufacture of porcelain in his *Description . . . de l'empire de Chine*, published in Paris in 1735 and in translation in London in 1738. Extracts from this work were later copied into Josiah Wedgwood's Commonplace Book, [3] but long before this the secret of porcelain manufacture had been discovered in Germany.

Porcelain of a sort had been made in Tuscany under the patronage of Francesco de' Medici, but it was a 'soft-paste' or 'artificial' porcelain containing quantities of sand, glass and powdered rock crystal. Nothing more is known of European porcelain until 1664, when Louis XIV granted a fifty-year monopoly on its manufacture to Claude Révérand. Just seven years later a patent for the manufacture of 'transparent earthenware commonly known by the name of Porcelain or China' was granted to John Dwight of Fulham. Since no single specimen of porcelain has been found that can reliably be attributed to either potter, it is now considered unlikely that Révérand or Dwight ever succeeded in making it. Louis Poterat of St-Sever, near Rouen, made small quantities of soft-paste porcelain between 1673 and 1696, and in the following seventy years factories were established at St-Cloud, Chantilly, Mennecy and Vincennes. None succeeded in making 'hard-paste' or 'true' porcelain before about 1768.

The re-invention of 'true' porcelain came about as an unlikely result of the search for the philosopher's stone, the occult elixir which had the power, under certain conditions, to turn base metals into gold. Johann Friedrich Böttger, a young apprentice apothecary in Berlin who was reputed to have discovered the elixir, fled to Saxony to escape the attention of Frederick the Great. There he was imprisoned for several years until his release was ordered in 1705 with the specific intention that he should work on the discovery of porcelain. [4] If he could not make gold, he could perhaps make the material next to gold in his master's affections.

Augustus the Strong,* Elector of Saxony and King of Poland, possessed the largest collection of oriental porcelain in Europe and spent so much on it that China became known as the 'bleeding bowl of Saxony'. He is alleged to have swapped a regiment of dragoons for forty-eight porcelain vases† from the King of Prussia's collection, and taxes were raised to pay for his extravagant passion. It would have been a positive economy to finance the necessary experiments to discover the

---

*He is recorded as having fathered 350 children.
†The so-called 'dragoon vases' still preserved at Dresden.

secret of true porcelain and to set up a royal manufactory for the production of this 'white gold'.

Böttger's work was supervised by Ehrenfried Walther von Tschirnhaus, one of the advisers entrusted by Augustus with the development of Saxony as a manufacturing nation. Tschirnhaus, who had studied mathematics, physics and natural history at the University of Leyden, had visited Dutch potteries at Delft and, during a number of visits to France, had observed the making of soft-paste porcelain at St-Cloud. He had also located local materials and conducted experiments with them. Böttger continued this work in conditions of extreme secrecy in the dungeons of the Jungfernbastei, the eastern fortifications of Dresden.

On 15 January 1708 Böttger privately recorded the production of a white translucent ceramic body, but he waited a further fourteen months before he felt confident to report his discovery of 'fine white porcelain with the very finest glaze and all accessory painting, and it should be at least of the same quality as East Indian* ware, if not superior to it'.[5] The announcement of the founding of the Royal Saxon Porcelain factory at Meissen was delayed a further ten months. It was then published in four languages. English was not one of them.

Böttger's porcelain was made from a white clay of the kaolin type from Colditz (and later from Aue, near Schneeberg) and a local fusible rock similar in properties to the Chinese petuntse. The nature of these ingredients was kept secret and for many years no one but Böttger was privy to the recipes for the body and glaze or the processes of manufacture. The superb quality of Meissen porcelain and of the decoration, particularly in the Kakiemon style, applied to it gave the factory a supremacy in European porcelain manufacture that was to last until Frederick's occupation of Dresden at the beginning of the Seven Years War.

Long before then the secret had been sold by a defecting workman to Vienna and carried to Venice, where it was stolen and spread to factories in Alsace, Bavaria, Württemburg and the Palatinate. It did not reach Sèvres, where the finest soft-paste porcelain was made, until 1761, and it was another seven years before kaolin and a suitable fusible rock were found in France in sufficient quantities to make production profitable.

The earliest surviving piece of English porcelain was made at Chelsea: a cream jug in the form of a recumbent goat, bearing the incised

---

*A common, if confusing, European description for all goods imported through the East India Companies.

date '1745'; but factories at Bow, Derby, and the Pomona site and Longton Hall, both in Staffordshire, were producing soft-paste porcelain before 1750. Others soon followed at Worcester, Lowestoft, Plymouth, Bristol and Caughley. Of these, only the Plymouth and Bristol factories made hard-paste porcelain, the secret of which was discovered independently by William Cookworthy of Plymouth.

It seems almost certain that Cookworthy's search for porcelain was significantly helped by Andrew Duché, who had found both petuntse and kaolin in Virginia and may be credited with being the first to produce 'true' porcelain in America, possibly as early as 1739. In an undated memoir, probably written in 1768, Cookworthy implies that his first find of kaolin was made in 1748 but adds that 'immense quantities both of the Petunse stone and the Kaulin' were discovered by him in the parish of St Stephen's, between Truro and St Austell in Cornwall.[6] In 1768 he was granted a patent giving him the monopoly on the use of the Cornish materials he had found. This temporarily hampered the development in Staffordshire of both porcelain and the refined earthenware known as creamware, and Josiah Wedgwood took a leading part in its amendment six years later.

The Bow porcelain patent granted to Edward Heylyn and Thomas Frye in 1744 specified one of the principal materials used as 'an Earth, the product of the Cherokee Nation in America called by the natives Unaker'. It is evident that Duché's kaolin and Frye's unaker are the same clay and it was this 'Cherokee clay', as Josiah chose to call it, that he imported in a small quantity at enormous cost in 1768.

By the middle of the eighteenth century all of Europe was seized by the mania for porcelain. Karl Eugen, Duke of Württemburg, who founded the Ludwigsburg factory, declared that a porcelain factory was 'an indispensable accompaniment of splendour and magnificence' and believed that no prince of his rank should be without one.[7] Others appear to have shared this view, for the Berlin factory was the property of Frederick the Great; the Nymphenburg factory belonged to the Elector of Bavaria; Charles III, King of Naples and Spain, founded one at Capo di Monte; and his son Charles IV, who was also the grandson of Augustus the Strong, founded another at Naples. In France, Louis XV subsidised the factory at Vincennes and later at Sèvres, finally assuming total ownership in 1759. And such patronage was not confined to kings. Almost every princeling, duke and bishop had his factory for 'white gold'. Almost every nobleman felt obliged to own it. Table services of several hundred pieces were commissioned and ornamental objects were created by mounting jars and bowls in silver-gilt or ormolu.

Such intense demand from the richest patrons should have helped to create one of the most lucrative industries imaginable, but it did not. Production costs were crippling. Materials were expensive, especially gold and the rarest pigment, cobalt,* used for all the finest blue decoration; skilled potters, particularly throwers, were slow to train and commanded high wages; painters who could create landscapes, botanical studies or designs in the Kakiemon style, or copy in miniature the work of François Boucher, Antoine Watteau or Nicholas Berchem could never be found in sufficient numbers and could often name their own rates. But worst of all were the losses sustained in firing porcelain at the high temperatures† required to obtain one of its most essential qualities: translucency. The most disastrous losses were suffered by the makers of soft-paste porcelain, but all forms of porcelain were costly in firing.

Porcelain factories almost invariably operated at a heavy loss and were kept in being by ever heavier subsidies from their patrons. Such patronage implied control, not only of the factory itself but often also of the conditions under which it operated. The Vincennes factory, removed to Sèvres in 1756, provides an instructive example of the value of the right patronage. From 1753, soon after Louis XV became a substantial shareholder, regular sets of prohibitions were issued forbidding the manufacture of porcelain elsewhere in France and severely restricting the types of decoration that might be applied to French earthenware (faïence). These restrictions continued until the death of the Marquise de Pompadour, one of the most enthusiastic patrons of the factory, in 1764. Two years later, the prohibition against the manufacture of porcelain was lifted, but decoration in competing factories was limited to blue or shades of monochrome (en camaïeu), the use of gilding was forbidden, and the making of figures was restricted to the royal manufactory. Thus internal competition was eliminated and the added prohibition or tight regulation of imports ensured that competition from abroad was negligible. But in spite of special treatment, many Continental porcelain factories failed.

Such favourable conditions were never available to porcelain manufacturers in England, where no royal patronage on this scale existed.

This lack of the patronage enjoyed in European countries and the

---

*The best quality cobalt was to be found in deposits in Saxony. Quantities were kept artificially small and expensive by total prohibition or rigorous control of exports. Smuggling was punishable by death. See p. 157.

†Chinese porcelain and European hard-paste porcelain were fired at around 1350–1400°C; soft-paste porcelain rarely above 1100°C. In China the glaze was commonly fired with the body; when, as was usual in Europe, the body was fired first ('biscuit') and the glaze applied before a second firing, the temperature for the 'glost' firing was lower.

even more crippling production losses associated with soft-paste porcelain ensured the failure of many English factories, even of those whose porcelain was of excellent quality. The owner of the Bow factory was made bankrupt in 1763, Pomona lasted only about ten years,[8] Longton Hall was closed in 1760, and Chelsea was bought by Derby in 1770 and the original workshops closed in 1784. Less notable factories lasted even less well. Porcelain manufacture was not an investment for the amateur, the underfunded or the timid. The lessons of the Pomona and Longton Hall factories were not lost on those earthenware potters in Staffordshire who might otherwise have been tempted to join the race.

The almost universal craving for porcelain, and its great price, opened up a vast new market. The majority of the population desired porcelain but could not afford it. It was the dream of every ambitious potter to develop a fine, white earthenware that could imitate the appearance of porcelain without incurring destructive losses in production. Such a development involved substantial improvements in both the materials used and the techniques of production. In Staffordshire, the local clays, or marls, generally produced a red, brown or greyish-white body after firing. White-burning clays were obtainable from Dorset and Devon but supplies were limited and comparatively expensive until the opening to traffic of the River Weaver, some 20 miles from the Potteries and connecting with the port of Liverpool, in 1733.

Important technical advances were made in the 1740s with the introduction of liquid lead glaze,* slip-casting† and separate firings for biscuit and glost (glazed). The last, although it added the cost of a second firing, greatly enhanced the quality and scope for decoration while saving the substantial costs of glazing and decorating goods that were already faulty. Other improvements were made to the preparation of materials: the refining of clay and the grinding of flint, an essential ingredient of white stonewares and of liquid glazes.

---

*This replaced the powdered, calcined lead ore applied to the ware before it was fired. The liquid glaze was not only easier to apply but far less hazardous to health. Lead poisoning and silicosis (from the use of powdered ore and calcined flint) were the principal causes of death in the Potteries until recent times.

†Slip is clay mixed with water to a creamy consistency. Slip is poured into plaster of Paris moulds, which absorb the water leaving a firm layer of clay adhering to the mould. The surplus clay is poured away and the cast piece allowed to shrink in drying until it can be removed from the plaster case. This technique gradually replaced that of press-moulding in which clay was pressed by hand into moulds of plaster or fired clay, though the older process is still used for certain types of ornament, especially Wedgwood's.

The principal disadvantage of early lead glaze was its colour, a definite yellow, varying in shade according to its thickness and the whiteness of the underlying fired clay. The only alternatives in use were tin glaze, an opaque white based on tin oxide and used on most European pottery (*maiolica*, *delft* or *faïence*, according to its country of origin) or saltglaze, a hard, transparent deposit obtained by throwing salt into the kiln when it reached maximum heat. Both produced fine results. The opaque tin glaze could be, and generally was, used to disguise the colour of the clay to which it was applied, and it was exceptionally suitable as a ground for the finest decoration, such as the work of the *istoriato* painters of Urbino, Gubbio and Deruta; but it was soft and easily chipped. Saltglaze, being transparent, revealed the colour of the underlying clay body, which, for the purpose of imitating porcelain, must be a good white, but had a distinctive, pitted 'orange-peel' surface. Neither provided a satisfactory imitation of the hard, smooth, transparent glaze obtainable on porcelain.

In its challenge to the supremacy of porcelain, Staffordshire salt-glazed stoneware was superior to all but the finest tin-glazed wares. At its best the saltglazed stoneware body was white, strong and beautifully potted, and the introduction of plaster of Paris moulds and slip-casting made it possible to reproduce the most intricate shapes, which might be further enhanced by enamelling in colour. Ornament could be added from metal stamps or applied by hand after removal from moulds, a process known as 'sprigging' that was later the basis of all Wedgwood's applied ornament. John and Thomas Wedgwood of the Big House, Burslem, were among the most highly respected manufacturers of saltglazed stoneware, and another distant cousin, Aaron Wedgwood, with his brother-in-law William Littler, invented a remarkable form of decoration: a beautiful cobalt blue colour in which objects could be dipped before firing.

The first Staffordshire saltglazed ware was made about 1692[9] and such was its quality, and so varied the form and decoration achieved in it, that it might have been expected to continue in production almost indefinitely. In fact, by the third quarter of the eighteenth century it had been superseded and a rapid decline in its popularity followed. The ceramic body which supplanted saltglazed stoneware, virtually extinguished the manufacture of tin-glazed earthenware in Europe and was accepted by monarchs and their courtiers and imitated throughout the Western world, was cream-coloured earthenware, or creamware. It was to the ultimate development of this useful product that Josiah Wedgwood devoted the greater part of his energies during his early years as a professional potter.

CHAPTER THREE

Wedgwood with Whieldon

In 1754, when he took Josiah Wedgwood into partnership at his factory at Fenton Vivian,[1] near Stoke, Thomas Whieldon was thirty-five years old. His new partner was twenty-four. Whieldon had already been in business as a potter for at least fourteen years and had achieved some financial success as well as a considerable reputation. He owned and worked a pottery at nearby Fenton Low, which he let to tenants between 1750 and 1761; he leased the considerable property at Fenton Vivian in 1747 and bought it outright a year later; and in the following year he added Fenton Hall and its flint mill to his holdings. These are not the transactions of a potter whose business was failing for want of enterprise. Indeed, it is far from clear why a potter of Whieldon's experience, already on his way to acquiring a substantial fortune, should have wanted to share his business with a younger and less experienced partner. The conclusion must be that, despite the shortcomings of his first partnership with Harrison & Alders, Josiah had already acquired a remarkable reputation for industry and creativity.

Whieldon's production at this period is described in the Introduction to Josiah's Experiment Book.[2] Because of its significance in the early development of Wedgwood wares, it is quoted here in full:

This suite of Experiments was begun at Fenton Hall, in the parish of Stoke upon Trent, about the beginning of the year 1759, in my partnership with Mr Whieldon, for the improvement of our manufacture of earthen ware, which at that time stood in great need of it, the demand for our goods increasing daily, and the trade universally complained of as being bad and in a declining condition.

White stone ware (viz. with salt glaze) was the principal article of our manufacture; but this had been made a long time, and the prices were now reduced so low, that the potters could not afford to bestow much expence upon it, or to make it so good in any respect as the ware would otherwise admit of. And with regard to Elegance of form, that was an object very little attended to.

The article next in consequence to Stoneware was an imitation of Tortoiseshell.* But as no improvement had been made in this branch for several years, the country was grown weary of it; and though the price had been lowered from time to time, in order to increase the sale, the expedient did not answer, and something new was wanted, to give a little spirit to the business.

I had already made an imitation of Agate;† which was esteemed beautiful & a considerable improvement; but people were surfeited with wares of these variegated colors. These considerations induced me to try for some more solid improvement, as well in the *Body*, as the *Glazes*, the *Colours*, & the *Forms*, of the articles of our manufacture.

I saw the field was spacious, and the soil so good, as to promise an ample recompence to any one who should labour diligently in its cultivation.

This account generally confirms the information in Whieldon's surviving notebooks and the evidence accumulated from excavations of the Whieldon factory site, but with three important omissions. Wedgwood makes no mention of red stoneware, glazed red earthenware or creamware, all of which are known, from shards excavated at Fenton Vivian, to have been made at Whieldon's factory at about the time of the partnership. From these shards it is plain that the greater part of the Whieldon–Wedgwood partnership production was in saltglazed stoneware, tortoiseshell and agate. The evidence of plain creamware is slight and it is likely that the lead glaze was neither of good enough colour nor sufficiently reliable in firing to allow the creamware body to be marketed in quantity without tortoiseshell or 'surface agate' decoration to disguise the faults. The range of shapes recorded in Whieldon's Account and Memorandum Book for 1749–53[3] includes coffeepots (some as large as 3-quart capacity), bowls, ewers, sugar dishes, pails, piggins,‡ plates of various sizes and quantities of toys.§

Wedgwood's claim that he had already made a form of agate ware

*Mottled decoration on creamware produced by the application of metal oxides to the ware before glazing.
†Agate was made in two forms: wedged coloured clays (solid agate); and stained slip ('surface agate' or 'marbled').
‡Small handled pails used as dipping bowls for milk or cream.
§In the eighteenth century, 'toys' were understood to be an enormous variety of metal trinkets, such as snuff-boxes, seals and buckles. The centre of production in England was Birmingham, where forty-eight such manufacturers were listed in 1770. The same word was also used less popularly to describe miniature pieces of pottery, but these were not made in great quantities in Staffordshire before 1800.

before he joined Whieldon is confirmed by Simeon Shaw, who states that, while still in partnership with Harrison & Alders and lodging with the Mayer family, Wedgwood had 'supplied the tradesmen of Birmingham and Sheffield with Earthenware hafts for Table knives &c in imitation of Agate, Tortoiseshell, Marble, and other kinds'.[4] It may have been the quality of these imitations of natural stones that encouraged Whieldon to take Josiah into partnership.

If Wedgwood's account in his Experiment Book is accurate, his work with Whieldon was largely experimental and concerned with improving bodies, colours and forms. Since the saltglazed stoneware body had already been brought to a high degree of perfection by others, including the Wedgwoods at the Big House, it is clear that the ceramic body with which Josiah was principally involved was creamware. The problem in its manufacture was not the body, which was already an acceptable white colour, but the development and application of a suitable lead glaze. This varied in colour from a dark syrup to bright green, ruining the appearance of the white body, and was difficult to apply evenly. The colours which Josiah's experiments were intended to improve were those of glazes and stained clay slip. The success of these experiments proved to be crucial to Wedgwood's future.

None of Whieldon's pottery was marked, and the certain identification of it, and therefore of the shapes he favoured, depends largely on the evidence of shards recovered from the Fenton Vivian site. Production evidently included forms based on contemporary silver and pewter shapes, both press-moulded and cast decoration, and probably a few rare commemorative pieces celebrating, for example, the capture of Portobello by Vernon in 1740 and the marriage of George III in 1761. It is clear that both shapes and decoration became more sophisticated in the 1760s, but to what extent this may be attributed to Wedgwood's influence is unlikely ever to be certain.

What is undeniable is Whieldon's ability to attract to his employment some of the most important figures in the early history of Staffordshire pottery. Aaron Wood, reputedly the best ceramic block-cutter in the country and 'modeller to all the potters in Staffordshire at the latter end of this time that . . . white stoneware was made',[5] was briefly with Whieldon; Josiah Spode, founder of a great factory that came to rank second only to Wedgwood's, was Whieldon's apprentice;[6] William Greatbatch, creative potter, block-maker and ceramic printer, who supplied Wedgwood with a variety of wares in the early 1760s, was another.[7]

Whieldon was remarkable also for being probably the first employer in the Potteries to provide rented accommodation for his work-people.

As early as 1750 he was letting to his employees houses and cottages within comfortable walking distance of his factory.[8] The advantages of this incentive were not lost on Josiah Wedgwood, who is usually given the credit for being the first to introduce it.

During the first thirty years or so of the eighteenth century Staffordshire pottery was sold principally to local markets and borne by the 'poor crate-men who carry them on their backs all over the countrey'.[9] As the quality of the tortoiseshell and saltglazed stoneware improved, so the market for it expanded, and by the 1750s it was being delivered to London in substantial quantities and even reaching customers in Europe.[10] The obstacle to this trade was no longer the low standard of the ware but the difficulty of transporting it to markets further afield.

There were three main routes by which goods might leave the Potteries. All involved a combination of road and river transport to ports and the coastal trade. The first was by road to the River Weaver, a journey of about 20 miles, and thence to Liverpool; the second, about twice as far by road to Bridgnorth, reached Bristol via the River Severn; the third, another distance by road of about 40 miles, took the River Trent from Willington ferry to Hull on the east coast. The same routes in reverse were used for materials arriving in the Potteries. On the road, crates were carried, one at a time, by pack-horse, and this slow form of transport continued to be used until improvement to the roads made its gradual replacement by carts or waggons practicable.

The roads were deplorable. Contemporary accounts are unanimous in condemning their condition. One correspondent complained in 1752: 'A gentleman in the country or a citizen in London, thinks no more of visiting his relations than traversing the deserts of Nubia.'[11] Even sixteen years later, when several turnpike roads had been built in the area, Arthur Young complained: 'it is impossible to describe these infernal roads in terms adequate to their deserts.' The road between Knutsford and Newcastle-under-Lyme was

> in general a paved causeway, as narrow as can be conceived, and cut into perpetual holes, some of them two feet deep measured on the level; a more dreadful road cannot be imagined, and wherever the country is the least sandy, the pavement is discontinued, and the ruts and holes most execrable.[12]

Turning aside to avoid a cart that was overthrown and almost buried, he was obliged to hire two men to support his own chaise to prevent it from overturning. The road between Newcastle and Burslem was even worse – deeply rutted with wide pits in the clay surface. The principal cause of this was the long tradition, abandoned only in 1720, that any freeholder of Burslem had the right to dig coal or clay, at any time and in any quantity, wherever he might find it on unenclosed land. All the resulting holes in the streets and lanes had not been filled a century later.[13]

The prohibition of digging for local clays and coal and the increasing reliance on the whiter clays transported from the West Country merely increased the traffic on the roads. Arthur Young was writing in 1768 when he complained that even the comparatively new turnpike roads were no great improvement:

> . . . let me most seriously caution all travellers who may accidentally purpose to travel this terrible country to avoid it as they would the devil, for a thousand to one but they break necks or limbs by over-throws or breakings down. They will here meet with ruts, which I actually measured, four feet deep, and floating with mud only from a wet summer; what must it be after winter? The only mending it in places receives is the tumbling in of some loose stones which serve no other purpose but jolting a carriage in the most intolerable manner.[14]

The charge for transporting a ton of goods from Burslem to the Weaver was 18s and to the Willington ferry 34s. To these costs must then be added the rates for transit by water, on the rivers and down the coast to the final destination. A further expense, and often the largest, was incurred in breakages and theft. The loss of goods on the road was frequent and river bargemen were notorious for their dishonesty. These were problems that persisted throughout the century.

Some improvement in transport was possible by the construction of turnpike roads, but these were often strenuously resisted by local merchants, who saw their interests being injured by roads that passed by their towns instead of through them. The potters were supported by influential coal owners. Whieldon was among those who subscribed in 1759 to the first turnpike road in the neighbourhood of the Potteries, an 8-mile stretch between Tittensor and Talke, on the old London post road near Kidsgrove. It was a small beginning but one on which Josiah Wedgwood soon determined to build.

There is a tradition, unsupported except by hearsay evidence, that, during his five-year partnership with Whieldon, Josiah became seriously ill and was unable to work in the pottery for several months. The causes and length of this illness are not known, though it has been authoritatively diagnosed as the result of a widespread inflammation following the bruising of his injured right leg.[15] Much has been built upon this story, published for the first time more than 100 years after the supposed event, to show that this was the time when he acquired his extended education:

> He saw clearly that this was a golden time, though a brief one, in which he might supplement the narrow limits of his education. . . . He saw clearly the great philosophical fact . . . that the sources of truth and knowledge are limitless. With his usual sagacity and humility of spirit, he began this self-culture. . . . He improved his constructive knowledge of his native tongue, as also of arithmetic. He read such histories of his country as were then extant; made himself well acquainted with its social and industrial features, and its commercial and political relations to other countries. . . . He had a passion for chemical analysis and philosophical speculation . . . [16]

In all of this, he was, it is said, helped by his sister Catherine's husband, the Reverend William Willet, who was the Unitarian minister in Newcastle. While Josiah thus educated himself in bed at his lodgings, he was examined, so the story goes, by the young Erasmus Darwin, who had recently settled in Lichfield and was already making a name for himself as a fine diagnostician.[17]

It is not a likely story. It is not easy to believe that any injury or illness serious enough to keep Josiah from his work would have left him well enough to make a thoughtful study of so many subjects. Nor would there have been time for them all if the period was 'a brief one'. Darwin did not take his MD degree at Edinburgh until 1756 and he moved to Lichfield in November of that year. True, he had scored a startling success with one of his first patients[18] and given a well-received paper to the Royal Society in March 1757, but, although he and Josiah Wedgwood were to become intimate friends, there is no evidence that they met before 1764. By that time Wedgwood had been in business on his own for nearly five years.

The Whieldon–Wedgwood partnership is an important one in the history of Staffordshire pottery and it is unfortunate that so little evidence has survived of its organisation and development or of the relationship between the two men. Its particular significance for Wedgwood evidently lay in the experience it gave him of the administration of a successful firm, of the improvement of existing types of ware and the expansion of markets for them, and in the opportunity for experiment.

He remained with Whieldon for about five years. While there can be no doubt which of the two partners was the senior and exercised control over the business, there is also no doubt which was the more inventive. Whieldon's production appears to have altered little between 1759, when Josiah left him, and 1780, when the factory was demolished. In the same period, Wedgwood could boast the invention of at least one original ceramic body and the development to something close to perfection of no fewer than six others. Said to have accumulated a fortune of £10,000, Whieldon retired from potting about 1780 and became High Sheriff of Staffordshire in 1786. He died nine years later at the age of seventy-five.

In 1758 Josiah finally decided to become a master potter in his own right. He remained with Whieldon, however, until May the following year and his Experiment Book shows that his first important invention, a brilliant translucent green glaze, was completed during this period.

After the treaty of Aix-la-Chapelle in 1748, peace in Europe trembled on an ill-constructed edifice of defensive alliances. British policy, the principal aim of which was the security of Hanover and the North Sea ports, was founded on the 'old system', the alliance of Britain, Holland and Austria against France, which had worked well enough in Marlborough's time but was now out of date. Prussia had grown strong and Austria no longer saw France as her most dangerous enemy. During this interlude, the colonies of France and England had been left to fend for themselves. This they had done with far-reaching consequences. It had long been a convention that limited colonial action could be regarded as something apart from European politics and thus that a minor clash between the forces of England and France in distant territory did not necessarily constitute an act of war.

In India the commercial feud between the rival East India Companies had led to open warfare. The victories of Robert Clive and Stringer Lawrence in the Carnatic, however, so alarmed the French that Dupleix, their governor in Pondicherry, was recalled in disgrace and, by the agreement of the two parties, further military action was suspended.

In America the clash of interests was even more violent. The colonial ambitions of France were founded on her claim to the entire Mississippi basin, her possession of Acadia and the islands in the Gulf of the St Lawrence in the north, and a sickly settlement at New Orleans in the south. The French aimed to connect these settlements by a chain of forts which would, in theory, give them the effective occupation of the vast hinterland to the west of New England, confining the British colonies to their narrow Atlantic strip. This would reserve to France the monopoly of the valuable fur trade centred on the Great Lakes and the Ohio valley. The design was impressive but it took no account of practical considerations. The French colonies in America were an artificial creation, underpopulated, heavily subsidised and wholly subservient to centralised administration in France. In spite of their administrative unification and a provision for compulsory military service, the colonies were weak. The retention in France of the power to make all decisions affecting their development had robbed the people of much of their vigour and initiative.

In contrast, the New England colonies, founded haphazardly and left by ignorant or indifferent statesmen to look after themselves, bred a hardy race of healthily independent people – proud, jealous and stubborn, difficult to weld into a cohesive body for any mutual purpose, but potentially formidable. They had not the slightest intention of giving up the fur trade and rightly saw the building of a line of French forts round the Great Lakes as a threat to their own existence. Early in 1754, a first attempt to halt the building of these forts and to protect the fur interests of the newly formed English Ohio Company was entrusted to a young and inexperienced major of militia, George Washington. It failed. Washington unwisely divided his small detachment and was soon obliged to surrender to superior French force. He and his men were released on ignominious terms to return to Virginia.

In the autumn of 1754, an expedition was planned to remove the French threat to the colonies. This was officially defensive and retaliatory, and it was essential that it should be regarded in this light if war with France in Europe were to be avoided. In practice the operations, which were aimed to end French control of the Ohio valley, break the chain linking the colonies of the north and south, and prepare the way for the expulsion of the French from Canada, looked suspiciously like a deliberate offensive. Major-General Edward Braddock, who commanded the force sent to America, chose as his chief adviser the officer least qualified for the task, George Washington. Braddock sailed in January and six months later his army was ambushed and all but annihilated. Braddock himself was mortally wounded. Meanwhile, the French succeeded in sending 3000 regular troops to Canada.

In Europe, the diplomatic house of cards collapsed. Frederick the Great abandoned his alliance with France and signed the Convention of Westminster by which Britain and Prussia mutually guaranteed the security of their possessions in Germany; France and Austria concluded the Treaty of Versailles guaranteeing their possessions and frontiers. At the end of the year, reliable intelligence was received that French troops were being concentrated in Normandy and Brittany for the invasion of England. On 18 May 1756 war was declared.

The invasion fleet never sailed but the French instead took Minorca. The British attempt to recapture the island was an inglorious failure for which Admiral Byng was blamed and summarily shot. The Duke of Newcastle and his ministers could not escape responsibility. The government fell and was replaced by one led by the Duke of Devonshire. But the new ministry was shortlived and, after a fruitless search for an alternative, the king was obliged to accept a coalition of the Newcastle and Pitt factions and William Pitt, whom he loathed, as Secretary of State for the South, responsible for the conduct of the war.

Pitt at once made clear the unconventional strategic principles on which his direction of the war was to be founded. Britain, he argued, was a maritime and mercantile power and her strength lay not in her army, which could not be raised on the Continental scale, but in her fleets and in her wealth from trade, which could be used to buy armies. Frederick must be supported, if for no better reason than to guard the Electorate of Hanover, but it would be the 'result of the great struggle between England and France that will determine the conditions of the future peace'.[19] That struggle would be won at sea and in the colonies.

Pitt's strategy was founded on four interrelated aims: the security of England as a base; the preservation of the alliance with Prussia; command of the sea; and the conquest of Canada. Three were attainable without further military action; the fourth required the capture of Quebec. On 26 July 1758, after a daring, energetic and well-led campaign, Lord Amherst accepted the surrender of the almost impregnable fortress of Louisbourg; but supplies were short, more than 5000 prisoners must be transported to England and the fleet was in no condition to undertake a second campaign against Quebec. James Wolfe, who had served as Amherst's junior brigadier-general and distinguished himself in the Louisbourg campaign, wrote prophetically:

> This will, some time hence, be a vast empire, the seat of Power and Learning. They have all the Materials ready, Nature has refus'd 'em nothing, & there will grow a People out of our little spot (England) that will fill this vast space.[20]

Next year he laid the corner-stone himself.

The gateway to Canada had been forced and the destruction of the French empire in North America was now a realistic ambition. In addition, the capture of Louisbourg had demonstrated that combined operations requiring the cooperation of the navy with the army need not end in stalemate, as they had at Minorca. With efficient planning and determined leadership, qualities notably absent in earlier operations, there was every possibility of success. In India, too, the French had come under pressure. Clive's victory at Plassey in 1757 and his subsequent capture of Chandernagore gave the British control of Bengal, the great resources of which were crucial in the destruction of French power and influence in the Carnatic. Within three years, the French had been unceremoniously ejected from India.

Pitt's strategy produced less spectacular but still useful results in Europe. The Prussian alliance was preserved, the French were contained and the Russians forced to withdraw into Poland; the British army carried out eccentric attacks, or nuisance raids, on Emden and French coastal defences; and, most urgently, the navy gained control in both the Channel and the Mediterranean. The ebb and flow of hope and disappointment, success and failure, continued through much of 1759. The Russians took Frankfurt and inflicted a crushing defeat on Frederick's main army at Kunersdorf but withdrew into Poland leaving Frederick to regain the rest of Saxony. The Austrians took Dresden. The allied army under Prince Ferdinand of Brunswick, driven back into Westphalia, turned to rout the French army at Minden on 1 August. Meanwhile, Pitt's policy of nibbling away at French colonial territories deprived the French of Goree, Senegal and the richest of the West Indian sugar islands, Guadeloupe.

Another invasion plan was thwarted when the French fleets from Brest and Toulon, concentrated to protect the convoy of transports, were soundly defeated at Lagos and Quiberon Bay in November. The greatest prize was Wolfe's capture of Quebec. This made certain the final destruction of French power in North America. Had it been understood that the inevitable consequence of this conquest would be the loss of the American colonies, celebrations in London might have been less joyful.

'Can one easily leave the remains of such a year as this?' asked Horace Walpole on 21 October. 'It is still all gold . . . Our bells are worn threadbare with ringing for victories'.[21] It was a suitable year for the birth, in May, of Pitt's younger son, William. Josiah Wedgwood chose to celebrate it by founding his own factory.

CHAPTER FOUR

Useful Partners

On 30 December 1758 Josiah Wedgwood signed a formal agreement to employ his cousin Thomas as a journeyman.[1] Under the terms of this agreement, Thomas was to start work on May Day the following year at an annual salary of £22, to continue until 11 November 1765. Four years Josiah's junior, he was the sixth child of Josiah's uncle Aaron Wedgwood and was already working as a journeyman in Worcester, probably at the 'Worcester Tonquin Manufacture', where Dr Wall had been making a form of porcelain* for about seven years. Josiah's experience was confined to pottery and to decoration consisting of moulded or applied patterns with coloured glazes. Practical experience of porcelain-making and knowledge of the techniques used in its decoration would have been especially attractive to a potter ambitious to improve and refine creamware. Thomas was to prove during the next thirty years, however, that he possessed personal virtues that would be even more valuable than his understanding of porcelain.

May Day 1759 was also the date from which Josiah hired his first potwork. The 'House and Workhouses', known as the Ivy House, were rented from John Wedgwood of the Big House for one year at £15.[2] This term was later extended to Martinmas 1762 and there is evidence that Josiah did not quit the premises until Christmas or the New Year.[3] Rent for the first year, almost a quarter of which was settled in goods, was paid in five instalments, the last being received on 9 January 1761. The rent for 1762, from May Day to Martinmas, was also late, by a full nine months, a delay which suggests either inattention or some difficulty in settling debts.[4]

It would be useful to have reliable examples of Wedgwood's pro-

---

*Worcester porcelain of this period contained a high percentage of soaprock in place of the feldspathic rock of true porcelain.

duction during this period. According to Simeon Shaw, he continued to manufacture the same type of ware that he had made during his partnership with Whieldon: 'Knife Hafts, Green Tiles, Tortoiseshell and Marble Plates, glazed with lead ore, for his previously formed connections'. This does not suggest a period of energetic innovation. Shaw continues: 'his attention to their demands soon secured him such a share of business that he engaged a second small factory only across the road . . . Here he manufactured the White Stone Pottery, then increasing in demand.'[5] No evidence has yet been found to support the last statement, but it is unlikely that Josiah would have neglected to produce saltglazed wares, and these would have required a separate oven. The Ivy House is recalled[6] as being equipped with two ovens, but one of those would have been needed for lead-glazed wares and the other was probably used for red wares.

What is surprisingly lacking in Shaw's account is any mention of ware decorated with the green and yellow glazes perfected by Josiah before March 1760.[7] These were used on the 'greengrocery' of Wedgwood's production, principally between 1760 and 1763; teawares made in imitation of cabbages, cauliflowers, melons, pears, apples and pineapples, the rococo fruit and vegetable shapes already popular in the porcelain of Chelsea and Longton Hall. Unable to produce all the types of ware he wished to be able to offer, Wedgwood followed the well-established custom of buying-in goods from other manufacturers, including Whieldon.[8]

Whatever may have occasioned Wedgwood's early difficulties in paying his rent, he was sufficiently successful in his first three years to move to a larger potwork. By the beginning of 1763 he was able to rent from the Adams family the Brick House Works, later known also as the Bell Works from Josiah's habit of summoning his workmen by bell instead of the horn customarily used in the Potteries. Three years later he expanded production further, renting the 'Red Workhouses', again from John Wedgwood, for £10 a year from March 1766. He used these premises for six years.

Valuable evidence has survived of Wedgwood's production at the Brick House and it is clear that this was an important period of development. The most significant improvement was made in the production of creamware which, by 1765, had been brought to such a high standard that it superseded saltglazed ware and, in due course, ruined the trade in tin-glazed wares, not only in Britain but throughout Europe. Wedgwood had conducted countless experiments to improve the colour and quality of both the body and the glaze and his business was so successful that he was obliged to buy large quantities of creamware from

William Greatbatch, who had been employed by Whieldon during and immediately after the Whieldon–Wedgwood partnership. One of the most versatile potters in Staffordshire, Greatbatch had set up his own pottery in 1762. He became one of Josiah's most trusted employees and his connection with Wedgwood lasted for the rest of his life.

In addition to his improvements in the body and glaze of creamware, which brought it closer in appearance to porcelain, Wedgwood had started to apply to it styles of decoration then in use at the porcelain factories. The most popular type of English porcelain decoration was in blue, painted under the glaze, generally in designs intended to appear Chinese (*chinoiserie*) but it was rapidly discovered that on creamware the blue pigment fired to a disagreeable greenish-black, and so it was seldom used. It was also the style of decoration most typical of the tin-glazed earthenware manufacturers, and Wedgwood had good reason to wish his creamwares to be easily distinguished from European delftwares. He found the style he needed in transfer-printing,* a method of decoration new to the Potteries.

The technique of transfer-printing was invented independently by John Brooks, a London mezzotint engraver, in 1752, and by John Sadler, a Liverpool printer, in 1756. Brooks's invention was used at the Battersea Enamel Works and the Bow and Worcester porcelain factories. Sadler's, soon copied by other Liverpool printers, some of whom had been his apprentices, was applied to Liverpool tin-glazed tiles, some saltglazed wares and, according to his own statement, to Wedgwood's creamware only. 'You may rest assured,' Sadler wrote to Wedgwood on 11 October 1763, 'that we never printed a Piece for any Person but yourself.'[9] Printing was usually in black, but a rust-red and purple were also used. Sadler's printed patterns for Wedgwood included traditional narrative scenes (some complete with appropriate verses), floral centres and borders, exotic birds, sporting scenes, classical landscapes, masonic emblems and a number of important historical and commemorative pieces, often with engraved portraits of royalty or contemporary heroes such as George III and Queen Charlotte, Frederick the Great, Pitt, Wesley, Wilkes and Keppel. Wedgwood's plain creamware, fired and glazed, was sent to Sadler and his partner Guy Green in Liverpool, where it was printed and fired again before being returned to Burslem. Some of the finished stock was sold direct from Liverpool, much of it going to export. Trade between the two firms began early in 1762 and by the end of 1763 was averaging £30 a month. Eight years later it

---

*The technique of transferring a pattern to fired ware by means of an engraved copper plate, prepared ink and tissue paper. The transferred design must be fixed by a second firing.

amounted to £650 a month, representing more than 20,000 individual pieces. Although he was later to change his mind, Josiah was not at first interested in making crested services ('armorial ware'). 'Crests', he wrote in 1766, 'are very bad things for us to meddle with, and I never take any orders for services so ornamented.' Faulty goods, or 'seconds', of regular patterns could be sold at reduced prices, but faulty crested goods would be unsaleable and therefore 'as useless as most other Crests, & Crest wearers are'.[10]

The other principal method of decoration was by handpainting. By 1763 Josiah was in touch with a Leeds firm, Robinson & Rhodes, who traded in 'a good Assortment of Foreign China, and a great variety of English China . . . and all sorts of Fine Earthenware' as well as undertaking repairs 'without rivetting' and enamelling china, earthenware and saltglazed wares.[11] They bought various types of ware from Wedgwood, principally colour-glazed teapots in the moulded fruit and vegetable shapes then fashionable, for resale, and in turn supplied him with copper dust for use in his own green glaze. By the end of November 1764 Wedgwood was sending Rhodes quantities of teapots and coffeepots for enamelling in colours. The decoration was at first fairly primitive painting in iron-red and black, and dumpy figures, some of which appear to be levitating, but these were soon replaced by more sophisticated flowers and some striking 'Calico' and banded and diaper patterns.

In the spring of 1762, on one of his periodic visits to Sadler & Green in Liverpool, Josiah was either taken ill or accidentally damaged his vulnerable right knee.[12] For whatever reason, he was confined to bed for some days, where he was attended by Dr Matthew Turner, a surgeon, chemist, scholar and conversationalist and, seven years later, one of the founders of the Liverpool Academy of Art.[13] On one of his routine visits, Turner brought with him his friend Thomas Bentley. It was a chance introduction, probably made without any motive beyond providing agreeable company for his patient, but its consequences were extraordinary.

Wedgwood was a man of exceptional energy and invention: inquiring, practical and tenacious. Bentley was educated, cultured and sociable, already well known in Liverpool, where his lively intellect, wide experience, liberal views and personal charm made him a welcome member of a burgeoning society. He had travelled in France and Italy and spoke both French and Italian, and, at Findern Academy near Derby, he had been given the grounding in the classics then considered the essential foundation of a gentleman's education. But there was a commercial side to his life as well. He had spent seven years indentured to a wholesale merchant in Manchester, acquiring a sound training in accountancy, and for a further eight years had been in business on his own account as a general merchant with premises in King Street, Liverpool.

It would have been surprising if this connection with the valuable export and coastal trade had not especially interested Wedgwood. The two men, so different in their social background and education, found that their personalities were both compatible and complementary. Their first meeting was the beginning of a friendship of unusual depth and intimacy which led to one of the foremost manufacturing partnerships of English industrial history.

Soon after his return to Burslem, Josiah wrote the first of more than 1000 letters he was to send to Bentley in the course of the next eighteen years:

> My much esteemed Friend
>
> If you will give me leave to call you so & will not think the address too free, I shall not care how Quakerish or otherwise antique it may sound, as it perfectly corresponds with the sentiments I wish to continue towards you; nor is there a day passes but I reflect with a pleasing gratitude upon the many kind offices I receiv'd in my confinement at your hospitable town. My good Doctor [Turner] & you in particular have my warmest gratitude for the share you *both* had in promoteing my recovery.

Bentley had recently written a piece on the subject of female education, which he had allowed Wedgwood to read in manuscript when he was in Liverpool, but he was reluctant to see it published because he thought it not yet perfect. 'Why', Josiah demanded, 'should *you* or the *Publick* expect it should be so? Do you know any publication, *on this side Rome*, that is so in every respect? I can honestly tell you, & from some experience that it is perfect enough to do a great deal of good.'[14]

The style of the letter, which continues at some length, already shows an unusual ease and, as their friendship warmed, Josiah wrote with unfettered freedom. Within five months he was addressing Bentley as 'dear Friend' but it was several years before their letters to one another became almost a daily event. There is evidence that Bentley was as frequent a correspondent as Wedgwood,[15] and Josiah kept all his letters, which he had bound and kept by his bedside.[16] All are now lost. Wedgwood's letters, on the other hand, unbound and discarded, have survived almost intact as the result of an extraordinary accident of fortune.

In 1848 Joseph Mayer, a native of Newcastle-under-Lyme who had moved to Liverpool and prospered as a silversmith, discovered a large quantity of manuscript material being sold by a Birmingham scrap merchant to local grocers for use as wrapping paper. Bought by the merchant from Francis Wedgwood, Josiah's grandson, the enormous pile contained almost the entire series of Wedgwood's letters to Bentley besides a great number of invoices and other valuable records of the business. Mayer bought the lot and the collection now forms the greater part of the Wedgwood archive relating to the eighteenth century and also the foundation of all studies of Josiah Wedgwood and his business.[17]

Almost at the start of their friendship, Wedgwood warned Bentley what a 'troublesome correspondent' he was likely to become. 'I will be quite honest & tell you what you have to expect from me,' he wrote in October 1762, 'that I may as the Vicissitudes of Life may furnish occasions, sometimes call upon you for advice, – at other times I may want your assistance to settle an opinion or to help me form a probable conjecture of things beyond our kenn, & sometimes I may want that Valuable, & most difficult office of Friendship, reproof.'[18] Later he was to describe Bentley's letters as 'my Magazines, Reviews, Chronicles, & I had allmost said my Bible'.[19] Already, within weeks of meeting Bentley, Josiah was asking for and following his suggestions for his reading and his library, wishing, as he said, 'to furnish a shelf or two of a book-case'.[20] He admired the work of James Thomson, described as Bentley's 'favourite Author', and sought Bentley's opinion of Rousseau's *Emile*, which he proposed to buy 'notwithstanding his Holiness has forbid its entrance into his domains'.[21]

In April Josiah was in London for two weeks, a length of stay that suggests he was content to leave the factory in his cousin Thomas's charge. He visited both houses of Parliament, went to the theatre and bought some clothes and household goods, but a more practical reason for his visit may be found in his expenditure on teapots and china plates.[22] Throughout his working life, Josiah took a close interest in the products of his competitors and was never above flattering them by imitation. His extended visit to London was no doubt principally to see his elder brother John, but he sensibly took advantage of it to look at, and where prudent to buy, examples of fashionable china and earthen-ware which he might copy.

Throughout 1763, and probably with less urgency several years earlier, Josiah had courted his distant cousin, Sarah Wedgwood. Her father, Richard Wedgwood of Spen Green, was the eldest brother of Thomas and John Wedgwood of the Big House, Burslem, and probably the richest of all Josiah's relations. A successful cheese factor in Cheshire, where he owned an estate of 75 acres,[23] Richard had become a general merchant. He lent substantial sums to his brothers and £1900 to Sir William Meredith, a large loan that led to an acrimonious dispute and nearly to a duel. His account book shows monthly receipts of £1200–1800 in the 1760s.[24] In 1763 he was a widower in his sixty-third year and his heirs were his son, John, still unmarried at the age of thirty-one, and Sarah, just two years younger. While he was no doubt pleased at the prospect of his daughter's marriage, for she was rapidly approaching an age when it would be justifiable to assume that she was destined to remain a spinster, Richard was always aware that she was a target for fortune hunters. He viewed his young kinsman with some suspicion.

Josiah explained the situation to Bentley on 9 January 1764:

I had . . . hoped by waiting a post or two to be able either to tell you of my happiness, or at least the time I expected to be made so, but 'O Grief of Griefs' that pleasure is still deny'd me, & I cannot bear to keep my friend in suspence any longer, though I own myself somewhat asham'd, and greatly mortify'd, to be still kept at bay from those exalted pleasures you have often told me (& I am very willing to believe) attend the Married state. If you knew my temper, & sentiments on these affairs, you will be sensible how I am mortify'd when I tell you I have gone through a long series of bargain makeing – of settlements, Reversions – Provisions &c: &c: Gone through it did I say: would to Hymen I had. No I am still in the Attorneys hands, from which I hope it is no harm to pray 'good Lord deliver me'. Miss W: & I are perfectly agreed, & could settle the whole affair in three lines & so many minutes, but our Pappa, over carefull of his Daughters interest, would by some demands which I cannot comply with, go near to separate us, if we were not better determin'd. – On Friday next Mr. W: & I are to meet in great form, with each of us our Attorney which I hope will be conclusive, you shall then hear farther from

Your obliged & very affectionate friend[25]

The negotiations were protracted and it is said that in order to obtain Richard Wedgwood's permission for the marriage Josiah was obliged to match Richard's settlement of £4000.[26] No document has been found to support this statement. Nor is it likely that Josiah could have raised such a sum unless by loans which his future father-in-law would not willingly have approved. A marriage settlement was none the less agreed and Josiah wrote jubilantly to Bentley to announce that his fondest hopes had been realised:

> All things being amicably settled betwixt my Pappa elect & myself I yesterday prevail'd upon my dear girl to name the day, the blissful day! When she will reward all my faithfull services & take me to her arms! to her Nuptial Bed! to – Pleasures which I am yet ignorant of, and you my dear friend can much better conceive than I shall ever be able to express. In three words we are to be married on Wednesday next. On that auspicious day think it no sin to wash your Philosophic evening pipe with a glass or two extraordinary, to hail your friend, & wish him good speed into the realms of Matrimony. Adieu my good friend, I am very busy today, that no business may intrude on my pleasures for the rest of the week.[27]

Josiah and Sarah Wedgwood were married two days later, on 25 January 1764.

By twentieth-century standards, Josiah's postponement of marriage until his thirty-fourth year might be thought unusual and his clearly implied lack of sexual experience before that age seems almost incredible. In the eighteenth century, however, neither would have been considered exceptional. Late marriage had long been normal among the poor and lower-middle classes of north-west Europe, where it was the custom for couples to set up their own homes as soon as possible after marriage. This required either a prolonged period of saving or the inheritance of property from parents. Most marriages took place after the death of one or both parents of the husband.

By the middle of the century, late marriage had also become the norm among the professional classes and the younger sons of landowners. Sexual experience was inhibited by the absence of reliable methods of contraception and the social disgrace of bastardy. Condoms, generally of leather, were uncomfortable and not easily available outside the cities and they were used primarily as protection against venereal disease. Even allowing for low fertility resulting from poor diet, reluctance to report illegitimate births and some inaccuracy in the records, the low incidence of bastardy until the 1780s, when increased employment and higher wages for both sexes allowed couples to save more easily and therefore to risk the possible consequences of intercourse, is a fair indication of the sexual restraints of the day, especially in country areas where prostitutes were few. These restraints were often relaxed after betrothal but this period of greater freedom was, in the case of the Wedgwoods, a matter of only a few days.

Bentley, whose wife, Hannah Oates, had died in childbirth in 1759, must have viewed Josiah's manoeuvres with amused concern. After the death of his wife, his sister-in-law Elizabeth Oates had kept house for him. Josiah had met her shortly after his introduction to Bentley and frequently sent his 'best respects' to her. His equally frequent teasing references to Bentley's solitary bachelor state continued until the latter's second marriage, to Mary Stamford, in 1772.

There is ample evidence that the marriage of Josiah and Sarah Wedgwood was a happy one. Sarah was intelligent, shrewd and better educated than her husband. They apparently shared a sense of humour and a strong sense of family duty. Her portraits show her to have been more handsome than beautiful, and later generations found her presence commanding, even awe-inspiring.[28] After four months of marriage, Josiah wrote that he and Sarah were 'two married Lovers happy as this world can make them'.[29]

It is nevertheless undeniable that his marriage was of enormous financial importance to him. In spite of his success in the previous five years, there is no reason to suppose that he had been able to save any substantial sum of money, and the obstacles put by Richard in the way of the marriage are evidence enough of the inadequacy of Josiah's means. According to a knowledgeable family source, Sarah's brother John lent Josiah £500 in 1764 to improve the Brick House Works.[30] No provenance is quoted for this statement but, if true, it adds weight to the belief that Josiah's capital was extremely small. By continuing custom, though less definitely in law, Sarah's marriage settlement and any other money or property of hers would have come under Josiah's control after their marriage. Her brother died unmarried in 1774 and her father in 1782. She was sole heiress to both men and there can be no doubt that her inheritance was great: it is said to have been £20,000.[31] This, too, would have come under Josiah's control, which would account for the comparatively small size of Sarah's estate when she died.

It can be shown that Wedgwood's business prospered between 1764 and 1769: sales increased greatly with the improved quality of his goods and the influential patronage he succeeded in attracting, but it is significant that Josiah's entry into public life, as a subscriber to charities and turnpikes and a prime mover in the building of canals, and his intention to buy land on which to build his own factory rather than renting premises from other owners of potbanks, all date from after his marriage.

Sarah had not been spoilt by her comfortable family circumstances.

She was happy to exchange her father's much grander home for the simpler Brick House and to make herself useful in her husband's business. She set about learning the code used by Josiah to record his experiments so that she could help with their transcription. As Josiah told his brother John in 1765:

> I have just begun a Course of experiments for a white body & glaze which promiseth well hitherto. Sally is my chief helpmate in this as well as other things, & that she may not be hurried by having too many *Irons in the fire* as the phrase is I have ordered the spinning wheel into the Lumber room. She hath learnt my characters [code], at least to write them, but can scarcely read them at present.[32]

He added, as if casually, 'This business I often think if you could but once enter into the *spirit* of it, would be the prettiest employment for you imaginable.'

Sally, meanwhile, combined her domestic duties with those of Josiah's secretary and adviser. She was as ready with an opinion on property values as she was with suggestions for the shapes of teapots or the decoration of vases, and the value of her practical approach to matters of design was often acknowledged by Josiah. He told Bentley: 'I speak from experience in Female taste, without which I should have made but a poor figure amongst my Potts, not one of which, of any consequence, is finished without the approbation of my Sally.'[33] She helped with the business accounts and, whenever Josiah was ill or unable to deal with them himself, she wrote his letters for him.

In spite of this concern with the business, she found time for her family. She was regularly pregnant and occasionally miscarried, but she took childbearing cheerfully and bore seven children who survived infancy. Their first child, Susannah, was born on 3 January 1765. Known to the family as Sukey, she turned out to be as independent and mettlesome as her mother and appears always to have been a firm favourite with her father. John sent a gift of lobsters from London, especially appreciated by Richard Wedgwood, who spent three days with the family for the christening.[34] The Wedgwoods' second child and eldest son was born the following year and christened John on 2 April 1766. Josiah gave Bentley a graphic account of the arrival of the last child, Mary Anne, born when Sally was forty-four:

> I have now the pleasure to acquaint you that Mrs Wedgwood yesterday presented me with another fine girl & with as little trouble to herself & family as could be expected. She sent for the midwife whilst we

were bowling (after making tea for us as usual in the afternoon) without so much as acquainting me with the matter, slipt upstairs just before supper, & we had not risen from the table before the joyfull tidings of a *safe delivery* & *all well* was brought to us & as soon as the young visitor was dressed she joined the company in the dining room. The mother eat her supper, went to sleep, & all are in a very fine way this morning, but from a sort of decorum established among the sex, originally intended, no doubt, to impose upon us poor men, & make us believe what sufferings they underwent for us & our bantlings, I believe she does not want to come down to dinner to-day, but I shall endeavour to perswade her that the farce will no longer pass upon us in this enlightened age, & as for mere etiquette it is not worth preserving. Mrs Bent, our first surgeon, & man-midwife's wife has made some bold strokes at the silly custom & Mrs W. follows her up pretty closely, but these innovations do not pass without much whispering & shaking the head amongst good gossips of the country.[35]

Sally Wedgwood's constitution was as strong as her will. She suffered from bouts of severe rheumatism but she was seldom ill and lived to an advanced age. Josiah's many surviving letters contain occasional hints that Sally's temperament was not always serene, but in only one, written to her, does he show any impatience with her behaviour: 'I must thank my dear Sally for her last favour, though she did not conclude it so meekly as one might wish, but with a Toss of her head crys, I shall not trouble my head – Oh Fye Sally Fye, wilt thou never mend?'[36] The reproof is good-humoured and gentle but there is a strong suggestion that the problem is not new. Shy and somewhat austere to her children and to all but her closest friends, Sally was a spirited and sometimes headstrong woman who did not automatically fall in with her husband's wishes.

Between 1763 and 1765 two more members of Josiah's family joined his firm. The first was his sister Margaret's son, Tom Byerley. The early death of her husband, who held a post in the Excise, left Margaret and her three children in straitened circumstances. With the help of her brothers she opened a millinery shop in Newcastle-under-Lyme and must have welcomed her youngest brother's offer to employ Tom, then fifteen years old. After a lengthy stay with his uncle John in London, Tom accompanied Josiah to Liverpool, where he met Bentley and, no doubt, visited Sadler & Green. Back in Burslem, his trunks were unpacked to reveal the astonishing and unwelcome knowledge that Tom had ambitions to be an author. 'What we shall now do with a Lad of his turn of mind I cannot tell,' Josiah wrote in dismay. 'What can be done with so young a subject of Authorism: so terribly infected with the Cacoethes scribendi as to take possession of a Garrett at fifteen!'[37]

For a time young Byerley settled down to helping with accounts at Burslem and learning French so that he might help his uncle with translations and correspondence. Josiah described him as 'a very good boy' and believed that he would become 'a usefull member of Society',[38] but his confidence was premature. Another visit to London distracted Tom from his job and he returned chastened to Burslem, where Josiah was paternally forgiving. 'Tom arriv'd here last night . . . & I hope will settle again,' he wrote to his brother on 6 March 1765, 'he was grown really fond of his business before your giddy Town set his spirits afloat again, but I have great hopes a little encouragement, – a set of *new* books, & one months serene air will bring them to subside again.'[39] A month later Tom still appeared 'very well satisfy'd' and Josiah wrote that he would have no objection to paying him handsomely except that Tom had not 'the least notion of the value of money, nor would keep a farthing any longer than an opportunity offer'd of parting with it'.[40]

It was too good to last. Tom still had oats to sow and unsatisfied passions to pursue. In 1766, after an abortive attempt to join a Dublin stage company, he attached himself to a band of strolling players but soon tired of the life and became convinced of his *'inability to succeed in any tolerable degree'*. He wrote penitently to Josiah, asking if his uncle could obtain for him a place as a clerk in the Honourable East India Company. 'I do not know', Josiah wrote with laudable moderation to Bentley, 'what we shall do with him, to keep him out of mischief, & put him in the way of being of some use in the World.'[41] It was finally decided that he should be shipped to Philadelphia to try his luck as far away as possible from the temptations of London and the English stage. On Bentley's advice, Josiah did not insist that young Byerley travel steerage, where conditions were even more primitive than Josiah had imagined, and he sailed at the beginning of July 1768, armed with a generous letter of credit for £70, arranged by Josiah through Bentley's contacts in Liverpool.[42] 'I hope', Josiah wrote without obvious optimism, 'that he will perform his promises, my best wishes attend him, & that is all I can now do for him.'[43]

Tom Byerley's capacity for getting into trouble remained undiminished, however. He spent wildly, was jailed in Philadelphia, probably for debt, and moved to New York, where he found work as a schoolmaster. Josiah sent him a pair of Adam's patent globes 'with the latest improvements' and some books with which Tom was extremely pleased, but less than a year later he was home in Staffordshire.[44] Taking warning from the rapidly deteriorating situation in America and the brief but violent engagement between British troops and New England colonists at Concord in April, Tom preferred to 'run away than stay and fight in so disagreeable a service as he must have been engaged in'.[45] He was glad to settle again in Burslem, in the job he had left some nine years earlier, but this time he stayed. He was to become a dutiful and loyal partner in the firm, and, for some years after Josiah's death, he carried the entire burden of its management.

The second of Josiah's family to join him was his brother, though he did so on an informal basis and from good will rather than any notion of salaried employment. Nine years Josiah's senior, John Wedgwood had prospered in London as a partner in the warehousing firm of Wedgwood & Bliss at the Sign of the Artichoke in Cateaton Street.[46] He sold his share of this partnership towards the end of 1764 or early in 1765[47] and it was from about this time that Josiah began to drop hints that John might usefully be employed on his business in London. Early in March 1765 John himself suggested that he would gladly transact business for his brother,[48] an offer which Josiah immediately accepted and lost no time in exploiting. From this time on, his letters to his brother, always affectionate and often humorous, contain more and more details of his business, and he consulted John on matters of behaviour towards some of the aristocratic patrons he was gradually acquiring as well as on matters of commerce. He wrote to him at least once a week[49] and, whatever the sobriety of his subject, he could never resist interrupting his train of thought with entertaining comment or gossip, as when their cousin Thomas Wedgwood of the Big House made belated plans for marriage:

> A VOICE this moment breaks in upon me with – NEWS, NEWS, NEWS, & what do you think it is? why truly, the Marriage writeings are making between my [wife's] Unkle Thomas, and my Cousin Molly, both of venerable memory, this may serve as *a Choice drop of Comfort to Old Maids & Batchelors*[50]

Thomas Wedgwood was then sixty-two and his wife, Mary (daughter of Dr Thomas Wedgwood, a Burslem potter of drab saltglazed ware), forty-six.

John was soon making himself useful, paying bills, delivering invoices, obtaining books of designs such as Robert Dossie's *Handmaid to the Arts*, supervising shipments for export through the Port of London and arranging for the engraving of copper plates for the use of Sadler in Liverpool. It is apparent that by mid-June he was obtaining business for his brother as well as transacting it and was effectively acting as Wedgwood's London agent.[51]

Josiah wrote that he could not spare John from London during the summer for a proposed visit to France. He was concerned for his brother's health, which had suffered from overwork in the unhealthy city atmosphere, but his principal reason was an order that he had received from a Mr Smallwood of Newcastle, who had brought it to him, Josiah believed, because no one else in the Potteries would undertake it. Placed by Miss Deborah Chetwynd, daughter of the Master of the Mint and 'sempstress & Laundress to the Queen', the order was for 'A complete sett of tea things, with a gold ground & raised flowers upon it in green' for Queen Charlotte. As Josiah told his brother, it was an order about which he wanted to ask a hundred questions, but had 'never a mouth but yours in Town worth opening upon the subject'.[52]

The principal problem, and the one which was certainly the reason why other potters had refused the order, was the application of gold to earthenware. It was difficult enough to obtain a satisfactory result in lines or bands on porcelain, but no one in Staffordshire at this period had any experience of trying to lay it down as a solid background in the manner indicated in the order. Gold was also extremely expensive. Josiah asked his brother to buy for him 'a few pennyweights by way of tryal' of a gold powder 'such as is burnt in upon China', obtainable only from a Mr Shenton at 7 guineas an ounce. He added hopefully: 'Mr Shenton may perhaps give you instructions about the best manner of useing it.' Josiah had already ordered a similar quantity of gold leaf from another London dealer and was anxious to begin experiments with it. He urged his brother to 'put on the best suit of Cloaths you ever had in your life, & take the first opportunity of going to Court' to call on Miss Chetwynd with his list of detailed questions about this prestigious order.[53]

The importance of this order to Josiah can scarcely be overestimated. He had understood almost from the first that the production of cream-ware of such a quality – in material, form, decoration and finish – that it might be used instead of porcelain by the greatest people in the land was not enough. Those same people must first be made aware of it and then, most essentially, be persuaded that it was fashionable. 'Fashion', he wrote some years later after considerable experience of it, 'is infinitely superior to *merit* in many respects.' Although he was never content to allow fashion to dictate his production, he was never so improvident as to ignore its commercial value and he took care that, through the exploitation of 'proper sponcers',[54] fashion was regularly given a friendly nudge in his direction.

Although no evidence has ever been found to corroborate the story, there is a long tradition that Josiah had earlier presented a 'caudle set'* to Queen Charlotte, probably in 1763, but if this unsolicited gift was intended to interest Her Majesty in his developing creamware it clearly failed to do so. The green and gold creamware teaset, on the other hand, which was finished to his satisfaction and delivered complete with matching coffee cups,† candlesticks and fruit baskets, brought him an accolade of incalculable value: his official appointment as Potter to the Queen.[55] No better sponsor could have been discovered in Britain.

The successful execution of this order is a measure of the remarkable improvement Wedgwood had achieved in the quality of creamware. His continuous experiments with clays, glazes and firing temperatures had resulted in a reliable body of an attractive creamy-white under a glaze that was both clear and even, and he created for it shapes – often adapted from Sèvres, Meissen or Chelsea porcelain – that combined utility with elegance to a degree seldom previously encountered in Staffordshire pottery. His creamware, renamed 'Queen's ware' from 1766 in honour of his most distinguished patron, had a further inestimable advantage: it was cheap to produce. The greatest costs of production were in the decoration, and prices could be adjusted to them.

Where the Queen had led, others, including the King and lesser members of the royal family, soon followed. Sales of Queen's ware in Britain and to the continent of Europe increased hugely. Little more than a year after the formal announcement of his appointment, Josiah was able to write to Bentley:

The demand for this said *Creamcolour*, Alias *Queen's Ware*, Alias *Ivory*, still increases. It is really amazing how rapidly the use of it has spread allmost over the whole Globe, & how universally it is liked. How much of this general use, & estimation, is owing to the mode of its introduction – & how much to its real utility and beauty? are questions in which we may be a good deal interested for the government of our future Conduct . . . For instance, if a Royal, or Noble introduction be as necessary to the sale of an Article of *Luxury*, as real Elegance & beauty, then the Manufacturer, if he consults his own interest will bestow as much pains, & expence too, if necessary, in gaining the former of these advantages, as he would in bestowing the latter.[56]

---

*Caudle was a warm, sweet drink of eggs, sugar, spices and bread or oatmeal mixed with ale or wine, generally for invalids.
†At this period, and well into the nineteenth century, a teaset included coffee cups which were matched with the same saucers as those used for the teacups in the set.

Josiah was not slow to realise that distinguished patronage was more readily to be found in London, where most of the aristocracy kept a house for occupation for that part of the year when the Court was in attendance on the King and Queen at St James's Palace, than in the West Midlands. The capital was also by far the greatest centre of both wholesale and retail trades. It was already clear that, although he was goodnaturedly glad to look after Josiah's interests in London, John had no desire to live there indefinitely. Nor was he looking for full-time, energetic work but rather, as Josiah put it to one of his most generous patrons, for 'a genteel employment not attended with too much fatigue'.[57]

Josiah was beginning to think in more ambitious terms of some form of permanent representation in London. He wrote to John in August 1765: 'You know I have often mention'd having a man in London the greatest part of the year shewing patterns, takeing orders, settleing accounts &c. &c. & as I increase my work and throw it still more into the ornamental way I shall have the greater need of such assistance & should be glad to have your advice upon it. Wo'd £50 a year keep such a Person in London & pay rent for 2 Rooms'. . . about so much I think it might answer for me to give.'[58] He told his brother just five days later that the Duke of Marlborough and Lord Spencer, both great-grandsons of the 'great' Duke of Marlborough, had visited the Brick House Works with Lord Gower and expressed surprise that he had no 'Warehouse in London where patterns of all the sorts I make may be seen'.[59]

After an uncharacteristic hestitation of three months, Josiah decided to drop a careful, disguised hint to Bentley: 'My Brother is now with me,' he wrote on 15 October, '& is very certain that if you would come to London, & enter a second time into the holy estate of Matrimony that you might choose your Lady, have your Chariot, lead the World in a string, & do what seemeth good in your own eyes . . . every wife, maid and widow that hath seen Mr Bentley in London join in this opinion.' Finding that this produced no satisfactory response to indicate that Bentley had understood the message, he tried again with less delicacy: 'the Reason for my stay in London was the very same that has prevented you from doing many things – My Concerns & Business have Prevented me, & I had no hand I cou'd well leave it in.'[60]

Ignoring the implied personal invitation, Bentley recommended Peter Swift for employment. Josiah was unwilling to take on a married man and pay 'London wages to one who must keep house there'[61] but engaged him in 1766 to work in Burslem, for three years at £25 a year, rising to £30 in the third year. This released William Cox, his unmarried book-keeper at the factory, to take charge of the premises he rented at 5 Charles Street (now Carlos Place), London.

Josiah's ambitions were not satisfied by the acquisition of an office and small showroom in the capital. His business was already expanding and he confidently expected an even larger increase from his growing reputation in London. Nor was there any obvious reason why the purchase of such a reasonably priced product as Queen's ware should be confined to the rich. The 'middling class' could comfortably afford it and even the poorer families need not be wholly excluded. He supposed also that a London showroom would have a satisfactory effect on his trade to Europe.

Such a great increase in sales as he anticipated could be serviced only by buying-in, in enormous quantitites, goods that might be of inferior quality, or by greatly expanded and improved production in his own factory. In fact, if he were not content to allow his business to stand still, and then inevitably to decline, the time had come to buy, or possibly even to build, his own factory.

There was another important consideration, hinted at in Josiah's letter to John in 1765, when he wrote of increasing his work and directing it 'still more in the ornamental way'. He had noticed a remarkable omission from the long lists of objects made by English earthenware potters: although they included large and sometimes complicated pieces such as pharmacy jars, there were no ornamental vases such as were expensively available from the porcelain manufacturers By 1765, he was already making some cream-coloured ornamental vases and was sufficiently confident of their excellence to send a few examples of them to the Queen in July,[62] but he had far more adventurous plans for the exploitation of this opportunity. His cousin, Thomas, had already proved himself invaluable in the development of Queen's ware and quite able to organise the production of tablewares. The manufacture of these 'useful wares', later defined by Josiah as 'such vessels as are made use of at meals', was allotted to Thomas as his particular task. He was made a partner in the firm in 1766 and given a '1–8th share of the proffits'.[63] By this single action Josiah freed himself to plan his new factory, to develop original and profitable forms of ornamental ware and to carry out the experimental work that would be essential to the success of these new enterprises.

CHAPTER FIVE

Commercial Communications

In March 1765, Josiah wrote to John Wedgwood that he was looking out for 'an agreeable and convenient situation elsewhere'.[1] It is possible that he was referring to his need for greater oven space, temporarily relieved in March the following year by renting the 'Red Work-houses' from Cousin John of the Big House for £10 a year,[2] but this is more likely to be the first signal of his intention to move and build his own factory. By the summer of 1766 he had found what he wanted and, in an apparently offhand postscript to his letter to Bentley on 18 July, informed him that he had bought the estate he had previously described to him for £3000, completion of the sale to be at Michaelmas.[3]

His announcement was premature. The Ridgehouse Estate, a property of about 350 acres near Burslem, overlooking the valley towards Newcastle-under-Lyme, was owned by a Mrs Ashenhurst, an intractable old lady who proved to be a tougher businesswoman than Josiah had anticipated. 'She scolds & huffs away at a large rate,' he told Bentley a year later, '& seems to be in a good way for making me a hard bargain. I have wrote to Her by Mr Hodgson,[4] & instructed him to treat with her. If he succeeds, I hope yet to be able to build . . . at the latter end of this summer.'[5] In this, too, he was disappointed, and Mrs Ashenhurst continued to hold out for a higher price. The stalemate might have been prolonged indefinitely but for her timely death, which allowed the executors of her estate to settle with Josiah at the original sum at the end of 1767.

The Ridgehouse Estate was probably not the only property of a suitable size to be offered to Josiah in this period and he was unusually patient in his negotiations for it. The reason for his perseverance became clear when the approved route of the Trent and Mersey Canal was made public. The Ridgehouse Estate lay directly in its path.

For several centuries the local craft of pottery had survived in Staffordshire in almost entirely local markets but, from about 1740, as the range and quality of the goods began to be transformed by technical advances in the bodies, glazes, shapes and methods of decoration, and when it became possible to make and fire larger quantities with less risk, potters had started to demand better roads and more reliable shipping. An industry was gradually emerging which required improved communications with the principal cities of Britain for trade, and with its great ports for the transport of raw materials to the factories and finished goods to the outside world.

Josiah became a leading figure in the fight for turnpikes against local opposition. He enlisted the help of Lord Gower, one of the county's most influential magnates, whose ownership of vast coal resources gave him a particular interest in the transport of freight. Granville Leveson-Gower, who had succeeded his father as 1st Earl Gower in 1754, had been Member of Parliament for Westminster and later for Lichfield, and a Lord of the Admiralty from 1749 to 1751. After his succession to the Upper House, he was twice appointed Lord Privy Seal, on the second occasion in the Younger Pitt's administration, and twice President of the Council. He was created Marquis of Stafford in 1786. During the early 1760s, when Wedgwood was most in need of his advice and the weight of his influence, Gower was established close to the royal family as, variously, Master of the Horse, Keeper of the Great Wardrobe and Chamberlain of the Household. He was the most powerful ally Josiah could have found and he was one of his earliest aristocratic patrons. He had a high regard for Wedgwood's abilities and products and he entertained him frequently at Trentham Hall, his Staffordshire seat between Newcastle-under-Lyme and Stone.

Through Gower's influence a petition was presented to Parliament in February 1763 for a turnpike to connect the existing Liverpool–London road to the north of the Potteries and the Derby–Uttoxeter–Newcastle-under-Lyme road to the south. This would avoid the detour of nearly 10 miles made necessary by the state of the road between Burslem and Lawton on the northern turnpike. The petition, which Josiah probably helped to draft, contains useful information about the Potteries and their existing arrangements for the transport of raw materials and finished goods.[6]

According to the petition, there were nearly 150 separate potteries in the area providing 'constant employment and support' for as many as 7000 people. It was claimed that their ware was:

> exported in vast quantities from London, Bristol, Liverpool, Hull and other seaports to our several colonies in America and the West Indies

as well as to every port in Europe . . . Many thousand tons of shipping, and seamen in proportion, which in summer trade to the northern seas, are employed in winter in carrying materials for the Burslem ware; and [an allusion guaranteed to appeal to the exchequer ministers] as much salt is consumed in glazing one species of it as pays annually near £5000 duty to government . . . and every shilling received for ware at foreign markets is so much clear gain to the nation, as not one foreigner is employed in, or any material imported from abroad for, any branch of it.[7]

The route suggested for the new turnpike would have diverted traffic and trade from Newcastle-under-Lyme to Burslem and Stoke, and the petition was strongly opposed by the inhabitants of Newcastle. Wedgwood addressed a public meeting of the 'Gentlemen of Newcastle' in the Town Hall, severely reproving them for conduct that, if they persevered in their objections, would be 'unneighbourly and ungenerous', adding, 'and whether you carry your point or not, it cannot be to your advantage'. This was indeed true, for he had warned them that, faced with continued opposition, he and other potters would repair the road privately by subscription 'without an Act of Parliament and then travellers will have a stronger inducement to come our way if the tolls were equal'.[8] The Act was finally passed, but only after a compromise solution had been found, and the road terminated at the southern entrance to Burslem instead of running on to join the Derby–Newcastle turnpike.

Almost exactly two years later Josiah wrote to John that he was mounted on his hobbyhorse again 'and a prancing rogue he is at present', to have the Burslem and Uttoxeter turnpikes joined and two other major routes converted to toll roads:

£2000 is wanting for this road. My [wife's] Uncles Thomas and John have – I am quite serious – at the first asking subscribed – I know you will not believe me, but it is a certain fact – *five hundred pounds!!!* – I have done the like intending 2 or 300 of it for you, & if you choose any more you must let me know in time, it will not be wanted 'till Summer though it must be subscribed now.[9]

Evidently John did not reply, for Josiah wrote to remind him in March, reassuring him that the subscriptions would attract interest at 5 per cent '& good security'.[10]

This time local objections were more easily overcome and the Act was passed, once again with help from Lord Gower, without amendment. During the following eighteen years Wedgwood successfully led the pottery owners in their demands for a network of turnpike roads serving the Potteries. As a result of this pressure, six Turnpike Acts affecting the Six Towns* were passed in 1766 alone. Josiah and his three sons were among the 130 trustees of the 1779 Act, and Wedgwood, Whieldon and Spode all attended the first recorded meeting of the committee of trustees in July 1791.

These improvements were in line with developments throughout the country; indeed, in comparison with much of England, the Potteries were backward in their demands. It was understood that one of the reasons why Prince Charles Edward Stuart's army had been able to advance as far as Derby in 1745 had been the atrocious state of the roads, which had hindered the movement of the King's regular forces. This was but one of many factors that caused the government to take a more active interest in road-building, but it is significant that a Turnpike Act of 1751 specifically directs that the road between Carlisle and Newcastle-upon-Tyne shall be 'proper for the passage of troops, horses and carriages' in all seasons.[11] The number of Turnkpike Trusts rose from 160 to 530 in the twelve years to 1760, and in the following fourteen years Parliament passed 452 Acts regulating the building and maintainance of roads in Britain. The dramatic effect of all this activity is reflected in a contemporary account published only two years after Wedgwood's successful campaign to have the Uttoxeter and Burslem turnpikes linked:

> There never was a more astonishing revolution accomplished in the internal system of any country, than has been within the compass of a few years in that of England. The carriage of grains, coals, merchandise, etc., is in general conducted with little more than half the number of horses with which it formerly was. Journeys of business are performed with more than double expedition. Improvements in agriculture keep pace with those of trade. Everything wears the face of dispatch, every article of our produce becomes more valuable, and the hinge upon which all these movements turn is the reformation which has been made in our public high roads.[12]

The new turnpikes made it possible for raw materials and finished goods to be carried by cart and waggon rather than by pack-horse, but road transport nevertheless remained expensive. A cheaper method of moving large quantities of heavy goods to and from the Potteries was

---

*Tunstall, Burslem, Hanley, Stoke-on-Trent, Fenton and Longton.

urgently needed if the fledgling industry was to achieve its potential growth. That need was met by the creation of an inland waterway system.

The concept of canals for irrigation and transportation was an ancient one; canal systems were in use in Europe, especially in France, Italy* and the Low Countries, long before any serious proposal was made for such a system in England. One of the first was published by Andrew Yarranton, a brilliant but eccentric visionary, in 1677. He urged that the rivers of Britain should be made navigable 'in all places where art could possibly effect it' and that the principal waterways – the Thames, Severn and Trent – be linked by canals.[13]

During the next eighty years some useful work was carried out on rivers, including the Mersey, Trent and Derwent, whose courses ran close to developing cities, but the first canal to be cut for the particular purpose of transporting goods and materials, the Worsley Canal, was not completed until 1761.

The Worsley Canal was the creation of the Duke of Bridgewater, who financed it, and James Brindley, who designed it and supervised the engineering work. Both had a connection with Staffordshire: Bridgewater as Lord Gower's brother-in-law and a regular visitor to Trentham; Brindley as a millwright, settled in Leek, where he had been employed in the past to construct and repair windmills and water-wheels used to crush flint for the Potteries.† Like Lord Gower, the Duke of Bridgewater owned large deposits of coal, but the cost, after extracting it from his mines at Worsley, of transporting it by pack-horse to Manchester (between 9 and 10s. a ton for a journey of less than 7 miles) was prohibitive. In 1758–9, after consulting Brindley, he obtained an Act of Parliament permitting him to cut a canal from Worsley to Manchester. Completed in two years, the canal started in the underground galleries of the Worsley mines and crossed the River Irwell on an aqueduct 40 feet above the water. It was regarded with awe as one of the engineering masterpieces of Europe, and Brindley, whose extraordinary ingenuity and practical application had persuaded the Duke to provide resources for what appeared to be an impossible plan, was hailed as a genius. In 1767 the canal was extended to the Mersey, halving the cost of transport between Manchester and Liverpool.

By this time Brindley had become involved in another project which took him back to the Potteries. As early as 1717 Dr Thomas Congreve of Wolverhampton had published a project for a canal between the

---

*Leonardo da Vinci completed the six locks uniting the canals of Milan in 1487.
†These mills were originally made to grind corn and had to be adapted for use with flint.

Rivers Trent and Severn and a survey of the route had been carried out in 1755. A fresh survey was made four years later by Brindley at Lord Gower's expense, but the magnitude of the task, the complex problems and the enormous costs involved did not encourage support for the project, which was shelved. The success of the Worsley Canal and the immediate commercial advantages achieved by it persuaded a number of interested parties in Staffordshire to examine the prospects for a canal to link the Trent with the Mersey. Such a waterway would carry Gower's coal and the products of the Potteries direct to the ports of Liverpool on the west coast and Hull on the east as well as providing access at greatly reduced costs for the materials brought from the West Country. The quantity of goods carried would quickly allow subscribers to recoup capital costs and show a profit on their investment.

Josiah wrote to his brother on 11 March 1765:

> On Friday last I dined with Mr Brindley the Duke of Bridgwater's engineer, after which we had a meeting at the Leopard on the subject of a Navigation from Hull, or Wilden Ferry to Burslem agreeable to a survey plan before taken. Our Gentlemen seem very warm in seting this matter on foot again, & I could scarcely withstand the pressing solicitations I had from all present, to undertake a journey or two for that purpose.[14]

When a hobby horse presented itself, Josiah was the first to mount it. With this one he involved both Bentley and a newer friend, Dr Erasmus Darwin.

It is not certain when Wedgwood first met Darwin but it is likely that they were first introduced by Matthew Turner after Josiah's return from Liverpool in May 1762. Darwin was to become one of Josiah's most intimate friends as well as the physician called upon whenever there was serious illness in the family. His originality of thought and interest in scientific and mechanical invention made him an especially attractive companion to Josiah, whose inquiring mind and almost continuous experimentation equally recommended him to Darwin.

The Trent and Mersey Canal, or, as Brindley called it, the 'Grand Trunk' Canal, proved to be a more complicated venture than even Wedgwood had anticipated. Rival schemes were proposed and there was obstinate opposition from the proprietors of the River Weaver Navigation (the 'Cheshire Gentlemen'), who saw obvious advantages in a canal that terminated at the Weaver but none in one that continued to the Mersey, offering much lower transport costs than their own.

They did their argument little good by at first refusing to consider any reduction in their charges, and then, in response to a proposal to cut the new canal direct to Liverpool, alternating offers of concessions with threats to construct another canal along a parallel route.

Bentley's first contribution to the campaign was in the form of advice about the most politic manner of approaching the Liverpool authorities for their support. Josiah transcribed part of this in his own letter to Darwin:

> . . . the first application should be made to the Mayor, Jno Tarleton Esqr. The application of the Trade duty, which is the Fund I suppose you must expect assistance from, will depend a good deal upon his influence, & if he and the Council begin, I dare answer for the concurrence of the other [Sir William Meredith's] party, though if the other party were to begin, the M—& his friends would be sure to oppose you. Suppose you was first to write to the Mayor & desire his advice & opinion upon the subject, and in the mean while prepare your plans & scheme to be introduced by him and laid before the Merchants at large. You may honestly pay him some compliments upon his public Spirit & known attention to the interests of Commerce &c. &c. – I presume without fear of offence – Good things go down better with a little seasoning . . . [15]

Josiah solicited Darwin's help with Lichfield Council and invited him to be 'Generalissimo in this affair', adding, 'in this, as well as every other step, we shall be govern'd by your advice'.[16] He later had cause to regret this declaration in favour of Darwin's superior judgement.

Meanwhile, he made approaches to the councils (whom he invariably described as 'the Gentlemen') of Newcastle-under-Lyme and Birmingham, where 'a very intelligent Gentleman', Samuel Garbett, a manufacturer of industrial chemicals and a man of some influence in Birmingham business circles, had given him relevant figures for the savings to be made by the 'Russia Merchants' trading in iron and flax. 'This scheme of Navigation', Josiah told his brother on 3 April 1765, 'is undoubtedly the best thing that could possibly be plan'd for this country & I hope there is a great probability of its being carried into execution.'[17]

Both Darwin and Bentley urged Wedgwood to send them factual information about current use of road and river transport: the volume and value of all manner of goods and materials;* the costs of moving them; the anticipated increase in volume following the building of the canal; and the savings per ton to be expected. These Wedgwood gathered assiduously and passed on with other news of his intentions and activities. Figures of particular interest to the Staffordshire potters included the freight costs of clay and flint, to be reduced from 15s. to 2s. per ton, and the carriage of earthenware from 28s. to 12s. Darwin was insatiable in his demands for details until Wedgwood finally wrote to him: 'I have no more facts for you, if you are short you must create some'.[18] Letters were written to newspapers; landowners, Members of Parliament and city councillors were lobbied; petitions were presented; and Bentley's skilled advocacy was enlisted in a pamphlet which he wrote to publicise the benefits of the canal.

This pamphlet was published in October 1765 and ran to several editions, but not before Erasmus Darwin had subjected it, and its author, to a stream of criticism, which threatened to postpone publication indefinitely. Darwin's strictures were characteristically blunt and devoid of tact and Josiah, retailing to Bentley Darwin's comment that 'the style was too flat & tame', asked him to remember that the opinion came from one who was 'himself a Poetical Genius'.[19] But worse was to come. Bentley's use of formal styles was dismissed as bourgeois: 'nobody writes Grace, & Rt. honourable, but Taylors & such like folks'.[20] The Octagon Prayer Book, with which Bentley had been intimately concerned, was condemned as 'astonishingly deficient in Language'.[21] 'It is', Darwin wrote, warming to his task of demolition, 'no Discredit to Mr Bentley, that he does not write agreeably and concisely. But it is no Credit to him that he does not know it.'[22] Bentley was a founder of the Octagon Chapel, opened in June 1763 in Temple Court, Liverpool. It was a place of worship intended primarily for nonconformists who chose some emancipation from orthodox creeds and ritual. The special liturgy, of which Darwin was so scathing a critic, was drawn up so that it might be used, without offence, by both dissenting 'Octagonians' and more conventional Churchmen. Bentley is likely to have had a hand in drafting or revising it and Darwin either knew this to be so or guessed at it.

Perturbed by the quarrel that appeared to be brewing between two of his closest friends, Josiah appealed to Bentley's sharp sense of the

---

*The freight was listed in the pamphlet under three headings: 'natural productions of the countries that lie near the canal'; 'Cultivated commodities and manufactures'; and 'Imported materials'. It included coal, clay, stone, slate, lead, copper, marble, alabaster, corn, timber, cheese, ale, hides, charcoal, lime, flint, iron ore, tobacco, rum, wine, salt and sugar.

ridiculous: 'I doubt not but you have received . . . a long critical epistle from our ingenious & poetical friend Doctor Darwin, which . . . if it be such as he generally favours his friends with, hath afforded you entertainment & shook your diaphragm for you, whatever it may have done respecting your pamphlet on Navigation.'[23] Darwin's criticism was, however, 'below a Man of Letters' and he added, 'I fancy the Author was sore.'[24]

In such a situation, as Wedgwood suspected, Bentley was well able to take care of himself, displaying an enviable capacity for the ironical riposte and silken diplomatic reproof. He wrote to Darwin on 11 October:

> Mr Bentley never had the pleasure of seeing Dr Darwin, but shall think himself much honoured by his friendship & future Correspondence. . . . In every work that can bear the Expence I think it would always be prudent to print a few copies with large Margins first, to put into the hands of Critics. This is the only way of bringing a Work to any Degree of Correctness. . . . I have found this by Experience, in a considerable Work, which I transcribed for the Press, after the Corrections of a Hundred contending Critics – no two of which were hardly ever of the same Opinion, about the Elegance of an Expression . . . the Misfortune is, those who can write best, seldom know much of such Subjects.[25]

He was, however, stung by Darwin's harsh comments on the Octagon Prayer Book:

> You say the Liverpool Liturgy was not read, because it was *ill-written*. And yet that book was written by Gentlemen of as much Learning as any we shall find for this Pamphlet; and had all the advantages of *Reviewing* (from which you seem to expect too much) that a Work could have. It received the Corrections of many Gentlemen who were as well qualified as any in this Kingdom for that Purpose; and by many good Judges, it is thought to be excellently *well written*. So much do Men of Learning & Taste differ in their Judgements![26]

The two men were too sensible to allow this disagreement to fester into animosity and they were united in their aim, if not in the detailed means to achieve it. They composed their differences and the pamphlet was sent for publication. With all its additions and amendments it had become, as Bentley described it, 'a piece of Patch-Work',[27] part-Bentley, part-Wedgwood and part-Darwin. 'Mankind are seldom ungrateful to those who *apparently* employ themselves in promoting the public Welfare.'[28]

While others bickered and criticised, it was Wedgwood who pushed and drove and led, argued and persuaded, canvassed and enlisted influence and help, and all the while continued actively to manage his business. 'I have scarcely read anything at all, or thought of anything at all but Pottmakeing & *Navigateing*, & when it will be otherwise with me I cannot tell,' he told Bentley in October.[29]

This is the earliest evidence that survives of Wedgwood's extraordinary energy and capacity for work. When he was mounted on one of his hobby-horses he gave himself no rest and it is not surprising to learn that he outrode his strength and fell ill in November, while staying with his brother in London. His breakdown was serious enough for Sally to write his letters for him, but he insisted on adding his own postscript to Bentley, 'lest you should think me dead, lame, or very lazy'. 'I shall', he wrote, 'for the future be very cautious how I hook my friends into such thankless, profitless business again, & how I engage in them myself too, but there is no retreating now without both loss & shame therefore must make the best of a bad matter . . . we hope to leave this dismal, smoaky place on monday next.'[30]

His return to the comparatively clean air of Burslem failed to complete his recovery and Darwin was called in to treat him. 'I am got pretty well but not perfectly recover'd,' he wrote to Bentley on 18 November. 'Dr Darwin who stop'd all night with me at Burslem last week hath prescrib'd something for me which he says will strengthen the machinery & set it all to rights again. The Dr acknowledg'd he had wrote you two or three very rude letters, & said you had drub'd him genteely in return, which he seem'd to take very cordially, & to be very pleas'd with his treatment.'[31]

The 'bad matter' was entering its final phase. Promoted by the Duke of Bridgewater and Lord Gower with influential support from other local grandees – the Earl of Stamford (of Enville) and his brother, Lord Grey, Sir Walter Bagot of Blithfield, Sir William Wolseley and Thomas Anson of Shugborough – all personally enrolled by Josiah, the arguments in support of the canal had found favour with all the city councils concerned, but the opposition of the Cheshire Gentlemen, some landowners and others with vested interests in river navigation was strengthening.

A significant factor in the Duke of Bridgewater's support was his plan to cut a canal, named after him, to link Manchester with the Mersey, finished by the indefatigable Brindley in 1767, and agreement that the Trent and Mersey Canal should be linked with it, adding

Manchester to the network. The Duke was a wholehearted supporter of the Trent–Mersey scheme but his enthusiasm for it was tempered by his own financial straits. Josiah, who spent about eight hours with him early in December,[32] did not fully appreciate the situation and mistook the Duke's hesitancy for doubt. Meanwhile, the Weaver Navigation proprietors offered to reduce their tonnage charges and there were rumours that they were considering the construction of a rival canal to join Hull to Liverpool by a different route and to extend it from Stafford to the Severn. Josiah believed that 'this bustling affair' was a bluff aimed at obtaining a compromise in favour of the Cheshire Gentlemen, but it later appeared that they were in earnest and that the threat was real.[33]

His letters to Bentley at this period began to take on a flavour of secrecy which was later to be a familiar feature of their correspondence. Thefts of letters were common and Josiah trusted none of his most confidential information to the mail unless it was in his private code. 'I am ordered', he wrote, 'when our battle waxeth hot, which it soon will do, to keep 4 or 5 running footmen at my elbow & trust nothing of consequence to the post.'[34] More and more he was discovering the true worth of Bentley's friendship and balanced advice; repeatedly he told him of his pleasure in reading his 'very valuable letters'; but, as later in their relationship, he wished most for Bentley's company. 'I cannot come to Liverpool,' he wrote in December, '& yet I would do allmost anything to spend an evening with you, cannot you possibly come to Burslem once in your life? pray let me know where & when we can with the greatest convenience to yourself spend a day together.'[35]

Meanwhile, subscriptions were pouring in; £20,000 had been raised for the canal by the end of 1765, before any contribution from Liverpool. Preliminary expenses, however, which included surveys and fees incurred in obtaining the essential Act of Parliament, were likely to be heavy, and only £500 had been subscribed for these. Josiah calculated that about four times this sum would be needed, but councils were as reluctant as individual subscribers to advance money for a bill that might not become law.[36]

Early in the New Year he was able to assure Bentley that he no longer had any fear that the full sums required would not be raised,[37] and he wrote to the Mayor of Liverpool that applications to the land-owners all along the proposed route of the canal 'even in Cheshire . . . an Enemy's Country', had met with success, all but one having 'consented or promis'd not to oppose'.[38] The campaign outside Parliament was almost complete.

The petition for the Trent and Mersey Canal was presented in the House of Commons on 15 January 1766 and referred to a committee of the House. The Duke of Bridgewater's petition to link the Bridgewater and Trent and Mersey cuts at his own expense was likewise referred, and the committee began to hear witnesses on 15 April. Wedgwood, Bentley and Brindley were among those called. Six days later, the arguments of the opposition having been demolished, the bill received its third reading. It passed through the Lords without amendment and received the royal assent on 14 May.

Under the Act, two governing bodies were appointed to administer the new canal: the Company of Proprietors, 101 subscribers headed by the Duke of Bridgewater and Lord Gower and including Thomas Whieldon, William Willet and John Wedgwood of Smallwood (two of Josiah's brothers-in-law) and John Wedgwood of the Big House; and 816 Commissioners, twenty-two of whom were potters. The Executive Committee, entrusted with the active management of the canal, had only seven members, all but one of whom were salaried: James Brindley as Surveyor-General at £200 a year; Hugh Henshall, Clerk of the Works, at £150; John Sparrow, Clerk to the Proprietors, at £100; and T. Nailor, R. Parrott and T. Bateman, respectively Clerks to the Cheshire, Stafford-shire and Derbyshire Commissioners, at one guinea a day when employed on canal business. The single exception was Josiah himself, appointed Treasurer, as he ruefully told his brother, 'at £ooo Per ann. out of which he bears his own Expences'. For this privilege, and although he expected never to handle more than £5000–6000 at a time, he was obliged to offer security of £10,000.[39] As an acknowlegement of his tireless work and the successful outcome of a campaign that had been peculiarly his, he was permitted to cut the first sod of the canal when work on it was officially begun on 26 July 1766.

The Grand Trunk Canal was not completed until 1777, when it extended to 93 miles with seventy-five locks. The total cost was £200,000. The price of coal in Manchester was halved and the Duke of Bridgewater's profits from his mines rose from £406 in 1760 to £48,000 in 1803. 'A navigation', he said with understandable satisfaction, 'should have coals at the heel of it.'[40]

Brindley did not live to see it completed. Josiah wrote to Bentley on 2 March 1767:

> I am afraid he [Brindley] will do too much, & leave us before his vast designs are executed, he is so incessantly harassed on every side, that he hath no rest, either for his mind or Body, & will not be prevailed upon to take proper care of his health . . . I think Mr Brindley – The *Great*, the *fortunate, money-getting* Brindley an object of Pity! & a real sufferer for the good of the Public. He may get a few thousands, but

what does he give in exchange? His *Health*, & I fear his *Life* too, unless he grows wiser, & takes the advice of his friends before it is too late.[41]

A month later, Brindley was not well enough to attend a meeting of the committee or to undertake a journey to Ireland and Scotland for Samuel Garbett. Josiah tried to persuade him to 'be idle for a season that his stay amongst us may be the longer for it' and Brindley took his wife to Buxton for two weeks, from which he returned 'a good deal better'. But Josiah was far from satisfied: 'his constitution requires more than a fortnights rest.'[42] In spite of diabetes, from which he had suffered for at least seven years before Darwin diagnosed it, Brindley survived another five years of overwork. Josiah, who had visited him regularly during the previous ten days, wrote sadly to Bentley on 26 September 1772: 'Poor Mr Brindley has nearly finish'd his course in this world. He says he must leave us, & indeed I do not expect to find him alive in the morning.'[43]

Brindley died at about noon the next day and Wedgwood paid him a generous tribute:

> What the Public has lost can only be conceiv'd by those who best knew his Character & Talents – Talents for which this Age & Country are indebted for works that will be the most lasting monument to his Fame, & shew to future Ages how much good may be done by one single Genius, when happily employd upon works beneficial to Mankind. . . . Millions yet unborn will revere & bless his memory.[44]

By 1790, the great canal work for which Brindley had laid the foundations was complete: London, Liverpool, Hull, Birmingham and Bristol were linked.

The key to Britain's industrial growth in both the eighteenth and nineteenth centuries was the transformation of inland communications. 'Good roads, canals and navigable rivers are the greatest of all improvements,' wrote Adam Smith in 1776, 'as by means of water-carriage, a more extensive market is opened to every sort of industry than what land-carriage alone can afford it, so it is upon the sea coast, and along the banks of navigable rivers, that industry of every kind begins to sub-divide and improve itself.'[45] The improvements in provincial roads brought about by the turnpikes encouraged traffic and reduced travelling times but did little to cut costs of transportation, which were calculated on mileage, not on time taken in delivery.

Until the middle of the century, there was no regular passenger coach service between Staffordshire and London and the journey on the scarce coaches on the route took at least four days. The charge was about 3d. a mile, passengers inside the coach generally paying twice as much as those 'on top'. By 1766 there were thirty stage coaches running daily between London and Birmingham and the journey from Liverpool could be accomplished in three days by the Warrington 'flying coach'. Burslem was brought within a full day's travel from London.

Even more important to businessmen was the improvement in the postal service but, like the rates for road transport, the charges were high. The London penny post extended only to a radius of 10 miles from the General Post Office and the rate for a letter to Staffordshire rose from 4d. to 6d. in 1784 and further to 8d. in 1796. Such rates generally encouraged frugality in the use of the Royal Mail, but Josiah, in spite of frequent reminders to his correspondents to be economical, continued throughout his working life to send letters of immense length to his friends, most particularly to Bentley.[46]

In contrast to turnpike roads, the canals reduced costs of transportation for all goods, and the consequent reduction in prices at the point of distribution in turn produced a proportional increase in demand. As a result of the completion of the Trent and Mersey Canal, the freight costs for raw materials and finished goods to and from the Potteries were reduced from 10d. to 1½d. per mile.[47] When this significant benefit became available, Josiah Wedgwood intended to be so placed as to take maximum advantage of it.

His campaigns for improved communications, essential though they had been, had taken too much of Josiah's strength and time. He told Bentley in January 1766, 'As to my private concerns I have almost forgot them. I scarcely know without a good deal of recollection whether I am a Landed Gentleman, an Engineer, or a Potter, for indeed I am all three & many other characters by turns.'[48] He was ready to give his full attention to the expansion of his business.

Although he had not yet, as he at first believed, succeeded in his negotiations for the purchase of the Ridgehouse Estate from Mrs Ashenhurst, Josiah immediately began to make ambitious plans for the building of a new factory. The price of the land was £3000. The initial cost of the factory was estimated at nearly £4000 and of Josiah's house, Etruria Hall, a further £2660.[49] No evidence has survived to show how these considerable costs were financed but, had a large loan been negotiated, it is likely that some hint of it would remain, either in Wedgwood's colossal correspondence with Bentley or in the remaining manuscripts referring to his dealings with his bankers, Ashton, Hodgson & Co. Such a loan might have been made to Josiah by his father-in-law but there is no evidence of interest payments to Richard Wedgwood at any period. Nor, in spite of his rapidly growing business, is there any indication that Josiah could have saved such a large sum from his profits. On the contrary, the evidence is that he spent more than he could easily afford on his campaigns for turnpikes and the Trent and Mersey Canal.[50]

Proof of an entirely domestic transaction would not be expected and no such proof has been found, but the inference is inescapable that this heavy expenditure, which Josiah entered upon with such confidence and so little anxiety, was financed from his wife's fortune. Until the Married Women's Property Act of 1882 gave wives the same rights as spinsters and widows, married women had no rights in common law over matrimonial property or children. The authority for this, as for almost everything else in English law, was Sir William Blackstone, whose *Commentaries* were published between 1765 and 1769: 'In marriage husband and wife are one person, and that person is the husband.' So that there might be no possible misunderstanding, he added, 'the very being, or legal existence of the woman is suspended in marriage'. The principle that he enunciated with such clarity was well established and, although not invariably practised, it had the respectability of custom, usage and the law.

In 1762, Bentley had introduced the work of his own favourite author, James Thomson, to Josiah, who had been struck by the poet's 'extensive benevolence & goodness of heart'.[51] It is likely that he, though perhaps not Sally, admired Thomson's portrayal of the ideal wife:

> Well-ordered Home Man's best delight to make;
> And by submissive wisdom, modest skill,
> With every gentle care-eluding art,
> To raise the virtues, animate the bliss,
> And sweeten all the toils of human life:
> This be the female dignity and praise.[52]

Sally's fortune was considerable, and was evidently to be even greater in the future. It would have been extraordinary if Josiah had not used part of it for the factory that was to provide their enhanced standard of living, and for the house that he was also to build on the same land, and it would have been even more extraordinary for a dutiful and sensible wife to complain.

One member of the committee of the Proprietors whom Josiah had come to know during the previous year[53] had been Matthew Boulton, whose Soho, Birmingham, factory was already one of the most success-ful in the Midlands. Boulton is credited with coining the advice, 'Don't marry for money but marry where money is', a precept which he had made his own* and which Josiah had followed while still unaware of it.

Born in 1728, Boulton had inherited his father's toy-making business in Snow Hill, Birmingham, in 1759, the year in which Wedgwood had started his first factory at the Ivy House, Burslem. 'Toys' in the Birmingham metal trade were differently defined from those in the Potteries (see page 19n) and comprised a wide variety of products, both useful and decorative, in polished iron, steel, brass, copper and silver, ranging from the tools and instruments used by carpenters, plumbers, millwrights and other such craftsmen to buttons, buckles, candlesticks and watch keys. Boulton's factory was concerned with the production of ornamental and decorative objects, of which he became the leading manufacturer, and by 1766, when he moved to his second, newly built factory at Soho, he claimed to employ 500–600 people and to have a turnover of £15,000. This figure was doubled in twelve months at the new factory,[54] which almost immediately came to be regarded as 'one of the wonders of the industrial world'[55] and attracted a throng of fashionable visitors.

Since 1762 Boulton had been in partnership with John Fothergill who evidently had no capital resources but appears to have had experience, probably as a travelling salesman, of trade in Europe, and useful connections in the financial world. Although it was seldom allowed to interfere with Boulton's ambitious plans for the partnership, Fothergill's natural caution, which amounted to timidity, acted as an occasional brake on his partner's runaway expenditure. When Fothergill died, insolvent, in 1782, Boulton had already lost much of his interest in the ornamental metal trade and was increasingly concentrating his energies upon the engine trade and his partnership with James Watt, which dated from 1775.

The topographer William Hutton, who settled in Birmingham in 1741 at the age of eighteen and was responsible for the city's first circulating library ten years later, was impressed by the fine buildings and burgeoning industry of the growing city but even more by the energy of its population:

> I was surprised at the place but more so at the people: They were a species I had never seen: They possessed a vivacity I have never beheld: I had been among dreamers, but now I saw men awake: their

---

*His two wives, Mary and Anne Robinson, were sisters and the daughters of a wealthy Lichfield mercer. When Mary died in 1759, Anne, whom Boulton married two years later, became sole heiress to a fortune of £28,000.

very step along the street shewed alacrity. Every man seemed to know
& prosecute his own affairs.[56]

In 1765 Boulton was already a leading figure in Birmingham business, and his Soho Works, which cost £10,000 and consisted of more
than sixty workshops for the great variety of specialised production
processes, extensive warehouses and two water-mills, made him
famous. No contemporary plan of the factory has been found, but the
principal buildings, believed to have been designed by William Wyatt,
were contained within four squares with accommodation for 1000 work-
people. Wedgwood determined to be taken round the Soho factory
before the plans for his own were too far advanced.

After this first visit to Soho in May 1767, Wedgwood described
Boulton as 'the first – or most complete manufacturer in England, in
metal. He is very ingenious, Philosophical, & Agreeable.' Boulton
invited Josiah to make another, more extended visit later in the year
and, in return, Josiah invited him to Burslem, 'but this year he is too
much immers'd in business to indulge he says in anything else'.[57]

They were to find much in common. Neither had been given an
opportunity for much formal education but both were men of exceptional intelligence whose boundless energy and endless curiosity led
them to educate themselves. Both were inventive and ambitious. Both
were trained in their fathers' trades and transformed them; and both
married heiresses. Both were men of unusual integrity who trusted one
another. Both had yet to discover the deficiencies in their managerial
skills. When those were revealed, the decisive difference between the
two great manufacturers became apparent. Wedgwood found solutions
and continued to prosper; Boulton failed to understand the problem
until it was too late.

CHAPTER SIX

The New Etruria

While Josiah was treating with Mrs Ashenhurst for land on which to build his factory, he was also negotiating a new partnership with Thomas Bentley. Just three months after his premature announcement of the successful purchase of the Ridgehouse Estate he had casually let fall his first hint to Bentley. When this fell on ears that were strangely or deliberately deaf, he had dropped another, to which Bentley had responded with characteristic good will by recommending Peter Swift.

He was not to escape so easily. Josiah had found the partner he wanted and he was determined to overcome all objections. They were already doing useful business together. Within two years of establishing his partnership with Samuel Boardman at the Manchester Stocking Warehouse, Liverpool, in 1764, Bentley had begun to build up a trade in Wedgwood wares. At first the amount of business was small and Josiah gave him a simple discount of 10 per cent on all the products of his own factory. Soon, however, it became clear that Bentley & Boardman could take valuable orders also for the wares of other potters, and not only those who were Wedgwood's neighbours in Staffordshire. Josiah wrote to Bentley on 26 June 1766:

> I am extremely happy in the thoughts of haveing our connections increased in any way & the pleasure will grow in proportion as those connections can be made more agreeable or more advantageous to you, & as you are to be a Pot merchant you may rest assured that everything I can make or purchace you shall be able to serve to your friends to the utmost of their wishes, so take in orders for anything this country produces. . . . With respect to commission or profit upon the goods you sell I shall very readily conform to any plan you may have determin'd upon, or if you have not settled that matter, I would

make a proposal a very simple one to you respecting this new branch
of Trade betwixt us, which is that whatever goods I purchace to send
you we divide the profitt laid upon them equally betwixt us which is
to pay you for the trouble of selling & me for that of buying the goods.

For goods of his own manufacture, the 10 per cent commission previously offered would be continued. He made a special point of his
need to know whether the goods were for wholesale or retail customers
so that they could be priced accordingly, and agreed that, on goods for
export, their profits must be reduced. A discount of 5 per cent would
be allowed for cash on all wholesale transactions.[1]

This simple and informal, but no less practical, arrangement is
typical of Josiah's common-sense approach in his commercial dealings.
If he believed he could trust the other party to hold to an agreement,
the terms were brief and immediately comprehensible; if not, then he
either refused the business or gave it up as soon as possible.

In effect, Bentley & Boardman became Wedgwood's agents in Liverpool, displaying his products, taking orders, receiving payments and,
in addition, seeing his shipments of clay through the port of Liverpool
and on to Burslem. In return, Wedgwood acted as agent for Bentley &
Boardman in the purchase of pottery which he was unable to supply
from his own factories.

Five months later he proposed the partnership that he had evidently
had in mind for at least twelve months. Bentley replied at some length
on 1 November 1766, stating his objections: he pleaded 'total ignorance
of the business'; his partnership in Liverpool, after a slow start, was
now making promising progress; the business Josiah proposed was as
yet untried and, if the profits failed to measure up to expectations,
Bentley would be the prime loser for having neglected a more certain
source of profit; he could offer little or no capital to the partnership;
and finally, he would be obliged to move from Liverpool, where he
was happily settled, away not only from his business but also from his
friends.[2]

All but the last objection Josiah swept aside. He firmly denied
Bentley's ignorance of the business, adding, 'You have taste, the best
foundation for our intended concern, & which must be our *Primum
Mobilie*, for without that all will stand still, or better that it did so, &
for the rest, it will soon be learn'd by so apt a scholar. The very air of
this Country will soon inspire you with the mere Mechanical part
of our trade.' He admitted that it was impossible to judge the effect of
Bentley's absence from his business in Liverpool against the prospects
of the new partnership, there being 'no data to proceed upon, but

probabilities of future contingencies, which we cannot investigate, or command', and agreed that Bentley would be the loser if profits were not up to expectations. As to the capital investment, Josiah would make whatever arrangements were required: 'The money objection is obviated to my hand, & I doubt not in a way that will be agreeable to us both.' The wording of this proposal is not precise but it later became clear that he intended to raise all the necessary capital himself.

Perhaps in genuine concern, perhaps as a deliberate smokescreen, Josiah chose to depict the last objection as the most serious:

> But the leaving of your friends, & giving up a thousand agreeable connections, & pleasures at Liverpool, for which you can have no compensation in kind (indeed my friend I know from experience you cannot) this staggers my hopes more than everything else put together . . . can you part with your Octogon, & enlightened Octogon-ian bretheren, to join the diminutive & weak society of a Country Chapel? Can you give up the rational & elevated enjoyment of your [Liverpool] Philosophical Club for the puerile tete a tete of a Country fireside? – And to include all under this head in one question Can you exchange the frequent opportunities of seeing, & conversing with your learned & ingenious friends, which your present situation affords you, besides ten thousand other elegancies, & enjoyments of a Town life, to employ your self amongst Mechanicks, dirt, & smoke?[3]

It was not an especially enticing picture and it was one that was to be radically altered to accommodate Bentley's social and intellectual needs. Meanwhile, Josiah countered his own arguments by reminding Bentley of the opportunity that was offered, not only of 'proffits . . . in proportion to our application', but to 'be the Creator as it were of beauty, rather than merely the vehicle, or medium to convey it from one hand to another', a gentle comparison between his own occupation as an innovative producer and Bentley's as a warehouseman.[4]

He listed the types of goods that he intended the new partnership should make. These were to include 'ornamented & plain' flower-pots and 'essence pots', snuff-boxes, 'Fish, Fowl, & Beasts, with two leged Animals in various attitudes' and, most significantly, vases.[5] This is the first clear indication of the nature and scope of his proposal. The partnership was to manufacture ornamental goods only, leaving the production of tablewares to his partnership with his cousin Thomas.

It was already evident that Josiah expected vases 'of various sizes, colours, mixtures & forms, ad infinitum'[6] to be the principal product of the new factory, which he was soon describing as a 'Vase work'. A little more than two years later, he was confiding to Bentley his ambition to become 'Vase maker General to the Universe'.[7]

The peculiar importance of this proposed concentration on ornamental wares, and particularly vases, was that it was new to the pottery industry in England. In China and Japan decorative vases had been made both for use and as altar vessels for several centuries before such objects were known in Europe, where the vase as an ornament was largely the invention of the eighteenth century. The sophisticated Greek vases made some 3000 years before Josiah's birth were made for use: the *alabastron* was a practical jar; the *krater*, a mixing bowl; the *amphora*, a wine-cooler. It was specifically in the eighteenth century that these objects came to be prized for their ornamental qualities.

The first purely decorative vases in European pottery or porcelain were made at Meissen in the first quarter of the eighteenth century. The fashion for vases spread across the Continent and through the porcelain factories and was further developed at Sèvres, where superb rococo vases were produced after the removal of the factory from Vincennes. European potteries, including those at Berlin, Fulda and Höchst, made decorative vases also in earthenware between 1730 and 1750, but there is no evidence that British potters made any serious attempt to follow the porcelain fashion and there is nothing that can accurately be described as a decorative vase* in English tin-glazed earthenware or creamware before 1765, when Josiah Wedgwood sent examples of his vases, 'Creamcolour engine turn'd, & printed' to Queen Charlotte.[8] This is the earliest recorded evidence of Wedgwood vases and although the porcelain manufacturers, notably Chelsea, Bow and Worcester, were making fine vases before that date, it appears to be the first for any English potter. Even if Josiah was not the first earthenware potter to produce decorative vases in Britain, there is no doubt that he was the first to include them as a material part of his production plan.

Josiah's vision and optimism were boundless and his enthusiasm infectious. In spite of serious reservations, Bentley was persuaded. By February 1767, informal agreement had been reached[9] and the 'Basis of the Agreement between W & B' is set out in a memorandum in Bentley's hand dated 15 November 1767.[10] Vases are listed first among the objects to be manufactured by the partners.

Bentley was to choose his own time for moving from Liverpool to

---

*Large vessels, some of them similar in form to vases, exist in English pottery as early as 1724: for example the dated 23-inch punch bowl with domed and tiered lid in the Fitzwilliam Museum, Cambridge (Glaisher).

the Ridgehouse Estate, where Josiah proposed to build a house for him. In September 1766 he invited Bentley to view the estate:

> My Sally says your *fat sides* require a good shakeing & would recommend a journey on *horseback*, not in the Coach, to Burslem . . . she will not fix upon a spot for either your house or Gardens no not even the Stables 'til you have viewed & given an opinion of the premises, so now my dear Sir you are invited to the Ridgehouse Estate in the quality of a *Brown*.* . . . Ten guineas if I remember right is the price of a single call without the advantage of his direction, to make a Lawn & piece of water here – Cut down that wood & plant it there, level the rising ground, & raise yonder valley.[11]

This was a full twelve months before the purchase of the land was completed but Josiah never planned for failure. In November he told Bentley that it would be at least a year before the factory could be built and supposed that he would 'choose to have a house, with so much of a farm as will keep you a Horse, a Cow & a Pig, with a few other domestic Animals, all of which will take some time to get ready'.[12] The house was built, but Bentley never lived in it, and there must be at least a suspicion that he viewed the delay in settling him as a Staffordshire potter-farmer with something less than dismay.

By August 1767, even Josiah was becoming seriously concerned at the delays in planning and building occasioned by Mrs Ashenhurst's obstinacy. She was threatening to accept another offer for the Ridgehouse property. William Hodgson had warned Josiah that he must not depend upon reaching any agreement with her, 'so', he told Bentley, 'I must build Elsewhere, for build I must'. He had his eye on 'a sett of works to be let in a few weeks, with a tolerable smart house to them' and was prepared, if necessary, to abandon his plans for the Ridgehouse Estate.[13] Fortunately, it was not. By the middle of December, the death of Mrs Ashenhurst had removed the obstruction and the land was his. By the end of the month he had discussed a plan with his architect, Joseph Pickford, in Derby and spent a day with William Henshall, Brindley's assistant engineer in the planning of the Grand Trunk Canal, laying out the course of the canal through the estate. 'The fields are unfortunately so very level that the Canal will run in a straight line thro' them,' he told Bentley, 'at least so it is set out, for I could not prevail upon the inflexible Vandal [Henshall] to give me one *line of*

---

*Lancelot 'Capability' Brown (1715–1803), architect and landscape gardener, laid out the gardens at Blenheim and Kew. He was employed by Lord Gower at Trentham, where Josiah met him in May 1767.

Grace – He must go the nearest, & the best way, or Mr Brindley would go mad.'[14]

He had also renamed the estate 'Etruria', under the misapprehension, generally shared, that some of the finest Greek pottery found in tombs in Etruria, in central Italy, was Etruscan. It seems to have been a word that he had heard before he saw it written for it appeared as 'Hetruria' in his letters until corrected, presumably by Bentley, in 1768.[15]

With his letter to Bentley of 17 December Josiah enclosed an outline ground plan of the proposed buildings. It is no longer merely a 'Vase work' but a complete factory for wares designated as *'usefull'* (table-wares) or ornamental, housed in three blocks, linked by walled courts or yards, at the corners of which are a total of eight 'hovels' containing the ovens or kilns. The whole stretches to a length of about 150 yards along the intended course of the canal. The 'hovels', as he reminded Bentley, might be round towers or domes instead of the conventional beehive shape. The central building (designed for 'useful' ware, and rather larger than those on either side for 'Plates & dishes only' and for ornamental wares) and the two linking courts were provided with wide gateways for the delivery of clay and coal and the removal of rubbish. From this lightly sketched ground plan Bentley was invited to draw an elevation.[16]

On Christmas Eve Josiah wrote again, this time enclosing a sketch map of the estate, traced from Henshall's survey. This shows the same buildings, but in reverse order in relation to the canal, and the suggested site of the wharf and of Bentley's house on the farther bank. It shows also the lane to Newcastle and the land beyond it, then owned by a Mr Egerton of Tatton, who was considering selling it. Josiah immediately proposed to add it to his Etruria estate. 'I believe', he wrote, 'you will think me allmost out of my senses for thinking of buying more Land, and indeed it is not because I shall have money to spare that I would make this purchase, but firstly (for I have many reasons) it is full of limestone . . . secondly I would have the wharf on that side of the lane, & perhaps my works too, & thirdly if I do not buy it for those purposes somebody else will who may be very disagreeable neighbours.'[17]

The plan of the factory and the proposed layout of the Hall and of Bentley's house were discussed in detail between the partners in their letters, and both Erasmus Darwin and Bentley's sister-in-law, Elizabeth Oates, were consulted. So, of course, was Sally.

Josiah had sent Bentley a series of sketches for the hovels, showing a variety of shapes, ranging from beehive to pepper-pot and from milk churn to crenellated castle keep.[18] Not all were intended to be taken seriously and he was alarmed when Bentley chose the last. 'Will not Gothic Battlements to buildings in every other respect in the modern taste be a little heterogeneous?' he asked, after complimenting Bentley on the drawing of the elevation that he had sent, and added hastily, 'I do not think any other finish looks so well for the hovels but had given it up on account of its incongruity (pardon this hard word) with the rest of the building.'[19] This, and many other matters, were settled by Joseph Pickford when, at last, he visited the site in the fourth week of January and examined the suggested elevation and ground plans. He and Josiah were able to agree on plans for the factory and the Hall, but Pickford's revised plan for Bentley's house, to be called the Bank House, was rejected as soon as both partners had seen it.

Nothing could be finally settled without Bentley. Josiah wrote towards the end of January: 'I think there never was more necessity for your presence here than now. . . . I shall expect to see, or hear from you on Monday that you are on the road. . . . Adieu my dear friend – put on your boots, mount your Rosinanty, & let me see you at Hetruria in a day or two.'[20]

The cutting of the canal was now making good progress and Josiah reported with delight on some of the objects found in the clay: 'a prodigious rib, with the vertebrae of the backbone of a monstrous sized Fish, thought by some connoisieurs to belong to the identical Whale that was so long ago swallowed by Jonah!', stone that was so hard that it must be blown up with gunpowder, and a great variety of fossils of fern, crowsfoot, hawthorn, yew and withy.[21]

On 3 March Josiah sent Bentley new plans for both houses and a revised estimate for the cost of building the Bank House, which was to be reduced to £350. The design of Etruria Hall was altered to be 'more in the Modern, & I think *true* taste' at a saving of between £500 and £700. In spite of these economies, the total estimate, excluding the Bank House, was more than £9000.[22] It was now urgent that building should begin without further delay and Bentley was warned not to 'alter a line, or Angle in the whole Fabric, for I have sworn not to waver any longer & so help me – Bentley – to Create new Vases for the payment of my Architect'.[23]

An unexpected and disagreeable hitch occurred in April. As Josiah explained:

Some of my good Neighbours have taken it into their heads to think I shall have too pleasant, & valuable a situation by the side of the Canal as it is plan'd & executing thro' my Estate, – This has raised a

little envy in their breasts, & as they are Proprietors thay have represented to the Committee that the Canal ought to be made along the
Meadows, as that is the shortest, & most natural course for it. – That
it will receive more water, & retain better what it does recieve as the
upper course is over sloping banks & sandbeds.

A select committee, appointed to make a survey of the alternative
courses, favoured the lower route through the meadows but, fortunately, decided to order a professional survey from James Brindley. 'I
know my cause is good & feel my self a match for them all,' Josiah
wrote, plainly perturbed. 'Mr Brindley's Brother is at the head of this
affair, but . . . I know *Brindley the Great* to be *an honest Man* & that he
will give a true state of the case let the event be what it will.'[24]
    This dispute, which threatened the siting of the factory beside the
canal, a crucial factor in Josiah's decision to buy the Ridgehouse Estate,
was no sooner settled than a far more serious problem threatened to
demolish the entire project. On 30 April Josiah wrote to William Cox
that he had 'over walk'd & over work'd' his knee lately and must rest
it before he could undertake another journey to London.[25] Just four
weeks later he had his right leg amputated. At the foot of an invoice
from Burslem, Peter Swift added a succinct note to William Cox in
London:

> Sir, Your favour of the 26th is just come to hand, but can make no
> reply to the contents. Mr Wedgwood has this day had his leg taken
> of [*sic*], & is as well as can be expected after such an execution.[26]

Five days later, the Wedgwood's second son, Richard, died. He was
just a year old.
    Josiah's leg was amputated, in his own house, by James Bent, a
local surgeon, probably with Erasmus Darwin in attendance.[27] Bent was
evidently an accomplished surgeon, but without the use of anaesthetics
or benefit of asepsis the operation involved appalling pain and extreme
hazard to the patient's life. Many amputees died of shock and many
more of gangrene. In spite of acute anxiety for her husband and grief
for her dead child, Sally was reported to be keeping 'her Spirits up to
a tollerable degree' and, when the doctors removed the dressings from
Josiah's stump for the first time on Thursday 2 June, just five days after
the operation, the wound was seen to be healing perfectly and there
were 'the greatest hopes for a perfect cure'.[28]
    While Josiah was invalided, supervision of the business was divided
between Tom Wedgwood and Bentley, who stayed in Burslem until

the immediate danger to his friend was past, dealing with Josiah's correspondence at least until 13 June. On that day Josiah was able, for the first time, to add a short paragraph in his own hand to a letter written for him to William Cox.[29]

By about the 17th, however, Josiah was strong enough to resume control of his affairs and Bentley was able to return to Liverpool. Josiah wrote to him there to express gratitude and 'brotherly love & affection':

> Though I may be prevented telling you so, as often as I should wish to do it, yet I trust you know my heart too well, to think that I could for a moment cease to love, & be grateful to you. Now I am recover'd so far as to be able to write, I find myself over head & ears in debt that way, & every post is increasing the heavy load. . . . At present I am well even beyond my most sanguine expectations, my leg is allmost healed, The wound is not quite 2 inches by one and ½, I measur'd it with the compasses this morning when I dress'd it. Yes, when *I dress'd it*, for I have turn'd my Surgeon adrift & Sally & I are sole managers now, only we give him leave to peep at it now & then, when he lifts up his hands & eyes, & will scarcely believe it to be the wound he dress'd before.[30]

Within three days the upper part of the wound had healed and he had given up taking laudanum to ease the pain. He had been to the Brick House and to Etruria, where the building was being delayed by bad weather, and had 'two Airings in a chaise'. By the first week in July he had been 'rambleing into Cheshire two or three times'.[31]

Later in the month he came across a mathematical instrument-maker and caster of printing type who wore a wooden leg. It transpired that this was of his own making and he readily agreed to carve several legs for Josiah, who, meanwhile, proposed to employ him to make and repair machinery for the factory.[32]

By mid-September, in spite of the cold and wet summer, the new factory buildings were ready for roofing and there was talk of covering the Hall and the Bank House before winter. However, trouble was brewing with the architect. Pickford had shown a disquieting reluctance to produce formal estimates for his work, putting off Josiah's inquiries with such rigmaroles as that 'he thought it not right to give such things to Noblemen, or Gentlemen' and assurances of 'very different (much lower) terms than he did for Gentlemen', which Josiah found neither reassuring nor complimentary. Finally Pickford produced an estimate for Bentley's house that was exactly double his original figure. Josiah 'talked a good deal to him upon the subject of his two estimates & told him the difference betwixt them was the most extraordinary thing'. When he went on to particularise 'several articles . . . which were extravagantly charged', Pickford made an abject admission that 'he had been guilty of an Error, was sorry for it & would do every thing in his power to make the House agreeable to us both, that he would make us a present of the surveying & desire to be paid barely what it cost him'.[33] Josiah's arguments were seldom more persuasive than when he believed he was being cheated.

The problems with Pickford about the Bank House continued, but on 6 November Josiah was able to report to Bentley:

> The works are cover'd in, & they are begining upon the Cellar Arches, & the Chamber & ground floors, as soon as these are finish'd I shall order them to be fitted up & put some men into them to make sagars*, prepare Clay, build ovens, &c &c that we may begin to do something *in earnest* as soon as possible. The Partnership books should be open'd on Monday the 14th inst. as some hands (Potters) will begin there at that time.

He urged Bentley to 'leave home – Liverpool I would say, for I must now consider Etruria as your home' to arrive in Burslem no later than the 12th.[34] By 21 November Bentley was installed at Burslem and his Etruria partner was writing to him from London: ''tis a pitty but we could be alltogether in this fine world here . . . but it cannot be, somebody must take care of the Etruscans.'[35]

By April 1768 Josiah was already running short of money, yet the Ornamental Works, Etruria Hall and the Bank House were unfinished and the building of the new 'Useful' Works not yet started. He urged William Cox to '*make hay whilst the sun shines*', in collecting debts, and wrote personally to a number of good customers who were 'a little tardy'.[36] By November of the following year he was in far more serious trouble. He had been given notice to quit the Brick House Works and needed a further £3000 for the completion of the Etruria factory. He wrote in some desperation to Bentley, by then in London: 'Collect – Collect my friend – set all your hands, & heads to work – send me L'Argent & you shall see wonders. . . . Aye £3000 not a farthing less will satisfy my Architect for the next years business, so you must either *collect* or take a place for me in the Gazett.'[†37]

---

*Saggars are boxes of highly refractory fire clay used to protect ware from coming into direct contact with the flames during firing.
†The *London Gazette* contained government and legal notices, including notices of bankruptcies.

The Etruria factory was formally opened on 13 June 1769, when Josiah threw six 'First Day's Vases' while Bentley cranked the wheel for him. It was not, however, until 1772 that the Brick House and 'Red Workhouses' were finally vacated and the 'Useful' Works transferred to Etruria. Until then, Etruria remained a 'Vase work' or factory for ornamental wares, and Josiah was obliged to ride frequently between his three factories, besides, from time to time, having to transfer workmen temporarily from one to another to deal with occasional shortages of labour.

Josiah was determined that his new factory should be the most modern and the most efficient in Europe. In March 1768 Erasmus Darwin had designed a novel form of windmill with sails rotating in a horizontal plane which he proposed to Josiah for use in grinding colours. As Darwin explained to Dr Peter Templeman, Secretary to the Society for the Encouragement of Arts, Manufactures and Commerce*, his model produced a third more power than any vertical-sail windmill of comparable span, was easier to maintain and repair because of its simplified wheelwork and would move three pairs of grinding stones.[38] He constructed a model which he showed to Wedgwood at Lichfield on 10 March 1768. Josiah was impressed with this 'very ingenious invention' and sent a primitive sketch of it to Bentley,[39] There were, however, obstacles. Darwin estimated that the full-size windmill would require 68,000 bricks, 4800 feet of 1-inch deal boards, a 30-foot shaft 12 inches in diameter, and two sails. This was an unwelcome expense at a time when Josiah's capital was apparently close to being exhausted. He was also concerned that the principle on which it was constructed was imperfect but he was nevertheless keen to build it at Etruria.[40] On 15 March 1769 Darwin, with typical frankness, advised against it. He had learned, in the interval, of James Watt's experiments with his 'Fire-Engine' and wrote to Wedgwood: 'I am of opinion it will be a powerful and convenient Windmill, but would recommend steam to you if you can wait awhile as it will on many Accounts be preferable.'[41] The proposal for a horizontal windmill was revived in 1779, when Darwin was helped by Watt and Richard Lovell Edgeworth to perfect its design.[42]

Whether Darwin's windmill was ever erected at Etruria is doubtful. Josiah wrote to Bentley in April 1773 that he was going to erect a windmill in front of one of his workshops to grind materials,[43] and a watercolour of Etruria by Stebbing Shaw dated 1794 shows the sails of a conventional windmill. This was demolished before the end of the

*Founded in 1754; now known as the Royal Society of Arts.

century by which time it had been superseded by steam engines. The first of these, a Boulton & Watt Sun and Planet machine ordered in April 1782 and erected two years later, drove the clay and flint mills as well as grinding colours. The second was a 10-hp engine, installed in 1793 and used for the same purposes and for pounding broken saggars to a powder. Eight years later even this proved to be too small for the task and Josiah II replaced it with a 30-hp engine.[44]

From the start, the Etruria factory was equipped with a water-wheel, supplying power by water drawn from the canal. It was not until after Josiah's death that the final decision was made to abandon the use of water and wind and to rely solely on steam.

Another important innovation at Etruria came in the improved use of the engine-turning lathe. The simple lathe, originally a development of the potter's wheel, has been used for turning (shaping and thinning) wood since the Bronze Age, when the pole lathe was employed, and the technique was later developed for turning metal. In spite of its close connection with the art of throwing on the wheel, it does not appear to have been used for pottery until the end of the seventeenth century when it was reputedly introduced to Staffordshire by John Philip Elers. He and his brother, David, are believed to have been saltglaze potters in the Rhineland before they settled in England about 1690. After opening a pottery in Fulham, both were cited in 1693 for an infringement of John Dwight's patent. They then moved to a factory at Vauxhall in Surrey and John Philip started a pottery in Staffordshire, renting Bradwell Wood, near Newcastle-under-Lyme, probably in their joint names, from the Sneyd family of Keele. The brothers were famous in their own time and are remembered now for the fine quality of the red stonewares they made from clay found there. Although the introduction of lathe-turning to the Staffordshire Potteries has been attributed to others, Josiah certainly believed that the credit was due to Elers,[45] and he made use of the lathe to refine the shapes of his earliest creamware teapots.[46]

In 1746 he introduced the more complex technique of engine-turning to the Potteries.[47] The engine-turning lathe is similar in concept to the simple lathe but the motion is eccentric, allowing geometric and fluted patterns to be cut into a 'leather-hard'* clay object as it rotates on the lathe. Josiah sent a sample of this type of decoration to Bentley in May 1764. 'This branch hath cost me a great deal of time & thought & must cost me more,' he wrote. 'I have got an excellent book on the

---

*Also known as 'cheese-hard': the state of unfired pottery after the evaporation of some of its moisture content. In this condition it remains firm but pliable.

subject in french & latin.' The book was J. Plumier's *L'Art de Tourner*, published in Paris in 1701, and, try as he might, Josiah was unable to make much of it. Tom Byerley was learning French so that he might be able to help his uncle with correspondence, but Josiah could not wait for him to succeed.[48] He sent a chapter of the book to Bentley with a request for a translation and he soon mastered the technique for the decoration of red stoneware teapots and creamware vases.[49]

A further refinement was rose-engine-turning, which involved fitting a series of special tools ('roses' and 'crowns') to the lathe, enabling the operator to cut repetitive curved patterns. The variation of patterns made possible by the creative and skilful use of these tools revealed exciting possibilities for the decoration of pottery, and in particular of vases. Josiah first saw such a lathe in operation in 1767, when he visited Matthew Boulton's Soho factory. It had been made for another customer who no longer wanted it and Wedgwood immediately offered to buy it. Later in the year he showed it to John Wyke, a Liverpool watch- and tool-maker who made metal punches and runners for him, and they considered the possibility of Wyke's making a second lathe, but by February 1768 Josiah was planning to make his own lathes in Burslem, where he had 'an ingenious & indefatigable smith' already working for him.[50]

In April 1769, when the building of the Etruria factory was nearing completion, Josiah turned his attention to the siting of the turning room, which was rapidly becoming one of his most important workshops. He wrote to Bentley:

> I have altered my opinion . . . & unless you think of any objection shall fix the lathes in the lower corner room under that we before proposed. Here the lights are high enough & a ground floor is much better for Lathes than a Chamber story the latter are so apt to shake with the motion of the lathe, & as we shall want so very often to be steping into the Lathe room, for there the *outline* is given, it will be more convenient, especially for me to have it without any steps to it.

The layout of the room was of particular concern:

> Though it may not be of much consequence for common things, [it] will, I think, be a great help to the workman in turning plain Vases, where a true outline, free of any irregular swellings, or hollows, are of the first consequence. The alteration I propose, is to set the Lathe so that the turner shall have an *end light* instead of a *front one*, which

they now have. If you hold a Mug both these ways to the light, you will see the advantage I propose from this alteration.[51]

It was just this attention to detail that made the new factory efficient and the quality that Josiah aimed for attainable. Six months later there were three lathes in constant operation at the ornamental works at Etruria and Josiah admitted that he had 'committed a Sad Robbery upon my Burslem works. . . . We have not one Engine Turner left there now. . . . Poor Burslem. . . . They tell me I sacrifice all to *Etruria and Vases.*'[52]

He had built a factory that was second to none in Europe for its location and the practicality of its design. He had acquired for it the most modern machinery and mastered the newest techniques. While these aims were being achieved, he had taken a leading part in improving communications to the area on land and by water. The little time he had been able to spare from these activities had been taken up by the invention and improvement of earthenware and stoneware bodies. With these he would conquer the market for 'useful' wares for the table, create a new fashion for vases and other ornaments and, as he promised Bentley, 'surprise *the World* with wonders'.[53]

CHAPTER SEVEN

Vase-maker General

By the middle of 1767 Wedgwood was satisfied that his Queen's ware was of such quality that little improvement was required. Problems seldom arose in its production and those that did were quickly solved by 'Useful' Thomas, who had proved himself an efficient and practical manager, more than capable of running the Burslem factory. The most serious obstacle to the production of Queen's ware was the patent granted in 1768 to William Cookworthy of Plymouth for the exclusive use of Cornish china clay and china stone. This right to monopoly was sold to Richard Champion who applied for an extension of fifteen years from 1774. Josiah led the Staffordshire potters in a petition to the House of Lords. In the face of such powerful opposition, Champion amended his application to refer only to the manufacture of porcelain.

The threat to essential supplies of white clay was, however, serious enough for Josiah to seek them elsewhere. He travelled extensively in the Midlands, rattling about in his carriage over appalling roads in search of suitable materials, and solicited samples from such friends as Brindley, Watt and Fothergill. John Whitehurst and James Hutton were among the geologists who sent him specimens of rocks and minerals, and samples of clay from various parts of the British Isles were given to him by Peter Templeman and his successor, Samuel More, of the Society for the Encouragement of Arts, Manufactures and Commerce. More obtained for him a sample of Chinese clay but so tiny that it was lost in the straw in Wedgwood's warehouse.

Wedgwood even considered importing clay from America.[1] The agent he chose was Thomas Griffiths, brother of a good friend, Ralph Griffiths, founder, proprietor and publisher of the *Monthly Review*. Thomas set out in 1767 and survived an expedition of considerable hardship in North Carolina, returning to England in the spring of 1768.

He brought with him a bare 5 tons of clay at the staggering cost of £615 19s. 3d.[2] At such a price it could scarcely be used for anything less expensive than porcelain and it seems certain that Wedgwood knew that the clay was indeed kaolin and that he intended it for use in his first porcelain trials. There was, in any event, no possibility of obtaining further supplies of this 'Cherokee clay' as he called it, and he learned later that quantities of it had previously been obtained by porcelain factories in France and in England, 'where they could make nothing of it'.[3] Josiah, on the contrary, was to make much of it.

Although experiments to whiten the colour of the Queen's ware body in closer imitation of porcelain were continued, its development after 1768 became primarily a matter of design: the introduction of elegant new shapes and of decoration in keeping with current fashion. The monochrome prints applied in Liverpool by John Sadler and, after his retirement in 1770, by Guy Green, retained their popularity throughout the rest of the century. The printing was of the highest quality and Wedgwood had a monopoly of their work on cream-ware.[4]

The early styles of painted decoration, however, were less endur-ing. David Rhodes* joined Wedgwood from Leeds in 1768, first as his tenant in premises in St Martin's Lane and in 1770 as manager of the decorating studio set up in Cheyne Row, Chelsea. The types of decor-ation associated with him were unsuitable for plates and dishes and too individual and too expansive for the more restrained taste that was becoming fashionable. By the early 1770s Wedgwood's Queen's ware was being decorated with simple continuous borders based on natural objects – foliage, flowers, fruit, seaweed or shells – or on designs of respectable classical origin frequently copied or adapted from architec-tural details or the painted decoration of antique vases. These made possible the decoration of full sets of tableware and were more in keeping with the growing taste for classical simplicity. The lighthearted and flamboyant rococo associated with France and 'frippery' was giving way to the more austere neoclassical or 'true' style. This change was reflected not only in Wedgwood's decorative style but also in the shapes of his tablewares. Only the serving pieces – such vessels as tureens, teapots and coffeepots, known in the Potteries as 'hollowware' – retained in their knops, handles and terminals clear signs of a declining fashion. After a visit to London in September 1769, Josiah wrote of his 'firm resolution to *simplify*' and as a first move he intended to discard

*See p. 31.

the 'twiggen* and flower'd' handles from all his shapes except the ornamental baskets.[5] He was probably the first Staffordshire potter to understand and exploit the changing fashion.

Even less enduring were the coloured glazes and the 'greengrocery' shapes that were so redolent of rococo. In 1766 Josiah cleared his warehouse of 'Colour'd ware', which he was 'heartily sick of', and offered his remaining stock of dessert sets at a large discount to Bentley for sale to the West Indies, where gilded green-glazed wares were still popular.[6] By the spring of 1768, while most other earthenware potters in Britain were still producing quantities of rococo shapes decorated with coloured glazes, Wedgwood had given them up altogether and had no old stock left.[7]

Having redesigned the style of his tablewares, Josiah turned his attention to the production of ornamental pieces, which he considered 'an inexhaustible field'. In July 1767 he was able to assure Bentley that he had 'improved bodys enough for Vases'.[8] Among them was certainly his 'fine Black Porcelaine, having nearly the same properties as the Basaltes, resisting the Attacks of Acid; being a Touchstone to Copper, Silver and Gold, and equal in hardness to porphyry'.[9] This body was in fact a stoneware of entirely different composition from any porcelain, and the name 'basaltes', by which it was identified, was a variant on 'basalt', the hard black igneous rock used by the Egyptians and others for sculpture.

Two months later Josiah wrote that he had new 'tryals' which he was anxious to show to Bentley but could not send them to him nor even describe them in a letter because letters were 'liable to Accidents'.[10] This was a reference to theft and industrial espionage, two serious problems of which Josiah was obliged to be constantly aware. The 'first fruits' of his experiments, '2 Etruscan bronze vases', were sent to his new partner in August next year. Such vases, he told him, could be made to sell at 18s. a pair, and smaller sizes down to 7s. 6d. 'They cannot be afforded at less to have a *living* proffit – at the rate we live.'[11]

Wedgwood's first name for this black body, 'Etruscan', indicates that he may have shared the popular misapprehension that the ancient pottery then being recovered in Italy was Etruscan work, but it is also possible that he had seen illustrations of Etruscan *bucchero nero*, with moulded or incised ornament, dating from the eighth century BC. Although he was later to claim the invention of the black basaltes body,

---

*'Twiggen' handles and knops, usually known as 'crabstock' or occasionally 'crabtree', were moulded to represent the gnarled branch of a crab apple tree. Adapted from the Chinese, the shape first appeared in Staffordshire saltglazed wares about 1745.

a red earthenware that burned black in firing had been known in England since the Iron Age, and a hard black-stained pottery had been made in Staffordshire since the middle of the eighteenth century. Black basaltes was a refinement of the latter, but so improved as to be almost unrecognisable, and Josiah felt justified in calling it his own.

Within a month of sending the first good vases to Bentley he was supplying them to William Cox in London, carefully admonishing him not to forget to call them 'Etruscan' and mentioning that he would be sending some black teapots of the same body to his 'good Patroness Miss Chetwynd', who had sent him the order for the Queen's teaset three years earlier.[12] He readily admitted that the prices were unusually high but told Cox that heavy losses in production made it impossible to sell them for less. In the early stages of the production of basaltes he was losing about 85 per cent in firing.[13]

The surface of his 'Etruscans', as he affectionately called his first vases, was smooth with a lustrous sheen that could be added by polishing with a leather or the use of steel burnishers before firing. This dense, even surface was essential for two new methods of decoration for which he took out a patent in 1769. The first, 'bronzing', required the application of brown varnish and a mixture of bronze powder* and lampblack to produce an 'antique' bronze effect similar to that of verdigris. This preparation was a closely guarded secret and, because it was not fired on, was at best semi-permanent. The second was the so-called 'encaustic' decoration, which Wedgwood had perfected in imitation of the Greek red-figure style of painting. His technique was simple and it enabled moderately skilled painters to make surprisingly satisfactory copies of antique red-figure vase painting using black basaltes as a ground. The pigments used by Wedgwood were of his own invention, part enamel and part slip, and, according to his original specification, contained a proportion of the precious Cherokee clay brought home by Griffiths from North Carolina.

The inspiration for this style of decoration were the *Recueil d'antiquités égyptiennes, étrusques, grecques, romaines et gauloises* by Anne-Claude-Philippe, Comte de Caylus, published in seven volumes in Paris between 1752 and 1757, and the lavishly produced four-volume set, *Antiquités étrusques, grecques et romaines*, by Sir William Hamilton and P. H. d'Hancarville, published in Rome in 1766–7. As Ambassador to the Court of Naples from 1764 to 1800, Hamilton took a close interest in the excavations at Herculaneum and Pompeii and formed a remarkable

---

*Prepared by dissolving pure gold in a mixture of hydrochloric and nitric acids and adding bronze filings.

collection of Greek and Italian vases, which he later sold to the British Museum. Pierre-Germain Hugues, self-styled Baron d'Hancarville, was a French adventurer, antiquarian and art historian, whose dubious reputation for scholarship was confirmed by his later *Recherche sur l'origine, l'esprit, et les progrès des arts de la Grèce* which was full of inaccuracies.

It was Hamilton's collection that was illustrated and described in what Josiah generally referred to as 'Hamilton's Antiquitys'. How Josiah became aware of this work, which was not then available in England, is not certain, but he told Bentley in March 1768 that he had met Lord Cathcart in London and spent several hours with him. 'We are', he wrote, 'to do great things for each other.'[14] Charles, Lord Cathcart, who had succeeded to the title on the death of the 8th Baron in the ill-fated Cartagena expedition in 1740, had married Hamilton's sister Jane in 1753 and had recently been appointed Ambassador to St Petersburg. He and his wife proved to be among Wedgwood's most beneficent patrons and, as first evidence of their practical favour, Cathcart lent Josiah prints from his brother-in-law's folio volumes. Having seen them, Josiah was anxious to obtain the whole set.[15] By August 1770 he had acquired sets of both Caylus's and Hamilton's works, the first volume of the latter being presented to him by another generous patron, Sir Watkin Williams Wynn.[16]

In the introductory remarks to his 1779 Catalogue, Josiah explained in some detail the development of his 'Encaustic Painting'. His colours had been invented, he wrote, 'not only . . . completely to imitate the Paintings upon the Etruscan Vases, but to *do much more*; to give to the Beauty of Design, the Advantage of Light and Shade in various Colours; and to render Paintings durable without the Defect of a varnished or glassy Surface'. This was, he modestly observed, 'An Object earnestly desired by Persons of critical Taste in all Ages, and in modern Times, without Success'. His technique of painting in his invented pigments on black basaltes bore no relation to the original method of 'encaustic' painting, described by Pliny the Elder in *Historia Naturalis* and copied by Caylus, and Josiah candidly admitted, 'It is evident that this kind of Painting, in *coloured Wax*, has little or no Resemblance to ours but in Name.'[17]

Once perfected, the technique was extended to include a wider palette of colours and applied to tablets for chimneypieces, other ornamental, though practical, pieces such as inkstands, lamps and candlesticks, and even to trays, teasets and coffeesets. The vase shapes and their decoration of painted figures, groups and borders, were at first copied directly from pieces illustrated by Caylus or Hamilton, but it was not long before both shapes and designs were being adapted to suit customers' wishes or the requirements of production.

Wedgwood was the first eighteenth-century potter to reproduce this antique style of painting and he valued it highly. He chose it for his 'First Day's Vases', commemorating the opening of the Etruria factory; he gave the decorated vases the prized name of 'Etruscan', previously allotted to the plain basaltes; and it was the principal subject of the only patent application he ever made. It was also the subject of one of the rare lawsuits in which he was involved when, in 1770, his rival, Humphrey Palmer, whose factory was at Hanley, began to make his own red-figure vases, apparently in open contravention of the Wedgwood patent. Josiah had already had cause to complain of Palmer's copying of his black basaltes vases, supplied to Hanley by a London dealer within a fortnight of their being delivered in London.[18]

Competition seldom disconcerted Wedgwood. He was supremely confident in the superiority of his products and in his ability to stay ahead of the field. Palmer, however, offered a more serious threat than any contemporary potter to Wedgwood's burgeoning market for ornamental goods. Josiah frankly admitted that Palmer's black stoneware body was 'very good' and 'the shape & composition very well', and it was galling to realise that his new technique could have been copied so quickly. 'We must proceed', he told Bentley, 'or they will tread upon our heels'.[19]

The proceeding he had in mind was through an appeal to the Courts, but it proved to be a more complicated matter than he had supposed. Palmer's vases were being marketed by James Neale, then his London agent, later his partner and successor in the business. Although it was easy to show that Neale was selling red-figure vases, it was less so to prove that Palmer was making them, or, if he was, that he was responsible for the decoration contravening the patent, which might have been painted by a freelance artist in London.[20] An injunction was granted but, after protracted negotiations carried on without much acrimony, a compromise was reached. In return for an unrecorded sum paid to Wedgwood & Bentley, Palmer was declared to be a 'sharer in the Patent'.[21]

Another potential challenge came from an unexpected quarter. There was talk of Boulton & Fothergill's making 'black Vases . . . and building works for that purpose' but Josiah was unperturbed. 'It doubles my courage', he told Bentley, 'to have the first Manufacturer in England to encounter with . . . I like the Man, I like his spirit. – He will not be a mere snivelling copyist like the antagonists I have hitherto had.'[22] The following year, in return for some metal candle branches for vase-candelabra, Wedgwood agreed to make some painted 'Etruscan' urns for Boulton to mount as tea-urns.[23]

The second style created by Wedgwood for vases and other ornamental ware was a variant on old-established Staffordshire techniques to produce variegated effects in imitation of marble, agate or similar natural stones. Two principal techniques were employed: the wedging of stained clays of two or more colours, a method used by the Romans and seen in Chinese pottery of the T'ang period; and the use of stained slips of different colours, trailed on to the surface of unfired ware and 'combed' into patterns, a less venerable technique used in medieval times and common in eighteenth-century Staffordshire.

John Dwight had used the wedging technique at Fulham towards the end of the seventeenth century and it had been brought to a high degree of artistry by Böttger at Meissen. As an aspiring young potter, Wedgwood had made 'an imitation of Agate; which was esteemed beautiful & a considerable improvement'[24] and this early experience could be put to good use in the creation of a range of ornamental vases. The original idea may well have been inspired by his visit to Boulton's factory in 1767. Boulton's interest in vase-making at this time is shown in his subscription, in July, for the Hamilton and d'Hancarville volumes,[25] and it is certain that he would have discussed the subject with Wedgwood, when the latter bought his rose-engine-turning lathe.

During his second visit to the Soho Works in March 1768, Wedgwood discussed with Boulton the possibility of decorating his Queen's ware ornaments with printed designs in purple and gold and mounting them in metal, a suggestion that, he told Bentley, 'will certainly be of importance to us, but it should not be mention'd at present'. He added:

> Mr Boulton tells me I should be surprised to know what a trade has lately been made out of Vases at Paris. The Artists have even come over to London, picked out all the old whimsical ugly things they could meet with, Carried them to Paris where they have mounted & ornamented them with metal, & sold them to the Virtuosi of every Nation, & Particularly to Millords d'Anglise for the greatest raritys, & if you remember we saw many such things at Lord Bolingbrokes which he brought over with him from France.

He recalled especially seeing 'two or three old China [Chinese] bowles . . . stuck rim to rim which . . . looked whimsical & droll enough'.[26]

Wedgwood's view that the ornamental combination of clay and metal was an almost limitless field for exploitation[27] was shared by

Boulton, who listed 'Etruscan ware' among the bodies suitable for mounting in metal.[28] In November the two manufacturers together visited the shop of Thomas Harrache, a dealer in porcelain and jewellery in Pall Mall, and Josiah reported Boulton as 'picking up Vases' to make in bronze. Boulton now proposed 'an alliance betwixt the Pottery & Metal branches, Viz, that we shall make such things as shall be suitable for mounting, & not have a *Pott look*, & he will finish them with mounts'. Wedgwood was clearly unsure how to respond and asked Bentley for his opinion: 'Perhaps you would rather he would let them alone. Very true, but he will be doing, so that the question is whether we shall refuse having anything to do with him, & thereby affront him, & set him doing them himself.' Or he might obtain similar goods elsewhere. The alternative seemed to be to exercise some control by producing for Boulton 'such things as nobody else can & thereby make it his interest to be good'. 'We can', Josiah told Bentley, 'make things for mounting with great facility, & dispatch, & mounting will enhance their value greatly in the *eye of the Purchacer.*'[29]

Bentley's reaction to this proposal appears not to have been favourable. Just one month later Boulton sent an order for 'one, two or three dozen pair of the vessel part of some good formed vases' and wanted to know if Wedgwood would make for him a few pairs to match a French vase sent from London: 'The vessel part is made of china . . . exactly the colour of the blood stone, I mean the green blood stone that hath a few red specks in it. The form I know you will say is hugly but nevertheless when mounted it is a handsome vase.'[30] Josiah could see no way of refusing him without offence but, on Bentley's advice, he did so, in spite of receiving a second order on 17 January.[31] Boulton & Fothergill later made their displeasure clear to William Cox, when he visited the Soho factory in September. After refusing to show him their vase work they told him of their proposal to make their own black vases and dropped heavy hints of an agreement with the Chelsea porcelain factory.[32]

Although he made a jocular show of taking the threats lightly, writing to Bentley that they must 'not sell the victorie too cheap, but maintain our ground like men, & indeavour, even in our defeat to share the Laurels with our Conquerors',[33] Josiah was induced to give new thought to the speed of his inventions and improvements and the almost equal speed and facility of his rivals and imitators in copying them. He suggested to Bentley that they should 'proceed with some prudent caution' so as not to 'glut the curiosity & spoil the choice' of their customers nor to give their imitators 'so large a field to fight us in'.[34]

This field was increasing in size almost daily. Josiah's trials of vases made from wedged clays had moved naturally into experiments in the use of stained slips to produce mottled, veined and other 'variegated' patterns. These had resulted in a remarkable variety of handsome effects and colours to which he gave names such as 'agate', 'marble', 'pebble', 'granite', porphyry, and 'lapis lazuli'. Each example was, in a sense, unique since the decorating process could be controlled only within certain limits. Even without further decoration or ornament, no two vases were ever identical and the variations of shape and ornament were almost infinite.

Such diversity may have helped to produce an impression of extra-ordinary creativity and allowed customers to believe in the singularity of their purchases, but it was the cause of exceptional difficulties in the organisation of orders, production and costing. It was not long before Josiah was obliged to attempt a solution to some of these problems by defining the most popular styles and colours. Such descriptions as 'Jaune Antique' and 'Holy Door Marble', however precise they may have been to Wedgwood & Bentley, have never since been certainly identified with the decoration of any vase.

The staining of clay and slip was not the only decoration possible. Many of the early vases were enriched with gold on the handles and knops, and the square plinths might be of black basaltes or a gilded white stoneware. The latter, a development of the body used earlier for saltglaze, was a new ceramic composition of great strength and hardness which Josiah named 'terracotta'.* In production from 1771, it replaced creamware for vases and was also used extensively for cameos, medallions and plaques.[35]

The shapes of Wedgwood's vases were seldom original but he usually presented them in altered or adapted form with ornament or decoration that helped to disguise his sources. These were both books of engrav-ings and actual examples in porcelain or metal which he either bought or had copied. The principal sources were the engravings illustrating the work of the Comte de Caylus and the collection of Sir William Hamilton but Wedgwood made use of shapes designed and published by many European artists, including Bernard de Montfaucon, Jacques de Stella, Stefano della Bella, Joseph Marie Vien, Fischer von Erlach and Edmé Bouchardon, as well as the British architects James 'Athenian' Stuart, Sir William Chambers and the brothers Adam.

Early in June 1767 Josiah wrote that he was 'picking up every

---

*'Terracotta' (meaning no more than 'baked clay') is not necessarily an orange-red, as is generally supposed, but may be any colour natural to clay, including many shades of grey, brown and red as well as white.

design, & improvement for a Vase work' and about eighteen months later Sally Wedgwood, accompanying her husband and Catherine Willet on a visit to London, complained to Bentley, 'My good man is upon the ramble continually and I am almost afraid he will lay out the price of his estate in Vases he makes nothing of giving 5 or 6 guineas for but you will see them soon and judge for yourself, if we do but lay out half the money in ribband or lace there is such an uproar as you never heard.'[36] Wedgwood would spend a whole day 'curiosity hunting' in London with Boulton[37], and never hesitated to ask permission to take drawings or moulds from any vases that took his fancy in the private collections of his patrons.[38] He told Bentley that he had seen some Italian vases in London and 'liked them vastly', a sure sign that he was about to copy them; he borrowed engravings from the sculptor Sir Henry Cheere; and one of his painters in London was despatched to take drawings of the handles of Sèvres vases in a shop in Arlington Street.[39]

The ornament used by Wedgwood took the form of bas-relief, at first cast with the body of the vase and later applied separately from moulds, consisting primarily of festoons, swags, cameos and single classical figures or groups. In addition there were impressed running borders of classical motifs and patterns cut into the body of the vase by engine-turning. With a variety of suitable handles and finials which, like the rest of the ornament (and, in the case of the variegated vases, the colours) could be transposed and interchanged at will, the diversity of designs was virtually unlimited.

By the spring of 1771 Wedgwood had five principal types of vase currently in production: plain creamware, variegated, ornamented basaltes, bronzed basaltes and encaustic-painted basaltes; and within these categories there were almost endless subdivisions of ornament and decoration. By August 1772 he was able to boast that he had 'upwards of 100 Good Forms of Vases for all of which we have the moulds, handles and ornaments'.[40] It is not surprising that such a multiplicity of shape and decoration should have led to difficulties in the warehouse and the saleroom.

The task of the factory would have been complicated enough if vases had been the only ornamental wares that Wedgwood made at Etruria, but they were not. Among the earliest of his productions were 'gems' in cameo and intaglio, and these were soon augmented by medallions, figures, large oval and circular 'pictures' with their own frames and tablets of various shapes to be inset in chimneypieces.

The collecting of antique gems – precious or semi-precious stones carved in cameo or intaglio with classical or mythological subjects or portraits – was almost as fashionable in eighteenth-century Europe as it had been in ancient Rome. Pliny the Elder wrote of the large-scale reproduction of such gems in a deceptive form of glass composition and this technique was revived by the sculptor and modeller James Tassie, using a coloured glass-paste that he had invented while working in Dublin with Dr Henry Quin.* He settled in London in 1766 and supplied Wedgwood with seventy casts in sulphur and two in 'enamel' (white glass-paste) in November 1769.[41]

Both Tassie and Wedgwood subsequently produced gems in enormous quantities. Raspe's catalogue of Tassie's work, published in 1791,[42] lists 15,800 subjects reproduced from the antique, nearly 900 small portraits and 114 portrait medallions with heads about 1½ inches in height on oval grounds of 'enamel' or painted glass. Wedgwood's last catalogue, printed in 1787, is a more modest affair with 1091 cameos and intaglios, 648 small portraits (including 257 heads of popes) and 233 portrait medallions, a few on ovals measuring about 10 inches in height. Unlike Tassie's, which were intended to reproduce as nearly as possible the colours of the original gems, Wedgewood's early cameos and intaglios were produced in black basaltes or white terracotta and, even when their backgrounds were coloured with enamel or stained slip, bore no more than a superficial resemblance to the originals. They were nevertheless popular, not only among collectors and those who had been on the Grand Tour and bought them in quantities for their 'cabinets', but also for mounting as jewellery, in fobs, brooches, buckles and pins, and as ornament for snuff-boxes and sword hilts.

Boulton & Fothergill, recovered from their pique at not being regularly supplied with vases, bought the white terracotta cameos, but coloured the backgrounds to make them more attractive. As Josiah explained to Bentley:

> They sell very well in Tortois-shell boxes, which is the only way they have try'd them at present. I have mention'd several more to them. In Pedestals for vases, Candlesticks &c. Cameo Buttons Mr Fothergill believes would sell abroad for the sleeves, Cloaks, and Ladies' dresses and provided they could be made cheap enough would sell in large quantities. I am perswaded we can make them very cheap *in a way to answer their purpose*. They set them all under Chrystals† & would there-

*Henry Quin, who had studied medicine at Padua, was King's Professor of Physic in the Dublin School of Physic from 1749 to 1766. He was an accomplished musician and had his own private theatre at his house on the north side of St Stephen's Green.
†Watch glasses

fore be content with them of white Bisket, without polish or colour'd Grounds, as they would do the latter themselves *in water colors*. They have done some cameos for boxes in that way, & they look much better than our burnt in grounds, & being covered with a Glass are sufficiently durable . . . Sets of Gems, & Gem Pictures may be done in the same manner in Metal mounts very cheap.[43]

Five days later he was jubilant because he had been told that 'there was two suits at the last Birth Day* with Buttons of Miniature painting – the Ladies eminent for Beauty – This I think is a fine leader to wearing Cameo's.'[44] This particular commercial seed seems not to have taken root, for his list of 'modern' cameo portraits contains only those of Queen Charlotte, Mrs Laetitia Barbauld, the Queen of Naples and the Duchess of Portland, all ladies of undoubted merit but none 'eminent for Beauty'.

Once again, Bentley raised objections to supplying Boulton with goods that he would be free to decorate to his own taste and, once again, Josiah was concerned not to offend either his partner or his rival, particularly as he knew that Boulton was already colouring black basaltes cameos as well as the terracotta because he thought them too dull. He warned Bentley that Boulton & Fothergill had connections with the Worcester porcelain factory which might begin to produce similar objects in biscuit porcelain in direct competition.[45] On this occasion Bentley was overpersuaded, the cameos were supplied and the friendly relationship between Etruria and Soho was preserved.

Wedgwood's cameo and intaglio subjects were of three main types: classical, modern and ornamental ciphers or initial letters. The sources of many were original gems in the private collections of Josiah's friendly patrons. Of the first 414 catalogued, more than half came from Sir Watkin Williams Wynn, and Josiah solicited plaster casts from many other collectors, including the Duke of Marlborough. At first more interested in copying gems for the decoration of vases than in producing collections or 'cabinets' of them, Josiah soon understood their wider commercial potential. 'Gems', he wrote in September 1769, 'are the fountain head of fine & beautiful composition.'[46] They were also to be one of the cornerstones of his ornamental work.

The success of his black basaltes and terracotta cameos encouraged Josiah to try for more impressive pieces. By 1772 he was starting to replace the technique of casting bas-relief subjects in one piece with their grounds with that of applying them from separate moulds. This

*The King's Birthday levée at St James's Palace on 4 June.

method yielded reliefs of greatly superior quality and the skilful sharpening of detail before the piece was fired – a technique which Josiah called 'undercutting' – further improved them so that they appeared to have been sculpted or cut by a lapidary.* He soon embarked on an extensive gallery of relief portraits, including 'medals' of all the popes and the kings and queens of England and France and small oval medallions, between 2 and 4 inches in height, of historical figures – 'Kings & Queens of Asia Minor, Greece &c'; 'Statesmen, Philosophers, and Orators', 'Poets'; and 'Emperors from Nerva to Constantine the Great'. The likenesses were often imaginative and some bore so close a resemblance to others as to make recognition improbable. The twelve Caesars, for example, display a family likeness that those familiar with their history must have found surprising; and the almost identical portraits of two great Athenians reflect Josiah's baffled irritation at finding that he had no likeness of Solon 'other than what we have called Demosthenes'.[47]

Of far greater iconographical interest are the 'Heads of Illustrious Moderns from Chaucer to the Present Time', of which one of the earliest was that of Sir William Hamilton. Most of these were based on authentic likenesses and a few are unique portraits 'taken from life'. The largest portrait recorded as having been made by Wedgwood in the eighteenth century is the medallion of Peter the Great, which was produced on an 18-inch oval. The portraits were not only of the great and the good, though Wedgwood & Bentley did a brisk trade in European rulers and national heroes. Introducing the portraits in their 1774 Catalogue, they offered to undertake private commissions: 'A model of a portrait in wax† . . . from three to six inches diameter, three, four, or five guineas. Any number of portraits . . . not fewer than ten . . . at ten shillings and sixpence each.'

Even more ambitious were Wedgwood's large medallions, plaques and tablets. Like the cameos and portraits, the earliest of these were cast in one piece and the classical subjects were obtained as plaster casts from specialist suppliers. These professional makers of plaster casts, which they sold to the public, were not always flattered to have their work used for the production of replicas in a more durable material, considering, not unreasonably, that their own businesses

---

*A lapidary was employed later at Etruria but for polishing, not cameo-cutting (see page 153).

†Many of the portraits reproduced by Wedgwood (and by Tassie) were originally modelled in wax. These models were supplied by the artist or the sitter, or commissioned by Wedgwood, and plaster casts taken from them. The cast was used as a first matrix for commerical reproduction in stoneware or glass-paste.

would be likely to suffer. One of them, Mrs Mary Landré, who from 1769 unwittingly supplied Wedgwood with casts both in plaster and metal, was, he warned Bentley, 'the D——l at finding out Pirates . . . If once she finds me out I shall never be able to get a Cast from her.' As her invoice of January 1769 shows, his orders were placed for him by Bentley.[48]

Among the first subjects chosen for reproduction were sets of Renaissance bronzes after Guglielmo della Porta and fourteen 'Figures from paintings discovered in the ruins of Herculaneum'* taken from a set of plaster bas-reliefs brought to England by the Marquis of Lansdowne. Eight of the fourteen are circular plaques, 11½ inches in diameter, and all were available with cavetted frames of the same material. They were described as 'fit for inlaying, as Medallions in the Pannels of Rooms, as Tablets for Chimneypieces, or for hanging up as Ornaments in Libraries &c for which purpose some of them have rich Compartments of the same Material, modelled and burnt together with the Bas-reliefs'. The grounds of the black basaltes and terracotta plaques were sometimes coloured brown or orange-red, 'antique' colours which emphasised the high relief of the figures and the contrasting fluted frames.

The first Wedgwood & Bentley Catalogue, issued in 1773, contains a list of eighty plaques and large medallions, the largest 11 inches high and 20 inches long, after antique or Renaissance sculpture or from work by such artists as François Duquesnoy ('Il Fiammingo'), Claude Michel ('Clodion') or J. C. Cobaert. Later Wedgwood was able to commission artists to model original work for his exclusive use.

Josiah was never satisfied with the 'rich Compartments', as he chose to call his frames. Occasionally coloured and more often gilded, they continued, in his opinion, to look like 'Crockery', and they were more easily damaged than wood or metal frames. 'I think', he wrote in January 1775, 'it is impossible for us to make any frames of *Pottery* however fine, or color'd that will not degrade the gem or Picture. Metal Frames Gilt, though they may tarnish in time, are the best frames in use.'[49]

The appearance of polished black basaltes was so close to that of bronze that its use for figures was almost inevitable. It was not, however, easy to accomplish. Figure-making depended not only on the

---

*The 'Herculaneum Paintings' were first illustrated in Le Antichita di Ercolano Esposte, written by an anonymous group of scholars commissioned by Charles III of Spain and published in nine magnificent folio volumes between 1757 and 1792. These catalogued the finds from the systematic excavations of the buried city of Herculaneum begun in 1738.

availability of suitable models but also on the skill of craftsmen known as 'repairers', whose job it was to dissect a clay, wax or plaster model, take moulds from the various parts, cast them separately, reassemble the parts, and prop the finished figure so that it did not collapse in the heat of the oven during firing. Josiah made fruitless enquiries at the Derby porcelain factory and asked Bentley to ask at Bow, but was doubtful of finding 'one *sober* figure maker' capable also of training young assistants. Meanwhile, he did the best he could, transferring one of his best modellers from Burslem to Etruria to work on small figures for the finials of vases and larger models of 'a Sphynx, Lyon & a Triton', the last a fine figure for a candlestick lent to him by Sir William Chambers.[50]

By 1773 the problem had been overcome. The Catalogue describes an eclectic collection of twenty-seven figures (eight in pairs), including a 2-foot high 'Neptune', smaller figures of Bacchus after Sansovino and Michelangelo, a set of five figures of reclining boys after Duquesnoy, and an elephant. Several of these figures have not been found and it may be assumed that the less popular among them were made in very small quantities. An example of the elephant, 14 inches high, was sold in 1770 but almost immediately returned by the purchaser. 'I . . . will send you no more such cumbrous Animals', Josiah wrote to Bentley, 'as the Lady said I fear we made a Bull when we first made an Elephant.'[51] During the next twelve months a pair of pug dogs was added, copied from Louis-François Roubiliac's model of William Hogarth's dog Trump.

Even more surprising than the odd mixture of figures was the inclusion of 'Egyptian Lions' and 'Egyptian Sphinxes'. One of the early European travellers in Egypt, Charles Norden, had written in 1743, 'Let them talk to me no more of Rome; let Greece be silent. What magnificence! What mechanics! What other nation [but Egypt] ever had the courage to undertake work so surprising!'[52] Norden's enthusiasm was not, however, immediately shared by more than a small number of adventurous explorers and informed antiquarians, most of whom had studied antiquities in Rome. Neither Greece nor Egypt was included in the regular itineraries of the Grand Tour and knowledge or understanding of Egyptian art was minimal.

In England the Egyptian style was an exotic taste before the end of the century. The undated and unused design by Sir William Chambers for a gateway with sphinxes at Sherborne Castle[53] was probably drawn about 1770, and Robert Adam's entrance screen for Syon House, incorporating sphinxes in the design, was not built until 1773, the year in which the first Wedgwood & Bentley Catalogue advertising Egyptian sphinx figures and candlesticks, Egyptian lions and cameos of subjects from Egyptian history was published. Wedgwood was therefore among the first to use Egyptian subjects in the applied arts and the first seriously to introduce them into English pottery.

Second only to vases in importance for their commercial value and their prestige were Wedgewood's library busts. Like the larger plaques and the reproductions of Renaissance figures, these took full advantage of the bronze-like appearance of black basaltes; and, like the portrait medallions, they catered to the taste of a people who had come to appreciate the importance of the individual and his family heritage and to revere history and the antique. If this was the great age of monuments and of the desire for personal, visible and lasting memorials, not only of public heroes but also of family ancestors, it was also the age when a classical education was the necessary equipment of a gentleman. No well-ordered country house could be without its library, and the architecture, interior decoration and furniture design of the period provided numerous settings for busts of classical authors or modern poets, composers, artists and architects, actors and dramatists, statesmen, divines and military heroes. The centre of the broken pediment, one of the most fasionable of design devices for doorways and bookcases, provided a suitable space for a bust or ornamental vase, and the semicircular 'shell' or 'fan' recesses so often moulded in plaster above Adam bookcases were intended, as drawings in the Soane Museum show, for the display of busts.

Wedgwood obtained moulds of busts of Cicero and Horace from the London plaster-cast makers Hoskins & Oliver in 1770 but he was evidently concerned that his models should not be too commonly available in painted plaster and wrote to Bentley about six months later: 'I suppose those [busts] at the [Royal] Academy are less hackney'd & better in General than the Plaister shop can furnish us with; besides it will sound better to say – this is from the Academy, taken from an Original . . . than to say, we had it from Flaxman.'* But sculptors were not much in evidence in the first years of the Academy, founded less than three years earlier, and Josiah concluded that 'We must be content to have them [moulds] as we can.'[54] He was, however, anxious to buy original moulds, prepared especially for him, and would pay a good price for them. This was a departure from his normal method and obviated any possible complaint that, by reproducing busts in a more

---

*John Flaxman senior (1726–95), modeller and maker of plaster casts. See pp. 294–5.

attractive and durable material, be would be destroying the business of any plaster-cast maker who supplied him with moulds.

Josiah located some 'divine busts' in the collection of Lord Rockingham, who was content to lend them to him, but he had no one at Etruria sufficiently skilled in taking moulds from original works of art to be able to take advantage of the opportunity. Oliver's moulds, on the other hand, were 'horrid dear'.[55] By 1773, only three busts were ready: Horace and Cicero, both 19 inches high, from the moulds bought in 1770, and a fine 10-inch bust of George II, cast from a carved ivory by John Michael Rysbrack[56] in the possession of the King's sergeant-surgeon, John Ranby. This was slow progress by Wedgwood's standards and next year he added thirty-two, including among the classical portraits busts of Palladio,* Francis Bacon, Ben Jonson, Sir Walter Raleigh, Sir Isaac Newton and Robert Boyle. The variety of subjects suggests that the first choices were made largely on the basis of what was available from the plaster-cast makers' yards. By 1779 there were eighty-seven busts of eighty-two subjects, nearly half of them 'modern', ranging in size from 25 inches to miniatures 4–4½ inches high.

The Wedgwood & Bentley Catalogue published in 1773 is proof of the extraordinary progress made by the partnership in inventive production during the first years at Etruria. In the form of ornamental vases, busts, figures, plaques, medallions and cameos, Wedgwood's black basaltes was scarcely recognisable as a development of the 'Egyptian black' earthenware produced in Staffordshire from about the middle of the century, and his variegated vases bore no obvious relationship even to the finest of 'agate' or 'marbled' knife handles. Decorative styles as handsome and fashionable as those that Wedgwood was introducing at Etruria could have been found elsewhere in Europe or among the English porcelain factories, but the entire concept of ornaments of such quality was essentially new to the Staffordshire pottery industry. Like his Queen's ware, they were imitated and copied in England and the rest of Europe, in Scandinavia and even in Russia; but few of his rivals ever successfully competed with Wedgwood for invention or quality of production,[57] and no potter, and few contemporary manufacturers, could match Wedgwood & Bentley in marketing.

---

*This is an 'invented' bust, accepted as a true likeness until 1970 and probably based on a fake by Leoni and Sebastian Ricci.

CHAPTER EIGHT

Elegance and Truth

Although the partnership books were opened in November 1768, the formal indenture of the agreement between Josiah Wedgwood and Thomas Bentley was not signed until August 1769, two months after the official opening of the factory at Etruria. In all respects except the provision of capital, the whole of which was subscribed by Wedgwood, it was to be an equal partnership, but Wedgwood was to receive interest at the rate of 7½ per cent on his investment in building the ornamental works and 5 per cent on money advanced to Bentley for his share of the starting capital.[1] These were high rates at a time when the rates of interest on government securities were exceptionally low. The usury laws imposed a strict limit of 5 per cent on commercial interest rates after 1714* but, in these two transactions, only the money lent to Bentley would have been considered a loan. The rate to be paid from profits on Josiah's investment in buildings and machinery may be compared with the 3 per cent Consolidated Stock introduced in 1757.

The partnership was specifically for 'making and vending Ornamental Earthen Ware', and the provision of a house for Bentley on the Etruria estate suggests an intention that he should be regularly concerned with production, at least while Wedgwood was away 'curiosity hunting' or searching for materials. This arrangement did not turn out to be practicable any more than it was ever likely to be agreeable to a man of Bentley's tastes. He never occupied the Bank House, which became home to Josiah and his family until Etruria Hall was completed, and, after a visit to Burslem, Bentley settled in London in August 1769. Since the autumn of 1766 William Cox had been in charge of

---

*Government stocks, which were immune from this legislation, paid 3–4 per cent in peacetime and tended to rise during time of war. The least favourable period for borrowing in eighteenth-century England was in wartime, during the last quarter of the century.

Wedgwood's London warehouse at 5 Charles Street between Berkeley and Grosvenor Squares. Although situated in a fashionable area, these were modest premises comprising two rooms with little enough space for samples of tablewares and none suitable for the proper display of the new ornamental pieces. By May 1767, only a few months after renting the Charles Street rooms, Josiah was looking for larger accommodation which could provide offices and satisfactory showrooms. He considered taking some empty auction rooms in Pall Mall but Bentley advised strongly against premises that had been 'a place of public resort'. Wedgwood was quick to take the point that it would be difficult to exclude the public from rooms to which they had previously enjoyed free access and he had no wish to expose his customers to the risk of mixing with 'the rest of the World any further than their amusements, or conveniencys make it necessary to do so'.[2]

He had clear and original ideas about the display of his ware. He wanted a *'Large'* Room:

> not to shew, or have a large stock of ware in Town, but to enable me to show various Table & desert services, completely set out on two ranges of Tables, six or eight at least such services are absolutely necessary to be shewn in order to *do the needfull* with the Ladys in the neatest, genteelest & best method. The same, or indeed a much greater variety of setts of Vases should decorate the Walls, & both these articles may, every few days, be so alter'd, revers'd, & transform'd as to render the whole a new scene, Even to the same Company, every time they shall bring their friends to visit us.[3]

He emphasised to Bentley the 'many good effects this must produce, when business, & amusement can be made to go hand in hand'. Having tried the idea, in attenuated form, in the restricted space available at Charles Street, he had sold three sets of vases which had been in stock for between six and twelve months 'and wanted nothing but arrangement to sell them'. But besides room to display his stock, he must, he told his partner, 'have room for *my Ladys* for they sometimes come in very large shoals together, & one party are often obliged to wait till another have done their business'.[4]

Suitable premises were not easy to find and he was not successful until March 1768. Meanwhile, his elder brother John, who had admirably represented the firm in London between 1765 and 1766, was killed in tragic and mysterious circumstances. Josiah's grief was undisguised: 'Your friend, & my poor brother is Dead, is no more, is no longer the warm & benevolent friend, Affectionate Brother, or Chearfull Companion, but is now a lifeless, insensible Clod of Earth,' he wrote in real distress to Bentley on 14 June 1767. 'And what has greatly heighten'd the shock to his surviving friends is the circumstances attending this Meloncholly event.' In the evening of 10 June 1767, as Josiah explained, John had been to see the fireworks at Ranelagh,* afterwards dining at the Swan at Westminster Bridge, where he had stayed until about midnight. Unable to find a bed there for the night, he had left to seek one elsewhere. His body was found in the Thames early next morning, and it was supposed that 'in passing the River side . . . he slipp'd in'.[5] The streets of London were no place for walking after dark and the proprietors of pleasure gardens, including Ranelagh, provided escorts to take their patrons safely home at night. While it was assumed that John's death was an accident it was tacitly understood that it was possible that he had been murdered. Certainly, in one of Josiah's letters to William Hodgson, who was the first to be informed of John's death and was entrusted with the arrangements for the funeral, there are hints that John might have in some way contributed to his own death, and the inference may be that he was drunk.[6]

In his desolation, Josiah turned naturally to Bentley, who had also been his brother's friend: 'I need not tell you', he wrote, 'how doubly wellcome a few lines will be at this time from a real, affectionate, & sensible friend, such a one as you have ever been to me since I had the happiness of being known to you. Let us now be dearer to each other if possible than ever, let me adopt you for my Brother – & fill up the chasm this cruel accident has made in my afflicted heart – Excuse me my dear friend, the subject is too much for me. I am your miserable friend . . .'[7] It was a further grief to him that he was unable to attend his brother's funeral, but Sally was about to give birth to their third child and was not well enough for Josiah to consider leaving her.[8] Instead, his eldest brother Thomas led the family mourners. To another close friend, Ralph Griffiths, who wrote to commiserate with him, Josiah admitted that he had 'long grieved' for John 'as one who from an unhappy combination of circumstances could enjoy or relish few of the comforts of life',[9] but what those unhappy circumstances were is not suggested.

For several weeks after his brother's death Josiah exhibited symp-

---

*Pleasure gardens and fashionable place of entertainment in Chelsea. The princi-
pal structure, erected in 1742, was a wooden rotunda accommodating 6000
people, designed in imitation of the Pantheon in Rome, where patrons promen-
aded or supped in the boxes that lined the walls. After about 1785 Ranelagh
declined, becoming a favourite haunt of pickpockets and prostitutes, and the
gardens were closed in 1804.

toms of reactive depression, most noticeably an uncharacteristic listlessness and reluctance to work combined with the 'bilious complaint' from which he suffered regularly in times of severe stress and which, as he told Bentley, 'sunk my spirits, & dishearten'd me greatly in the prosecution of my schemes'.[10] In July he recovered, imposing on himself a strict regime of exercise, riding up to 20 miles a day, and a diet of 'Whey, & yolks of Eggs in abundance, with a mixture of Rhubarb & soap just to keep my body open'. He was just thirty-seven years old and already beginning to show a serious concern for his health.[11] This later developed into the hypochondria that was a recognisable legacy of Josiah Wedgwood to generations of his descendants.

Josiah found little time during the remainder of the year for the active expansion of his London business but, in March 1768, he spent ten days in the capital searching for suitable premises for his showrooms. He wrote to Bentley on 24 March that he had succeeded beyond his 'most sanguine expectations', acquiring the lease of a house near the lower end of St Martin's Lane, 'quite convenient for Westminster, & within a 12d ride of St. Pauls Ch[urch] y[ar]d'. The accommodation was larger than he required and he proposed to use the surplus rooms as 'habitations for a Colony of Artists, – Modelers Carvers &c'. He had, indeed, already agreed terms with one 'very useful Tennant, A Master Enameler, & China piecer [restorer], – he joins old valuable pieces of China, not with Rivits, but a white glass . . . & they are as sound as ever they were'.

This 'sober & steady' man was David Rhodes, who had moved from Yorkshire to work in London. Josiah lost no time in securing his services before he should be employed by any of the china companies. He explained to Bentley that he already had a long-established connection with Rhodes, who painted 'flowers, & Landskips very prettily', had a 'tolerable notion of Colours' and could prepare good powder gold for gilding. Rhodes would bring with him an apprentice and a second assistant. 'The having such a Man as this under the same roof with the warehouse, to do Crests or any other patterns by order – to take sketches &c – is the most convenient thing imaginable,' he wrote, '& nobody but our selves will know what he is doing.' He proposed to look for a modeller, who could be employed in making copies of 'any Ladys favourite Antique'.[12]

In spite of this enthusiastic report, these premises were never occupied by Wedgwood. A week later, Josiah informed his partner that he had found another house, even better suited to his purpose, on a corner at the other end of St Martin's Lane, '60 feet long, the streets wide which lye to it, & carriages may come to it from Westminster or the

City without being incommoded with drays full of timber, Coals &c which are allways pouring in from the various Wharfs, & making stops in the Strand, very disagreeable & sometimes dangerous'. The rent was substantial, 100 guineas a year, but Josiah's friends assured him that it was 'the best situation in all London' for his rooms.[13]

Josiah sent his architect Joseph Pickford to London to advise William Cox on the sale of one house and the redecoration and fitting of the other, explaining, 'He is a Londoner & knows all their tricks.'[14] His own involvement in these transactions was curtailed by his having 'over walk'd & over work'd' his knee, leading to the amputation of his leg a month later, but work on the new warehouse and showrooms proceeded without him.

By the middle of June the preparation of the new rooms was sufficiently advanced for Josiah to be sending extra hands to London to help Cox with the move. One of these was John Wood from Stockport, hired for three years at £15 a year with 'Meat, Drink, Washing & Lodging'. 'His Diet at home', Wedgwood told Cox, 'is chiefly Milk, Bread & Butter &c, & as he is not of a very robust Constitution he shou'd not make much Alteration in his way of Living.' He could write 'a good hand' and was therefore to be employed as a clerk. Cox had drawn up an advertisement informing customers of the new address but this was something that Wedgwood already had in hand, including in his own design an 'Acknowledgement of royal Patronage'. This he desired Cox to show to Deborah Chetwynd (see p. 41) for her approval and then, with the advice and help of Ralph Griffiths, to have it published in the *St James's Chronicle* for a fortnight and 'that Morning Paper which is mostly taken in by People of Fashion, & which I suppose is that wherein the Plays are advertised' for a week before the opening of the new rooms. Meanwhile, he was preparing stocks of tableware to be sent by sea to the new London warehouse and already had '1000 dozen of Plates . . . for that purpose'.[15] Apart from a few lines added at the foot, this letter, written just sixteen days after 'St Amputation Day', is in Bentley's hand, but the tone of instruction and organisation is unmistakably that of the recuperating Wedgwood. A week later, free of pain-killing drugs, he was ready to believe 'the present to be an Age of Miracles'.[16]

In August he was in London for the opening of his new showrooms at 1 Great Newport Street. The building consisted of two shops with fronts on to the street, one of which, facing St Martin's Lane, was sublet to a linen draper. The other, facing Newport Street, was used by Wedgwood for the sale of 'useful' wares from stock. The showrooms occupied the whole of the first floor above both shops, and displayed tea, dinner and dessert services laid out, as Josiah had previously proposed, on tables. Ornamental wares of the Wedgwood & Bentley partnership were arranged on shelves around walls lined with paper in colours carefully chosen to enhance shape and decoration. Josiah favoured yellow as a background for basaltes and blue or green for Queen's ware. Green baize was used on some of the tables.[17] The finest vases and the most recent productions were kept in a small, locked room to the rear, where they were shown only to customers selected for their social importance, knowledge or taste.

As their invoices confirm, Wedgwood tablewares and Wedgwood & Bentley ornamental wares could be bought in London only at the Newport Street showrooms, where sales were strictly for cash. Twelve months after the rooms were opened, Bentley settled permanently in London, and William Cox, who had managed Wedgwood's business in London since November 1766, returned to Staffordshire to work at Etruria.

Thomas Bentley's arrival in London to take charge of all business, for both the 'useful' ware and ornamental ware partnerships, signalled the beginning of Wedgwood's greatest period of achievement. Josiah had proved his ability as an entrepreneur and he had laid sound foundations for the expansion of his markets. His Queen's ware tablewares were already 'spread allmost over the whole Globe', rapidly superseding the European tin-glazed earthenwares and even providing some competition with porcelain, and he had attracted powerful patronage. Much of this had been achieved by the effective use of his considerable native wit and boundless enthusiasm and an exceptional capacity for creating opportunity and exploiting advantage. What he lacked in formal education and social polish he was able, to a remarkable degree, to supply by application and charm. But his particular talents, the unique contributions which lifted both partnerships above all competitors, were his inventiveness and his managerial skills, and even he, driven by unremitting ambition, could not find time for all he must do. For the next eleven years it was Bentley who played the principal role in the discovery, exploitation, organisation and even the creation of markets for their goods, and it was during this period that Wedgwood made the most original and enduring invention of his life.

Bentley's education, taste, commercial experience, entrepreneurial skills and social graces were only the most evidently valuable of his contributions to the partnership. He was able to combine the stimulus of original ideas with a practical and restraining good sense and he was alone in being permitted to curb Wedgwood's almost untameable enthusiasms and to unseat him from his hobby-horses. Their friendship, fuelled by their almost daily exchange of letters, was even closer than the partnership which united their complementary abilities. Josiah was not exaggerating the case when he told Bentley, 'when we have been together some time I feel but like half my self when we are separated'.[18]

It is clear that the business being done through the London show-rooms was already increasing enormously even before the move to new and improved premises.[19] Cox was in effect replaced by two men: Bentley as director of all London operations, and a new head clerk, Ben Mather.

Bentley's influence was immediately apparent. He had Josiah's authority to make whatever changes he pleased in the showrooms and he at once introduced glass-fronted showcases for the display of the more expensive ornaments.[20] Within a month of his arrival at Great Newport Street he had rented a house in Cheyne Row, Chelsea, and in December he set up a decorating studio there, complete with muffle* kiln, moving David Rhodes and his painters from Newport Street. This perfectly accorded with Josiah's idea for a 'Colony of Artists' and both partners set about finding suitable painters, able not only to decorate simple Queen's ware services but also to paint the more sophisticated figures and groups on the black 'Etruscan' vases.

The principal painters in London at this time were David Rhodes and his partner William Hopkins Craft. They remained independent until March 1770, although it appears that most, if not all, of their work was for Wedgwood. After that date they were employed directly by Wedgwood and Rhodes was appointed manager of the Cheyne Row Studio. Rhodes continued under the day-to-day direction of Bentley for ten years, becoming one of the firm's most valued employees, entrusted with closely guarded secrets and with confidential negotiations and purchases.[21] Rhodes or his assistants were probably responsible for much of the charming, but somewhat primitive, painting on teapots of this period and he is believed to have worked on important tableware. He is reputed also to have had a hand in the painting of the First Day's Vases, though it is far from certain that he was sufficiently skilled to have painted the figures.[22]

Craft was both more difficult and more talented. None of his work for Wedgwood has been identified with certainty and his reputation therefore rests on a few references in Josiah's letters and some fine

---

*A muffle is a refractory (for example, fireclay) box, similar in principle to a saggar but a permanent part of a kiln, used to protect ware from direct contact with the flames. Muffle kilns (made unnecessary by clean modern fuels) are used especially for firing delicate colours.

signed miniatures which have survived.* He was at first entrusted with some administration at the Studio and the training of less skilled and experienced painters, but he soon showed unwelcome signs of artistic temperament and dissatisfaction. By the end of December 1769 he was being blamed for neglecting his work for Wedgwood & Bentley in favour of better paid employment elsewhere, and this at a time when there was more than enough for him to do in painting 'Etruscans'. While admiring Bentley's superior patience, Josiah was furious with Craft. 'Why,' he wrote in disgust, 'if he had been a Nabob himself we could not have behaved with more respect, & caution towards him, & between friends I believe that is the very thing which has spoiled him. . . . I shall not easily forgive him. . . . He too will find in the end, as such people allways do, that he is *penny wise & pound foolish.*'[23] Craft demanded, and was given, £200 a year, which Josiah considered 'too extravagant to be lasting'[24] and, the following October, when Craft threatened to leave to join the Derby porcelain company, it looked as if he would be proved right. Nevertheless, Craft was probably the most skilled painter in the Studio and Josiah had grudgingly to admit that 'If that Coxcomb Crofts† would be made any way bearable I apprehend we could find him constant employment.'[25] Craft finally left in 1771 to become an independent enameller. By then the Decorating Studio had been so strengthened that it was altogether more comfortable to be without him.

In June 1769 Josiah had engaged Ralph Willcox and his wife Catherine, both of whom had worked at Liverpool porcelain factories, where they had painted underglaze blue patterns, and at Worcester, where the greater part of their work was in blue but may also have included some painting in polychrome. Ralph made a good impression: 'I like his appearance much,' Wedgwood wrote, 'he seems a sober solid man, & has nothing flighty or Coxcomical in his dress, or behaviour of which most of this Class [painters] are apt to contract a small tincture.' Catherine, the daughter of Thomas Frye, the mezzotint engraver who was also one of the founders of the Bow porcelain factory, was, as her husband readily admitted, by far the more skilled of the two and 'an excellent copyer of figure & other subjects'.[26] Three months later Josiah suggested that Mrs Willcox should join the painters in London to try

---

*Portraits of George III, Queen Charlotte and Sir William Hamilton and a pastoral scene (British Museum); a self-portrait is in the National Gallery of Ireland.

†Josiah's inability to spell this name later led to some difficulty in identifying 'Crofts' with the miniaturist W. H. Craft. This was resolved by the discovery of signed invoices for his work for Wedgwood.

her hand at painting vases, and she and her husband joined the Chelsea Decorating Studio in December. Evidently she was employed for more than a year painting border patterns but Josiah thought her talents were not being used to best advantage: 'Mrs Willcox should be doing *figures* rather than borders,' he told Bentley. 'She will paint much better figures . . . than any I have seen upon *real Etruscan Vases*.'[27]

Another valuable acquisition to the Studio was James Bakewell, who joined Wedgwood at Burslem in the summer of 1768 and was at first employed in drawing the shapes of vases for reference purposes.[28] From this mechanical work he graduated to flower painting and may have been responsible for developing an individual style of botanical painting using a rose-purple pigment mixed by Rhodes and a striking combination of black and yellow. Josiah was not entirely satisfied with the quality of Bakewell's work but nevertheless wrote to Bentley: 'Bakewell has set his mind on being a *good enamel Painter* and really improves very much in flowers and in Coppying figures. I have not taken him from his painting of some time past he has set his heart so much upon it, & makes so quick a progress both in improvement & in a dispatchfull method.'[29] Wedgwood sent him to London with one J. Simpcock, 'a new made flower painter who promises to have a very dispatchfull hand', to work under the supervision of Rhodes.[30]

This was fairly typical of Josiah's method when he was able to recruit painters. He was conscious that the quality of work that he demanded was often superior to that accepted by other manufacturers. As he told Bentley in May 1770, 'You observe very justly that few hands can be got to paint flowers in the style we want them. I may add, nor any other work we do – We *must make them*. There is no other way. We have slipped forward beyond the other manufacturers & we must be content to train up hands to suit our purpose.'[31] This became all the more evident as the high quality of Queen's ware increasingly came to be recognised and appreciated. Wedgwood's supremacy in this field was largely dependent on quality of decoration – the printing of Sadler & Green and the painting of his enamellers – and he valued them, in spite of their tiresome airs and tantrums, accordingly. 'It is,' he wrote, 'the *Elegance, & truth* of the pencil, & not the labour which ravisheth fine eyes.'[32]

It was indeed to 'fine eyes' that Wedgwood most wanted his Queen's ware to appeal and in April 1770 he was rewarded by an order for a large dinner and dessert service for the Empress Catherine II of Russia. The pattern chosen was a botanical centre surrounded by a border of husk festoons painted in a rose-pink on the shapes created for Queen Charlotte in 1765,[33] with a matching dessert service of scat-

tered sprays of boldly painted flowers on shell-edge shape. This important order, which was transmitted to Wedgwood by Alexander Baxter,
a Scotsman acting as Russian Consul in London, was undoubtedly
owed to the influence of Lord and Lady Cathcart, who had lost no time
in making good their promise to 'do great things'. Having supplied the
Cathcarts with a set for their own use, Josiah had wanted to send them
some examples of his vases. These, it was made clear, were intended
as display samples from which he might hope to obtain orders from
Russian noblemen, but he was uncertain how to achieve this. 'There
seems to be difficulty how to *deliver* these Vases to Lady Cathcart,' he
wrote. 'They must not be *presented*, & we must not pretend to charge
them, so that they must neither be *given* nor *sold*.' His solution was
characteristically ingenious: 'we must borrow a pair of her Ladyship's
chimneypieces to shew them upon'.[34]

This order for Catherine the Great was all the more welcome
because Wedgwood's early attempts to supply goods to Russia had not
been entirely successful. The Russians, he was told by one of the
Cathcarts' staff in St Petersburg, liked 'anything of Gilding & shew'.
This was later confirmed by Lady Cathcart, who advised him that 'all
sorts of Gilding & Colouring' would find a ready market. Josiah found
the Russians still in love with the rococo and complained that his teasets
were too elegant for one of his customers who wanted only 'shewy,
tawdrey cheap things, cover'd all over with colors'.[35] This did not fit in
at all with his intention to 'simplify' his designs, nor with the advice
he was given from other quarters, but the potential of the Russian
market was too tempting to ignore and the best he could do was to
compromise by adding gilding to some of his patterns.

A second difficulty was transport. The first order received through
the good offices of the Cathcarts suffered considerable damage when
the *Dolphin*, the ship carrying it, was wrecked while entering port and
was not unloaded for two months. Lady Cathcart wrote:

> Since the frost has been hard enough to get at it the things have been
> taking out & are still, but in miserable confusion & loss of the perishable
> commodities besides that while no body from the Petersburg side could
> get at it, some Pirates from Islands near at hand have Plunderd many
> things which most people say will not be recover'd.

Under the circumstances, it was perhaps fortunate that any of Wedgwood's goods arrived at all, but Lady Cathcart, who sent Wedgwood
a full list of damage and replacements required, reported that she heard

'nothing but complaints & disappointment' from the customers she had so carefully cultivated.[36]

The fault lay as much in the packing as in the accident to the ship. Those goods, including all the vases, which had been packed in boxes, survived almost unscathed, but the dinner services ordered for noblemen at the Imperial Court had been sent in 'hampers'.

Last, delivery in January 1770 of orders placed in London the previous June was criticised as far too slow, and Jane Cathcart bluntly agreed: 'I have', she wrote early in February 1770, 'realy had discouragement in this attempt to be useful to your Manufactory, however if you will point the way I shall gladly follow it if I can be of service. Certain it is that the Nobility of this Country express the highest approbation whenever they see any of the Queens ware at our House.' Both she and her husband were keen to promote British goods and she took some trouble to give Wedgwood accurate advice. Much of the 'Husk' service made for Catherine the Great has been preserved and is displayed in the palace of Petrodvorets (Peterhof). It is the earliest Wedgwood table service to have survived in such quantity and provides a great deal of valuable information about the quality of Wedgwood's Queen's ware and the work of his painters at this period. Its production was the cause of heavy anxiety to both partners, primarily because they still had too few skilled painters to decorate Queen's ware services as well as 'Etruscan' vases, and only one oven in London for firing-on the decoration. 'I tremble as well as you for the Russian service,' Josiah wrote to Bentley, '& would rather Mr Rhodes set up two or three iron Kilns than it should not be done in time. I think hands may be got to do it, if you are short I could send you three from hence who can paint flowers very well from good patterns . . . all I can say any farther is that you shall not want the *plain ware*.'[37]

Two Liverpool painters, Joseph Cooper and Ralph Unwin, were engaged at 48s. and 27s. a week and sent down to London as 'outside passengers' on the coach in May, and two more, Joseph Barrat and Thomas Glover, walked to London from Burslem, a distance of about 150 miles, at the end of the year.[38] To avoid drawing unwelcome attention to the partners, Rhodes was instructed to advertise '& mention that any hands who had been employ'd in painting figures or flowers upon Coaches, Fans, Waiters [trays], or China might have constant employment by applying to him in Little China Row Chelsea'.

With the exception of Mrs Willcox, who was employed in a single package, as it were, with her husband, all the painters were men. 'And what', Josiah demanded, 'has become of your scheme for taking in Girls to paint?' He reminded Bentley that it was almost impossible to find anyone in the Potteries who could achieve their standards without further training: 'Where amongst our Potters could I get a complete Vase maker? Nay I could not get a hand through the whole Pottery to make a Table plate without training them up for that purpose & you must be content to train up such Painters as offer to you & not turn them adrift because they cannot immediately form their hands to our new stile, which if we consider what they have been doing all their life we ought not to expect from them.'[39] Josiah had 'a *Waking notion*' of starting up a 'regular drawing, & modeling school to train up Artists' by taking on 'likely Boys of about 12 years old' as apprentices for eight or nine years until they were capable of painting vases to the highest standards. It was an ambitious project: 'The Paintings upon these Vases are from the W & B school – So it may be said 1000 years hence.'[40] In the meantime, the most suitable painters were to be found at Liverpool, rather than at Worcester where the jobs of the porcelain painters were threatened by the introduction of blue printing, and Josiah commissioned James Bakewell to 'ingage half a doz or half a score' of the Liverpool painters.[41]

Matters were further complicated by an explosion, which wrecked the oven at the Chelsea Decorating Studio, and Bentley complained irritably, 'We are always too much in a hurry to do anything right. . . . Things done in a hurry are never done well.' 'Who says so?' Josiah rejoined. '*Never*? . . . first thoughts are often best, & many things must be done *now* or *never*, – Take time by the forelock or he will slip through your fingers – And – but I have not time for any more old proverbs or I would string you as complete a neclace of them as ever Sancho hung round his Master's neck.' For good measure he added: 'It was not precipitation in *making* but in fireing the Kiln at Chelsea which blew it up.'[42] A week later he was impatient to get started again: 'I hope you will have a kiln of some sort up soon that we may drive away like Jehu the son of – somebody.'[43] Bentley was already beginning to feel the goad of Wedgwood's sense of urgency.

As early as April, when the order for Catherine the Great was received, Josiah was planning to take full advantage of the prestige attached to it by 'shewing, & making the most of this service at *home* as well as *abroad*',[44] and he could not resist the temptation of a visit to London in July to see it for himself.[45] It was duly inspected and approved by Alexander Baxter and despatched to St Petersburg, where it was evidently received with satisfaction by the Empress. Although it had not proved possible to exhibit the service publicly as Josiah had wished, Bentley had been able to arrange for it to be viewed by the King, for whom a similarly decorated service had been commissioned, and shards from another set of about this period excavated at Williams-burg show that the 'Husk' pattern was not reserved to Catherine II. The full significance of this order, however, was not revealed until nearly three years later.

In little more than twelve months Wedgwood and Bentley had consolidated their partnership in London by setting up offices, a ware-house and showroom, and a working studio of artists. Bentley was already displaying a quick grasp of the business and was not short of ideas for its promotion. Between them the partners had acquired and successfully produced one of the most prestigious orders ever com-missioned from a pottery manufacturer. It seemed to be a period of extraordinary achievement and brilliant promise. And so it was; but beneath the surface there were problems of inexperience and neglect that threatened the very structure of the business.

CHAPTER NINE

Crises of Management

For eleven years, since the founding of his own pottery, Josiah had enjoyed almost unbroken business success. It was a period of great personal strain, in which he had survived a painful and dangerous operation and experienced the anguish of bereavement, but it was also one in which he had established a supreme reputation for innovation and style. The greater part of this achievement had been his own. Bentley's influence, noticeable some years before the beginning of their partnership, was not evidently formative before 1768. Queen's ware had been brought to a degree of refinement acknowledged through Europe as unrivalled by any other pottery; black basaltes, in its various painted and ornamented forms, dominated the market generated by its development; Wedgwood's vases had inspired a new fashion which was being profitably exploited; and his mind was filled with ideas for invention and improvement which lacked only time for experiment. He could look towards the future with confidence.

The problems that arose might have been anticipated. The fact that they were not is less a measure of Wedgwood's lack of foresight than of his inability to find time to do all that was needed by himself or to recruit anyone to whom he could safely delegate the administration of the business. It had outgrown his own experience and he was obliged to learn, or as often as not to invent, solutions to problems as he encountered them.

By far the most serious of these concerned his partnership with Bentley. The setting up of the Chelsea Decorating Studio had been Bentley's work in anticipation of large orders for 'encaustic' painted vases and the consequent benefits to the partnership, but the skilled painters he had assembled had been employed for two months on the 'Husk' order for the Empress Catherine. Although decorated in London, this was 'useful' ware produced at the Burslem factory and thus part of the Josiah Wedgwood and Thomas Wedgwood partnership in which Bentley had no beneficial interest. In June 1770 he wrote to express his first doubts about the profitability of the Wedgwood & Bentley partnership. Josiah attempted to reassure him, putting Bentley's misgivings down to anxiety for his sister-in-law, Elizabeth Oates: 'I have not the least doubt of it,' he wrote on the 13th, the first anniversary of the official opening of the Etruria factory, 'nor do I think you will now our good sister is recovering. I could *feel* the impression her illness made upon your spirits by sundry expressions in your last letters, however there is nothing like demonstration, & if you will let us have the accounts up to 10th August next (when it comes) we will then see what we have with certainty.'[1]

Bentley's patience was further tried when he suggested that some erncaustic-painted black teapots might be made at Etruria. Josiah had no objection to the idea in principle but pointed out that his agreement with Thomas stipulated that he should have a one-eighth share of the profits on all 'useful' ware and that he had spent much of his time in the development of black basaltes teapots at the Brick House Works: 'though I believe he would not deny me if I asked him to give up the black T.pots &c to us, yet I have some fear of its being a tender point with him'.[2] Thomas's reaction to the proposal was, as Josiah had expected, unfavourable. Bentley, who clearly considered it unnecessary to refer the matter to Thomas, was unexpectedly angry and reverted to his earlier argument that his new partnership with Wedgwood, while taking up almost all of his time and energies, yielded little in profit compared to his Liverpool business with Boardman, which he was obliged to neglect in its favour.

Caught between the demands of his two partners and their own separate partnerships, Josiah was obliged to exert all his powers of diplomacy and persuasion: 'I told you in my last', he wrote on 3 September from Etruria, 'that my choice was to have the Etruscan Teapots made here, rather than at Burslem, but thought my self obliged to consult my partner T:W accordingly I spoke to him and ordered some to be made here last week.' Nevertheless, he reminded Bentley that when they had taken out the patent for encaustic decoration it had been agreed between them that, while the ornamental ware should be made by Wedgwood & Bentley, profits on any 'useful' ware decorated in this manner should be credited either to Wedgwood alone or to the J. and T. Wedgwood partnership, the expense of the patent being charged to them in proportion to their use of it. At the time he had told Thomas that there was a strong possibility that they would want to make considerable quantities of 'painted Etruscan *usefull ware*' and

that he should have his share of the profit. 'From both these circumstances', he wrote, 'I hope it will appear to you, as it did, & does still
to me, that however inclinable I was my self to the measure in question,
yet I ought to mention it to T:W before it was put into execution.'[3]

In spite of the delicacy of the situation and his affection for his
partners, Josiah found himself unable to conceal his irritation:

> With respect to the difference between *Usefull ware* & *Ornaments* I do
> not find any inclination in myself to be over nice in drawing the line.
> You know I never had any idea that Ornamental ware should not be
> of *'some use'*. You knew this from all that we have done hitherto, from
> the many conversations we have had upon this subject, & from the
> list we wrote in your commonplace book of the uses to which ornamen-
> tal vases might be put: I could have wish'd therefore that you had not
> repeated this idea so often, & asked me if my Partnership with T:W
> would exclude our making Stella's Ewers.* Tell me my dear friend,
> did you ask me this question for information or were you really as
> angry with me as the question accompanied with any other idea would
> seem to import. I hope you were not, for I should be very unhappy
> to think you would be angry with me lightly or that I had given you
> any just occasion for the warmth some parts of your letter *seem* to
> express. I say *seem* for I hope I am mistaken & shall rest in that hope
> 'till I have the pleasure of hearing from you again. But as this question
> has put me upon thinking a little more upon the subject, & the situation
> I am, or may be in, betwixt two Partnerships it may not be amiss to
> enter a little deeper into it.[4]

He agreed to 'attempt something like a line in *Theorie*, though I hope
we shall none of us be too rigid in our adherence to it in *practice*'.[5]

His solution was typical of his solidly practical approach to every sort
of difficulty but it was, almost inevitably, one which favoured Bentley
at Thomas Wedgwood's expense. The fact was that the 'Useful' partnership was already a commercial success and the production of Queen's
ware had become both profitable and, as long as suitable materials
were available and the factory was efficiently managed, comparatively
trouble-free. Its further development depended on fashionable design
and the expansion of markets, for both of which Bentley's contribution
was certain to be crucial. The 'Ornamental' partnership, on the other

---

* Vases modelled from illustrations (title-page and Plate 10) to Jacques Stella's
Livre de vases, Paris, c. 1667, etched by his niece, Françoise Bouzonnet Stella.
This book was in the Wedgwood & Bentley library by August 1770 (WMS.
55–31201).

hand, was barely out of the cradle. Wedgwood was likely to be able to sustain it with inventions and improvements but its proper presentation to the public at the most valuable levels of society was Bentley's particular task and it was scarcely possible to contemplate it without him.

Josiah sought to 'chalk out a path' between the partnerships, 'at present separate, & of which my situation renders me the connecting link, without giving offence to either' by common-sense definitions:

> . . . first Negatively. I do not think that *fineness*, or *richness*, or *price*, or *colour*, or *enameling*, or *bronzeing*, or *gilding* can be a criterion for our purpose, for though we make a Table, or desert service, ever so fine, rich or expencive, though they are every piece rich enough to adorn a Cabinet, they are, in my opinion, *usefull ware* still, & I think the same may be said of a teapot, or a Chamberpot. Suppose, for instance, that I should make pebble* desert ware, & vein, or edge it with gold. . . . This would be as rich as the Vases, but must, I apprehend, be class'd as *usefull ware* still: & on the other hand, though we make a flower-pot, Vase Candlestick† &c ever so plain, it is still in the Class of *ornamental ware* & clearly within the partnership of W & B only, & I should think I did wrong in making them at Burslem in any occasion without first asking your consent.[6]

This was a sound enough principle on which to base new definitions, but it was also, as he frankly explained, an attempt to protect the interests, and thus to maintain the loyalty, of 'Useful' Thomas:

> If degrees of richness, or elegance of form, were to constitute the difference in question, & consequently the making of it to be transfered from Burslem to Etruria upon its improvement beyond such a pitch: this would not only lay the foundation for frequent disputes, but must also have the same effect upon my usefull works, as the King of Frances Edict‡ has upon the Potteries in France to prevent their rivalling his works at Seve, for T:W might with reason in that case say, I have such, or such an improvement to introduce into the desert, or Tea-ware, but I shall then lose the Article, or if I improve such a single article any farther, it is gone! . . . there seems to me to be a more distinct criterion to distinguish betwixt *Usefull ware* & *Ornaments* . . . May not usefull ware be comprehended under this simple definition,

* Variegated decoration, principally for vases, like 'agate' and 'prophyry' in imitation of natural stones.
† A vase with a reversible lid to form a candleholder.
‡ See p. 15.

of such vessels as are *made use of at meals*. This appears to me the most simple & natural line, & though it does not take in Wash-hand basons & bottles or Ewers, Chamberpots & a few such articles, they are of little consequence, & speak plain enough for themselves: nor would this exclude any superb vessels for sideboard, or vases for deserts . . . as these articles would be rather for *shew* than *use*.

He offered this as a solution to the immediate difficulty, and it is probable that he had already obtained Thomas's agreement to it, but he affirmed his willingness to consider any objection or alternative: 'I am perfectly open to conviction & am so far from wishing to *limit* our undertaking, or to render it too trifleing for your attention that I wish to extend it by every means.'[7]

Although Josiah referred to the dispute as 'haggleing . . . about trifles', he was aware of its seriousness and of the damaging consequences of a failure to settle it. Bentley had written of the business 'certainly coming to nothing upon the present plan' and Cousin Thomas was unsettled and aggrieved by the proposed change. The letter was one of the longest Josiah ever wrote and contained a moving appeal to Bentley's friendship and for sympathy in his predicament: 'Next to my *Wife & Family*, my *Partners* are those with whom I must be at peace.'[8]

Finally, Josiah called for patience. The accounts for the Wedgwood & Bentley partnership for the twelve months to 10 August 1770 showed a profit of £2560 18s. 1d. but the bulk of this was in increased stock; the cash profit amounted to about £500.[9] 'If', Josiah wrote, 'the first year of a business pays all expences, & furnishes any proffit at all, I should not call it a bad one, but if beyond this, it likewise gives a proffit of £500, or £1000 in Cash for goods *really sold* & an increase in stock . . . of one to two thousand pounds more, surely we ought to be more than barely content. I think we have reason to rejoice.' The justice of this argument and the irony of Josiah's comment that ornament was 'a field [on] which . . . you have bestowed one years close attention . . . & I many' would not have been lost on Bentley, but he was adamant and he had his way. In his own records, written after discussions at Etruria: 'The Difficulty was easily settled: & the Etruscan Tea Pots made by ye Company [Wedgwood & Bentley] at Etruria. The Company very much wanted some such constant selling Article.' In fact he obtained for the partnership not only the 'Etruscan' painted teapots, which he had originally demanded, but the whole of the factory's production of black basaltes and the later coloured stoneware bodies – cane, rosso antico and jasper – whether apparently 'useful' or 'ornamental'.[10]

This trouble came upon Josiah while he was still recovering from another personal crisis. He feared that he was losing his sight.

On New Year's Day 1770, replying to Bentley, who had also experienced some difficulty with his eyesight, he described the symptoms as 'Atoms . . . which appear when I look at the sky' and 'little clouds . . . still before my eyes when I look at the Sky or any distant object, as usual & *sometimes* upon the paper when I am reading or writeing . . . These things do not allways appear before my eyes, & never in the dusk of the evening or by Candlelight, but I can allways find them (in the day time) by looking for them in the Air, or against a cieling . . . the little Atoms are lucid, fill the whole compass which the eye takes in, & are ever twinkling, & in motion.' He had consulted the family physician, James Bent, and also Dr John Eliot, 'the most famous in this branch of the healing Art of any Man in England', who had successfully treated the Duke of Bedford and the Duchess of Norfolk for the same malady. His prognosis was hopeful but he warned Wedgwood that there was 'always *some danger* in these cases'. He diagnosed *muscae volitantes*, interpreted by Wedgwood as 'Mice Volanti', prescribed a 'Collyrium consisting of Elder flower water, Spirit of Wine Champorated – Sugar of lead & something else which I have forgot' to be used three times a day to rinse the eyes and told Josiah to see him again in March.[11]

Josiah's friend John Whitehurst, the geologist, horologer and maker of scientific instruments, had suffered from a similar complaint and admitted that he thought he 'was going blind immediately'. He consulted Erasmus Darwin, whose diagnosis and advice were typically blunt and uncomforting: he told Whitehurst he was 'very safe – that everybody at one time of life or other had the same appearances before thier eyes, but everybody did not *look at them*'. Instructed that he would soon be well again, Whitehurst obediently recovered. Wedgwood's experience, he believed, would be no different.[12]

Josiah was less confident. For two months he was deeply depressed, writing despondently to Bentley of his 'affliction', of the 'disorder which must totally incapacitate' him. Dr Bent had prescribed a 'perpetual blister, or a caustic' to be applied behind the neck, saying 'with great earnestness & several times over he believ'd [this] to be *absolutely necessary for my safety*'. On 15 January Wedgwood wrote: I am often practising to *see* with my *fingers* . . . but shall make a wretched walker in the dark with a single leg', and a week later he was persuaded that his life as well as his sight was in danger. He told Bentley: 'I find this disorder . . . nearly as often deprives the miserable patient of one as the other.' He had heard of two deaths from this cause in the neighbourhood and was certain that there were many more which he had 'made no enquiry after'. 'If the disorder is seated near the brain which is often the case, Vertigoes, convulsions &c put a period to life & sight together.' He resolved to face his fate with 'resignation & fortitude'.[13]

Bentley, who probably wished that his friend would listen to Darwin, advised rest, but he knew Josiah too well to suppose that such counsel would be heeded. It was, Josiah replied, 'very difficult to see things going wrong without feeling *uneasy sensations* & exerting the *necessary* force be it *more* or *less*, of the *head* or *hands* to set them right again . . . to keep 150 hands of various professions, & more various tempers & dispositions, in *tolerable* order is no easy task.'[14]

His fears, which he confided so frankly to Bentley, were no less real for being, as Darwin would have told him, unfounded, and they formed the basis for attacks of reactive depression which recurred in times of stress throughout his life. This was a particularly serious and prolonged period of despair and on 10 February he was preparing for the worst: 'when you have settled matters in the best manner you can in London & Chelsea,' he wrote to Bentley, 'I could wish you to be at the manufactory awhile to learn the Art of Pott-making, whilst I am able to go thro' that branch with you, which I shall do with great pleasure & hope you will carry on to great perfection those improvements which I have been endeavouring to lay a foundation for, & shall be happy in leaving them with you. Do not think by what I have wrot that my eyes are worse, but I am sensible of my danger, & the last attack may be sudden & not give me an opportunity of communicateing many things which I would not have die with me.'[15]

There is a gap in Josiah's correspondence with Bentley between 21 February and 5 March, probably attributable to Bentley's visit to Etruria at Josiah's request, and a second gap, between about 6 March and mid-April, is accounted for by Wedgwood's extended stay in London. Bentley's reassuring company and generous hospitality, a change from the daily pressures of the two factories, and perhaps even the release from family concerns, worked the cure. After a cursory comment early in March that the condition of his eyes was 'much the same',[16] Josiah did not mention the problem again. Only in September, when the argument with Bentley was cause for acute anxiety and irritation, did Josiah return to the subject of his health, describing his life as 'a very precarious one'.[17]

The dispute with Bentley, though primarily one of definition, was closely related to a part of the business with which neither Josiah nor his partners were sufficiently familiar: the accounts. Bentley, it is clear, was accustomed to leaving such transactions to Boardman and his clerks, while Josiah was content to supervise the work of Peter Swift and the less reliable William Cox.

Deficiencies in the system began to show themselves early in 1770, when Wedgwood sent Cox to London to bring the accounts there up to date. In November 1769 he had warned Bentley of his lack of cash to pay his architect and within two months a rumour was circulating that Wedgwood was 'brok, & run away for no less a sum than Ten Thousand Pounds'. Although he assured Bentley that he was less concerned for ready money, which could always be borrowed, than for his good name, which 'when lost is scarcely redeemable', he was obliged to recognise that his debts – nearly £4000, swelled by about £100 a week draining out in wages and factory overheads – were frighteningly large. 'Where', he asked, 'must this tide of money flow from think you?' He calculated that he had packed about £12,000 worth of goods at Burslem in 1769 but remained 'nevertheless as poor as a Ch[urch] mouse'.[18]

In May he found it necessary to remind Bentley to collect from his customers: 'Pray do not let the good People escape you without paying their bills, I shall be set in the stocks if you do.' Four days later he added: 'Cash is a *weighty matter* . . . the Ultimatum of all our labours, & unless either you or I *know* that the accounting is kept right we should hardly be easy about it. . . . You know our ideas are the same respecting the effects of *good books* both upon ourselves & our customers.'[19] Wedgwood believed the problem was one of inefficient debt-collecting but it was more complex than either of the partners realised.

As so often happened, Josiah identified the true cause of his difficulties by explaining them to Bentley: 'How do you think, my dear Friend,' he wrote on 16 February 1771, 'it happens that I am so very *poor*, or at least, so very *needy* as I am at the present time, when it appears by the accounts that I clear money enough by my business to do allmost anything with.' The profits for 1770 had been more than £4000 from the Burslem factory alone and yet he was still short of cash and was likely to have to borrow to pay his debts. He had, however, discovered 'a vast increase' in stocks – more than £4000 of finished goods in London and a further £1200–1500 worth in Burslem and Liverpool. Such a huge accumulation was 'too much by one half and must be diminished some way or other'. It was particularly serious in the dim light of sales for the previous November and December: £500 in seven weeks, a total insufficient to pay the wages for the same period.[20]

This was a classic symptom of over-expansion with insufficient capital resources. In addition to the considerable costs of his London warehouse and the Chelsea Decorating Studio, Wedgwood was putting out cash for raw materials, transport and wages to satisfy a far greater demand than he had anticipated without collecting his bills fast enough to finance the increase in production. But the more dangerous problem lay deeper than that and it was more permanently rooted.

Josiah's investigations revealed that the pricing of ornamental ware was haphazard and commercially nonsensical, production runs were often too short to be economic, and the lack of a proper costing system had allowed the wasteful use of labour and materials to go unnoticed.[21] Instead of exploiting a profitable market, Wedgwood & Bentley had been exploited by it. As it declined, they were left with enormous stocks which locked up much-needed capital.

Josiah acted promptly, personally calculating detailed costings, which he called a 'price book of workmanship', showing 'every expence of Vase making as near as possible from the Crude materials, to your Counter in London upon each sort of Vase'. He examined the relationship between fixed overheads and prices and he had discussions with the foreman of the Ornamental Works with a view to increasing production runs and thus lowering manufacturing costs and prices to the public. The result was an exercise in self-taught cost accounting, one of the earliest documents of its kind in the history of manufacturing and certainly the first in the British pottery industry.[22]

Meanwhile, the burden of stocks had to be reduced and he wrote to Bentley: 'we must either find some new markets or new Warehouses or turn off some of our hands, which I should be very sorry to do as they are not easily made for our purpose'.[23] He proposed to plan production, instead of allowing it to be dictated by demand. For this to be successful he must create demand where he most needed it and this required a reversal of his previous policy of designing and making primarily for the richest in society. He could, he told Bentley, manufacture vases almost as regularly as ordinary tablewares and at about half the previous cost if he could make a dozen or so of the same design at a time instead of switching his throwers and ornamenters, painters and gilders wastefully from one shape, ornament or decoration to another, according to demand from London or elsewhere. 'The Great People', he wrote,

> have had their Vases in their Palaces long enough for them to be seen & admir'd by the *Middling Class* of People, which class we know are vastly, I had almost said infinitely, superior in numbers to the Great, & though a *great price* was I believe at first necessary to make the Vases esteemed *Ornaments* for *Palaces* that reason no longer exists. Their character is established, & the middling People would probably buy quantitys of them at a reduced price.[24]

His measures were effective. Costs were assessed with greater accuracy, production runs were lengthened and prices adjusted, new markets were exploited, especially among the 'middling class', and stocks were reduced. All, indeed, would have been well but for skulduggery at Great Newport Street.

Benjamin Mather had replaced William Cox as chief clerk and cashier at Newport Street at the end of September 1769. In August 1772 Josiah received an anonymous letter, which he passed on to Bentley, informing him that Mather was an embezzler. This report confirmed suspicions that Bentley had expressed some months earlier and was itself supported by the evidence of an employee at the factory who had worked temporarily in London. According to this witness, Mather had 'long been in a course of extravagance & dissipation' far beyond anything he could afford on his wages. He had been keeping bad company and entertaining 'young Bloods whom he calls Cousins', and his recent illness, for which 'he was so much pitied by us all', was 'the foul Disease'. Asked by Josiah why no one had reported this sooner, his informant told him that 'they durst not. The Violence and haughtiness of his [Mather's] temper over awed them, prevented them saying anything *to him*, & the high favour they thought him in with us prevented their saying anything *of him*. This last idea he would endeavour to keep up in order to prevent & intimidate his fellow servants from saying anything to his disadvantage – For nobody will impeach a Minister, nobody at Court I mean whilst he is in high favour with his sovereign.'[25]

The behaviour of both partners was embarrassingly at fault. It became plain that the cash and accounts books, which should have been constantly available in the Counting House at Newport Street for Bentley's inspection, were generally between three and five months in arrears and that the account of sales and cash received, due to Etruria for Josiah's inspection every week, had been sent only three or four times a year and was now a full five months overdue. 'These circumstances', Josiah explained tardily, 'have given me much uneasiness, & great reason to suspect that our Cashier was not fit to be trusted.' Bentley might be forgiven for wondering why Josiah had not mentioned this before, particularly since it accorded with his own suspicions, which he had reported. Nor was it clear why Josiah had not previously complained that he was, 'not able' to get from Mather the weekly reports which he had 'insisted upon'. Josiah, on the other hand, might well consider that Bentley's failure to examine the accounts in London for months at a time displayed a disquieting lack of managerial interest or performance. Further, as he questioned more of his employees, it became all too obvious that the indiscipline of the London staff was cause for serious concern.[26] This too was Bentley's responsibility.

It was, however, no time for recriminations between them. As Josiah pointed out, the solution was not as straightforward as it appeared at first sight. If Mather were to be summarily sent packing, he might collect thousands of pounds of debts from customers who were unaware of his dismissal. The first step must be to remove him from the scene so that the truth of the accusations might be discovered and the damage assessed. The second was to introduce new regulations which would prevent such dishonesty in the future. The third should be to reorganise Wedgwood's London offices and studios so that Bentley would no longer be obliged to supervise the work of employees in separate buildings several miles apart.

Mather was sent on an errand to Bath, where new showrooms had recently been opened, while stock was counted at Newport Street, and Peter Swift, who had become one of Wedgwood's most trusted servants as 'Cashier, Paymaster General and Accountant General',[27] was dispatched to London to supervise the stocktaking and to examine the accounts. The truth of the accusations against Mather was soon proved beyond reasonable doubt and fresh examples of his 'Villanie' were exposed. According to his records there had been 'scarcely a single parcel sold or sent from the Warehouse last summer'.

Although he agreed with Bentley that they could not continue to employ Mather, Josiah was still cautious about discharging him. His anxiety was not only for the damage that Mather might do to the firm by unauthorised debt-collection or by selling confidential information. He was also concerned for the man's future: 'If he is immediately turn'd adrift, with the total loss of his character, he may probably be driven to a degree of desperation beyond any effort of amendment. He should have *some hope left him* that upon a change of conduct he may be restor'd to the favor & confidence of his friends, which, if he has one ingenuous feeling left, will be a stronger motive for his reformation than any other he could possibly have, *when bereaved of that hope.*'[28] He decided to accept Mather's bond, or the best security he was able to offer, to repay or make good the missing cash.

This was extraordinarily charitable treatment of an employee who had systematically robbed his employer, and especially remarkable in view of Josiah's stern standards of moral behaviour. Stranger still was his decision after all to employ Mather, though no longer in a position which allowed him to handle cash, for a further eight years. His generosity was not rewarded. Mather's penitence was short-lived and his promises of reform only briefly fulfilled. When he finally dismissed him in 1780, Josiah described Mather as 'an abandoned worthless wretch . . . who is self devoted to destruction whither he would have brought us too'.[29]

If Josiah's leniency to Mather was influenced by a belief that Bentley's failure to provide adequate supervision was at least partly to blame, he gave no hint of it in his letters. Perhaps he recognised his own fault and was more concerned to reorganise the administration of his London showrooms than to apportion blame or dispense punishment. For the future, weekly accounts were unfailingly to be sent from London to Etruria and Josiah promised that he would take a closer interest in them than he had given to the bulky parcel of four or five months' accounts to which he had become accustomed: 'too formidable a volume . . . to attempt, besides it was something like reading an old newspaper'.[30]

There were to be other reforms to secure the buildings and their contents and to regulate the behaviour of the employees working in them. 'Stockport' John, who had fallen under Mather's malign influence, had been rescued by 'Nanny', the housekeeper, only, it was reported, to become her lover. Josiah disapproved of this situation and thought it 'an awkward one on the Lads side' since Nanny was some years John Wood's senior. He was, however, obliged to admit that the relationship had possibly saved Wood from ruin and he feared the consequences 'if it was to be suddenly broke, & against his will'. This reinforced his belief that the lack of proper supervision of the Newport Street house was 'rather unfavourable to Virtue & good order in young men'. 'What avails all our industry & care', he asked Bentley, 'if we must finally lodge all the fruits of it in the hands of unprincipled Boys & spendthrifts, who we see are debauching & ruining themselves, & perhaps a score of their acquaintance at our expence.'[31] The solution was evident: the two London establishments must be amalgamated as soon as possible so that Bentley could conveniently oversee the staff and the work of both.

In the meantime, Josiah suggested that the introduction of commission payments on sales made at Newport Street would ensure 'the interest of the sellers to take care that order was preserv'd in the House'. If commission were paid only after the receipt of payment for goods, this would provide an additional spur to the collection of cash and accurate accounting. This system might also encourage a reduction in staff, which then numbered twelve 'including Nanny'.[32]

The search for new premises began again in earnest and it was, for a time, likely that Wedgwood & Bentley would occupy part of the Adelphi, a prestigious new development planned by the brothers

Adam* between the Strand and the Thames, near Charing Cross. At the end of 1770 Josiah had told Bentley that Matthew Boulton was planning to establish showrooms in London and had spoken to Adam about rooms at the Adelphi, professing 'a good deal of pleasure' at the possibility that Boulton & Fothergill and Wedgwood & Bentley might be neighbours. Wedgwood was less enthusiastic. He discussed the merits of such an arrangement with the architect James 'Athenian' Stuart, with whom he was on friendly terms, and they concluded that the competition would be favourable to Wedgwood & Bentley, 'that those customers who were more fond of shew & glitter, than fine forms, & the appearance of antiquity would buy Soho Vases, and that all who could tell the effects of a fine outline & had any veneration for Antiquity would be with us – But these we were afraid would be a minority'. Not content with this conclusion, Wedgwood enlisted Stuart's help to imagine a third group of customers who, preferring 'shewy, rich & gawdy things', would nevertheless allow themselves to be *over ruled by their betters* and directed by their architects in matters of taste. These, too, would favour Etruria over Soho. In case this argument should be insufficiently persuasive, he added that Wedgwood & Bentley were capable, if need be, of adding *'richness and splendor'* to compete with anyone. Stuart, however, attempted to steer Wedgwood towards another house nearby in which he appears to have had a personal interest.[33]

Boulton abandoned his proposal to take rooms in the Adelphi by the autumn of 1770, when he arranged, instead, a sale of stock at Christie & Ansell's in Pall Mall. The sale of new ornamental goods by public auction was a regular method of stimulating business and acquiring valuable publicity among the fashionable audience who frequented Christie's rooms. Boulton's sale in 1770 was a success and he held others, with greater preparation, in the following two years. From a purely financial point of view, both were failures: the proceeds were disappointing, many pieces were knocked down at prices below the value that Boulton had estimated and some of the finest remained unsold. The value of the publicity, on the other hand, was incalculable. Boulton withdrew temporarily from the London market-place and concentrated his efforts on selling his ormolu ornaments abroad.[34]

Josiah is unlikely to have ignored the lessons of these sales and he continued his search for a permanent warehouse and showrooms. Sir William Hamilton had strongly urged him to reduce, or altogether to

*The two eldest, John and Robert, were primarily concerned with the architectural practice in London while James spent much of his time in Scotland and William managed the family firm set up in 1764.

banish, the 'offensive gilding' which enriched many of the Wedgwood & Bentley variegated vases and, acknowledging the value of this advice, Josiah countered Bentley's favourable estimate of the work then being offered at auction:

> I make no doubt of your Friend Mr Boultons things being very excellent, both in contrivance and execution, & wish him every encouragement his ingenuity, spirit & industry deserve, but Mr Cox* has so far *outshone* him that I am afraid he will be under some little bit of an eclipse. . . . I am not without some little pain for our Nobility & Gentry themselves, for what with the fine things in Gold, Silver & Steel from Soho, the almost miraculous magnificence of Mr Coxes Exhibition, & the Glare of the Derby & other China shews – What heads, or Eyes could stand all this dazzling profusion of riches & ornament if something was not provided for their relief. . . . I have some hopes for our black, Etruscan, & Grecian vases still . . .

He advised Bentley to hang a curtain in front of the shelves of variegated vases to '*moderate the shew*' and hide the gilding from those customers who might find it offensive while, incidentally, preventing the gilding from tarnishing.[35]

In April the Adelphi was still being considered. Josiah and Bentley had taken measurements and prepared detailed plans of the showroom and offices that could be obtained from one of the buildings and Josiah expressed his satisfaction with them. Adam was asked to submit an estimate of costs. Within a month Josiah had changed his mind: 'it can never be settled so as to answer all our wishes in *quantity* & *disposition of the parts*'. And yet, in spite of the 'great risque & a certain great expence', he was still tempted by the opportunity of being so permanently and 'nobly situated'. A firm decision was once again postponed until an accurate estimate of costs could be completed. At last, towards the end of November 1772, after nearly two years of discussion, the Adelphi plan was abandoned.[36]

By then the Adam brothers were in considerable financial difficulties. What their nephew William described as 'the underground stream of loss and expenditure'[37] gradually bore them towards bankruptcy. The financing of the scheme had depended substantially on the leasing of the underbuildings to the government, but fears of flooding put an end to that intention. After the most extreme measures – including a loan on the family estate and the sale of their collection of pictures –

*James Cox was a jeweller and maker of spectacular ornaments and automata.

had failed to raise enough money to pay their creditors, the Adams resorted to the curious, but not uncommon, contrivance of disposing of their entire assets, except for the Adelphi estate, by lottery. This expedient, which required the permission of Parliament, granted in 1773, saved them from ruin, allowed them to complete the Adelphi scheme* and even brought in enough for them to buy back part of their art collection.

Meanwhile, Bentley had been busy looking for other suitable accommodation. Wedgwood considered, and for varying reasons rejected, a number of grand buildings, previously the town houses of noblemen. These included Newcastle House,† built in 1685 on the north-west corner of Lincoln's Inn Fields, Monmouth House and Carlisle House, both in Soho Square. Monmouth House, demolished a year later, was refused because the rent of £400 a year was excessive. Carlisle House, on the east side of the square, was owned by Teresa Cornelys, an Austrian singer, who had been imprisoned earlier in the year for debt. For the past ten years the house had been used for concerts, masques and assemblies which had once been fashionable but had lately become less than respectable. The search continued. The Strand, where several houses became available, was considered by Josiah 'a Vulgar place' and too crowded for easy access.[38]

The final choice was the largest of them all – Portland House, a late seventeenth-century mansion in Greek Street. Since 1734 the Dukes of Portland, after whom the house had been renamed, had owned the freehold of Soho Fields, the area of Soho Square and those streets, including Greek Street, running to the south. Among the previous lessees of Portland House had been the third Viscount Chetwynd, father of the amiable 'Deb' Chetwynd, Wedgwood's first mediator with the Queen, and James Cullen, a cabinet-maker of some distinction. Another had been Teresa Cornelys, who had used Portland House and the house adjoining for more of her assemblies and entertainments. Earlier in the century the district of Soho had become popular with the medical profession and during the 1760s Portland House had been sub-leased to a surgeon, who had built a dissecting room at the rear. The next house to the south, No. 13, was ocupied from 1774 to 1796 by a physician who had, similarly, added a laboratory.

Bentley had first described Portland House to Josiah in November 1773. The property was considerable: a four-storey brick house finished

*The Adelphi was demolished in 1936, only the arches of the underbuildings being left intact.
†Formerly Powis House, now 66 Lincoln's Inn Fields. Its condition deteriorated until in 1930 it was skilfully rebuilt by Sir Edward Lutyens.

with pilasters at the north and south sides, each storey with seven sash windows facing the street, and a frontage of nearly 55 feet; and behind it more buildings and two spacious yards to the east and to the north opening into Manette Street. Josiah was particularly attracted to the idea of adding a gallery to the dissecting room, and negotiations were put in hand to take a twenty-one-year lease from James Cullen.[39] This was achieved in June 1774 at a rent of £300 a year and a second lease gave Wedgwood & Bentley possession of No. 11, a much smaller house, recently rebuilt, as a residence for Bentley.[40] There was no time for the alterations that were planned and the partners could not even wait for the lease to be formally signed before occupying the building. For more than twelve months they had been working on the production and decoration of the largest, the most costly and the most celebrated service ever manufactured in earthenware, and they had been ordered to show it to the Queen before it was shipped abroad.

CHAPTER TEN

Landscape with Frogs

The courts of eighteenth-century European monarchies were the centre of their countries' culture. Catherine II understood, better than most autocratic rulers, the unique importance of her court as the focus of attention and therefore as the principal means at her disposal to influence opinion both at home and abroad. She gave her active patronage to literature, the theatre, painting, sculpture and architecture and, in spite of her reputation for being tone-deaf, to music. She separated the Academy of Fine Arts from the Academy of Science, to which it had been added as a subordinate department in 1758, and commissioned from Vallin de la Mothe and the Russian architect Kokorinov one of the most beautiful of the buildings in St Petersburg to house it. She encouraged the exchange of ideas with the intellectual élite of Western Europe, inviting d'Alembert, the mathematician, philosopher and *encyclopédiste*, to supervise the education of her second son';* she cultivated the admiration of Voltaire, who called her 'Our Lady of St Petersburg' (a rather less ambiguous sobriquet than 'the Semiramis of the North') and wrote in support of the Russian invasion of Poland; and she not only invited Diderot to continue in Russia the publication of the *Encyclopédie*, when it appeared that it would not be permitted in France, but also bought his library, while allowing him the use of it for life and paying him a pension as her librarian.

As a collector and patron of the arts, Catherine was already well known in 1772, when she bought the collections formed by Pierre and Joseph-Antoine Crozat and the duc de Choiseul, but her most brilliant acquisition was the Houghton collection. 'To be sure', Horace Walpole wrote to Sir Horace Mann about the sale of his family pictures for more

---

* D'Alembert declined on the ground that he was *'trop sujet aux hémorroides'*, the malady said to have caused the death of Peter III.

than £40,000, 'I should wish they were rather sold to the Crown of England than to that of Russia, where they will be burnt in a wooden palace on the first insurrection: here they would still be Sir Robert Walpole's collection.'[1]

From the early years of her reign Catherine showed a distaste for the florid baroque buildings favoured by the Empress Elizabeth and she employed foreign architects, as well as Russians who had studied in Italy, to introduce the new classical style to St Petersburg. Foreign painters too were encouraged to work in Russia and patronage was extended to Russian artists. Before Catherine's accession the Imperial palaces had been poorly furnished and equipped and the standards of comfort and elegance to be found in the houses of the nobility were primitive in comparison with those enjoyed in Western Europe. Catherine imposed discipline and economy, often criticised as parsimony, on her court and the housekeeping of her palaces; but, by the example of discriminating acquisition and patronage, she raised the aspirations of the urban nobility and prosperous merchants until the architecture and furnishings of their houses, especially those in and around St Petersburg and Moscow, could compare with the best in Europe.

Much fine furniture was brought into Russia and imitated by local craftsmen. Catherine patronised the great *ébéniste-mécanicien* David Roentgen, who received his first commission from her in 1783, and the French silversmith Jacques-Nicholas Roettiers, who was one of the first to adopt the neoclassical style. For porcelain she turned naturally to Sèvres, where, although the style remained unreformed rococo, the finest European porcelain was made. Less predictably, she chose to buy a large quantity of ornaments from Matthew Boulton. His first shipment to Russia in 1771, a collection of ormolu vases, was sent to Lord Cathcart, who succeeded in having them shown to the Empress. She bought the lot, expressing the opinion that Boulton's ormolu vases were 'superior in every respect to the French'.[2] 'I shall be very glad', Cathcart wrote diffidently to Boulton in February 1772, 'if I have been of any use in laying a foundation for the reception of your manufacture in a country where a great deal is imported from France, inferior in quality and dearer in point of price.'[3] In October Count Orlov, one of the five brothers* who had been most active in Catherine's *coup d'état* in 1762, visited the Soho Works.

Wedgwood's successful introduction to the Russian market, also through the good offices of Lord Cathcart, had resulted in Catherine's order for the 'Husk' service. Evidently the quality and design of this

---

* The second brother, Grigory, was Catherine's lover from about 1761 to 1772.

service pleased the Empress, for in 1773 Josiah's 'Great Patroness in the North'[4] sent Alexander Baxter an even larger and more important commission for him.

In 1770, when Wedgwood & Bentley were preparing to ship the 'Husk' service to Russia, there was apparently some difficulty with Baxter, whose haughty behaviour had prompted Josiah to describe him as a 'Bashaw like Gentleman'. Bentley's firmness and tact had, however, prevented a rupture and ensured that a cordial relationship was maintained.[5] His patience was rewarded and in March 1773 Josiah asked Bentley to pass on to Baxter his 'best compliments & thanks' for 'this very supurb commission'. By any standards the size of the order was formidable – 680 pieces and a similar dessert set of 264 pieces – with a rich variety of tureens, 'glaciers',* monteiths† and decorative fruit baskets. The size and the complexity of the service was not, however, the most challenging problem. Each piece was to be decorated with one or more paintings of English landscapes and crested with a green frog emblem to represent the site known as Kekerekeksinen or La Grenouillière (the frog marsh), where the Chesmenski Palace was built.

Conscious of the important part that the Chelsea Decorating Studio would play in the production of this service and of the mistake he had made with the 'Husk' service, Josiah lost no time in offering Bentley a share. A special shape, a variant on the 'Royal' shape produced for King George III and thereafter known as 'Catherine', was created for the service, and two decorative borders were designed – oak-leaf and acorn for the dinner service and ivy for the dessert – both broken to accommodate the frog emblem. Josiah guessed that production would take between two and three years and would cost £1000–£1500. Nothing of the kind had ever before been attempted by any potter.

His estimate of costs proved to be low. No one in England, or even on the Continent, had at that time any experience of producing so large a quantity of topographical painting on pottery or porcelain, and neither Wedgwood nor Bentley had any accurate notion of the costs involved in acquiring suitable landscape drawings, or where they might be obtained. As Josiah wrote: 'Why all the Gardens in England will scarcely furnish subjects sufficient for this sett, *every piece having a different subject.*'[6] In fact, this was an understatement of the problem: the serving

---

* 'Glacier' or, as often, 'glaucier', appears to have been Josiah's own name for a four-piece ice-cream pail.
†A deep oval bowl with scalloped rim used to cool the bowls of wine glasses suspended from the rim by their feet, their bowls resting in chilled water. The name is derived from a Scotsman who, during the reign of Charles II, wore a cloak with a scalloped hem.

pieces – the tureens, covered dishes, 'glaciers', monteiths and sauce-boats – all required more than one landscape view and some as many as four. In the event, 1244 different views* were painted on 952 pieces.

Baxter was disquietingly vague about the price that the Empress would be prepared to pay and Josiah was correspondingly anxious. His fears were increased when the Consul, after receiving a first estimate, at once began to suggest economies. Josiah was outraged by any suggestion that he should produce less than his best for the Empress: 'The Consul should not talk of *doing them* [the landscapes] *as much lower as we can* – If his Mistress heard him she would rap his knuckles.'[7]

There was a further, and greater, anxiety: production of the entire service represented an investment of no more than £51 8s. 4d. in plain Queen's ware,[8] but the costs to be incurred in acquiring suitable engravings or original drawings, a large number of which might have to be commissioned especially for the service, and in painters' wages, would be formidable. The partnership also had to consider the loss of ordinary business and the disruption to everyday production caused by occupying so many of the most skilled painters in decorating the service when they might otherwise have been more profitably employed on the decoration of vases.[9] All costs for materials, wages and production had to be laid out in cash long before payment could be requested and there was always the appalling possibility that, for some good reason or poor excuse, either settlement would be delayed or liability repudiated.

Josiah wrote to Bentley at the end of March:

I think we should have some assurance that no revolution in the North, should affect the Validity of the Consuls order to us. To paint a number of pictures which can only suit one particular situation, to the amount of one or two thousand pounds without any assurance of this being accepted farther than a verbal order which may be countermanded at pleasure, is too great a risque. And as these paintings will inhance the value of these pieces so monstrously beyond the prices of *Earthen Ware* Dishes & plates ought to bear, this alone if there is not a thorough understanding of this circumstance with the Consul before the execution, may furnish a plausible excuse for rejecting the order when completed.[10]

Less obvious but equally frightening possibilities occurred to Josiah, any one of which might be sufficient to invalidate the commission:

* Although all the views appeared to be different, it was sometimes found possible to take more than one view from a single engraving.

Other causes, *many* other causes may have the same effect – The Death
of the Empress, a revolution in her Government or *ideas*, A War, or
bad understanding with our Government – The Death – or change of
the present Consul, or even our offending him (a very possible chance
you know) may cause a countermand of this order unless it be given
in some way to make it binding.

He proposed to discuss the matter with his lawyer, John Sparrow, a
partner in Sparrow & Caldwell, attorneys of Newcastle-under-Lyme,
and Clerk to the Proprietors of the Trent and Mersey Canal.[11]

His fears were not unfounded. For the past four years Russia had
been at war with Turkey, a war which had already involved French
troops, the partition of Poland and the crushing of an insurrection in
Greece, and which was constantly in danger of exploding into a wider
European arena. In 1773 Catherine's position was challenged at home.
At first dismissed by the Empress and her advisers as a tiresome peasant
disturbance of no consequence, the rebellion led by Emelyan Pugachev
threatened to spread through the country and develop into revolution.

Pugachev became a symbol of peasant discontent, of a revolt of the
poor against the rich, and gained not only the active support of disaf-
fected regular troops but the sympathy of many provincial clergy. As
the government failed in its attempts to put down the revolt, the movement spread towards the north and west and Pugachev was joined by
workers from the salt and copper mines. In July 1774 the rebel army,
about 20,000 strong, stormed Kazan, destroying the greater part of the
city. It was Pugachev's last important success. Within days his army
had been routed. The treaty of Kuchuk Kainardzhi, signed on 14 July,
ending the war with Turkey, only confirmed the certainty of his final
defeat. He was betrayed by two of his own followers and handed over
to government troops in October. Sentenced to be quartered alive, he
was, on the secret instructions of the Empress, first beheaded.

News of Russia's long and costly war with Turkey and the dangerous Pugachev rebellion did nothing to lessen Wedgwood's apprehensions concerning the order for the 'Frog' service. He was determined not
to embark on such an extravagant investment without some satisfactory
guarantee. That this was forthcoming is suggested by the absence of
any further mention of this particular anxiety in his letters. The context
of his acknowledgement in July of the 'good account from St Petersburg'
makes it clear that the problems of price and quality, as well as that of
a guarantee, had by then been agreeably settled. 'The Empress', Josiah
wrote with satisfaction, 'has again prov'd her self to be what we had
before all the reason in the world to believe she was – A Woman of

sense – fine taste, & spirit.'[12] He was having some original drawings, 'real views' as he called them, prepared for Bentley's painters to copy.

The price agreed and the investment secured as far as any contract with the Empress could be, the greatest remaining difficulties were the number of landscapes and the quality of painting required. Painters of sufficient competence could be found for the frog emblems and borders, but the painting of more than 1200 fine landscapes could not be entrusted to amateurs. Nor was it obvious where so many attractive views were to be found at short notice and at affordable prices. On reflection, Josiah and Bentley agreed that only a small proportion could be commissioned: the rest must be copied from existing prints or drawings and it was evident that the majority would be copied from published engravings. Many were already available in the form of books or portfolios. Some were known to be in preparation and might be borrowed before publication. Such sources certainly included George Bickham's *Beauties of Stowe*, Sir William Chambers's *Views of the Gardens and Buildings at Kew in Surry*, Thomas Pennant's *Journeys to the Hebrides* and Buck's *Antiquities*.[13]

It was equally plain that, while even the most skilled of painters could not be expected to reproduce landscapes in accurate colour from monochrome originals, the reverse was not so. It followed that the views applied to the Queen's ware blanks must be in monochrome. This would have the additional advantage of reducing painters' time and thus helping to keep costs under control, but it might have the disadvantage of producing the appearance of printed landscapes, like the Sadler & Green black-printed services already seen in Russia. To avoid this invidious comparison, the partners settled on a colour which Bentley described as 'a delicate black' and others have called mulberry, grey, purple or 'off-black which contains much dark purple-brown'. The only additional colour was the pale green enamel used for the frog emblems, which appear on all pieces of the service.[14]

Bentley made the rounds of artists, publishers, booksellers, printers and engravers in London, borrowing and, where necessary, buying from George Barrett senior, John Boydell (who probably also supplied views by the French artist J.-B. Châtelain), Thomas Major and others. John Pye, already known to Wedgwood through his engravings for Sadler & Green, supplied prints, a volume of views and 'sundry drawings'.[15] Meanwhile, Josiah canvassed his patrons and friends for views of their country seats. Lord Stamford lent sketches of Enville, his Staffordshire estate, 'taken by an Eminent hand'. 'These views', Josiah wrote in delight, 'are exactly what we want. The inside of Pleasure Grounds taken with great taste and made perfectly picturesque.'

Thomas Anson, for whom Wedgwood had made a colossal black basaltes bowl three years earlier, lent him views of his Shugborough estate, probably the set of watercolours by Moses Griffiths which are still in the house.[16] A large number of prints and drawings appears to have been acquired in this manner, but these two last owners proved to be particularly accommodating and useful: eighteen views of Enville and fifteen of Shugborough appear on various parts of the service.

In comparison with the quantities of engravings, original sketches painted by artists employed specially for the purpose were few. Only two such artists are recorded: the first, Edward Stringer, was a distant kinsman of Josiah's, and a member of a Knutsford family of painters:[17] the work of the second, a nephew of William Henshall, Brindley's assistant, has not been identified and may not have been used. 'Young Stringer', as Josiah usually referred to him, was first introduced to Bentley in April 1770, when Josiah suggested that he might be put to painting a few vases 'to pay his expenses in Town'.[18] Evidently he showed signs of some talent for he was one of the first to be consulted about the 'Frog' service three years later and was probably responsible for convincing the partners that, without almost unlimited financial resources, very little could be done by the direct employment of free-lance artists. Josiah nevertheless asked Bentley to obtain a camera obscura and suggested that some views of London might be taken with it.[19]

Josiah accompanied Stringer on several of his sketching expeditions to Trentham, Keele, Swynnerton and Enville, and on Christmas Day 1773 reported that Stringer would shortly complete about fifty sketches for the 'Frog' service. The view of Josiah's own house, Etruria Hall, used for a serving dish, is almost certainly his work.[20]

All the painted views were to be identified by name and the selection was made with the intention of giving what Bentley described as 'a true and picturesque idea of the beauties of the country, both natural and artificial'.[21] The choice was limited by the cost of commissioning original work and by the subjects already available either in published volumes of engravings, or from existing paintings or drawings. A remarkably wide variety of subjects was nevertheless accumulated, ranging from the Queen's House, St James's Palace and Somerset House in London; Windsor Great Park (fifteen views) and Kew, Chatsworth, Blenheim, Shugborough and Tintern Abbey; through castles and cathedrals, to anonymous sketches of the Thames, the Lake District (then little appreciated) and such scenes of industrial progress as the Plymouth dockyard, a colliery and pump near Bristol and papermills at Rickmansworth.

Truth and picturesque appeal were not the only criteria applied to the choice of views. Wedgwood & Bentley also had to consider the often tender susceptibilities of their patrons. By November 1773 the news of their great undertaking had spread through much of Britain, and Josiah warned Bentley that the gentry of Staffordshire – and, it must be assumed, from elsewhere in the country – were planning to visit London for the purpose of seeing the 'Frog' service before it was sent to Russia. The dilemma was awkward. On the one hand, as Josiah explained, 'it would bring an immense number of people of Fashion into our Rooms – would fully complete our notoriety to the whole Island, & help us greatly, no doubt, in the sale of our goods, both useful & ornamental'. It would demonstrate the superiority of Wedgwood & Bentley's products and patronage over those of any other manufacturer. They would be able publicly to exhibit the compliments paid to their patrons by choosing to illustrate their castles, country seats and parks on the service 'and thereby rivet them more firmly to our interests'. But there was danger in this: 'Suppose a Gentleman thinks himself neglected, either by the omission of his seat, when his Neighbours is taken, or by [our] putting it upon a small piece, or not flattering it sufficiently. He then becomes our enemy.' It was not easy to see how it was possible to avoid giving offence in this manner; '*shew* or not *shew*, for if a Gentleman asks if we have taken his seat, we must tell him, & if he further asks to see it, I do not see how we can deny him'.[22]

The simple solution, to send the service abroad without showing it in London, was never a realistic option unless Catherine refused permission for an exhibition. When she gave her consent and this was reinforced by a command from Queen Charlotte, the partners could do no more than consult their lists of patrons and make prudent amendments to their choice of painted views.

By the end of February 1774, ten months after the order had been received in London, the work on modelling and manufacturing was almost complete and Bentley had made satisfactory progress in decorating the first pieces. The Chelsea decorating Studio was in a far better condition to carry out such a large commission than it had been three years earlier when the 'Husk' service for Catherine and a similar service for King George had been decorated. There were now eight experienced enamellers working under the supervision of David Rhodes, but Josiah was doubtful of their ability to produce painting of the quality required: 'Dare you,' he asked Bentley, 'undertake to paint the most embellish'd views, the most beautiful Landskips, with Gothique Ruins, Grecian Temples & the most Elegant Buildings with hands who never attempted anything beyond Huts & Windmills . . . And this too for the first Empress in the World?'[23]

Work was nevertheless begun with Catherine Willcox and James Bakewell painting landscapes and less skilled hands applying the borders. They were soon joined by others and the names of two more women, Miss Glisson and Miss Pars, appear on the worksheets as painters of landscapes. At least twenty-four painters were employed on the service, no fewer than seven of whom were women, an unusually high proportion of female labour in a department traditionally dominated by men. Their wages ranged from 31s. 6d. to 10s. a week, Mrs Willcox being the highest paid of the women with a weekly wage of 18s.[24]

Josiah spent part of May and much of June in London, helping Bentley to supervise the decoration and installation of fittings and furniture at the new showroom in Greek Street and seeing for himself the progress that had been made in Chelsea. Towards the end of May he sent a flurried note from Greek Street to Bentley in Chelsea: Lady Holderness had told him that the Queen was impatient to see the Russian service and the new showrooms. Although the service was not yet complete, sufficient of it was finished to make a fine show and it was therefore decided to advance the date of the exhibition. Advertising was put in hand and the showrooms were opened to the public on 1 June.[25]

News of the 'Frog' service attracted a great throng of fashionable society to Portland House, but Wedgwood & Bentley had taken the precaution of allowing admission by ticket only so that the rooms were never dangerously or even uncomfortably overcrowded. One of the visitors was the indefatigable diarist and correspondent Mrs Mary Delaney, who wrote a breathlessly enthusiastic and inaccurate account:

> I am just returned from viewing the Wedgwood-ware that is to be sent to the Empress of Russia. It consists I believe of as many pieces as there are days in the year, if not hours. They are displayed at a house in Greek Street, Soho, called 'Portland House'; there are three rooms below and two above filled with it, laid out on tables, everything that can be wanted to serve a dinner; the ground the common ware pale brimstone, the drawings in purple, the borders a wreath of leaves, the middle of each piece a particular view of all the remarkable places in the King's Dominions neatly executed. I suppose it will to come to a princely price; it is well for the manufacturer, which I am glad of, as his ingenuity and industry deserve encouragement.[26]

The Queen visited the showrooms in mid-July, accompanied by her brother, Prince Ernst of Mecklenburg, both, according to Bentley who sent a long description of the royal visit to Wedgwood in Staffordshire, 'expressing their approbation in pretty strong terms'.[27]

The price was indeed princely, as Mrs Delaney suggested: 16,406 roubles and 43 kopeks, or approximately £2700; but the total costs of production to both 'useful' and 'ornamental' partnerships, including Baxter's commission at 10 per cent, came to about £2290.[28] The profit was small and Josiah was relieved when he was able to put 'this tedious business'[29] behind him and return to more conventional manufacturing and to his experiments. Although enormous for an earthenware service, the price was scarcely to be compared with the 300,000 *livres* charged for Catherine's service of Sèvres porcelain in 1775 or the sum of nearly 1 million *livres* which was the cost of Madame de Pompadour's garden of porcelain flowers. But Wedgwood & Bentley were paid in full, whereas Sèvres never received more than a small payment on account, and the publicity for Wedgwood's Queen's ware and for the newly opened Greek Street showrooms was beyond price.

Sadly, Jane Cathcart, who had done so much to introduce and promote Wedgwood's Queen's ware and ornamental wares in Russia, never saw the 'Frog' service. She had died suddenly in St Petersburg in 1771 and, shortly afterwards, her husband gave up his post as Ambassador to return to England. Without the help of the Cathcarts it is doubtful if either Wedgwood or Boulton could have built up such a valuable trade with Russia, and, although useful business was later obtained through other British diplomats, only Sir William Hamilton ever approached the Cathcarts in intelligent activity on Wedgwood's behalf.

The subsequent history of the 'Frog', or 'Catherine', service is a patchwork of admiration and neglect. It was used intermittently by Catherine when she was in residence at the Chesmenski Palace and she made a special point of showing it to Sir James Harris, the British Ambassador, in 1779,[30] but after her death the palace was allowed to deteriorate and the service disappeared. It was not seen again until the early years of the twentieth century, when, through the persistence and persuasion of Dr G. C. Williamson, Tsar Nicholas was prevailed upon to order a thorough search for it. Remarkably, the greater part of the service was recovered intact and permission was granted for much of it to be exhibited in London in 1909. It is now displayed in the Hermitage, St Petersburg.

With the production of the 'Frog' service Josiah reached the peak of his achievement in Queen's ware. The colour of Queen's ware was refined from cream to ivory, a change often deplored as retrograde, and the progressively more mechanical methods of manufacture introduced during the following 200 years made possible a greater uniformity, but nothing in later years so satisfactorily combined quality and craftsmanship in such disciplined profusion. It was greatly admired in the eighteenth century and is justly the most celebrated earthenware service in existence. Wedgwood's became the creamware that all European potters tried to emulate and the earthenware tablewares of France, Germany, Italy, the Low Countries, Scandinavia and Russia provide ample evidence of his influence.

CHAPTER ELEVEN

Management and Security

By April 1772 the building of the Etruria factory was sufficiently advanced for Josiah to tell Bentley that he was beginning the move of the 'Useful' Works from Burslem. The 'Red Workhouses', rented from William Adams, were vacated first, followed by the transfer of the main tableware production from the Brick House.[1] By the end of the year Josiah had the manufacturing processes of both partnerships under his hand at Etruria. This enabled him to keep a close watch on the production of the 'Frog' service between 1773 and 1774 and it had also the advantage of placing his cousin Thomas where he was able to manage the whole factory in Josiah's absence. Josiah was impatient to get on with his experiments, work which had been necessarily interrupted by the building of the new factory, the establishment of the new partnership with Bentley and the creation of suitable ornamental wares for it, and the production of the 'Frog' service. From the summer of 1774 he was free to devote more time to invention. Much, however, depended upon the efficient working of the factory and a reliable, trained and properly controlled labour force.

Wedgwood's emphasis on training was unusual. In the Potteries, as elsewhere in Britain's developing industries, there were the customary apprenticeship agreements, but these had been neglected for many years and workers in the Staffordshire potbanks were generally trained on the job, often by older members of their own families. Not only were Wedgwood's standards of production higher than those of other manufacturers, he also insisted on more disciplined behaviour. And, in addition to the improvements in techniques introduced at Burslem and Etruria, of which the engine-turning lathe was the most striking example, he designed methods of working that were new, though not always welcomed.

Early in his career he had been, as he told his brother in 1765, 'teazed of my life with dilatory, drunken, Idle, worthless workmen which prevents my proceeding',[2] and he was determined that no such obstacles should stand in his way in the future. He did not, as other manufacturers of the period were known to do, treat his workpeople as slaves.* On the contrary, he planned and built an estate of houses – 'a Town for the men to live in'[3] – on the Etruria estate to improve their domestic conditions, and his attitude towards them was usually benevolent and paternal. He was, in fact, a model employer; but in return he expected loyalty and demanded regular conduct and the highest quality of craftsmanship.

The key to pride in the old style of craftsmanship was the knowledge that the craftsman was responsible for an object of his own making. The owners of small potbanks had been craftsmen potters, often doing every job from mixing the clay to decorating and firing. Josiah himself was by training just such a potter, but he understood better than any of his contemporaries the extent to which the making of pottery, and therefore the size of its potential market, had changed in his lifetime. The mixing of the necessary diversity of clays and glazes had become tasks that required expertise and experience. New techniques, such as slip-casting, engine-turning and transfer-printing, demanded specialisation. Josiah's reading among the works of d'Entrecolles and du Halde had informed him about the principles of division of labour. The industrial assembly line was the result, and the Etruria factory was the first pottery in Europe to be designed specifically for mass production on these principles. It was the first monumental acknowledgement that pottery in England had developed into an industry.

From the start Wedgwood had planned that the 'ornamental' and 'useful' factories, though housed for convenience in the same set of buildings and making use of centralised administration for such services as accounts and transport, should be complete, discrete and independent units for production. Each would employ its own hands, receive its own raw materials and manufacture its own goods. This system automatically separated different materials, workshops and ovens, and helped to keep apart the costs and profits of the two partnerships. 'The scheme of keeping each workshop separate, which I have much set my heart on', as Josiah described it,[4] was further extended to the internal organisation of the two factories and finally to the Greek Street show-

---

*The economist Josiah Tucker (1712–99) stated that the relationship between employer and worker often 'approached much nearer to that of a planter and slaves in our American colonies than might be expected of such a country as England'.

rooms. At Etruria each workshop was designed as a distinct unit, arranged with the others in sequence to avoid all but the minimum of inessential movement of hands or goods between departments. Thus materials were unloaded at the gates or from canal barges and progressed through the various workshops and kilns until they arrived back at the canal as finished goods for examination, counting, packing and loading.

The simplicity of this flowing line of production reduced errors in all stages of manufacture and accounting, and the division of workshops facilitated training and management. Local supervision was delegated to foremen who were responsible for the production of their workshops and reported direct to Josiah or Thomas.

It was occasionally necessary to make temporary transfers or loans of specialists, such as turners, from one partnership to the other,[5] and the vagaries of fashion sometimes reduced or extinguished the need for certain specialist skills,[6] but in principle it was acknowledged that every workman was trained for, and expected to remain at, the task in which he had acquired particular skill. Work requiring higher degrees of skill was separated from the less skilled and was rewarded with higher wages: 'the same hands cannot make *fine, & coarse – expensive & cheap* articles'.[7] Such skills, as well as the economics of manufacturing, were assisted by long production runs of the same article for, as Josiah reminded Bentley early in their partnership, 'there is no such thing as making now & then a few of any article to have them tolerable'.[8] By 1790, when Wedgwood's workforce numbered 278, only five were described as 'Odd men': all others – men, women and children – had specified tasks to perform.[9] Josiah intended to achieve, as nearly as possible, a regular, standardised perfection never previously seen in pottery; in short, 'to make such *machines* of the *Men* as cannot err'.[10] By this means, he aimed to achieve what potters through the centuries have attempted with rather less success: '*constant employment*'.[11]

These innovations were not invariably popular with the work-force. Specialisation was all very well if it resulted in increased wages, but this was not always so; and men trained in a particular skill, with no experience of other work, did not find it easy to change when, by reason of falling demand, change became necessary. The painters, on the other hand, made trouble because they understood, for the first time, the value put upon their work. The fashion for Wedgwood & Bentley's painted black basaltes vases and the special needs of the 'Husk' and 'Frog' services emphasised the rarity of skilled painters, who took advantage of it. Except for the instruction he had given to other painters, the influence of William Craft had not been beneficial.

James Bakewell found 'his good fortune too much for him' and Josiah considered him overpaid; Ralph Willcox was known to be as free with drink as he was with his tongue.[12]

Others, whose abilities were less, found the training too tedious and preferred easier work. This was especially the case when the new factory was first opened and men were transferred from the 'Useful' Works at Burslem, where they had been making familiar tableware objects, to Etruria, where they were required to learn new skills to make unfamiliar ornaments. 'We have now got thirty hands here', Josiah wrote in November 1769,

> but I have much ado to keep the new ones quiet – Some will not work in Black [basaltes]. Others say they shall never learn this new business, & want to be released to make Terrines & sa[uce] boats again. I do not know what I shall do with them, we have too many *fresh* hands to take in at once, though we have business enough for them, if they knew how, or would have patience to learn to do it, but they do not seem to relish the idea of a second apprenticeship.[13]

Such difficulties persisted for several years. In February 1773, Josiah reported 'some Fracas with our work men of late which have vexed me a little' and added: 'We have had a most uneasy time for many months past with our people. They seem to have got a notion that as they are come to a new place with me they are to do what they please.'[14]

Further problems arose when new techniques were introduced. In 1777 Josiah had more trouble with his painters, who feared that their jobs might be endangered by the introduction of print-and-enamel decorating techniques.* Guy Green experienced similar difficulties in Liverpool, when he tried to produce a print-and-enamel shell pattern for Wedgwood, and wrote that 'his Enamel painters were very jealous of a junction between printing & painting & asked an exorbitant price for colouring the groups of shells'.[15]

Workers had no understanding of the expanded markets for the goods they made and objected to the introduction of any new methods that increased output, believing that their hours of work would be threatened by them. In spite of all Josiah's attempts to persuade his painters to the contrary, they persisted in believing that their jobs were at risk and chose a period, twelve years later, when he was absent from the factory, to stage a strike. Wedgwood's twenty-year-old younger son, Josiah II, had been left in charge of Etruria and performed well.

---

*Transfer-printed outlines, the colours being filled in by hand.

He wrote to his father to inform him that the cause, so far as he could tell, was 'some disgust at printing' but settled the dispute before he received his father's reply and advice:

> I . . . said to the painters just what you now direct me to do, that printing would be their best friend & that as it was not a thing started up after you was gone, they ought to have objected to it whilst you was here or else stay untill you came back. . . . I desired them to state why they had an objection to printing, but this they could not or would not do; having asked from nothing but a foolish prejudice & gone into a passion without knowing why.

The young Josiah pointed to the warehouse filled with enamelled goods that his father had ordered for stock rather than leave the painters short of work and showed them how foolish it was to suppose that he would introduce a technique that would deprive them of their living. It was in his interest, as it was in theirs, that 'cheaper, more expeditious & better ways of doing the patterns should be made use of'. With justifiable pride, he added, 'I am glad I happened to do what was right & that it had the desired effect, for they have been very constantly at work ever since.'[16]

In fact their work continued for many years to be principally hand-painting. Print-and-enamel patterns were both easier and cheaper to produce but they were considered by many, including Bentley, to be inferior to handpainting, and the technique was not suited to all types of decoration. Josiah wrote, 'I make no doubt but Painting, & Printing may exist together, I hope we shall do both in quantities, both in Table & Tea ware. Many patterns cannot be printed, & those will employ the pencils.'[17] Surprisingly little remains of the early application of a decorating technique that was eventually to destroy the commercial use of free handpainting on English pottery and porcelain.

Painters were not the only ones to cause trouble. Other hands were incompetent, unpunctual, wasteful, avaricious or alcoholic. Josiah described one senior hand as doing 'pretty well when at work, & I am here every day, but he often leaves the works, & drinks two or three days together, & has no taste to direct, at anytime'. Another had 'been drinking for three days' and 'three Liverpool hands . . . have drunk half their time here'. In July 1772 all the men in the Ornamental Works met Josiah at the gates to demand higher wages. They refused to take orders from their foreman Daniel Greatbatch, and insisted on negotiating with the 'Master'. Josiah gave Bentley a full account of the dispute, intended no doubt to give his partner some useful hints about the management of his own workers, particularly the temperamental painters, in Chelsea:

> I then talk'd to them altogether about a quarter of an hour, & after produceing several instances of their extravagant charges I told them we would *make a new sett of hands* which they must be sensible was in my power to do rather than submit to give such prices as must in the end ruin the Manufacture . . . & they might either walk into the work shops, or go home again. . . . One of them a young fellow seem'd to take the lead for the rest, talk'd very pertly, and ask'd why I would not turn him away if I did not like his work. I told him I did not set so light by any servant I employ'd who was willing to do his duty . . . but as I was now convinc'd that he would rather leave his place than mend his work, he was perfectly at liberty to leave our place. This stopp'd his mouth & seem'd to have a good effect upon the rest for they all went quickly to their work.

Three months later Josiah and Thomas agreed to sack the ringleader of a similar revolt at the 'Useful' Works and Josiah was obliged to 'sweep the House of every servant we have in it', including his head farmer on the estate, for 'robing us of everything they could carry off'.[18]

Satisfactory supervision was a continuing problem. There was no doubt of his own authority: 'my name has been made such a Scarecrow to them, that the poor fellows are frighten'd out of their wits,' he told Bentley, referring especially to the London staff, 'upon our first meeting they look as if they saw the D[evi]l'.[19] The traditional story that 'Owd Woodenleg', as his workers called him, stumped through his workshops smashing with his stick anything that failed to meet his standards and telling the workmen, 'This will not do for Josiah Wedgwood' is probably true, though it is less remarkable than it has been made to seem. It was customary for potters to smash ware that was so substandard as to be unsaleable and there is ample evidence that Josiah disposed of original models, part-finished and finished ware in this manner; but there is also ample evidence to prove that he sold great quantities of substandard ware – 'seconds' and even 'thirds' – much of it for export to countries where, it was presumed, customers would be less particular.[20]

While Josiah was at the factory, discipline and therefore standards of production were maintained; but when he was away, the proper supervision of both factories was too large a task for 'Useful' Thomas and it was all less certain. To assist his foreman and to leave no doubt in the minds of his employees about what was required of them, Josiah drew up sets of rules and instructions to regulate their behaviour in the factory. These covered the duties of most of the workers and they are typical of the attention to detail that marked all Josiah's work. The job of the porter at the factory gate, who was to work with the occasional assistance of a 'Writing clerk', employed in the lodge to copy orders, became one of particular importance to the orderly functioning of the factory, and his daily routine was defined to give him responsibility and authority. He rang the bell, retained from the old Bell Works, at a quarter to six and chimed it for ten minutes from six o'clock to summon the workmen. Those who did not come to work in that time were admonished, and anyone arriving after six-fifteen was locked out until half-past eight, when the bell was rung again for breakfast. A similar system was followed for the dinner break at one o'clock and, for those working overtime, when they returned from the evening supper break at six-thirty, latecomers being admonished and anyone arriving more than fifteen minutes late finding the door locked against him until the next break. During the intervals, the porter made the rounds of the factory, checking his daily record of workers present and absent.[21]

As an alternative to this method, Josiah devised an elementary form of clocking-in, using name-cards or tickets for each worker, which were deposited at the lodge on arrival. The porter was also responsible for weighing and checking all materials delivered to the factory. The primary duty of the 'Writing clerk', who assisted the porter, was to look after the factory showrooms, known as the 'pattern room', waiting on visitors, supervising display and keeping records of stocks and sales.[22]

The whole system was reinforced by rewards and fines. The 'Clerk of the Manufactory', who was instructed 'to be first at the works in the morning & settle the people to their business as they come in', was directed to encourage those who arrived regularly in good time for work, 'distinguishing them by repeated marks of approbation from the less orderly part of the work people by *presents or other marks suitable to their age*'. On the other hand, those who were late were made to understand that their lateness had been noticed and were fined if they failed to reform.[23] There were also fines for evading the system by climbing over the factory walls or gates or forcing a way through the lodge after the gates were shut.[24]

Similar instructions and rules regulated the behaviour of everyone in the workshops and there were, in addition, standard fines of 2s. or 2s.6d for particular offences. Carrying 'Ale or Licquor' into the factory during working hours, 'writing obseen or other writing' on interior or external walls, or 'playing at fives' against any wall containing a window, all attracted fines; but striking an 'overlooker' provoked instant dismissal.[25]

Much of this was not new. Ambrose Crowley, iron-founder and in his time the largest ironmonger in Europe, Richard Arkwright at Cromford and other large-scale industrialists imposed fines and sanctions for misdemeanours, and especially for irregular attendance at work.[26] Arkwright drew up and successfully imposed a code of factory discipline. At Soho, Boulton was said to have trained his workers to such a pitch of regularity that any break or change in the rhythm of factory noise was enough to signal an accident or unauthorised stoppage. The use of machines and the division of labour made the sequence of manufacture dependent on the smooth functioning of every unit in the factory. Control and training of the work-force became the keys to mass production.

One of the crucial elements in the production of pottery and porcelain of high quality is cleanliness. The 'Clerk of weight & measures' at Etruria, whose duty it was to discourage waste and heavy potting by weighing clay before it was used, was ordered to 'lay it up with as much cleanness as if it was intended for food'. His further duties included frequent and irregular inspections of the slip and clay houses and the passageways to them to ensure that they were kept clean. In summer, they were to be watered to keep the dust down. In the workshops, every bench was to be scrubbed before use.[27]

The instructions were especially strict for the dipping house, where there was a serious danger of poisoning from contact with lead glazes. The floor was always to be sponged, not brushed; no food was to be allowed in the room; the dippers were to be supplied with smock-like garments to be worn over their work clothes and to be discarded whenever they left the room; and a pail of water, soap, brush and a towel were to be always at hand so that the dippers might scrub their hands and nails before leaving, a precaution that was particularly necessary at meal-times.

The Clerk of the Manufactory had widespread authority over materials, equipment and quality control, being responsible for checking everything from the correct storage of clay to the condition of lawns* and the proper use of tools and machinery. Like other supervisors, he was reminded 'no more [to] forget to show marks of his approbation than to reprimand those more slovenly and careless'.[28]

Josiah was always as keen to praise and reward as to reprimand or fine and he showed compassion and forgiveness to employees whose

*Fine-meshed wire or fibre used to sieve raw materials.

faults were not malicious or incessant. In return, he expected hard work, obedience, reliability, a satisfactory response to training, and loyalty. Nothing less would make his factory work and keep it working.

The loyalty of his workers was often tested. Not only were they sometimes privy to secrets or confidential information of considerable value to competitors, but they might be enticed away by offers of higher wages, better conditions or greater independence. In the first confident enthusiasm of his new partnership, Josiah had told Bentley that the copying of his work held few anxieties for him. He could wish to have 'all the Artists in Europe working after our models' and to be 'released from these degrading slavish chains, these mean selfish fears of other people copying my works'; but in the same letter he offered his partner the alternative policy of putting *'money geting'* before fame, proceeding with *'prudent* caution' and taking care not to show too much of their new work at once.[29] Bentley chose a compromise[30] and, as the years passed and his inventions were more and more widely imitated or directly copied, Josiah became more and more secretive. He was aware that the rich spring of invention was not inexhaustible. He was further aware of the value of the training that his workers had received at Etruria and he was extremely reluctant to see it used elsewhere.

The greatest danger came from abroad. The General Chamber of Manufacturers,* though 'sensible of the inestimable value of civil liberty, and that no restriction would be put upon it without an obvious and sufficient cause, such as the welfare of the state',[31] even advocated legislation to prevent the emigration of skilled workers.

Josiah took his own course, issuing in 1783 *An Address to the Workmen in the Pottery on the Subject of Entering into the Service of Foreign Manufacturers.* It contained a stirring appeal to patriotic loyalty, warnings against the easy acceptance of exaggerated promises of fortune and improved conditions, and a number of deliberately shocking stories concerning the fate of those who had been seduced to defect:

> Would it have no weight with you to think that you were ruining a trade which has taken the efforts of some thousands of people for more than an age to bring to the perfection it has now attained – a perfection nowhere else to be found – an object exciting at once the envy and emulation of all Europe? But they will ever be harmless to us whilst we are true to ourselves. . . . The enemy must first gain over some traitors and renegadoes among ourselves, before they can obtain any decisive advantage.[32]

*See Chapter 19.

The 'renegadoes' whose cautionary histories Josiah chose to relate were local men well known to many of his own workers. Bartlem, who had emigrated to South Carolina to set up his own factory, had spent more than three perilous and debilitating months at sea before he set foot in America, only to find that his men sickened and died faster than he was able to replace them. Young Allen of Great Fenton had been cast away. William Ellis of Hanley, the only one to return to England, had personally told Josiah that *the wages promised were good enough, a guinea a week with their board,* but that *they never received half of it*.[33] Some had been shipwrecked or drowned. Others had died, succumbing to the climate and disease or victims of 'a disease of the mind, peculiar to people in a strange land; a kind of heart-sickness and despair, with an unspeakable longing after their native country'. Others still had been imprisoned or, 'abandoned, at a distance of some thousands of miles from home, and without a penny in their pockets', had been reduced to abject misery and the 'hard necessity of begging in the streets'.[34]

To contrast the lot of workers in the Staffordshire Potteries, 'a land truly *flowing with milk and honey*', with that of emigrant potters, 'suspected, watched, despised, and insulted', obliged to subsist on no 'more substantial fare than frogs, hedgehogs, and wild herbs of the field', was perhaps laying on the propaganda a little too thickly, but there was substance in Josiah's argument. As he wrote in another pamphlet published in the same year and addressed to the 'Young Inhabitants of the Pottery':

> . . . ask your parents for a description of the country we inhabit when they first knew it; and they will tell you, that the inhabitants bore all the signs of poverty to a much greater degree than they do now. Their houses were miserable huts; the lands poorly cultivated and yielded little of value for the food of man or beast, and these disadvantages, with roads almost impassable, might be said to have cut off our part of the country from the rest of the world, besides not rendering it very comfortable to ourselves. Compare this picture which I know to be a true one, with the present state of the same country. The workmen earning nearly double their former wages – their houses mostly new and comfortable, and the lands, roads and every other circumstance bearing evident marks of the most pleasing and rapid improvements. From whence and from what cause has this happy change taken place? . . . Industry has been the parent of this happy change . . . [35]

In 1782, there were violent demonstrations in the country caused by the disastrous harvest. A riot broke out at Etruria after a barge loaded with flour and cheese for the Potteries was redirected to Manchester. This boat and another that followed were seized by the rioters and the contents sold at reduced prices, although the proceeds were duly paid to the owners. The rioters were finally dispersed by a company of the Welsh Fusiliers supported by Staffordshire militia. One of the ringleaders, Stephen Barlow, was later hanged. The twelve-year-old Tom Wedgwood sent his father a vivid account of the affair, ending with the reading of the Riot Act by Dr Falkener, who gave the rioters one hour to disperse. 'One hour gone & they did not disperse Dr. Falkener had got the word Fire in his mouth when two men dropt down by accident which stopt him. . . . Parson Sneyd had got about 30 men to follow him he huzzaing . . . but a woman cried Nay nay that wunna do that wunna do & they turned back again. It was agreed that the corn taken in the boat should be sold at a fair price.'[36]

There could be little doubt that conditions for workers in the Potteries, and especially at Etruria where new housing was provided for the majority of them, were not only improved beyond recognition from those that had obtained a quarter of a century earlier but also compared favourably with any likely to be found elsewhere in Europe or in America. While the most skilled workers in the porcelain factories of France, Germany and Italy could attract good wages, the living standards of most potters were not enviable. Visitors to Etruria almost invariably expressed their admiration for the elegance of the factory, its clean workshops, efficient layout and pleasant situation, while earthenware potters in Paris 'choisissent des rues étroites pour y avoir un logement moins cher. Ils ont leurs ateliers dans les salles basses, humides'. Like many of their English cousins they suffered from 'la gêne dans la respiration' and 'maladies de poitrine'[37] brought on by working in an atmosphere thick with clay dust* and exposed to poisonous lead, but the poverty of their living conditions undoubtedly contributed to their ill-health.

It was probably the example of Boulton, who had set up a sick club at his Soho factory, to which workers subscribed between a halfpenny and 4d. a week according to wages, that persuaded Wedgwood to start a similar scheme at Etruria. This was serviced by James Bent, the surgeon and apothecary who had amputated Josiah's leg in 1768, and his younger brother, William, who charged greatly reduced fees.[38] The cost to Wedgwood of a small subsidy was amply repaid in the improved health of his work-force and the reduction of hours lost to minor injuries and sickness.

*Silicosis ('potter's consumption' or 'potter's rot') remained a principal cause of death among both male and female workers in the Potteries until the twentieth century.

Josiah's care for the well-being of his workers was central to his policy of demanding their loyalty. He cheerfully attracted, or even enticed, workers away from other potters in Liverpool or the Bow, Chelsea, Derby or Worcester porcelain factories, but he was incensed if any of his own hands went to work for anyone else. He hated losing workers whom he had trained to his own high standards but, more than that, he feared the diffusion of secrets which he was not yet ready to share. An added advantage of the separation of the two Etruria factories and the further division of their workshops was the limitation of knowledge among the workers. This was central to an inventive manufacturer in a country where, except for formal apprenticeships, the enforcement of long-term contracts was illegal. There were laws to prohibit the export of machinery or the emigration of skilled artisans but these were generally ineffective and, among progressive manufacturers, it became critically important to prevent highly trained workers from moving to another employer or setting up their own factories elsewhere.

These considerations produced a dichotomy in the policies of manufacturers: on the one hand, they were keen to establish profitable export markets and ready to evade legal restrictions in order to do so; but on the other, they wanted to avoid the dispersal of technology. Often the loss of skilled artisans was the key to this dilemma, for, without them, the technology could not be used to its best effect. On the whole, manufacturers chose to supply machinery and expertise when it suited them, as individual firms, to do so, and without regard for the industry as a whole or the national interest. Boulton & Watt, for example, were granted a fifteen-year monopoly on the sale of their steam engines in France, their first contract being agreed in February 1779, twelve months after the French had signed a treaty of friendship with the American revolutionary states, entering the war against Britain. They were none the less energetic in their efforts to prevent the defection of skilled artisans to competitors at home or abroad and were as sensitive as Wedgwood to reports of foreign visitors spying on their factory or attempting to steal their workers. Arthur Young, travelling in France between 1787 and 1789, visited a cotton mill at Louviers run by four Englishmen formerly employed by Arkwright, a 'colony' of Englishmen nearby making copper plates 'for bottoming the King's ships' and an establishment at Nantes for casting and boring cannon, founded by John Wilkinson.[39] At Vicenza in October 1788, Young was conducted on a tour of a 'very famous woollen fabric, at present under the direction of an Englishman, and to a magazine of earthenware in imitation of Mr Wedgwood. It is surely a triumph of the arts in England to see in Italy

Etruscan forms copied from English models. It is a better imitation than many I have seen in France.'[40]

The important *faïence fine* factory at Douai was founded by Georges Bris with the help of two Englishmen, Charles and James Leigh, in 1781, and three years later a letter to Bris from Samuel Jones, one of the painters at Etruria, was intercepted and returned to Wedgwood. If terms could be agreed, Jones offered his own services and also those of four others, 'a turner a presser and handler a modeller and a man that can make as good a China glaze and Enamel coulers as any man in the country'. His risk is emphasised by his offer to negotiate on behalf of the others, all of whom were married – to 'run the hazard of anything happening from the masters in this country' – and by his providing only an accommodation return address in Derbyshire.[41]

There were English potters at the French creamware factories at Choisy-le-Roy and Creil, and probably also at Chantilly and Sarreguemines. English potters found their way, too, to Germany, Holland, Denmark and Russia, where they helped their new employers to imitate the fashionable English earthenwares and stonewares.

Josiah was well aware of the activities of spies. As early as 1767 he told Bentley, 'some of the subjects I do not care to trust in writing for fear of accidents', and a few months later he complained, 'our Post-masters open just what letters they please, & seem to have a particular curiosity to be peeping at mine'.[42] This was a continuing problem and he was obliged to invent a code[43] to ensure the security of technical developments and formulas. This he used to record all his experiments and to communicate secret information to Bentley in London.

The increasing stream of visitors to Etruria, from home and abroad, posed continuing problems of security which were not easy to solve without giving offence to potential customers. Josiah told Bentley in 1779 of 'several foreigners here lately & most of them extremely anxious after the composition of the black [basaltes] of which we make our vases & busts, & quite hurt & disappointed when they are told we do not shew that part of the manufactory'.[44] Six years later he complained to the secretary of the General Chamber of Manufacturers about

three different sets of spies upon our machines & manufactures . . . from different nations . . . some of them exhibited the greatest share of impudence ever known upon like occasions. For having been refused admittance by one clerk, they have come again when he has been absent, and almost forced their way to the machines they wanted to see. In another instance having been turned out at one door, they have waited an opportunity of entering in under different pretences at another. Sometimes they pretend to be possessed of improvements to the machines they want to take drawings or models of, at other times they procure recomendations from gentlemen who are not aware of their intentions, or even bring those gentlemen themselves with them, when they can prevail upon them so far . . . no time should be lost, nor any diligence on our part to prevent them.[45]

One of the most professional arcanists of the eighteenth century was Louis-Victor Gerverot.[46] Born in 1747 at Lunéville, he was apprenticed at Sèvres, but soon moved to the Niderviller (Lorraine) factory, where he was trained as a bird painter and began his career in industrial espionage. He subsequently moved in turn to Ludwigsburg, Höchst, Fürstenberg and Frankenthal, in Germany, and to Weesp in Holland, acquiring the secrets of the factories wherever they were inadequately guarded, and back to Germany to manage, with the benefit of the valuable information he had amassed, his own factory at Schrezheim, in Württemberg. When his lease there expired, he returned to Holland, becoming a partner with Johannes de Mol in a factory at Oude-Loosdrecht. After the death of de Mol in 1782, Gerverot's share was bought out and he moved to America. Four years later he arrived in England, richly equipped to sell the secrets of European porcelain and ready to steal those of English pottery.

It was a foregone conclusion that the Etruria factory would be among his most coveted targets. By his own account, he advertised the secret of Continental porcelain for sale to any potter who would make him a partner in its manufacture, and Wedgwood replied, offering to buy the secret and to employ Gerverot at Etruria. Gerverot declined these terms and agreed instead with John Turner of Lane End, a potter of fine creamwares and stonewares who was on terms of amicable rivalry with Wedgwood, that he should build a porcelain factory at Lane End. This was still uncompleted when Turner died in 1787 and Gerverot was sued by Turner's sons for failure to discharge his obligations under the agreement. Having extricated himself from legal proceedings, with the assistance of the Marquis of Stafford,* Gerverot retired in dudgeon to Germany, finally becoming manager of the Fürstenberg factory, where a form of black basaltes was added to production in 1796. The fact that for some interim years he also made 'English stoneware' on the Continent suggests that his time at Turner's

---

*Josiah's friend and loyal patron, Earl Gower, had been created Marquis of Stafford in 1786.

factory was put to good use and also that he may have paid rather more than a casual visit to Etruria.

This is corroborated by an unusually intimate description of the Wedgwood factory, contained in letters written to the directors of Für-stenberg and first published nearly a century later.[47] Gerverot writes that the factory is 'an enormous building, practically a small town . . . a marvel of organisation' and verifies many of the details contained in the 'Potters Instructions' and 'Regulations and Rules' as well as describ-ing methods of production. He is astonished at the quantities of goods produced daily and evidently filled with admiration for Josiah's per-sonal control of the day-to-day working of the factory: 'Wedgwood himself is its first workman' and he is 'nearly always present among his workmen on the factory floor or else engaged in preparing the clay body'. But he confirms too that the workmen have no savings and no property, spending all they earn on food and drink, taking their wages straight to the inn, 'momentarily rich and not knowing what to do with their money . . . They have no debts because nobody lends them anything.'[48]

It is possible that Gerverot was briefly employed at Etruria, but no evidence has been found to prove this. More probably, he visited the factory more than once and, in the best tradition of spies, made the most of opportunities for conversation with workers at Etruria. His account of Josiah's offer to buy the secrets of European porcelain is possibly true. Wedgwood knew how to make porcelain long before Gerverot's arrival in England, and by 1786 he had almost certainly abandoned any intention to produce it. He was, however, an inveterate collector of technical information and he would have been tempted by the opportunity to add details of so many different Continental por-celains to his considerable records of porcelain production.

Two years after Gerverot's return to the Continent, another pro-fessional spy was discovered at Etruria. Josiah wrote to Sir John Dalrym-ple, a Scottish judge distinguished in private life by his discovery of the secret of making soap from herrings:

> Our pottery here is at this time in a considerable ferment, occasioned
> by a person having lately been detected in seducing & bribing our
> workmen to give him drawings of our kilns, samples of our clays
> & raw materials, & specimens of our goods in the different stages
> of mfre [manufacture]. The person has made his escape, but we
> are endeavouring to take & prosecute him. The foreign agent, for
> such he proves to be, has been 16 years in England employed upon
> the same plan respecting the different mfres of G.B. & has taken

drawings of our machinery for mining & mfres from Cornwall to Yorkshire.[49].

To guard against the local spy, the newly employed worker whose sole object was to learn what he might of his employer's secrets and then to sell them elsewhere, Josiah determined that 'new hands should if possible be kept by themselves 'till we are better acquainted with them, otherwise they may do us a great deal of mischief if we should be oblig'd to part with them soon . . . We cannot avoid taking in Strangers & shall be oblig'd sometimes to part with them again, we should therefore prevent as much as possible their taking any part of our business along with them. Every different class should if possible be kept by themselves, & have no connection with any other.'[50]

It was more difficult to guard against local imitators. In 1790 Josiah uncovered the existence of 'a journeyman or somebody in London or Birmingham' who kept a room in the Potteries and boasted that he could supply casts of anything made by Wedgwood. His task was not especially difficult in the case of cameos and intaglios, which could be cast from samples bought or borrowed from the Birmingham 'toy-makers' who mounted cameos in silver and cut steel for jewellery, but Josiah was disturbed by the man's claim that he could as readily supply casts of Wedgwood's vases as soon as they were put on the market. Josiah also knew of a worker in his warehouse who supplied casts to a London intermediary.[51]

In the event, the most serious potential danger to the secrets of the Wedgwood & Bentley partnership was threatened by the defection or dismissal of skilled hands who had come with high qualifications and remained long enough to be trusted. One such craftsman was the modeller John Voyez, who was to give Wedgwood greater cause for anxiety than all the disputes about pay and conditions or any foreign visitors at Etruria.

Josiah Wedgwood had better cause for secrecy than any contemporary potter. He was the most inventive potter of the eighteenth century, constantly at work on experiments to create new ceramic bodies and forms or to refine those already in existence. For two years, beginning in December 1772, he was engaged in a series of experiments which led to the most important invention of his life.

CHAPTER TWELVE

The Great Invention

Towards the end of 1772, the ornamental ware business of the Wedgwood & Bentley partnership was suffering one of its periodic declines.[1] It was a market, dependent upon fashion, that required regular feeding with new designs and styles. Although the handsome black basaltes, 'encaustic' and variegated vases were still admired and the whole range of black 'gems', medallions and figures continued to sell, both partners were aware that something more was needed. Josiah and Sally made a point of greeting, and sometimes of entertaining, the more important of the visitors to the factory, but Bentley, in daily conversation with customers in the London showrooms, was even better informed about changing taste and developing demand.

The showrooms were always an attractive and respectable meeting place for fashionable society and Bentley soon realised that refined neoclassical styles, austere by comparison with the abundance and frivolity of the rococo, might seem almost joyless to feminine taste. Wedgwood's ornaments did not lack style but they were, particularly after the removal of 'offensive gilding', lacking in colour and vitality. Imitations of natural stones, however decorative, and of bronze, were not sufficiently appealing to 'the Ladies'. Nor were the partners ever likely to forget that, next to King George, their two most important patrons were Queen Charlotte and the Empress Catherine of Russia. The Dukes of Marlborough and Devonshire might be high on the lists of customers at Etruria and in London but it was likely to be their Duchesses who chose what they bought.

Bentley's suggestion, made in December 1772, was simply for a 'finer body for gems', something of greater decorative potential than black basaltes, and he evidently proposed porcelain. Josiah replied, 'I think a China body would not do. I have several times mixed bodies for this purpose, but some have miscarried, & others have been lost or spoiled for want of my being able to attend to, & go thro' with the experiments.' He was again overworked and exhibiting familiar signs of stress: 'At present I cannot promise to ingage in a course of experiments. . . . If I feel stronger in the spring, something may be done, but at present my health is in too delicate a situation & my life I believe may, at least, be set down *Double hazardous.*'[2] Since October he had been worried about a sensation of tightness across his chest combined with an uncharacteristic lassitude and sudden loss of weight. He consulted Erasmus Darwin whose prescription of good food, moderate exercise and 'to keep free from care & anxiety' is an accurate indication of his diagnosis.[3] Darwin was never renowned for his tact and treated many of his patients with an irascible bluntness that suggested insensitivity. With Wedgwood, however, he appears always to have been sympathetic and perceptive.

In spite of this renewed bout of depression, Josiah succeeded in perfecting the white terracotta body and this temporarily satisfied Bentley's need for more decorative gems. By then, however, Josiah had made some 'very promising experiments . . . upon fine bodies for Gems & other things'.[4] Production of the 'Frog' service and the search for and organisation of the Greek Street showrooms, added to all his tasks at Etruria, obliged him to put his experimental work away for some months, but in March 1774 he was back at work with his old enthusiasm. 'I have', he wrote to Bentley, 'for some time past been reviewing my experiments, & find such *Roots*, such *Seeds* as would open & branch out wonderfully if I could nail myself down to the cultivation of them for a year or two. And the Foxhunter does not enjoy more pleasure from the chace, than I do from the prosecution of my experiments when I am fairly enter'd into the field, & the farther I go, the wider the field extends before me.' Some of the roots had been 'selected & put into cultivation' but he knew that experimental work was both time-consuming and uncertain in its results. Teasingly, he reminded Bentley, 'you have given me many excellent lectures upon the bad policy of hurrying things too fast one upon another'.[5]

He was as cautious in exciting Bentley's hopes as he was in giving him any details of his work. The science of chemical analysis was in its infancy and all progress in the development of a ceramic body, or glaze or technique was, by necessity, empirical. The problems of identification and isolation of materials were the first to be overcome, before any work could begin on observing their behaviour. Nor was there, before 1782, any method for measuring accurately the heat of a pottery oven during the firing process.

It was a guiding precept of Josiah's that 'Everything gives way to experiment',[6] but during the next four years he must often have doubted its truth. By July he had, he believed, identified the materials he needed as moorstone, a feldspathic rock similar in properties to the Chinese petuntse, and carbonate of barium, which he called 'Spaith fusible', but both varied so greatly in composition[7] that he could not obtain consistent results with them. 'They have plagued me sadly of late,' he told Bentley. 'At one time the body is white & fine as it should be, the next we make perhaps, having used a different lump of the Spaith, is a Cinamon color. One time it is melted to a Glass, another time dry as a Tob[acco] Pipe.' He had decided that these materials would not, after all, serve his purpose and had begun a new series of experiments using others which were more easily available and more reliable in quality and behaviour.[8]

Just five weeks later he had his first samples ready and Bentley was able to see for himself what Josiah intended. This first attempt was a quantity of portrait medallions, modelled earlier in the year, of the two daughters of Lady Charlotte Finch.* They had been made, as Josiah explained, 'not only of the same materials, nominally, but out of the same Dish in which we grind these materials & all ground together, & all fired in the same sagar, & yet you will see what a difference there is amongst them'. Two could be described as 'pretty good' but even these were satisfactory in appearance only when the background was coloured and they were therefore little, if any, improvement on the white terracotta cameos supplied to Boulton in the previous November.

Josiah was disappointed: 'I cannot work miracles in altering the properties of these subtle & complicated (though native) materials.' But he remained determined and convinced that, with different materials, he would find a way to make attractive relief portraits of uniform quality. He was, as usual, impatient to obtain results and exasperated at being unable to give all the time he wished to his experiments: 'If I had more *time*, & more *heads* I could do something – but as it is I must be content to do as well as I can. A Man who is in the midst of a course of experiments *should not be at home* to anything or anybody else but that cannot be my case . . . I am allmost crazy.'[9]

Four days of successful experiments restored his confidence and he was once again certain that he would achieve a fine white ceramic body of consistent quality and at small cost, and forty-eight hours later he was promising to send by the next coach samples of gems, made of less delicate materials but 'so delicate a color & so fine in every other

---

*Governess to George III's daughters. Horace Walpole described her as 'the cleverest girl in the world' and 'a woman of remarkable sense'.

respect' that he was preparing a quantity of clay for further use.[10] Early in November he made the first small oval bas-reliefs of classical subjects and sent them to London for Bentley to experiment with background colours.[11]

It was now clear where Josiah's experiments were leading. The basic concept, white bas-relief ornament on a coloured ground, was a commonplace of decoration long before the Adam brothers had made it a fashion in interior decoration. Cameo-cutting, employing the layered colours of laminated stones, especially the sardonyx, is an ancient art, the effect of which was imitated in pottery and glass. It was used in the fifteenth century by Luca della Robbia for large enamelled terracotta subjects in high relief, and in the 1750s the Doccia factory under the direction of Carlo Ginori produced quantities of portrait medallions, the heads in white relief on a blue ground. No fewer than eighty-four such portraits of the Medici family adorn a large porcelain centrepiece celebrating the 'Glories of Tuscany'.[12] While it is extremely unlikely that Wedgwood or Bentley had ever seen this remarkable piece, or even an illustration of it, it is reasonable to suggest that they might have seen other similar Doccia medallions brought home from the Grand Tour by patrons such as Sir Watkin Williams Wynn, or in the possession of Sir William Hamilton or Lord Lansdowne.

The 'revival of the arts' or the 'true style', as the neoclassical style was then called; the popularity of 'Adam' colours – principally, though not invariably, pastel shades of blue, green, pink, yellow or grey – with white or gilded plasterwork; the fashion for collecting cameos and intaglio seals ('gems'); the growing demand for portraiture in a wide variety of media; and the failure of the European porcelain manufacturers satisfactorily to adapt to changing taste, all combined to offer a magnificent opportunity to a potter of vision and technical ability. How far either Wedgwood or Bentley was aware of such factors or understood the full nature of the opportunity it is impossible to judge. What is clear is that, until they began to exploit it, no other pottery or porcelain manufacturer showed any awareness of its existence. Wedgwood & Bentley were, above all, the potters of neoclassicism and they were without serious rivals in this field.

By the end of November 1774 Wedgwood was in no doubt about his objective, or that it could be achieved, but the troubles with his intractable materials continued. His composition was fired at a high temperature and was frequently ruined by 'blistering'. Once more he altered it, producing a single specimen, 'a seed of consequence' which he immediately sent to Bentley, of a fine white body of 'a beautiful Onyx color'.[13]

Meanwhile, in London, Bentley had continued with his own trials of enamel colours for the contrasting grounds to the white relief subjects. The colours were painted round the edges of the reliefs and there was difficulty in preserving the clean, sharp outlines essential to the desired cameo-cut appearance. With care, the grounds of portraits could be coloured satisfactorily, but the colouring of grounds to more intricate reliefs, such as figures, proved to be impracticable.[14] Josiah was obliged to think of some alternative method.

By 12 December there had been an important development, but Josiah was coy about telling Bentley what it was, only hinting at it by instructing him not to enamel any more 'onyxes' because he believed he could do better at Etruria. Six days later he disclosed his secret, sending '4 black & Blue onyx Intaglios' for Bentley's opinion. The colours were obtained by staining the clay, instead of by enamelling, and the body could be polished.[15] These few intaglio seals were the first specimens of coloured jasper, an entirely new ceramic body and the most significant innovation in ceramic history since the Chinese invention of porcelain nearly 1000 years earlier.

Josiah had already told Bentley of the increased importance that lapidary* polishing was likely to assume in their work and had suggested that, for reasons of security, it should be done in a room at Greek Street. By mid-December he was sure of being able 'to give a fine white composition any tint of blue, from the Lapis Lazuli, to the lightest Onyx' and, to obtain the cameo-cut appearance that he wanted, he would make the relief subjects and grounds separately, the relief in white and the ground in blue, and then fix them together. This method would allow the grounds to be polished separately before the heads were fixed.[16]

The most stringent secrecy was now more essential than ever before. Josiah was chiefly concerned with the need to obtain the materials for his new invention without 'making a noise' and he suggested that Bentley might get a friend to order it for delivery in London, where it could be disguised before being sent on to Etruria. This was a long diversion for materials obtained from Derbyshire, but, as he explained, 'if it was sent by the West Indies the expence would not be worth naming in comparison with other considerations . . . I dare not have it the *nearest way*, nor *undisguis'd*, though I should only wish to have it pounded & put thro' a coarse hair sieve, but even this I would not have done with your People, nor have them see it at all.' He

---

*A lapidary is a carver of hardstones, who makes use of the principle that any substance may be cut by another that is harder. Polishing is carried out with very fine abrasives.

proposed to Bentley that he should ask Samuel More, the secretary to the Society of Arts, to recommend 'some poor Man to work upon it in some of the uninhabited buildings at the Adelphi'.[17]

This was, Josiah believed, the period when his secret was most vulnerable: 'If our Antagonists should overtake us at this stage, we cannot again take another step before them, to leave them behind again.' Once the invention was perfected and jasper was marketed, however, imitators would be left 'at so great a distance & they will have so many obstacles to surmount before they can come up to us, that I think we have little to apprehend on that account'. He took it for granted that his competitors would eventually discover the composition of jasper but, by that time, he would have 'variety of subjects – Execution – Character, & connections in our favour sufficient to continue us at the head of this business'.[18]

On 15 January, because his letter was to be delivered by coach and not by the insecure postal service, Josiah gave Bentley a full description of his essential material: 'a white Chalky looking substance, in form generally flatt, about an inch or two inches thick, & often enclosing small lumps of lead Ore'. It was commonly known as Cauk and he had found it in great quantity at mines between Matlock and Middleton in Derbyshire when he and his father-in-law, Richard Wedgwood, had been searching for 'spath fusible'. The two materials, cauk and 'spath fusible' or 'wheat stone', were confusingly alike and Josiah was unsure which of them would prove to be the more suitable. Both are forms of barium: 'spath fusible', no. 19 in Josiah's code, being barium carbonate, or witherite; and cauk, no. 74, barium sulphate, barytes or heavy spar. The physical properties of these materials could not readily be discovered and their similarities and crucial differences were the principal cause of Josiah's difficulties, still to come, in the manufacture of jasper.[19]

On New Year's Day 1775 Josiah had told Bentley that he was now 'absolute' in the white jasper, blue in various shades, 'likewise a beautifull Sea Green, & several other colors for grounds to Cameo's, Intaglio's, &c', and was confident of being able to make bas-reliefs ranging in size from the largest oval black basaltes tablet (17 inches high) to 'the smallest gem for rings'. It was a claim that proved to be grossly over-optimistic. Apart from a number of technical difficulties still to be overcome, the most obvious of which was 'staining' or 'bleeding' when the ground colour 'bled' into the white reliefs, he had underestimated the complications and vexation with which his materials could still reward his efforts. Often they seemed to have a will of their own and Josiah was brought close to despair.

In July he was irritated that consistent use of unvaried materials had given him entirely inconsistent results. The following month he complained that he was 'almost crazed' by having so many different materials and compositions under his hands and no one to assist him with them. He had ordered 50 tons of white clay from Bruges and was experimenting with clay from Cornwall, proof that he was far from 'absolute' in his composition. The unpredictability of his product was still such that he was unable to market it. In August he admitted to Bentley that his experience of 'the delicacy and unaccountable uncertainty' of the new white body had made him less hopeful of achieving his goal. He was haunted by the spectre of Nicholas Crisp,[20] a jeweller and potter at Lambeth, who had ruined himself in vain pursuit of the secret of 'true' porcelain: 'Poor Crisp . . . Ever pursuing -- just upon the verge of overtaking – but never in possession of his favourite object! There are many good lessons in that good man's life, labours & catastrophe . . .' But he would not be beaten. He struggled on through 1775: 'Fate I suppose has decreed that we must go on – we must have our Hobby Horse, & mount him, & mount him again if he throws us ten times a day.'[21]

January 1776 brought more hope and more disappointment. Early in the month Wedgwood was able to send Bentley two fine large plaques in a new white composition which he considered the best he had ever made and some blue-and-white jasper medallions of Medusa, 'too fine to sell'. He believed that he had traced the previous faults to inconstant firing temperatures and had taken the necessary action to regulate them. Eight days passed before he wrote again, an unusually long break in his correspondence when he was at Etruria and one which indicated that he was too deep in experiments even to communicate with Bentley. At last, on 14 January, he wrote in triumph: 'I believe I can now assure you of a conquest & a very important one to us. No less than the firing of our fine *Jasper* & *Onyx* with as much certainty as our *Basaltes*.'

He had fired successfully nearly 100 portrait medallions, and the two bodies, blue and white, 'agreed perfectly'. Four days later, he was so confident of the composition that he was mixing 2 tons of it and laying it up in a cellar 'to ferment'. One unexpected property of the mixture was its coldness to the touch. Unlike other clays it did not appear to take up heat from the atmosphere and the old man employed to take it out of the tub complained of its being 'bitter cold'.[22]

Josiah was under the impression that, by adjusting the firing of his materials, he had solved his problems; but he had not. In February he reported a good kiln load, 'not a single piece discolor'd, blister'd, or shewing any tendency to either of these disorders, so that I may now surely be confident of our being absolute in firing this delicate substance,' but he was no longer sure of the colours he had prematurely claimed more than a year earlier. In March he discovered fresh difficulties with the varying surface finish imparted by different grinding of the composition and, worse, the bas-reliefs, applied to their grounds with a little water, while both were in the clay state, were cracking in firing and in cooling and some even failed to adhere to their grounds. Others, it seems, even cracked during the journey from Etruria to London.[23]

Nor were these the only problems still to be solved. In June Josiah wrote in frustration: 'This Jasper is certainly the most delicately whimsical of any substance I ever engag'd with.' The losses in firing were heavy and, he believed, unavoidable. Prices would therefore have to be high 'to make the living pay for the dead'. This, Josiah explained, 'we may the more easily do as we shall have no rival yet awhile, and those pieces that are good are fine enough to ask any price for'. Further, provided that his tight system of security was not breached, the more complex the difficulties that he surmounted, the longer it would be before any imitator would be able to follow him.[24]

The losses were frightening, however. Josiah was well aware that it was losses in firing, more than any other factor, that had been responsible for the ruin of many of the English porcelain manufacturers and he must surely have wondered if manufacture of jasper could ever be commercially practicable. Towards the end of May he had reported a 75 per cent loss in firing jasper tablets. He was again experimenting with the composition in an attempt to make it harder and firmer. 'These alterations', he admitted, 'cause me infinite trouble & vexation, & nothing less than the patience of Job could go through with them.'[25] He discovered that well-matured clay helped to prevent the bas-reliefs from cracking in cooling and he laid up tons of it to age in store. In August he was able to report to Bentley, then in Paris, that only one piece of jasper had cracked in the last five or six kiln loads although the expensive losses in larger pieces continued. Josiah was obliged to cease production of tablets altogether. 'I apprehend we shall never make a *Perfect* one,' he told Bentley sadly. It was small consolation that 'Very few fine large things are perfect. Perhaps none.'[26]

Bentley, meanwhile, remained staunchly loyal to his partner, encouraging him when trials proved successful and comforting him when they did not. He was at the receiving end of a share of Josiah's bursts of irritation and impatience and seems never to have expressed his own anxiety or dissatisfaction with the painfully slow progress of the experiments. His rare suggestions were not always received with gratitude and occasionally provoked an explosion: 'You ask me if I could not make a middle tint of Blue. But you told me in a former letter that nobody bought a *pale* blue if a full-color'd one lay near it, which induc'd me to attempt a deeper color, & the white has suffer'd by it [from 'bleeding'].'[27]

Josiah went ahead with his experiments for a deep blue but, at 36s. a pound, the cost of cobalt, from which this fine colour was made, was too high for regular production. This forced him to invent a method of 'dipping' white jasper 'blanks' in liquid dark blue clay ('slip') to give it a thin coat of the dark wash. In April 1777 he sent Bentley two portrait medallions with 'exquisite blue grounds' which he described as 'by far the finest grounds we have ever made'.[28]

The high price of cobalt was a continuing problem. Before deposits of good quality were found in Cornwall, the best cobalt, which was also used by potters for painting, blue-printing and staining, was obtained from Saxony. Supplies were kept small, and prices unnaturally high, by the regulation, or at times prohibition, of exports. Demand therefore always exceeded the permitted supply and smuggling was punishable by death. By the end of 1777 prices had almost doubled to 63s. a pound and, properly prepared and refined, it was sold for as much as £4. Josiah bought 3 pounds of it in March 1777 from 'a man who kept a warehouse in Altona [near Hamburg]' who had 'found a way of procuring it by means of some Jews, one of whom they say has been discover'd & hang'd for the practice'.[29]

In January 1777 Josiah was complaining that he was still unable to control the colour or texture of jasper. The number of his experiments for this single ceramic body was approaching 5000 but he was as confident as ever that complete success was within his grasp. Once again certain that nothing but better regulated firing stood between him and the final conquest of this capricious composition, he built a kiln exclusively for it. On 3 November he wrote, more soberly than usual, to Bentley:

> I have tried my new mixing of Jasper, & find it very good. Indeed I had not much fear of it, but it is a satisfaction to be certain, & I am now ABSOLUTE in this precious article & can make it with as much facility, & certainty as black [basaltes] ware. Sell what quantity you please. I would as readily engage to furnish you with this, as any pottery I make.[30]

It was a bold claim after so many frustrations and disappointments, and one which Bentley, who had read almost identical claims before, may have received with some scepticism, but it was one which Josiah was able to justify.

The jasper made by Wedgwood during the last years of the Wedgwood & Bentley partnership was unrivalled. To three shades of blue – a delicate grey-blue, 'mid-blue' and 'deep blue' – Josiah added green, yellow, lilac, grey and chocolate-brown, colours dictated largely by the metal oxides available for staining his clay composition but chosen also, as he told Bentley, 'to the colours of the rooms'.[31] The rooms he had in mind were, of course, the interiors designed by Robert Adam.* These were the fashionable colours among the most fashionable of architects and Josiah hoped that architects would be among his most regular customers. They were not, however, colours that necessarily appealed to Wedgwood & Bentley's customers. Nearly a year later, when he believed his triumph complete, Josiah entertained Lord Gower and the great landscape gardener Lancelot ('Capability') Brown at Etruria and showed them his latest invention:

> Both objected to the blue ground, unless it could be made into Lapis Lazuli. I shew'd them a sea green, & some other colors, of which Mr Brown said they were pretty colors, & he should not object to them for the ground of a room, but they did not come up to his ideas for the ground of a tablet, nor would any other color unless it was a copy of some natural, & valuable stone. All other color'd grounds gave the impression of color'd paper – painting – compositions, casting, moulding &c &c & if we could not make our color'd grounds imitate marble or natural stones, he advised us to make the whole white, as like to statuary marble as we could.

There is no disguising the disappointment in Josiah's single comment on this devastating criticism, which suggested nothing less than a return to the variegated grounds he had introduced ten years earlier for vases: 'This is certainly orthodox doctrine, & we must endeavour to profit by it.'[32] On reflection, however, he probably decided that Gower and Brown were not accurate barometers of taste. Certainly he paid little practical attention to their advice and, with hindsight, it is now plain that he would not have benefited by doing so. He pressed on with his experiments, anxious to add to the growing range of objects

*For example: the Library at Kenwood (1767–9); the ceiling of the second Drawing Room at 20 St James's Square (1772); the Top Hall at Nostell Priory (c. 1773–5); and the ceiling of the Drawing Room at Mellerstain (c. 1778). It is an error, however, to suppose that Adam's colours were invariably pastels: full, strong colours, including a rich crimson, were used for some of the rooms at Northumberland House (1773–5), and the Sculpture Gallery at Newby Hall (c. 1767–72).

that he could make in jasper of all colours. In particular, he had his sights set on making jasper vases.

The achievement of this ambition proved to be even more difficult than he had anticipated. While smaller objects, and particularly those such as cameos and medallions that could be laid flat in the ovens, could now be made with confidence, the larger plaques and tablets continued to give trouble, and hollow pieces – teacups, teapots and coffeepots – tended to collapse in firing. Vases invariably did so. In November 1777 Josiah invented a new method of making these pieces. It was an ingenious dissimulation, a deliberate but legitimate deception that was never acknowledged and so effective that it remained hidden for more than 200 years.[33] Pieces made of coarse-ground jasper would stand the fire but lacked the smooth finish required for sophisticated ornaments; while objects of fine-ground jasper, which would have yielded the smooth finish, collapsed in the kiln. Josiah's new process combined the two: the object was made of coarse jasper and 'dipped' or 'washed' in fine jasper slip of the same colour. The result was an object that was constructed of a coarse composition but which appeared to be of the same fine quality throughout. The method was no less legitimate than that of applying fine veneers to furniture constructed of cheaper timber, but it was better concealed and its secret was so closely guarded that it was unknown even to Josiah's descendants.[34] The greatest obstacle to the making of jasper had been overcome, but it was to be another four years before jasper vases could be offered to the public.

Meanwhile, Josiah indulged himself in a foolish and potentially damaging fancy. He was aware that the secret composition of jasper was attracting much attention, not all of it unwelcome since, to many of his customers, the mystery added to its attractions. To compound that mystery, and further to confuse any potter who considered imitating his jasper, he proposed to spread the story that jasper was made of the Cherokee clay obtained for him by Thomas Griffiths in 1768. The hazards of the journey, the reluctance of the Indians and the consequent impossibility of procuring any further supplies were to be emphasised in order to make it appear that there was a defined limit to the quantity that might be made. It followed, of course, that no one else would be able to make the composition at all. He added, in case Bentley should think this proposal disingenuous, that 'a portion' of Cherokee clay was in fact used 'in all the jaspers' and suggested that the King, who had on more than one occasion asked what use Josiah had made of the North Carolina clay, should be told the story.[35]

Josiah's letter outlining this plan has been the subject of much controversy. Given that the total quantity of Cherokee clay brought back by Griffiths was a mere 5 tons, that it was, according to the patent application of 1769, an ingredient of the pigment used on all 'encaustic' vases, and, as a nineteenth-century memorandum reveals, there was still a substantial quantity of unused clay in store some forty-eight years later,[36] it is scarcely possible to believe that the quantities used in jasper were ever greater than infinitesimal. Nor is it easy to understand Josiah's motive for wishing to set a limit to the number of pieces he could make when no true limit existed. The most charitable explanation is that this claim was based on the use of trifling quantities in the fine-ground 'dip', but it is not seriously to be supposed that Josiah himself imagined this to make any significant difference to its quality. It is difficult to regard this story as anything but a deliberate attempt to mislead, and the lack of any further mention of it strongly suggests that Bentley stamped on it before it could be more widely ventilated. It was unlikely to be believed.

From the beginning of 1778, when the composition of jasper and the techniques of its production were settled, and while he continued his trials of vases, Josiah, with Bentley's advice, decided on the range and variety of objects that he would manufacture in this new body. It was convenient that the method of ornamenting it, the application of separately moulded clay heads, figures and borders, was no different from that employed in the ornamenting of black basaltes and therefore already familiar to ornamenters in the 'black' workshops. The two bodies were also similar in their physical properties and the same moulds could be used for both. The first jasper pieces were little more than two-colour replicas of objects available in black. The difference in their appearance, however, was so marked that there was no need for further disguise. Useful as this ready stock of moulds undoubtedly was, not least among its virtues being economy, Josiah wanted to build on it, to create a pageant of new ornaments that would maintain the position of Wedgwood & Bentley as the foremost ornamental potters in the world.

In all its colour variations, jasper was already capable of great versatility. To this Josiah added the extra decorative effects obtained from the use of the engine-turning lathe – stripes and chequered patterns and stippled grounds – of which he had become master, and experimented with relief ornament in colours as well as white. Cameo and intaglio gems and seals, which Boulton had helped to make fashionable in painted terracotta and black basaltes with various metal mountings, took on new life in jasper with cut-steel, pinchbeck, silver, ormolu or gold. They were mounted for a multitude of purposes: for bell-pulls; in boxes; as brooches, buckles and buttons; in candlesticks, châtelaines, clock pendulums, combs, coach panels and door furniture; as hair pins and hat pins; in lockets, lamps and opera glasses; in rings, smelling bottles, snuff-boxes and tea caddies; in watches and watch keys; and set in fire grates, sword hilts and furniture of all descriptions. Wedgwood supplied them in great quantities to mounters and jewellers, especially in Birmingham, Uttoxeter and Wolverhampton, and to Henry Clay, the Birmingham japanner, who used them as ornaments for his 'paper ware'* trays, furniture and decorative boxes. 'The Ladies', Wedgwood (or perhaps Bentley) wrote helpfully in their 1779 Catalogue,[37] 'may display their Taste in a thousand Ways, in the Application of these Cameos; and thus lead Artists to the better Stile in ornamenting their Works.'

The catalogue listed 440 cameo subjects and 379 intaglio subjects in regular production, but customers who chose to have their own likenesses 'of proper sizes for seals, rings, lockets, or bracelets' might have as many durable copies as they chose 'at a moderate expense'.[38] The model of a portrait of suitable size for a ring cost about 3 guineas and copies could be reproduced for 5s. each. A similar offer was made to patrons who preferred portraits of a more imposing size (generally an oval about 3½ inches high) for framing, and a deft appeal was made to the 'middling' class to join their betters in the exercise of patronage: 'If the nobility and gentry should please to encourage this design, they will not only procure to themselves *everlasting portraits*, but have the pleasure of giving life and vigour to the arts of modelling and engraving. The art of making *durable copies*, at a small expense, will thus promote the art of *making originals*.' Any criticism of the business of commercial reproduction was summarily rejected: 'Nothing can contribute more effectually to diffuse a good taste through the arts than the power of multiplying copies of fine things, in materials fit to be applied for ornaments; by which means the public eye is instructed; good and bad works are nicely distinguished, and all the arts receive improvement. . . . Everybody wishes to see the original of a beautiful copy.'[39]

Substantial additions were made to the lists of portrait medallions, especially to the 'Heads of Illustrious Moderns from Chaucer to the Present Time', which were sold in various sizes at prices up to a guinea each. During the next ten years, Wedgwood assembled the most complete gallery of historical portraits ever attempted in any medium. The last quarter of the eighteenth century was the period when the British

---

*'True' *papier-mâché* is produced from pulped paper. Henry Clay's imitation was made by drying layers or panels of several thicknesses of paper in a hot stove.

passion for portraiture reached its zenith. Likenesses of popular heroes, of family and friends, were demanded in quantities that would have been astonishing in any previous century or in any other country. This desire for portraiture, amounting almost to mania, was the outcome of such disparate influences as the excavations at Herculaneum and Pompeii, the improvement of communications which provided for wider recognition of public figures, and the better opportunities for social advancement. It is best illustrated in the enormous sales of engraved portraits, but there was also an unprecedented market for portraits in oils, miniatures on ivory, busts in marble or bronze, profiles cut out or painted in silhouette, bronze medallions, and small busts in relief, carved, modelled or cast in wax, ivory, glass-paste, jasper or basaltes. Before the invention of photography, multiple reproductions of durable, authentic and recognisable portraits, which could be bought or commissioned at moderate cost, commanded a ready sale.

Wedgwood both commissioned and employed modellers to provide him with original portraits to copy and, in the business of manufacturing relief portraits, he had no considerable competition from anyone but James Tassie. Their rivalry, like Wedgwood's with Boulton, Turner and Palmer, was friendly, and they provided one another with portraits to copy in their respective materials. The choice of subjects was nicely judged. In Britain, the King and Queen provided subjects of surprisingly stable popularity and their portraits were modelled in several versions; leading politicians of Whig or Tory persuasion were a little less durable; naval and military heroes might gain a place in history or be soon forgotten; artists ceased to be fashionable; poets ceased to be read; great beauties grew old. Many portraits, such as those of Catherine the Great and Queen Maria I of Portugal, were modelled to flatter patrons or to cut a channel into foreign markets.

It was sometimes necessary to work at speed in order to catch the market. One example of Josiah's proper sense of urgency was the portrait of Admiral Keppel. After an indecisive engagement with the French fleet off Ushant in 1778, Admiral Keppel was charged with neglect of duty and tried by court martial. He was acquitted and, largely because of his known opposition to the government, immediately became a popular hero. There were riots in London in his support. The First Lord of the Admiralty, Lord Sandwich, was 'exceedingly terrified' and Pitt wrote to a friend, 'I rejoice to hear that the good People of England have so universally exerted their natural Right of Breaking Windows, Picking Pockets etc . . . I begin to fear that the Clamour may subside, and the King still be blest with his present faithful Servants.'[40] Wedgwood shared Keppel's politics and, just two weeks after the news of the Admiral's acquittal arrived in London, complained crossly to Bentley that he had failed to send a portrait of Keppel to be copied at Etruria, although it was 'advertised every day in shade-etching & wax . . . we should have had it a month since'. A week later he had an etching – 'an extreme bad impression', unsuitable for modelling from – and demanded a wax model. On 8 March he was still waiting for the model, but five days later his own jasper portraits, modelled from the engraving, were fired.[41] Thus, in spite of his difficulties in obtaining a portrait from which his modellers could work, Josiah had his portraits of Keppel on the market within a month of his acquittal.

Josiah made portraits of his wife and his friends – among them, his brother-in-law William Willet, Bentley, Erasmus Darwin and James Brindley – and three of himself; but, like the private commissions, these were not listed in his catalogues, the last of which, published in 1788, contained descriptions of 857 portrait medallions and medals of which 233 were 'Illustrious Moderns'. Portraits commissioned by friends, on the other hand, were likely to be as uneconomic as they were tiresome. He readily agreed to produce a memorial portrait, on a black ground, of his friend Richard Edgeworth's second wife, Honora, when she died in 1780, but Paul Elers was a regular pest with his extravagant claims on behalf of his father, John Philip Elers, and his importunate demands for free portraits of him. 'Mr Elers', Josiah told Bentley in July 1777, seemed 'disposed to write, & if I am not much mistaken to beg *without ceasing.*'[42]

The commercial success of the cameos and the portrait medallions was not repeated with Josiah's prized jasper tablets. By 1788 he had produced 275 separate subjects, most of them from classical sources, including one rectangular tablet ornamented with a relief of 'Diana visiting Endymion' 27½ inches long and 8½ inches high. It was something of a technical triumph to be able to fire such large pieces and the variety of subject, colour and shape available would, it was anticipated, make them suitable for use in interior decoration and especially for setting in carved wood chimneypieces and furniture.

These jasper tablets were of particular importance to Wedgwood & Bentley because they hoped, through their production, to gain access to a market which had, until then, given them little business. It was no accident that the colours developed for jasper so closely resembled those made fashionable for interiors by Robert Adam and James Wyatt; and Bentley, living in London, must have known even better than his partner the colossal sums exacted by architects from their patrons in the name of interior decoration. The 'disinterestedness & contempt for money' that Elizabeth Montagu* thought she discerned in James 'Athenian' Stuart,[43] and which caused her to prefer him above Adam for the building of Montagu House in Portman Square about 1775, was rare, if not unique, among architects. Stuart's frequent drunkenness and unprofessional conduct caused her to have the house finished by others, but not before he had ordered Wedgwood tablets for its decoration. Josiah wrote to Bentley to congratulate him on his 'conversion of the Athenian'.[44] Stuart, who was simultaneously rebuilding Belvedere, an early Georgian mansion in Kent, for Sir Sampson Gideon, installed three jasper tablets in a carved chimneypiece there.† By what has been justly described as 'a spectacular process of graft',[45] Gideon, whose father was a prosperous Portuguese Jew from the East End of London, was created a baronet at the age of thirteen. Josiah's comment that 'Jews, & Infidels & architects are in a fair way to being converted to the true belief – in our tablets'[46] was, however, over-optimistic.

Wedgwood & Bentley had been supplying white terracotta and encaustic-painted basaltes tablets for chimneypieces since 1772. Robert Adam had been among their first customers, buying a beautiful rectangular tablet and two smaller plaques, painted in an unusual variety of 'encaustic' colours after designs by Antonio Zucchi, for a chimneypiece in Sir Watkin Williams Wynn's house in St James's Square. At the time, Wedgwood had written, 'I suppose it is very much in Mr Adams's power to introduce our things into use & am glad to find he seems well dispos'd to do it.'[47]

These hopes turned out to be premature. Although Adam designed a number of chimneypieces incorporating Wedgwood & Bentley encaustic-painted tablets,‡ and there is some evidence that he may have used unglazed enamelled terracotta plaques in 1772,[48] there was no sign that he favoured jasper. Those of his rooms, such as the Drawing Room at Mellerstain, the remodelled Dining Room at Saltram in Devon and the Etruscan Dressing Room at Osterley Park, which seemed especially suited to the use of jasper tablets and plaques, remained closed to Wedgwood, and it appears to have been Josiah, rather than Adam, who persuaded Lord Scarsdale to insert an oval jasper tablet into a

---

*The wife of Edward Montagu, renowned for her beauty and her learning. The death of her husband left her the richer by £7000 a year and she lost no time in spending much of it on her commission to Stuart. She was related by marriage to Matthew Boulton. Wedgwood issued a portrait medallion of her in 1775.
†Belvedere was demolished in 1960 and the chimneypiece removed to Charleston, South Carolina.
‡The designs are now in the Soane Museum, London.

chimneypiece at Kedleston Hall, in Derbyshire, originally designed with a plain rectangular marble centre.[49]

There can be little doubt that it was also at Josiah's request that in October 1778 his friendly patron Sir William Bagot sent three pieces to his architect, James Wyatt, to install at Blithfield.[50] The following year Josiah visited Blithfield to view the result and described the occasion to Bentley:

> Sir Williams new room is hung round with Correggios, Raphaels, Guercinos, Bassan[o]s & many more masters. . . . Amongst other great works of art Sir William particularly pointed out the chimney piece to my attention, assuring me at the same time that he esteemed it the best piece in the room. . . . In looking at the tablet I was lamenting a little chip off the edge, which misfortune I suppose had befalen it in the hands of the workmen. Misfortune you call it says Sir William? We esteem it a very happy accident. It shows the merit – the fine texture of the composition which might otherwise have pass'd for a painted surface.[51]

In view of what is now known about the coarse texture of the tablets and other large pieces beneath the fine-ground jasper wash, Josiah's dismay on observing the chip is easily understood and he must have been greatly relieved that the difference in quality had passed unnoticed.

Another local patron for tablets was a Mr Heathcote, who was rebuilding Longton Hall and sent along Gardner, his architect, to discuss the matter with Wedgwood. Gardner was already well known to Josiah, having designed Etruria Hall for him, and was a ready convert to jasper tablets. He 'approv'd of [them] very much and did not doubt that great quantities would be sold to compose chimney pieces of 10 to 15 guineas price which, he said, were the chief run in all country gentlemens houses, & he would put some of them up in chimney pieces he now had in hand'. Gardner brought with him a 'stucco man', a master plasterer, who also was greatly impressed by the jasper tablets and plaques and agreed with Gardner that 'it was impossible to equal in marble, & that they had never seen anything so fine'.[52]

This was all most encouraging, but the admiration expressed by Gardner and a few others was not shared by Adam or Wyatt (in spite of Sir William Bagot's enthusiasm) or by one of the most influential architects of the day, Sir William Chambers. Both Josiah and Bentley were deeply disappointed that the Queen, who visited the Greek Street showrooms in June 1779, did not choose to order any jasper tablets for her palaces and Josiah firmly believed that the royal architects were to blame. 'We were', he wrote to Bentley in July, 'really unfortunate in the introduction of our jaspers into public notice, that we could not prevail upon the architects to be godfathers to our child. Instead of taking it by the hand & giving it their benediction they cursed the poor infant by bell, book & candle, & it must have a struggle to support itself, & rise from under their maladictions.'[53]

The setback was serious but temporary. Records have been found of 115 suites of tablets and plaques for chimneypieces[54] and it is clear that the list is far from complete. Nor were the rectangular tablets and the large roundels and ovals produced only for the decoration of chimneypieces. They were marketed also as 'Cabinet Pictures', supplied with frames of ormolu or other gilded metal, wood or, in spite of Josiah's reservations about them, jasper.[55] Josiah had faith in the importance of these pieces and persevered with them in spite of the expense and difficulties involved in making them and of the initial opposition of the architects. He employed the finest modellers he could recruit to make copies of classical subjects for them, and the work of the school of modellers that he set up in Italy between 1788 and 1790 was devoted largely to producing models on this scale (see pp. 295-7). He would not have indulged his fancy to such an extent of cost and trouble if, as has often been suggested,[56] the tablets and plaques were a continuing commercial failure.

Bentley, meanwhile, was anxious to pursue more popular and more profitable goods and it was evidently at his suggestion[57] that Josiah introduced tea and coffee wares, chocolate sets and small *déjeuner* sets,* although the 'dejunias' as Josiah usually described the trays which were an important part of such sets, were always 'very hazardous' to make.

In spite of Josiah's promises, little of this type of ware was made before 1780 and it appears that he was less interested in it than in the more prestigious and impressive tablets and his trials of vases. Nevertheless, by about 1785, jasper tablewares, which included sets of eggcups and covered custard cups, tea caddies, monteiths and a lavish assortment of shapes and bas-relief ornament, had become an important part of his business. Although there is some evidence that such pieces were used, it is plain that they were intended as 'cabinet pieces', no less ornamental than the candlesticks that were designed at about the same time. No large library busts were made in jasper, but a small number of miniature busts appeared, including Voltaire, Rousseau and

*Sets comprising a round or oval tray with tea, coffee or chocolate pot, sugar dish, cream jug and one or two cups and saucers.

166

Montesquieu among a short list of mythological characters, and a few standing figures were attempted, though extremely few have survived.

Interesting and sometimes beautiful, such pieces were to Josiah little more than continuing trials on the way to the achievement of his ambition, or comparatively trivial additions to the list after he had achieved it. His experience with black basaltes had convinced him that nothing would so decisively confirm Wedgwood & Bentley's leadership in the production of fashionable ornaments as jasper vases. When that ambition was finally achieved, it was, in a sense, too late and Josiah's triumph was chastened by grief.

CHAPTER THIRTEEN

Time for the Family

In the midst of starting his own business, of entering into partnerships, of building a factory and establishing a variety of production
unprecedented in any pottery, and in spite of constant innovation and
an almost continuous stream of experiments, Josiah seems to have
found time for his family. But even if he had not given his energy to
the campaigns for turnpikes and canals; even if he had not spent hours
of candlelight before dawn or late at night, when his tasks at the factory
were done, in the composition of lengthy and almost daily letters to
Bentley; even if he had never travelled in search of materials or visited
London in pursuit of business, that time with his family must have
been severely limited. The early upbringing of their children and the
organisation of their domestic life were primarily Sally's work. It was
she who moved the family, apparently without warning, into the house
originally intended for Bentley at Etruria in November 1769, and it was,
naturally, she who furnished Etruria Hall. There is no evidence that
Josiah took much interest in such matters and it is also plain that he
trusted her taste.

During their first struggles, Sally had been content to act as Josiah's
unpaid secretary and chemical assistant, in addition to her household
duties, but, as the business prospered, she became accustomed to living
more nearly in the style to which she had been accustomed in the
houses of her parents at Spen Green and her uncles at the Big House.
In later life, she lived better than any of them and held a position in
society that none of them could have matched. Much of this was due
to her father's industry and generosity during his lifetime and his
bequests at his death. In spite of his understandable misgivings about
his daughter's marriage, Richard Wedgwood soon came to like and,
more important, to trust his energetic and inventive son-in-law. They
had, in fact, much in common and Richard admired Josiah's courage,

his ambition, his determination to learn and his belief in his own abilities. They became friends, a generation apart but united in the will to make Etruria a famous success.

Richard travelled with Josiah on several of his journeys around the Midlands in search of clays and, on at least one occasion, took charge of the factory in Josiah's absence. When Richard was ill, Josiah helped to care for him. He stayed at Spen Green for two weeks in January 1770 until Richard was fully recovered from a fever, although this involved daily journeys to Burslem at a time when he was desperately anxious about his own health and believed he was losing his sight. Four years later, shortly after the death of his only son, Richard came to live with his daughter and son-in-law at Etruria and it was there that he died in 1782. Shortly before his death, his portrait,* 'a very strong likeness', was painted by George Stubbs.[1]

There can be little doubt that Richard's money, either directly or through the use of Sally's marriage settlement, was essential in the early financing of the Wedgwood pottery and especially in the purchase of the Ridgehouse estate and the building of the Etruria factory. It is also certain that, on the death of her unmarried brother, John, at the age of forty-two, Sally became her father's sole heir. That she and her brother were on terms of close affection is suggested by the story of his loan to Josiah in 1764, made at a time when his father was still doubtful of his new son-in-law and probably also wearied by demands on his resources.

During her brother's fatal illness, Sarah was in the final stages of pregnancy before the birth of her sixth child and was unable to travel. Darwin was summoned to attend John, who was 'emaciated extremely & . . . in the last stages of a worn out constitution', but could offer no hope for him. Josiah visited his dying brother-in-law daily at Smallwood, spending so much of the next ten days with him that his letters had to be written either in Cheshire, or after dark at Etruria. From there he wrote sadly to Bentley on 19 November 1774:

> I am just return'd to this place in time to tell you by this post . . . My
> poor Brother† died about seven O'clock yesterday morning to the great
> grief of his Father, & Sister . . . who can but lament to see a young

---

*The portrait, with other family portraits by Reynolds, Romney and Stubbs is now in the Wedgwood Museum at Barlaston.
†Josiah invariably referred to his wife's relations as to his own: Richard was 'my father', John 'my brother', and John and Thomas Wedgwood of the Big House, 'my uncles'. This habit, and the frequent repetition of first names in the family, has caused some confusion among Josiah's biographers.

man, the only son of an Aged and affectionate Father with everything
in his possession to render life agreeable & happy, cut off in the prime
of life.[2]

He was anxious that the shock might induce Sally to miscarry, but she
bore her grief bravely and, eleven days later, presented him with their
second daughter, Catherine. The birth was easy and Josiah expected to
see Sally up and about again after a few days, 'for it is becoming
fashionable here for the Ladies in the Straw to become well, & leave it
as soon as they are able; & even a Lady of Fashion may be seen in her
Carriage again, without shame, in ten days, or a fortnight after delivery'. On the strength of this he ordered two barrels of 'Good Porter'
and a 'Barrel of Oysters . . . of the smallish blue kind' to be sent to him
by land every other week.[3]

On 17 December he passed on to Bentley Sally's request that he
would 'spare a day sometime when you are not better employ'd, & do
her little Etruscan the honor of standing (do you not call it standing)
God-father to her'. He added persuasively: 'We will not be over rigid
in our exaction of *Vows* & *promises*. If you will promise to be a *good
Neighbour*, give her a gentle hint *in rhyme* when you find she stands in
need of it.'[4]

At this time Josiah and Sally Wedgwood had five children. The
eldest, 'Sukey', was nine years old, and her brother John, eight. Both
had been sent to boarding schools two years earlier: Sukey to Bolton,
near Manchester, and John first to Hindley and then to join his sister
and their cousins, Jenny and Kitty Willet, at Bolton.[5] Their younger
brother Richard, born in 1767 soon after the tragic death of Josiah's
brother John, had lived less than a year. Josiah II ('Jos') had been born
in 1769 and a fourth son, yet another Thomas Wedgwood, two years
later.

Sally had been rising thirty years old when she was married and,
when Catherine was born, she was forty. Her last two children, Sarah
and Mary Anne, were born in 1776 and 1778, at a time in her life when
it might have been considered unwise for her and for her children. In
fact Sarah lived to the ripe age of eighty, dying, unmarried like Catherine, when the next century was more than half done; but Mary Anne,
whose birth had been accomplished with such ease, was retarded and
subject to fits, which lasted up to thirteen hours, and temporary paralysis. Darwin ordered electric shock treatment, applied by Josiah himself
two or three times a day on the side affected by paralysis 'to be continued for some weeks', a prescription which was as disagreeable as it

was ineffective.* Meanwhile, the teething, thought to have been the cause of her convulsions, was eased by lancing her gums and keeping them open for the new teeth 'by means of the sharp end of an ivory modelling tool'. The child's suffering must have been horrifying and, satisfied of its futility, Josiah abandoned the electrical treatment, on his own initiative, after a week's unsuccessful trial. 'We have', he told Bentley in a letter which confided his distress, 'every reason to hope that her intellects have escaped in this terrible shock, as she knows what is said to her & begins to play a little as usual.'[6] At the age of six she was able to speak scarcely any recognisable words and two years later, after a life of suffering relieved only by dosages of opium prescribed by Darwin, she died.[7]

Josiah's favourite among his children was always Sukey. Unlike her less robust brothers, she had inherited his sense of humour and zest for life. She was, from the first, 'a fine sprightly lass' and 'The finest Girl! – So like her father', according to Josiah, and 'worth your coming 150 miles to see', according to her mother's message to Bentley.[8] Her natural high spirits came close to costing her life in June 1773, when she and her cousins were being brought home from Bolton by Josiah. She was 'playing her pranks upon a high Horse Block, miss'd her footing, & pitch'd with her head upon a Stone which was sharp enough to make a wound'. Five days later, Josiah wrote to Bentley of 'poor Suke with her broken head', adding, 'but I hope her skull is safe – it is certainly of the *thick*, than *paper* species, or it had been crush'd to pieces'.[9]

The Bolton school, run by the Reverend Philip Holland and his wife, seems to have satisfied Josiah for the next two years. In January 1775 'The young Ladies' could already 'point upon a Table or blank Paper where all the Counties in Great Britain lie – where the Rivers rise, what Towns they visit & where they empty themselve into – with several circuits & chief Towns in each County'. He took a hand himself, promising to send them 'some short account of what is peculiar to each County'.[10] Six months later, however, Sally decided to move her daughter, perhaps to an establishment in Derby, where it was thought that her music and drawing would receive better tuition. Before any decision was made, Josiah consulted Bentley. Having written a pamphlet on the subject of female education, Bentley was often asked for advice on the matter and on the subject of education in general. He suggested that Sukey might attend Blacklands School in Chelsea and

*Such use of electricity was mercifully rare at this period. Darwin had used it, apparently with some success, about a year earlier as an experimental treatment for jaundice (*Zoonomia*, Pt. I, 1794).

he and his second wife, Mary, generously offered to look after her at their home in Turnham Green during the school terms. This proposal was gratefully accepted and Sukey was educated in London until 1778, when she became ill. Josiah attributed the 'bad habit of her blood and juices' to the regimen at Blacklands and determined to remove her and to have her tutored at home.[11]

This change coincided conveniently enough with a decision to bring his sons, all three of whom were now at Bolton, home to Etruria to continue their education privately. In 1777, when the boys were eleven, eight and six years old, Bentley had warned against spoiling them 'for the exertion of their own facultys, if they are enabled to purchace the fruit of other mens'. Josiah replied that he would endeavour to 'give them so much pride & unquietness of spirit that they shall not be content with anything other people can do for them, if they have not a hand in it themselves'.[12] He had always been reluctant to expose them to the rigours of public school life. They were 'quite stout & well', and he admitted 'a school education has many advantages over the family one for boys in general', but he believed it to be unsuitable for his own sons. Although John seemed to have come to no harm, Josiah II ('Jos') had been unwell at Bolton and Tom was never strong. 'Their Constitutions are not of the Herculean kind', he told Bentley in November 1779,

> & tho' pretty well in general, require more attention than can be paid to them at a public school. They must there be dosed alike in their learning, food & confinement with boys of the most athletic make, whether such doses be too little, or too much, too weak or too strong, & whether they agree or disagree with them: but at home I can regulate the food & exercise both of their bodies & minds . . .
>
> Another material consideration . . . is, that their morals will be in better hands than at a public school, & one may daily, & imperceptibly be furnishing their tender minds, as they expand & open for instruction with such raw materials as one wishes them to improve & cultivate in future life. Besides, I can be instructing them, even by way of play & amusement, in the rudiments of chemistry & give them a turn to such studies, & enquiries as are most likely to be of use to them in their particular occupations: or if these are not determin'd, find out the bent of their minds, & what walk in life may be most suitable for them.[13]

Josiah's fears for the boys' morals were well founded. English public schools and the universities were notorious both for homosexual activity and for the lack of any moral supervision and it was not uncommon for fathers, who had experienced the often brutal conditions of public schools, to prefer a private tutor for their sons.

Although he had no definite plans for their future, Josiah had already made it clear that he expected to find his successor among his sons. All three were intended for 'genteel business, or manufacturers, but not for what are called the liberal professions of Law, Physic, Divinity or the Army'.[14] He had, of course, consulted Erasmus Darwin, who approved of his proposal to have the boys tutored at home and 'thought it a very idle waste of time for any boys intended for trade to learn latin, as they seldom learnt it to any tolerable degree of perfection, or retain'd what they learnt – Besides they did not want it, & the time would be much better bestowed in making themselves perfect in french & accounts'. For their tuition in French, he suggested that Josiah should try to obtain the services of a French prisoner-of-war.[15] It evidently did not cross his mind that Wedgwood's sons might not be destined for trade.

Josiah again sought Bentley's advice and listed to him some of the advantages of a knowledge of Latin: enhanced understanding of one's own grammar; classical knowledge; and the opportunity to read the classics, especially those authors whose work was not readily accessible in translation. But some of these advantages might be gained through translations or a proper study of English. The benefits of 'additional knowledge of the derivation of words, & some assistance in spelling' were accepted, but this was 'learning a *thousand* things to make use of one'. Summing up his own opinion, he wrote:

That a knowledge of the classicks is highly ornamental, in classical company & conversations, & that it may be usefull in the knowledge of inscriptions, motto's [sic], & latin quotations I grant in its fullest extent; but diamonds may be too dearly purchac'd, nay, may become ridiculous, when ostentatiously display'd, out of place, & character; & even pernicious, when they take up that time & attention which should be bestow'd upon more substantial objects. I estimate the learning of a language equal to an apprenticeship, or learning a business at least . . .

He did not overlook the danger that overmuch education might not be conducive to a desire for a lifetime career in the pottery business:

The probable sacrifice of health, in weak habits, in fourteen years close study, is not little, & what very frequently happens where the mind is benefited much by education.

> That time must be employ'd in education which should be devoted to learning a business, I mean from about 14 to 20 & what is more unfavorable still to the latter, the ideas of a long school & classical education, & the company kept, & habits acquir'd there, are almost incompatible with a life of drudgery, as it might be deem'd by a fine classical gentleman . . . [16]

The reasoning appeared to be sound, but Josiah was to discover that it was not only a classical education and public school environment that produced in a young man a disinclination for trade.

Meanwhile, he sent his boys temporarily to Lichfield to be taught with Erasums Darwin's son Robert. Darwin, who had engaged a young prisoner-of-war named Potet, who had 'got his exchange but chuses to remain in England,' wrote to Wedgwood in December: 'Your little boys are very good, and learn french and drawing with avidity – and hope you will let them stay, till we write you word we are tired of them.'[17] Josiah, however, had other ideas better suited to his own convenience. He decided to set up an 'Etruscan School' for Sukey, John, Jos, Tom and Kitty (Catherine), joined by the daughter and three sons of his partner 'Useful' Thomas. They were to be instructed by his nephew Tom Byerley, his accountant and cashier Peter Swift, and the Reverend Edward Lomas, a parson from Newcastle-under-Lyme. Potet, removed from Lichfield and engaged for one year at a salary of 50 guineas, was 'a young man, not twenty, of a gentle deportment, not fawning nor too bold', who was usefully qualified to teach Latin, drawing, fencing and dancing in addition to French. French classes were planned also for some of the clerks and for Tom Byerley to perfect his pronunciation. Bentley was again invited to give his advice and asked to obtain a set of Mrs Barbauld's* books for children because 'our little lasses are quite out of *proper* books to say their lessons in'.[18]

Bentley had already suggested that Josiah's plans for his sons should be kept in mind when the curriculum for the school was designed and, for the first time, Josiah set down his thoughts for their future employment: John to be 'settled as a gentleman farmer in some desirable situation, with as many acres for himself, & his tenants to improve as I can spare him. Joss & Tom to be potters, & partners in trade. Tom to be the traveler, & negociater, & Joss the manufacturer.'[19] Earlier in the year he had considered having his three sons painted by George Stubbs or Joseph Wright of Derby. They were to be portrayed

*Anna Letitia Barbauld, whose portrait medallion was among the earliest made by Wedgwood, was celebrated for her poems, a volume of which was published in 1773, and four books of an improving nature for children.

as if conducting a chemical experiment, in 'actions . . . exactly descriptive of their respective characters',[20] but this idea was dropped in favour of a larger composition to include the whole family.

Josiah busied himself with the timetable for the Etruscan school and sent Bentley a specimen of 'One days schooling for our own five scholars':

Rise at 7 in winter when I shall ring the school bell, & at 6 in summer
Dress & wash half an hour
The boys to write with Mr Swift one hour along with Mr T. Wedgwoods
(if I approve of company) in some room fitted up for the purpose at
the works
The little girls an english lesson with their nurse *in the school*, which
happens to be a room near the nursery. I would instill an early habit
of *going to school at stated times* in the youngest of our scholars as it
will make it so much easier to them by as much as it seems a
necessary & connected part of the routine or business of the day.
My young men are quite orderly in this respect since I let them
know it was indispensible, & they are very good in keeping my
eleventh commandment – Thou shalt not be idle.
    Breakfast as school boys.
    From 9 to 10 French
    From 10 to 11 Drawing
    From 11 to 1 Riding or other exercise which will include gardening
        – Fossiling, experimenting &c. &c.
Susan fills up these intervals with music besides her exercise.
    From 1 to dinner at half past 1 washing &c in order to be decent
        at table.
    Half past 2 Latin one hour
    Then french one hour & conversation in the same, in the fields,
        garden or elsewhere as it may happen half an hour, to 5 O
        Clock.
    From 5 to 7 exercise, bagging* &c
    At 7 Accounts one hour – Supper, & to bed at 9
The little lasses I had forgot they must have two more english lessons
    in the school, & Kitty as much french as she can bear.

Whether for convenience or from some wish to keep them apart, the Josiah Wedgwood and the Thomas Wedgwood children were to be

*Local description for food between regular meals, used later in northern counties, especially Lancashire, for high tea.

taught separately 'at their own houses', except for the first hour with Peter Swift, while the clerks were to 'attend the master in his own rooms, morning & evening'.[21]

Although Josiah had evidently conquered his aversion to the learning of Latin, Bentley remained less than wholly enthusiastic about either the intention in general or the proposed regime in particular. He was anxious also about the employment of M. Potet, doubtful about his morals and concerned that he might turn out to be an industrial spy. Josiah could say little about the young Frenchman's morals except that he seemed 'a very decent orderly man' and that Erasmus Darwin, who was seldom short of something critical to say on any subject, found no fault with him. To be on the safe side, Potet was not to stay at Etruria Hall with the family. As to his being a spy, Josiah told his partner, 'I should be as little afraid of this young man as any I ever saw as a spy upon a manufactory; because I do not think he has a single manufacturing idea about him.' For good measure, he added that Jos had learned so much French from him in three weeks at Lichfield that he 'construes the language & reads it in english to the astonishment of his sister Susan & us all'.[22] There was little doubt that M. Potet would earn his salary for, between the families of Josiah and his cousin Thomas, he was expected to teach for a full seven hours a day.[23]

Bentley's final advice was that John, both the oldest and the strongest of Wedgwood's sons, should be sent back to Bolton to complete his studies under Mr Holland and to prepare himself for further education by learning some Greek. This was accepted and, after a further period at Bolton, John was enrolled at Warrington Academy, a stronghold of Nonconformism and the focus of intellectual culture in Lancashire, a choice no doubt inspired by Josiah's friendship with Joseph Priestley, who had been tutor in languages and *belles-lettres* there in 1761. From 1781, when he was fifteen, John worked intermittently at the Etruria factory and in the London showrooms in Greek Street, learning the techniques of manufacturing and marketing. Whatever his plans for his eldest son, Josiah was determined that he should not be ignorant of the business that provided the family's wealth.

The two younger boys and their sisters began their studies at Etruria but it was soon discovered that M. Potet's qualities did not include an ability to keep lively pupils in order. He was evidently unsure of his position, veering between over-familiarity and sudden severity. As Josiah complained to Bentley, 'He plays his authority away in a boyish manner, & then is oblig'd to establish it again, for want of knowing a better way, by thrashing the boys.' Josiah was prepared to give the young tutor a chance to improve but, although he was careful not to tell them so, he insisted that his boys should not again be beaten, whatever the circumstances. A further problem was Tom Byerley's increasing involvement with the business, which left him too little time for teaching. His place was filled by Mr Lomas, whose knowledge of Latin was superior to Byerley's and who would, Josiah thought, benefit from 'some daily, bodily exercise, *which sedentary gentlemen are apt too much to neglect*', this last being a heavy hint to Bentley, whom he continued to tease about his weight and lack of healthy activity.[24]

Potet reformed his methods, the boys improved their behaviour,[25] and, although there is no evidence to confirm its continuance, the Etruscan school probably lasted at least until the completion of the young French tutor's engagement. By the beginning of 1781, however, Josiah no longer had time to give daily attention to the education of his Etruscans. The following year Jos was sent away to school in Edinburgh, where a few years later both he and his eldest brother attended the university. Tom, the youngest and most gifted of Wedgwood's sons, whose health had always been delicate, remained at Etruria, receiving private tuition of a progressively higher quality as his talents came to be recognised.

Sukey, too, remained at home with her younger sisters. She had grown into a pretty girl with the sharpened features of her mother, and was interested in natural history and music. But, like her youngest brother, who resembled her in looks, she was not strong and her temperament was volatile. She suffered occasionally from rheumatism and, in spite of her vivacity, was liable to periods of depression. In Josiah's indulgent remarks about Sukey there is more than a hint that she knew that he favoured her and that she was accustomed to getting her own way. There is some evidence that she was as headstrong as her mother.[26]

The Wedgwood family, as it was towards the end of 1780, is to be seen in the large portrait by George Stubbs. It shows Josiah and Sally seated beneath a tree in the park of Etruria Hall, the four eldest children mounted upon well-groomed horses and ponies, the three youngest daughters playing with a cart. There is about them a certain woodenness of pose and expression not quite in keeping with the unselfconscious confidence of the country gentry they seem, at first glance, to be. That this is not due to ineptitude on the part of the artist is sure because the same unease may be discerned in certain family groups by contemporaries such as Reynolds, Gainsborough and Devis. It is almost as if Stubbs, a master portrayer of class in eighteenth-century England,[27] had chosen to paint them as newly arrived. Only a black basaltes vase on the mahogany tripod tea-table at Josiah's elbow hints at manu-facturing.

Wedgwood had suffered grievously from the effects of smallpox in his childhood and bore the scars of it for the rest of his life. He was determined if possible to save his own children from this disease. The technique of inoculation with live virus had been brought to England from Turkey by Lady Mary Wortley Montagu in 1721, but fifty years later it was still considered unsatisfactory because, although less dangerous than an attack of smallpox, it nevertheless posed some risk to an infant, and it kept the disease alive without conferring certain immunity. However, until Edward Jenner was able to prove the effec-tiveness of his vaccination technique in 1798, no alternative form of protection was known and inoculation became common among the upper classes in the 1770s.

The treatment was probably recommended to Josiah by Erasmus Darwin, who is recorded as using it, though certainly not for the first time, in 1768.[28] He described it many years later in *The Temple of Nature*, first published in 1803. Darwin was convinced of the efficacy of the technique and carried out an experimental inoculation against measles on his third son, Robert.

Writing to Bentley on 18 February 1767, Josiah told him that the two-year-old Sukey and John, then aged ten months, had been inoculated at Newcastle and, in response to his friend's enquiry, described their symptoms: 'They both had Convulsions at the first apearance of the eruption, & have had a *pretty smart* pox as our Doctor terms it. I believe they have had no dangerous symptoms, but they have been so very ill that I confess I repented what we had done, & I much question whether we should have the courage to repeat the experiment, if we had any more subjects for it . . . I hope they will not have reason to wish their parents had acted otherwise.' In spite of their apprehensions, Josiah and Sally decided to have their second son, Richard, inoculated in December, when Josiah described him as having 'about forty of those things with an ugly name upon him & is likely to do very well'. The child's death the following year was unconnected with smallpox and some thirty months later the baby Jos was reported as 'at the height of the disorder, the eruption is of a good sort but tiezes the poor fellow sadly'.[29] Although firm evidence is lacking, it seems sure that all the Wedgwood children were protected by inoculation.

By 1780 Josiah had no brothers living. John's death in 1767 had affected him deeply but he was never so close to any of the others. His fourth brother, Aaron, died in Liverpool the following year. Always known to the family as 'the Alderman', probably because of his portly figure and correspondingly portentous manner, he never held any such appointment and was, on the contrary, dim-witted and lethargic. Josiah offered to build a house for him on the Etruria estate but Aaron died before it could be started.[30]

Thomas, the eldest, died in February 1773. He had been confined to his house for several months beforehand, suffering, according to Josiah, from 'Ailments of various kinds, which seem now to have resolv'd themselves into a Dropsy. His Legs & Body swell, his appetite is nearly lost, & he sleeps but little.' Darwin, called as usual to minister to the Josiah Wedgwoods and their nearest relations, diagnosed a serious liver complaint and forecast that Thomas would probably live only a few months. His patient was possibly discouraged by the prognosis for he died within the month. He left five children by his two marriages: 'a sad Rakish Boy' aged twenty-nine for an eldest son, two daughters and two more sons, the youngest being fourteen. At the urgent request of Thomas's wife, Josiah had stayed with his brother for several days, eventually succeeding in persuading him to make a will, but his fears that it would 'not be an easy matter to bring about a settlement to the satisfaction of all parties' were amply justified.[31]

His eldest brother's affairs took up a good deal of Josiah's time during the following month, when he was already in a state of the most acute anxiety about Sally's health. She was suffering from a recurrent fever, probably rheumatic, for which she had been treated by Darwin for several months. Darwin's absence, shortly after Thomas's death, increased Josiah's fears for his wife and he could well have done without having to take on his own shoulders the 'vexation and fretting' that he knew had worn down his brother's constitution during the previous ten years.[32] Not least of the causes of this was his sister-in-law, Jane.

Thomas's eldest son, the 'Rakish Boy' (yet another Thomas), responded well to his uncle's kindness, but the boy's stepmother was in 'a deplorable situation'. She confessed to Josiah that it had been 'her daily study', in which she had succeeded all too well, to set her husband against her stepson, that she had 'wrong'd him in every way & cheated her own Brother & sisters' and ruined her own children. After her husband's death she had taken money and valuables from the house and hidden them at a neighbour's so that her stepson should not have them. She threw herself on Josiah's mercy, admitting that she had been 'the vilest wretch that ever liv'd' and begging for help for her children. 'I will not blot my paper nor trouble you with a recital of her black misdeeds,' Josiah told Bentley. 'She has been a wretch in grain! but it is all come home to her with a vengeance. She . . . has really lost her senses, & is quite distracted, & what I shall do with her, & her eldest son, who is not one remove from an idiot, I do not know.'[33]

It was fortunate that Thomas's two daughters by his first wife, Isabel, were comfortably settled as the wives of potters.* Their only surviving brother was heir to the Overhouse pottery and was able, with Josiah's help and advice, to work it. He died in 1786 at the age of forty-two. This left the deplorable Jane, her retarded elder son, William, and his fifteen-year-old brother John, 'a sensible thoughtfull Lad', to be cared for. Against his uncle's advice, John decided to become 'a pot seller instead of a maker' but he died, unmarried, in 1782. Since the Overhouse business was making little profit, Josiah was obliged for several years to provide for his brother's deranged widow and the unfortunate William. The last of Josiah's brothers, Richard, who had enlisted in the army, died in May 1777, weakened by 'a long course of drinking and irregular living'.[34]

Another nephew who, in his youth, had caused Josiah considerable trouble and concern had been his sister Margaret Byerley's son, Tom. (see Chapter 4). After his various flirtations with the dubious professions of acting and writing and his not entirely happy experience of America, Tom had returned to Staffordshire a reformed and more serious character. Josiah had always regarded him with affection and Tom gratefully accepted his offer that he should return to work as a clerk at Etruria. It was time to repay his uncle's patience and generosity and this he did by becoming Wedgwood's most loyal, conscientious and reliable lieutenant. In 1778, when it was necessary to fetch Sukey from the Bentleys' at Turnham Green after her illness, it was Tom Byerley who was sent to escort her home, and it was he who was chosen by Josiah to make the first serious attempt, on the same journey, to act as a travelling salesman. An earlier journey with that intention had been made by Joseph Brownbill but it had ended in ludicrous and humiliating failure through Brownbill's timidity and his inability to manage a carriage, which had led to an accusation of 'hawking' from one of his customers.[35] Tom Byerley's slight success was therefore greeted with all the more satisfaction. When Bentley needed help in collecting debts in the London area, it was once again Byerley who was lent to him, although Josiah admitted that he could not well spare him from Etruria.[36]

Tom Byerley's experience and sense of responsibility had become invaluable. He was presentable, literate and well mannered, with a

*Sarah was married to John Taylor of the Hill Top pottery, and Mary to Josiah Wood, son of Ralph Wood the younger.

good knowledge of French and some Latin, and he had proved himself as a salesman. At the age of thirty-three he had developed into his uncle's most trusted and senior manager.

Among the older generation, Josiah's closest friend was his sister Catherine's husband, William Willet. He was a well-educated man and, although no firm evidence has been found to confirm it, he is believed to have helped Josiah with his successful efforts to educate himself. Certainly he had a substantial library of books, of which Bentley had a catalogue, and it is likely that Josiah had the use of it after Willet's marriage to Catherine in 1754. William and Catherine Willet lived in the Bank House, originally built for Bentley on the Ridgehouse estate, from 1765,[37] so they were Josiah's and Sally's nearest neighbours. Catherine accompanied them on several of their visits to London and it is evident that she was on terms of warm friendship with Sally with whom she joined in teasing Bentley.[38] Willet was nearly thirty years Catherine's senior but their marriage seems to have been happy and they had several children, two of whom – Kitty and Jenny – were among Sukey's dearest companions. She was so shocked by the early death of Kitty, 'her favorite cousin', in February 1780 that Josiah feared for her health. A third Willet daughter, Sally, who was diagnosed as consumptive later in the same year, died at the age of seventeen at the end of March 1781.[39]

In 1776 Josiah had his brother-in-law's portrait modelled by William Hackwood, his senior resident modeller, for reproduction in jasper. He told Bentley, to whom he sent one of the first medallions, that a stronger likeness could scarcely be conceived, but added sadly, 'You may keep it as the shadow of a good Man who is marching with hasty strides towards the Land of forgetfulness.'[40] Willet lasted nearly two years more but early in May 1778 Josiah reported that he was 'very ill' and not expected to recover. At this time his particular concern was for Catherine, for the old man refused to allow anyone else to nurse him. However, Josiah thought his last wishes should be indulged: 'His faculties are much impair'd, & old age should be render'd as easy & comfortable as possible in complying with its caprice when the sacrifice it requires is not too great.'[41] William Willet died nine days later. Josiah wrote to Bentley later the same day:

> This truly good mans death was of a piece with his life, calm, serene & to the last moment. A little after nine this morning I assisted him to drink a dish of tea as he sat in his chair, & a few minutes after he expir'd in one single sigh. He had no pulse this morning, gasp'd for every breath, yet after thanking his wife for all her goodness to him,

& telling her he knew he was dying, & believ'd he should go off in a slumber he still talk'd of coming down to take breakfast with the family which was scarcely out of his mouth before the lamp of life went out, merely thro' the want of a single drop of oil to sustain it another moment.[42]

Although her husband's death had been expected, Catherine was grief-stricken and her weeks of almost uninterrupted nursing had left her exhausted and ill. With care, however, she recovered her strength so well that she outlived all her brothers and sisters, dying at last in 1804 at the age of seventy-eight.

Sally's brother had died in 1774 at the comparatively early age of forty-two, and her father, Richard Wedgwood, one year younger than the century, died eight years later.[43] He had been failing for at least two years, had given up all meat and alcohol, and required almost constant attention.[44] With his death came the final substantial accretion of wealth to Sally, and thus to Josiah.

Throughout these years of toil, anxiety, frequent bereavement and grief, Josiah relied for comfort, advice and practical help on two unfailing supports: Sally and Bentley. When Sally became ill, and especially when she miscarried, he was distracted.[45] When, as happened with remarkable infrequency, his friendship with Bentley was soured, however temporarily, by disagreement, he felt himself disabled. Although he gave an unusual amount of thought to his own health and the possibilities of his death, he seems scarcely to have considered the shocking possibility that he might survive either of those whom he most loved and whom he considered to be his life partners.

CHAPTER FOURTEEN

Lunatics and
Other Enlightened Friends

A side from members of his own family and Bentley, Josiah's closest friends were men who shared his passion for enquiry, experiment and invention. All were members of the Lunar Society[1] of Birmingham.

Known agreeably as 'Lunatics', members of the Society met once a month at or near full moon to ensure sufficient light for members returning home after their deliberations. Meetings were held in members' houses, or occasionally at a Birmingham hotel, where they also dined, and seem to have taken the loose form of unsystematic exposition, demonstration and discussion to which suitable visitors might be invited. No minutes were kept or proceedings published and the only reliable evidence of the meetings, fragmentary as it is, appears in the remarkable number of surviving letters and memoirs of the members and their families.

One of them, Richard Lovell Edgeworth, with whom Josiah corresponded regularly, accurately described the difference between the Lunar Society and the many other literary, philosophical and scientific societies that flourished in both London and the provinces during the latter part of the eighteenth century:

A society of literary men and a literary society may be very different. In the one, men give the results of their serious researches and detail their deliberate thoughts; in the other, the first hints of discoveries, the current observations, and the mutual collision of ideas are of important utility. The knowledge of each member of such a society becomes in time disseminated among the whole body, and a certain esprit du corps, uncontaminated with jealousy, in some degree combines the talents of members to forward the views of a single person.[2]

The Lunar circle, as it was known when it was founded in 1765, was a select group, consisting of no more than fourteen members in its twenty-five years or so of existence. It developed slowly from the friendship which sprang up between Matthew Boulton and Erasmus Darwin, after the latter's arrival in Lichfield in November 1756. Darwin soon became physician to Luke Robinson, a wealthy local merchant, whose daughter Mary was Boulton's first wife.* An early acquaintance of both men was the Derby clockmaker and instrument-maker, John Whitehurst. Unlike Darwin, who had been educated at Cambridge and Edinburgh universities, Boulton and Whitehurst had little formal education, but both were possessed of engaging personalities as well as a thirst for knowledge and a natural gift for invention. The three were united by scientific curiosity. In May 1765, their triangle was squared by the arrival in Birmingham of Dr William Small.

William Small came from London and brought with him a letter of introduction from Benjamin Franklin, whom Boulton, Whitehurst and probably Darwin had met in 1758. Educated at Marischal College, Aberdeen, Small had been appointed Professor of Natural Philosophy at the College of William and Mary at Williamsburg. One of his pupils was Thomas Jefferson, who later wrote of him as 'a man profound in most of the useful branches of science, with a happy talent of communication, correct and gentlemanly manners, & an enlarged & Liberal mind'.[3] Although Small's abilities as a teacher and also as an organiser of courses are well documented, he was neither happy nor healthy at Williamsburg. In 1764 he returned to England, and in spite of a number of tempting offers in London, he was persuaded by Boulton, to whom he had been introduced by Franklin, to settle in Birmingham. There he came to know Boulton's partner, James Watt, and their correspondence ranged extensively over such subjects as steam-engines, barometers, microscopes and telescopes. He had obtained, on recommendation, an MD degree from Aberdeen and soon displaced Darwin as Boulton's doctor. Otherwise unmoved by the loss of an important patient, Darwin wrote cheerfully of him as, 'our ingenious friend Dr Small', in a letter to Boulton in March 1766, generously praising his originality of mind.[4] Never dedicated to his profession, Small became the axle of the Lunar Society.

A fifth member arrived in 1766 when Richard Lovell Edgeworth came to Lichfield with the intention of discussing with him Darwin's design for a carriage which, he had proved, was able to execute tight

*Like Edgeworth, Boulton, after the death of his wife, illegally married her sister.

turns without overturning. Their meeting was dramatic. Darwin being out when Edgeworth arrived, he was entertained by Mrs Darwin until a loud knocking on the door and commotion in the hall announced the return of her husband, apparently carrying the body of a dead man. He was not, however, dead but only dead drunk. Darwin had found him lying 'nearly suffocated' in a ditch, had him lifted into his carriage, and brought him home to care for him for the night. He was not less surprised than his wife when, candles being brought, it was discovered that the object of his attentions, whose life he had probably saved, was his wife's brother, Charles, 'for the first time in his life', Edgeworth was hastily assured, 'intoxicated in this manner'.[5]

Edgeworth describes Erasmus Darwin at the age of thirty-five: 'a large man, fat, and rather clumsy: but intelligence and benevolence were painted on his countenance: he had a considerable impediment in his speech, a defect which is in general painful to others; but the Doctor repaid his auditors so well for making them wait for his wit or his knowledge that he seldom found them impatient'.[6] Edgeworth was impressed by Darwin and entertained his host and hostess with some conjuring tricks that he had recently perfected. For his part, Darwin was delighted with his new 'mechanical friend', whom he described to Boulton as 'the greatest Conjuror I ever saw', adding in astonishment: 'He has the principles of Nature in his palm, and moulds them as He pleases. Can take away polarity or give it to the Needle by rubbing it thrice on the palm of his Hand. And can see through two solid Oak Boards without Glasses! wonderful! astonishing! diabolical!!!!' He urged Boulton to bring his wife and Dr Small to meet his remarkable guest.[7]

He introduced Edgeworth also to Anna Seward, the poetess later to be apostrophised as 'the Swan of Lichfield' but then just twenty-three and at the height of her beauty. She remembered that 'His addresses were gracefully spirited, and his conversation eloquent. He danced, fenced and winged his arrows with more than philosophical skill.'[8]

Born at Bath, Edgeworth was educated partly in England and partly in Ireland before entering Trinity College, Dublin, at the age of sixteen. He was hastily removed after six months, probably on account of his overdeveloped appetite for women, and transferred to Corpus Christi College, Oxford, where he was prudently housed in the town with a landlord of impeccable dullness. Edgeworth responded by eloping with the daughter, who became the first of his four wives and bore him the first of his twenty-two children, the novelist Maria Edgeworth. The Oxford landlord was Paul Elers, later to besiege Wedgwood with impracticable ideas and demands for free portrait medallions.

Edgeworth's talents went far beyond amateur conjuring. He had read both law and science at university and had a natural mechanical aptitude which led to his lifelong fascination with vehicles and their construction. In 1767, at the age of twenty-three, he designed a machine for land measurement which won him a silver medal from the Society of Arts and a mechanical telegraph which predated by a quarter of a century the work of Claude Chappe. His later work included the forerunner of the tracked vehicle, a conveyor belt for moving heavy loads, a hygrometer and an anemometer. Ideas flowed from him. The heir to wealth and property, Edgeworth was insufficiently motivated by profit to make the best of his inventions and his most important contribution was in education. Two of his books, *Practical Education*, written with his novelist daughter Maria and published in 1798, and *Professional Education*, which followed ten years later, are among the most influential in the literature of the subject. Darwin, who had first thought that his visitor was nothing more than an amateur carriage-maker, was agreeably surprised to find that he had invited to his house an educated man and an inventor. Edgeworth, with his gaiety, his friendliness, his open approach to invention and discussion, was a natural recruit to the Lunar circle.

It was, perhaps inevitably, through Edgeworth, the most eccentric of the Lunatics, that the least likely member was introduced. Thomas Day appears to have had few, if any, of the qualifications shared by the others. Although richer than most of them, he was deliberately unkempt and notoriously rude. He was no scientist and so ignorant of 'mechanicks' that, when Edgeworth introduced him to Darwin and Whitehurst, he was unable to add a word to the conversation for several hours. But when the conversation turned to other subjects, he 'displayed so much knowledge, feeling and eloquence as to captivate the Doctor entirely. He invited Mr Day to Lichfield, an invitation which led not only to intimacy, but to a very sincere friendship.'[9]

Edgeworth described his friendship with Day as 'founded upon mutual esteem, between persons of taste, habits, pursuits, manners, and connexions totally different'.[10] Their estates at Hare Hatch and Barehill, in Berkshire, were not far apart and, after their first meeting in 1766, scarcely a day passed, when both were at home, without their spending several hours together. There is little in Day's writings, the most famous of which were vapid and platitudinous stories for children, probably more popular with parents than youthful readers, to suggest that he was not didactic, sententious, pompous and priggish. And yet he enjoyed the friendship of Darwin, Small and Wedgwood, and Edgeworth wrote of him: 'I never was acquainted with any man who in conversation reasoned so profoundly and so logically, or who stated his arguments with so much eloquence.'[11] Of all his friendships, the closest was with the modest, unassuming William Small. The secret of his appeal to men who might otherwise have found his company irksome lay in the seriousness and intelligence of his conversation, his reforming zeal, his courage in declaring unpopular opinions and pursuing an unconventional course when he believed in it, and his generosity. The last virtue would have appealed especially to Boulton, Small and James Keir, to each of whom he lent money.

Captain James Keir was introduced to the circle in 1767. Born in Stirlingshire, he had been acquainted with Darwin when they were both students of medicine at Edinburgh. Keir did not graduate but, instead, joined the army and was commissioned in the 61st Foot (the South Gloucestershire Regiment), seeing active service in the West Indies during the Seven Years War and later being posted to Ireland. After eleven years as a soldier, he resigned his commission in 1768 and returned to the study of chemistry.

Keir visited the Wedgwood factory in 1767, introduced by Darwin as 'an old Friend of mine, a successful cultivator of both Arts and Arms', who hoped also to meet at Josiah's house 'our common Friend, the Philosopher, Mr Whitehurst'.[12] Apart from removing himself at the earliest moment from a profession in which his enthusiasm for learning was not shared by many of his fellow officers, Keir's immediate ambition was to set himself up as a manufacturer of synthetic alkali. The natural sources of alkali, principally wood and vegetable ashes, were no longer sufficient to satisfy the increasing demand from manufacturers of glass, soap, bleaches and fertilisers. Keir's outstanding abilities were immediately recognised and he was welcomed into the Lunar circle. He was introduced to James Watt, who described him as 'a mighty chemist before the Lord and a very agreeable man'.[13]

There was, however, a practical problem of competition to be overcome. Keir had confided the progress of his researches into the chemical production of alkalis to William Small, who was privy also to experimental work on similar lines already conducted by James Watt in co-operation with Joseph Black* and Dr John Roebuck.† To avoid a clash of interests which might leave him open to accusations of a breach of

*Scottish chemist and physicist, professor of anatomy and chemistry at Glasgow 1756–66; professor of medicine and chemistry at Edinburgh 1766–97. His portrait medallion was produced by Wedgwood after a model by James Tassie dated 1788.
†Inventor; established a factory at Prestonpans for the manufacture of sulphuric acid and formed the Carron company in Stirlingshire for the production of iron and subsequently of ordnance.

confidence, Small hastily warned both parties that they were on parallel courses and suggested that they should form a partnership. According to Watt, Joseph Black applied for and was granted a patent for the process of obtaining synthetic alkali from common salt and lime, but no such patent was registered and, sixteen months later, Keir obtained a formal prohibition against the granting of any patent for this process without prior notice.[14]

The evidence is incomplete, but it appears that Keir did not then join in partnership with Watt and Roebuck,[15] and the process, which yielded synthetic alkali in quantities too small to be profitable, was temporarily shelved. It was to be revived in 1780, when war interrupted supplies from America.

Meanwhile, Keir, who had already established his credentials in print by translating and publishing Pierre Joseph Macquer's massive *Dictionary of Chemistry*, a work, according to Edgeworth, 'made doubly valuable by the notes of the translator',[16] turned his attention to the manufacture of glass, becoming a partner in a Stourbridge firm. Small happily employed his time in writing to his friends to solicit orders for him.

Watt had been introduced to the Lunar circle about a year before Keir. The son of a Scottish ship's chandler, James Watt was born in Greenock, where he was educated. His early interest in mathematics, possibly an aptitude inherited from his Watt grandfather, who was a teacher in the subject, led him to train under John Morgan of Cornhill, London, as a maker of mathematical instruments, and, at the age of twenty-one, he was appointed mathematical instrument-maker to the College of Glasgow. There he made the acquaintance of Joseph Black, who was working on his discovery of the principles of Latent Heat, and who encouraged Watt's early experiments on the use of steam. In 1765 Watt invented the separate condenser, the crucial improvement to Thomas Newcomen's engine which enabled him to construct his own improved steam-engine. Two years later, at the suggestion of Black, he went into partnership with John Roebuck and in 1769 he patented his engine. After Roebuck's financial collapse following the bank crisis in 1772, his share of the partnership was bought by Matthew Boulton.

Watt's first appearance among the Lunatics, however, dates from 1767, when he was entertained in Birmingham by Darwin and Small and visited Boulton's Soho Works, which impressed him as the ideal factory for his new engines. He discussed this possibility with Darwin and Small, though not with Boulton who was absent during his visit. For the next seven years, until he settled in Birmingham, Watt maintained a steady correspondence with Small and Darwin, both of whom encouraged him to move to Birmingham and to make his machines there. Small offered to contribute to any partnership that might be set up and he assured Watt of Boulton's intention to have a part in the project.

In the summer of 1768 Watt paid a second visit to Soho, this time to meet Boulton and to discuss with him the possibility of forming a partnership in which the two of them would be joined by Small and Roebuck. Roebuck was prepared to offer Boulton rights to production of the machines for the three counties most convenient to Soho – Warwick, Derbyshire and Staffordshire – but Boulton did not consider the cost worthwhile. He wanted, instead, to build a new factory close to Soho, where he would 'erect all the conveniences necessary for the completion of engines, and from which manufactory we would serve all the world with engines'.[17] Negotiations continued until the end of November, when it was finally agreed that, as soon as experimental work on the engine was satisfactorily completed, one-third of the rights should be sold to Boulton and Small. The price was left to the parties to agree in twelve months' time but it was not to fall short of £1000.

Although it was already patented and he had made a working model, Watt's engine was far from ready for production. Three years passed while Roebuck, whose financial affairs were rapidly deteriorating, pressed for results. Boulton, on the other hand, had done a considerable amount of work on a steam-engine of his own, which, until he heard of Watt's patent, he had intended to manufacture himself. He was therefore less impatient of delays which he understood to be in the nature of developing any invention. He and Small also appreciated Watt's need to earn a living from other engineering work while his invention was perfected. Boulton's patience was rewarded when Roebuck's creditors obliged him, in May 1773, to release his share of the rights to Boulton in return for the renunciation of Roebuck's outstanding debts to the Boulton & Fothergill partnership. The following year Watt moved to Birmingham, the partnership of Boulton & Watt was cemented and the engine was completed. In 1775 the patent was extended to the end of the century. Of the extraordinary number of valuable, interesting, peculiar or extravagant inventions which flowed from members of the Lunar circle during its brief existence, none was of greater consequence.

John Whitehurst's wide scientific interests and his friendship with both Erasmus Darwin and Matthew Boulton immediately qualified him to be one of the founding members of the Lunar circle. His connection with Boulton was especially strong for it was he who had first drawn Boulton's attention to the decorative fluorite known as 'Blue John', mined in Derbyshire, which was extensively used at Soho for ormolu-mounted vases, and he also supplied many clocks, of his own design, for which Boulton made the decorative ormolu cases. Whitehurst's work as a geologist had made him the senior authority on the rocks and earths of Derbyshire, which were of particular interest to Wedgwood, and by February 1767 they were corresponding regularly and exchanging information. Whitehurst 'set his miners to work and put by . . . samples of Earths and Clays' for Wedgwood, who in return furnished him with 'all the curious productions, or facts' he acquired during the cutting of the canal at Etruria. Later in the year he spent a week with Wedgwood at Burslem and Etruria and in April 1769 a kiln was built at the new factory to Whitehurst's design.[18]

At this time Whitehurst was already working on his *Inquiry into the Original State and Formation of the Earth*, published in 1778. Josiah subscribed to two copies and, as he told Bentley, would have ordered more but for having no friends interested in the subject who were not also friends of Whitehurst's and likely to obtain their copies direct from him. 'Philosopher John', as Josiah dubbed him, was a guest at Etruria soon after the publication of his book. Having read it 'to the appendix', Josiah pronounced himself 'very much pleas'd & edified' but he was convinced that he saw in it 'as many alterations since its first formation by the *free philosopher* of Derby, as his world has suffered by earthquakes & inundations' and he was highly critical of Whitehurst's 'labour'd & repeated efforts' to justify 'against all infidels and gainsayers the truth & inspiration of the mosaic account of the creation, the flood & its various effects'. He detailed to Bentley other criticisms, which he wished to discuss with him and admitted that he would 'like to tumble a little of his [Whitehurst's] world about his ears, but am afraid it would hurt him, & shall forbear, for I love the man, though I have some objections to the manufacturing of his world'.[19]

Whitehurst's later work included investigations into heat, the medical use of electricity, ventilation, the construction of chimneys and garden stoves, and a design of a water-closet. Like other members of the circle, Edgeworth and Darwin in particular, his interests were varied.

Wedgwood's membership of this exclusive circle is unproved. On the negative evidence of Joseph Priestley, who, in spite of earlier connections with the circle and most of its members, did not join until 1780, when it had become formalised as a society, Eliza Meteyard decided that Wedgwood was never a member of the circle but 'was occasionally present at its meetings and probably contributed at intervals subjects for discussion'. Not unreasonably, considering Josiah's almost total preoccupation with his business and the exceptional discomfort he suffered in travel, she concluded that 'Etruria and Birmingham were too distant for any regular attendance'.[20] As proof of this, she quotes Priestley's statement:

> [In Birmingham] I had . . . the society of persons eminent for their knowledge of chemistry, particularly Mr Watt, Mr Keir, and Dr Withering. These, with Mr Boulton and Dr Darwin . . . Mr Galton, and afterwards Mr Johnson, of Kenilworth, and myself, dined together every month, calling ourselves the *lunar society* . . . [21]

The omission of Wedgwood's name is notable and Meteyard's assertion was generally unquestioned for nearly a century. It appears to be supported by James Watt's invitation to Josiah to attend one of the dinners of the society.[22] Edgeworth, however, states plainly that 'Dr Small formed a link which combined Mr Boulton, Mr Watt, Dr Darwin, Mr Wedgwood, Mr Day, and myself, together',[23] and it is hard to believe that his reference could be to any but the Lunar circle. Robert Schofield and Desmond King-Hele[24] are among those who state categorically that Wedgwood was a member of the Lunar circle, but neither cites documentary evidence to sustain his certainty. While it is clear from his own letters and from those of Darwin and Edgeworth that Wedgwood was on cordial terms with most of the members, the Lunar Society is not mentioned by name in any of Wedgwood's letters to Bentley and satisfactory proof of his membership seems to be lacking. Meteyard's objections are logical and it is entirely possible that Josiah, though always a welcome guest and perhaps counted a member of the informal circle, was never formally a member of the Society.

The event which persuaded the members of the circle to formalise their association and combine as a regular society was the death of William Small in February 1775. He had selflessly provided the other eight 'Birmingham philosophers', as Darwin called them, with a confidential clearing-house for their ideas, acting as unpaid secretary to the circle while offering self-effacing and sympathetic advice and enthusiastic help where it was needed. While he lived there had been no need for the restraints of regulation.

Small's death, at the age of forty-one, was a sad loss. His own considerable talents were subordinated to the needs of his friends but his breadth of knowledge and curiosity enabled him to discuss with them in detail an extraordinarily wide range of projects from barometers to steam-engines and from telescopes to synthetic alkali. He was both respected and loved by the Lunatics. Day and Darwin wrote elegiac verses to his memory. Keir described him as 'a gentleman of very uncommon merit . . . who to the most extensive, various, and accurate knowledge in the sciences, in literature, and in life, joined engaging manners, a most exact conduct, a liberality of sentiment, and an enlightened humanity'.[25] Boulton wrote that 'His virtues were more and his foibles fewer (for vices he had none) than in any man I ever knew.' He was so grieved that he told Watt, 'If there were not a few other objects yet remaining for me to settle my affections upon, I should wish also to take up my lodgings in the mansions of the dead; and those objects I am fearful of diminishing.'[26] Watt replied robustly with 'sentiments which that dear friend we lament expressed to me upon a similar occasion. It is our duty as soon as possible to drive from our minds every idea that gives us pain, particularly . . . where our grief can avail us nothing. Remember, my dear Sir, that our friend enjoys that repose he so much desired; and we ought not to be so selfish as to render ourselves unhappy by the perpetual recollection of our own misfortune, however great we may think it, for it is also irreparable and was inevitable.' He advised Boulton to immerse himself in his business and not to 'add to the griefs of your friends'.[27]

There were two more losses to the Lunar circle at this time, neither of them total but both reducing the number of members who could be counted upon regularly to attend meetings. John Whitehurst was appointed to the newly created position of 'Stamper of the Money Weights'* and moved to London. He was, however, a frequent visitor to Birmingham and succeeded in maintaining his association with Lunar members as well as attending occasional meetings and supplying many of his friends with standard weights.

Thomas Day, too, had left to live in London, where he had resumed his law studies. He was called to the Bar, apparently without any intention of practising, and dabbled with the writing of verse. He also took a wife, having previously subjected her to a written examination of her knowledge of philosophy and education. Prior to this eccentric exercise he had unsuccessfully courted, in turn, Honora Sneyd and her sister Elizabeth, who had subsequently become the second and (illegally) the third wives of Richard Lovell Edgeworth. Even more unconventionally, he had, by way of an educational experiment to be based on the ideas expressed in Rousseau's *Emile*, adopted two foundling girls, aged eleven and twelve, who came to live with him until one of them should be considered suitably groomed and educated to be his

---

*To supervise and regulate the standard of gold coin issued by the Mint. When the Mint was moved from the Tower of London to Tower Hill in 1811, to take advantage of steam power, Boulton & Watt were responsible for its installation.

wife. This extraordinary domestic *ménage* appears to have been accepted in Lichfield for as long as it lasted, which was until Day decided that the experiment had failed, pensioned the girls off and transferred his attentions to the Sneyd sisters.

With his severely tested wife, Day settled in Essex. Josiah wrote to Bentley to thank him for the news of Day's marriage and added perceptively, 'I hope he will contrive to be happy, & make his lady so. They are good people & I hope will not sacrifice real solid happiness to whim & caprice.'[28]

Darwin took almost immediate steps to fill Small's place in the Lunar circle. His choice was William Withering, a young doctor working at the Infirmary in Stafford. Like Darwin, whom he had known for about ten years, he had studied for his MD degree at Edinburgh and, when Darwin wrote to suggest that he should take over Small's Birmingham practice, Withering was completing a book of British botany, the first edition of which was published in 1776. Small's practice was worth about £600 a year, without undue exertion, and as Darwin described it, 'chiefly in the town, without the Expense and Fatigue of Travelling and horsekeeping, and without being troubled with visiting the people'. He thought it a 'very eligible situation'.[29] Evidently Withering agreed with him for he accepted it at once.

In one respect Darwin's choice, which appears to have been made without discussion with other members and unquestioned by them at the time, was shrewd. Withering's interest in botany and chemistry made him immediately acceptable, and as a physician he was soon to be ranked with Darwin among the most respected medical figures in provincial practice. His personality, however, was less attractive and he quickly found grounds for a quarrel with the well-intentioned but often clumsy Darwin. Withering's book, based on the Linnean* system and his own extensive collection of botanical specimens, was nearing completion, but he had not decided upon a title for it. Darwin, with typical insensitivity, wrote to insist upon a short title, easily remembered and distinguished from the work of previous authors, and declared that this could be easily settled when they next met at Boulton's 'with the assistance of Mr Keir & Mr Watt'.[30] Withering was not unnaturally irritated by this unsolicited assumption of authority and deliberately ignored the advice. He chose, instead, a title of bewildering density which fills twenty-four lines of the title-page.

*Carolus Linnaeus (Carl von Linné, 1707–78), the Swedish botanist and natural historian, introduced a system of classification which defined genera and species and the systematic naming of plants according to their nature. Wedgwood's portrait medallion of him was modelled by John Flaxman junior in 1775.

Although it was criticised at the time for being little more than a translation from Linnaeus, edited to include only those plants indigenous to Britain, Withering's *A Botanical Arrangement of all the Vegetables naturally growing in Great Britain . . .* was a substantial work, greatly improved in later editions, and certainly the most complete 'British Flora' then available. Darwin, no doubt stunned by the enormity of the title, was no less dismayed by Withering's bowdlerisation of all the sexual terms so that the book might safely be read by women. Darwin detested all such prevarication and use of euphemism and deplored the prim substitutions of 'chive' and 'pointal' for stamen and pistil. This was probably the beginning of a private rift between the two men which widened, ten years later, into a public quarrel.

Their relationship was not improved by competition. Boulton had already formed a collection of plants, Wedgwood was interested in plants and collected shells, both of which he used frequently as sources for decoration and ornament, and Edgeworth had wickedly mocked the subject with records of the quantity of bats' dung recovered from a grotto in France.[31] Now Darwin embarked on the study of botany, planting a garden and making his own collection, and soon afterwards beginning his immense two-part poem, *The Botanic Garden*, published in 1789 and 1791.

Withering was not so much disagreeable as withdrawn, shy and quick to take offence. Mary Anne Schimmelpenninck, the daughter of a Lunar Society member and herself a 'Demon of mischief-making', remembered him as a kind man, but she added, 'his great accuracy and caution rendered him less open, and it had neither the wide popularity of Mr Boulton's, nor the attraction of Mr Watt's true modesty'.[32]

It was clear that Withering was no replacement for Small and there was some anxiety that the Lunar circle would decay for want of a motivating force at the centre. With the proposals made by Boulton for 'new laws and regulations such as will tend to prevent the decline of a Society which I hope will be lasting',[33] the circle was accorded a new formality and status which helped to preserve it for a further fifteen years.

The new members who joined during that period were Dr Joseph Priestley, Samuel Galton junior, Jonathan Stokes and the Reverend Robert Augustus Johnson. By far the most distinguished of them was Priestley, and with his arrival the newly constituted Society reached new levels of invention and productivity.

Born in Yorkshire in 1733 into a family of Calvinist dissenters, Joseph Priestley was educated for the ministry in the dissenting Church. His formal studies of Latin and Hebrew, with some Greek and Arabic, augmented by his own application to mathematics and philosophy, were interrupted by illness, which he turned to advantage by studying French, German and Italian, and in 1751 he was enrolled at Daventry Academy. Seven years later, after a year in Suffolk, he was appointed minister at Nantwich, in Cheshire, and in 1761 he accepted an invitation to teach languages and *belles-lettres* at Warrington, soon to become one of the most celebrated dissenting academies in Britain. During the next six years he delivered lectures there on rhetoric, languages, *belles-lettres*, history and anatomy. He was elected Fellow of the Royal Society in 1766 and, the following year, when he also moved to Leeds as minister of Mill Hill chapel, he published his first important book, *The History and Present State of Electricity*. This book, and the experiments described in it, gained him the admiration of Benjamin Franklin and a nomination for the Royal Society's Copley Medal. It brought him recognition throughout Europe and its favourable reception persuaded him to begin a history of optics, the first in the English language, which was published in 1771. The subscribers included Wedgwood, Bentley and Franklin.

In Leeds, Priestley began also his most important work on pneumatic chemistry and photosynthesis, leading to the announcements of his discoveries of oxygen, nitrogen, sulphuretted hydrogen, sulphur dioxide, ammonia and nitrogen peroxide. If Watt's steam-engine was the most notable invention by any Lunar Society member, Priestley's were the superlative discoveries. While he was in the midst of this work, he received an offer from Lord Shelburne to employ him as his librarian and as tutor to his son. The duties were not arduous and the post was designed to allow plenty of opportunity for Priestley to continue his experimental work. During his first year with Shelburne, he accompanied him to France, where he met Lavoisier and was personally exposed, for the first time, to the new French school of chemistry to whose methods and findings he was later so opposed.

Priestley's work was known to Wedgwood as early as March 1767, when Bentley informed him of experiments that Priestley had made in the use of electricity in gilding, and it is clear that he was Bentley's friend for some years before he became Wedgwood's. In October 1772 Josiah wrote: 'I am glad to hear of Dr Priestley's noble appointment, taking it for granted that he is to go on writing & publishing *with the same freedom* as he now does, otherwise I had much rather he still remain'd in Yorkshire. I rejoice too on your account, as you will have one more of your friends within your reach, to enjoy & Converse with occasionally.'[34]

For six years Priestley lived at Calne, near the Shelburne estate of

Bowood, in Wiltshire. His report on the purification of water, completed while he was there, drew from Wedgwood a sprightly comment for Bentley's amusement; 'the ingenious & indefatiguable Doctor is to *make water* for all the Navy. An Arduous task – & I heartily wish his powers may be adequate to the employment.'[35] When he left, for reasons which are not certain but which may have had something to do with his published views on artificial social distinctions and the moral disadvantages of aristocracy, and even more with the almost hectoring tone of his dedication of *A course of lectures on oratory and criticism* to Shelburne's heir in 1777, Priestley settled in Birmingham. The Lunar Society gained one of the most distinguished scientists in Britain.

As soon as he heard of his move to Birmingham, Wedgwood offered to subscribe to the fund planned for the support of Priestley and his family so that he might give all his time to scientific research:

> I need not say to you how much I am rejoiced to hear of the liberal plan adopting by his friends in order to place the Doctor's mind in the situation it is best suited to, & best for us all that it should be in – nor that I shall be happy in having an opportunity of throwing in my mite, nay I shall think myself highly honor'd in being permitted to unite with this illustrious band.[36]

Nothing came of this proposal, probably because Priestley was unwilling to give up his religious work, which during the next ten years included preaching, the instruction of children and the publication of more than thirty volumes of sermons, religious history and theology, but it was revived in 1782, partly to pay for essential equipment for his laboratory.

Wedgwood had considered the possibility of making crucibles as early as 1762, when he had consulted Dr Matthew Turner* on the subject,[37] but he seems to have taken no further action for about fifteen years, and it is likely that his interest in the manufacture of chemical apparatus was reawakened by his reading of Priestley's *Experiments and Observations on different kinds of Air*, published between 1774 and 1777. Wedgwood read this with close attention, making copious notes in his Commonplace Book and adding comments of his own. As he observed, 'The Dr seems much at a loss for a mortar, not metal, for pounding in. Make him a deep one or two.'[38] Priestley's difficulty was a common one among chemists and apothecaries. Bell-metal mortars, imported from Holland or Italy, had been in use in England for at least 400 years,

*See page 31.

but the danger of poisoning from small particles of metal flaking into the substance being prepared had led to a search for safer alternatives. Marble mortars, suitable for dry mixtures, were not impervious to oil and were attacked by acid. By the end of March 1779, Josiah had developed a composition which appeared to be satisfactory and he was ready to send Bentley the first examples of Wedgwood & Bentley mortars and pestles.

Some difficulty was experienced with the new mortar body but the problems of composition and firing were soon overcome and it was not long before Wedgwood was able to make several sizes and shapes, including a triturating mortar, intended for mechanical operation, to a design supplied by James Watt, and he soon added other chemical wares such as retorts, crucible cups and pharmacy cups. It was his policy not to make any charge for chemical wares ordered for experimental work and he supplied them free to scientists, including Priestley. Indeed, in his last catalogue, issued in 1787, Wedgwood described the 'compact hard porcelain' of which his chemical wares were made as 'excellently adapted also for evaporating pans, digesting vessels, basons, filtering funnels, syphons, tubes, such as Dr Priestley uses in some of his experiments . . . retorts and many other vessels for chemical uses, which I have made for my friends . . . with some variations in the composition itself, according to the views for which they are wanted'.[39]

Priestley was a man of radical, even revolutionary, opinions, outspoken and uncompromising, who was both a rationalist and a Christian, a scientist who was also a theologian and who considered the two activities as not merely compatible but almost indivisible. He was, however, in spite of the reputation that has endured, foremost a theologian, but one whose insistence on rational analysis of nature and scripture was intended to demonstrate 'the *reasonableness and truth* of Christianity',[40] a direct echo of Locke. Of all the members of the Lunar Society, Priestley was most clearly a part of the movement known as the Enlightenment. There was no contradiction in his beliefs. Dissenters, like most *philosophes* and even the Church of England, had adopted Newton and Locke. As Roy Porter has observed, 'The simple fact is that Enlightenment goals – like criticism, sensibility or faith in progress – throve in England *within* piety. There was no need to overthrow religion itself because here was no pope, no inquisition, no Jesuits, no monopolistic priesthood with a stranglehold on children through education and on families through confession.'[41] It was in the end the unity of his beliefs that cost Priestley his house, his library and almost his life.

Beside the intellectual stature of Priestley, Galton and Stokes are dwarfed and Johnson is insignificant. Samuel Galton, the son of a Quaker gunsmith and banker of the same name, attended Warrington Academy from 1768, just too late to benefit from Priestley's teaching, before being employed in his father's firm. He quickly became manager of his family's gun foundry and substantially increased the considerable private capital made over to him when he reached his majority. In his early twenties he began to study science, attending Adam Walker's* lectures in Birmingham in 1776 and 1781 and forming a small private collection of scientific instruments. His own work in this field was of no lasting value and his name is remembered only in connection with the Lunar Society and two of his family: his daughter Mary Anne Schimmelpenninck; and his grandson, Sir Francis Galton,[†] founder of the science of eugenics. Mary Anne's name would no longer be in any way notable but for her memoirs, written at the age of seventy-five. Grossly inaccurate as her memory can be shown to have been, and maliciously inventive as she undoubtedly was, her memoirs contain unique contemporary accounts of Lunar Society meetings. Used with necessary caution, they provide valuable information about the 'little society of gifted men', the 'intellectual galaxy' of which her father was one of the least distinguished members.[42]

Dr Jonathan Stokes, a young friend and protégé of Withering's, took his medical degree at Edinburgh. He had a useful knowledge of pneumatic chemistry and zoology and a passion for orderly classification, which he applied successfully to his studies of botany and less happily to earths and metals. Although he achieved some reputation as a botanist and corresponded with many of the leading scientists of his day – including Keir, Priestley and Darwin before he was known to them as a fellow Lunatic – his principal contribution to the Society was probably the assistance he gave to Withering until violent quarrels with him and with Darwin put an end to their association and to his membership. He was described by the venomous Mary Anne as 'profoundly scientific and eminently absent'.[43]

The reason for Robert Augustus Johnson's membership is even harder to deduce. A soldier, who appears to have spent his brief professional career on exceptionally inactive service (he remained in England when his regiment was posted to Minorca), he married, while an almost penniless lieutenant, the widowed sister of Lord Craven, a

---

*Self-educated inventor and travelling lecturer in science, employed variously at Eton and Winchester.
†Third son of Samuel Tertius Galton and Frances Anne Violetta Darwin (eldest daughter of Erasmus Darwin by his second wife, Elizabeth Pole).

circumstance which so enraged the Earl that he swore never to speak to her again. Lady Craven later described Johnson as 'a mild and good man, but entirely governed by his wife'.[44] During the next fifteen years he fathered eight children but this could scarcely be considered a sufficient qualification for membership of the Lunar Society in 1787, or for election to the Royal Society, of which he became a Fellow in the following year. James Keir nevertheless wrote of him to Priestley as 'our ingenious philosophical friend',[45] and his certificate of nomination to the Royal Society describes him as 'well versed in chemistry and other branches of Experimental philosophy'. There is no surviving record of how or when he acquired such knowledge, or indeed of the extent of it, and his election to both learned societies remains a mystery.

Such aberrations aside, the Lunar Society was, as Mary Anne remembered it, an 'intellectual galaxy', and it maintained connections, through correspondence and invitations to its meetings, with the brightest stars of other galaxies. Benjamin Franklin, Sir William Herschel, Sir Joseph Banks and Dr Daniel Solander were among the many distinguished guests. Every one of the Lunar Society members but Small, Day and Stokes, all of whom were better qualified than Robert Augustus Johnson, was a Fellow of the Royal Society and therefore in regular contact with other Fellows pursuing similar avenues of research. The Lunar Society was not only a gathering of remarkable intellectual quality, a centre for the concentration and collision of ideas and a power house of invention, much of it applied to industrial development: it was also an assembly of some of the leading provincial figures of the British Enlightenment.

Although historians are far from unanimous in their definition and interpretation of the Enlightenment, it is widely agreed to have been one of the three great watersheds in Western thought since the rise of Christianity, which most evidently influenced the development of modern society. But, while the Renaissance and the Reformation were still concerned with man's fate in the next world, the Enlightenment focused on the quality of his life on earth; while the Renaissance and the Reformation were contained in Europe and left Russia and American untouched, the Enlightenment was geographically widespread and embraced both. Whether it is considered as a spring which had its source in England, in empiricism and pragmatism fathered by Bacon, Newton and Locke; or as a French development of Cartesian ideas, most easily identified in the work of the *philosophes*; or that its most admirable expression is to be found in Germany, in work stretching from Leibnitz to Kant, the essential conviction, however greatly altered in national practice, was that human understanding was capable of comprehending the universe and that such comprehension would enable man to master it. Essentially, empiricism deriving from scientific experiment and observation, and rationalism expounded most cogently by Descartes, led in the same direction: towards a concept of the world which was no longer centred upon God but which existed for, and could be mastered by, man. But, with few notable exceptions, Enlighteners refused to follow the example of Descartes and discard God altogether in favour of reason. Although sometimes anti-clerical, the movement was seldom anti-religious or predominantly anti-Christian; but religion was subjected to scrutiny, and superstition and metaphysics were objects of suspicion and scepticism. It was precisely this rationalism and search for scientific explanations that informed the proceedings of the Lunar Society and the activities of its members.

With scarcely an exception, the Lunatics were enthusiastic Enlighteners, and the manufacturers among them, notably Wedgwood and Watt, were not alone in applying their principles to the progress of industry. Wedgwood's endless chemical experiments, Watt's steam-engine, Edgeworth's and Darwin's improvements to carriage design, Darwin's horizontal windmill and Whitehurst's clocks, the last of which provided time-clocks for factories as well as movements for Boulton's ormolu cases – all were more or less successful attempts to advance local industries. Wedgwood, Darwin and Boulton, in particular, were active in the promotion and financing of canals. Keir developed the chemical production of synthetic raw materials.

Lunar Society members interested themselves in social and industrial improvement, in education, factory conditions and training, workers' housing, medical research and treatment. The British Enlightenment principles of humanitarianism and utilitarianism, of self-improvement and progress through scientific experiment and discovery, were articles of faith in a society whose membership was drawn so largely from scientists and manufacturers. Whitehurst's emphasis on 'the result of physical reasonings' and 'the universal laws and operations of nature'[46] was shared by all his Lunar friends. Wedgwood's dictum, 'Everything gives way to experiment' might as suitably have been the motto of the Lunar Society as it was a guiding principle of the Enlightenment.

The value to Wedgwood of his association with the Lunar Society cannot be doubted. He had made strenuous efforts to educate himself in chemistry, and his Commonplace Books and extensive records of experiments are witness to his rational methods, dedication and powers of accurate interpretation; but he lacked formal training or the opportunity to acquire a necessary breadth of scientific knowledge. His close friendship with Lunar Society members, and with successive Secretaries of the Society of Arts, enabled him to call on the scholarship, wisdom and advice of some of the finest scientists of his time, not only in England but also in Europe and America. He was the only British potter to have access to such a treasury of resources and the only one to have both the ability and the determination to make full use of them.

Wedgwood's name, like Boulton's, is so indivisibly linked with what has come contentiously to be called the Industrial Revolution, that his place in the Enlightenment has been ignored. The frontiers between the periods are ill defined and largely artificial, false boundaries erected between intense intellectual activity and the explosion of industrial development which followed, but Wedgwood is one of the rare figures who may now be seen to have played an active part in both.

CHAPTER FIFTEEN

Competition and the Market

The commercial success of the Wedgwood & Bentley partnership has been attributed variously to the originality of their ideas, the excellence of their product and to the extraordinary abilities, complementary and collective, of the two partners.[1] All were major contributory factors, but there was another even more fundamental element in their domination of the pottery industry: the application of innovative marketing techniques to an exploding consumer market.

Among the more remarkable aspects of English society in the eighteenth century were the wealth and power of the aristocracy. On 30 January 1649, when Charles I was executed in Whitehall, and perhaps even more definitely some three years later, when Cromwell assumed the powers of Protector of the Commonwealth, the aristocracy had seemed doomed to extinction. Their wealth dissipated in the King's cause, their property looted, destroyed or confiscated, deprived of titles and privileges and the House of Lords, which had helped to maintain their position, England's noble families, some united in loyalty and others divided by it, faced undignified decay. Little more than a century later, those which had survived wielded greater wealth and power than ever.

The sources of this renewed strength were the Crown, politics and land. Every cabinet was stuffed with peers and more than a quarter of the English peerage benefited from the perquisites of the state by holding government or Court offices. Fees from sinecures could be colossal.* Ministers, especially Paymasters General, handled enormous public funds, which they could borrow for private speculation for so long as they held office. Their duties often permitted them to take commission

---

*George Rose, for example, the Younger Pitt's friend, Secretary to the Treasury 1782–5 and 1784–1801, and holder of several lucrative cabinet posts in both of Pitt's ministries, held sinecures worth more than £11,000 a year.

on government contracts and the official gaze was tactfully averted from all but the most flagrant demonstrations of peculation. Lord Chancellor Macclesfield, one of the unfortunate few to be charged, was impeached and fined £30,000 in 1725 for the misappropriation of an estimated £100,000. The Duke of Marlborough, Sir Robert Walpole and Charles James Fox's father were among those whose fortunes were founded on the office of Paymaster General and the first Duke of Chandos is believed to have profited from it by more than £500,000.

Land values and rents, and the profits from agriculture, rose steeply in the second half of the century and these were not the only profits to be derived from land-ownership. Coal, timber, slate, building stone and clay were all commodities for which there was increasing demand,* and magnates such as Lord Gower and the Duke of Bridgewater, both of whom owned vast reserves of coal, willingly invested in schemes to improve road and water transportation to increase their revenues. Urban property development, especially in London and the growing cities of Edinburgh, Dublin and Bath, was another profitable form of investment, bringing in rents which grew with the rise in land and property values. No stigma was attached to making money, and the aristocracy, whose grip on political power and patronage and owner-ship of land gave them advantages denied in comparable measure to any other section of society, set about the business of enriching them-selves with undisguised enthusiasm.

If the nobility were eager in their pursuit of money, they and their families were no less fervent in the spending of it. Sir Robert Walpole spent £90,000 in four years, some £6,000 of which was on wine, and it cost him £15 a night in candles to light Houghton, one of the most lavish houses of its day and built from the proceeds of public office. Lord Hervey wrote of Walpole's 'congresses' in Norfolk that guests were 'up to the chin in beef, venison, geese, turkeys etc. and generally over the chin in claret, strong beer and punch'.[2] The Duke of Bedford spent £84,000 on the rebuilding of Woburn and the Marquis of Rocking-ham just £1000 less on Wentworth Woodhouse. The Duke of Devon-shire owned two great houses in London and four in the country besides Chatsworth.

Great houses required great decoration and furnishings: carving and stucco and gilding; furniture from the workshops of the finest

*For example, the consumption of coal in London alone rose from about 800,000 tons to 2,500,000 tons in the first ninety years of the century, while the tonnage mined leapt from about 4¼ million in 1750 to nearly 14 million in 1800. In the same period the population of England rose by more than 50 per cent to nearly 8 ¾ million.

English craftsmen or imported from France; porcelain from China, Meissen or Sèvres; carpets and tapestries; pier glasses and looking-glasses in handsome carved and gilded wood frames; longcase clocks and bracket clocks, clocks in decorative ormolu cases; elegant candelabra, tureens and teasets from English or French silversmiths; marbles and bronzes; and, above all, paintings.

The British aristocracy became collectors and patrons. Young lords on the Grand Tour, and older ones on the hunt for old masters to hang in new or newly redecorated houses, combed the great cities of the Continent for masterpieces. And, in addition to some genuinely great and many genuinely worthless paintings and drawings, and an enormous quantity of copies and forgeries, they brought home with them artists whom they sought to encourage or work which they had commissioned from them. They formed collections of jewellery, medals and 'gems', casts of sculpture, antique pottery, glass and metalwork, scientific instruments, geological specimens and, of course, books. The great houses of Britain were filled with material evidence of the wealth and culture of their owners.

Much conspicuous expenditure was less edifying. Political costs could be almost as great as the perquisites of office. The price of election and the acquisition and retention of political power could be too heavy for even the richest of grandees. The Duke of Newcastle squandered a great part of his vast fortune on politics and the 4th Duke of Marlborough liquidated the corporation debt of Oxford in order to obtain a seat there in 1768. In a period when fewer than four in every 100 of the population had incomes of £200 a year or more, Charles James Fox and his brother lost £32,000 in two nights' gambling. Horace Walpole recalled that at Almack's club in Pall Mall, 'the gaming and extravagance of the young men of quality was arrived now at a pitch never heard of . . . generally there was £10,000 in specie on the table . . . They borrowed great sums of Jews at exorbitant premiums. Charles Fox called his outward room, where those Jews waited till he rose, the *Jerusalem Chamber.'*[3]

Next to the aristocracy was the broad section of society that encompassed the younger sons of peers, the shire knights, country squires and landowners, whose birth and inherited possessions allowed them limited access to the society and the perquisites enjoyed by the peerage. Classed as gentry, they generally lived well and, at the upper band of the spectrum, they were at least as well educated and as cultured as

*The Jerusalem Chamber is part of the deanery of Westminster Abbey. Dating from the fourteenth century, it was originally the Abbot's parlour and its walls were hung with tapestries illustrating the history of Jerusalem.

the aristocracy, with whom many of them had shared their lives in childhood, at school and at university. They swelled the ranks of Englishmen on the Grand Tour, built fine town and country houses, and acquired possessions and collections that were less splendid and less extravagant but often chosen with greater discrimination than those of their grander cousins. At the lower band they were hard-riding, hard-drinking, coarse-mouthed bumpkins. Fielding's Squires Allworthy and Western were not caricatures of their class.

The divisions between classes were often blurred, none more so than those between the upper gentry and the lower ranks of the aristocracy, or between those gentry who chose to enter the professions and the 'middling class' who had made a similar choice. Nor were the classes exclusive in their social amusements. All might mix in the pleasure gardens at Vauxhall and Ranelagh, in gaming or betting or in pursuit of the fox.

The habits and tastes, if not precisely the behaviour, of the aristocracy and gentry were imitated by the increasingly prosperous 'middling class' of professional men, manufacturers, merchants, yeomen farmers and skilled craftsmen. It has been estimated that by the end of the eighteenth century there were about half a million such families in England and they excited the surprise and admiration of foreign visitors. This was partly because, although the middle class aspired to the standards of education and material comfort of their social betters, they showed remarkably little inclination to overturn the system. They preferred a stable society in which they might make an opportunity to acquire superior culture, values and status. The class structure was accepted as the essential framework of the community. Through achievement, preferment, acquired riches or marriage, men and women might move up it almost as freely as they might, through ruin or disgrace, tumble down it, but few ever considered its removal or how it might be replaced. As Samuel Johnson told Boswell, 'Sir, I would no more deprive a nobleman of his respect than of his money. I consider myself as acting a part in the great system.'[4]

The aspirations of the middle class were undoubtedly fed by the urbanisation of Britain, by the growth of Georgian cities, such as Bath, and the slightly less fashionable spas at Cheltenham, Harrogate and Buxton, with their elegant town houses and sophisticated and tempting shops. With the remarkable improvements made to the speed and comfort of travel, both the capital and the principal provincial cities became accessible to anyone with money for the fare. Staffordshire potters and their families, who would only doubtfully have ventured on horseback into neighbouring Cheshire or Derbyshire earlier in the century, were by the 1760s making regular journeys to London to shop or visit the theatre or spend time in the gallery of the House of Commons listening to a debate. Wedgwood, Bentley and Boulton were exceptionally successful but otherwise fairly typical examples of this class and, for this reason, they had an unusually acute understanding of its needs and desires.

Most crucially, however, they understood that the key to the market was fashion and that fashion moved downwards. Josiah's complaint that 'Fashion is infinitely superior to *merit* in many respects' was a disillusioned response to the refusal of the architects to give their blessing to his prized jasper tablets but, as a purely commercial view, there was substance to it. He continued: 'it is plain from a thousand instances that if you have a favourite child you wish the public to fondle & take notice of, you have only to make a choice of proper sponcers. If you are lucky in them no matter what the brat is, black, brown or fair, its fortune is made.' It was a happy coincidence that in the same letter that contained this judgement he was able to express his pleasure that the Queen had chosen a service of his new, whiter earthenware, which he had named 'Pearl White', and his hope that her purchase would 'have due influence upon all her loyal subjects'.[5]

Sponsorship at the highest level was a requirement on which Wedgwood had placed the strongest emphasis since he had first supplied the Queen with his improved creamware, and he lost no time in cultivating the greatest possible prestige from her continued patronage by obtaining permission to use her royal title both for the body itself and for one of his most popular shapes. In similar manner, the shape made for the King was named 'Royal' and that designed for the Empress Catherine was named after her. Later, he wrote to Bentley: 'A name has a wonderfull effect I assure you' and urged him to present a set of flower-pots to the famous beauty and political hostess, Georgiana, Duchess of Devonshire, and to 'beg leave to call them Devonshire flowerpots'. He added, 'You smile – Well call them Mecklenberg* – or – or – what you please so you will but let them have a name.'[6] The tone of this letter suggests that Bentley was not already persuaded that this method of promoting sales was appropriate or effective and it contradicts the notion that it was always he who was the active entrepreneur.[7]

It was Wedgwood, too, who encouraged Bentley to make 'a little

*Queen Charlotte was the second daughter of the Duke of Mecklenburg-Strelitz, and her brothers, Prince Charles and Prince Ernest, were popular figures in England.

push farther . . . with *due decorum*' and to consult Mrs Schwellenberg* about obtaining the appointments of Potter to the King and to the Prince of Wales.[8] This attempt was unsuccessful and it took him nearly twenty years to be allowed to add the names of the Dukes of York and Clarence to his firm's letterhead.

Both Wedgwood and Bentley very quickly learned that they need not wait to follow fashion but that they could often mould it, or even create it, themselves. Although it is arguable that the finest saltglazed stoneware and lead-glazed earthenware tablewares were finding an increasing market in the higher classes of society by 1765, it cannot truly be said that either had become fashionable. Wedgwood, and the grandeur of his sponsors, were wholly responsible for the fashion for Queen's ware and it was one which not only spread throughout Europe but also took root. The 'Royal, or Noble introduction' which Josiah deemed necessary to 'the sale of an Article of *Luxury*' was no less prime a requirement for the marketing of 'useful' wares. When, in 1771, the trade in earthenware tableware was 'going to ruin on the gallop',[9] Wedgwood's business was saved by energetic marketing and by the reputation he had acquired for goods of such excellence that they were bought by the royal houses and the nobility of Europe.

The same principles applied to the Wedgwood & Bentley ornamental wares. A form of black basaltes, known variously as 'black ware', 'black Egyptian' and 'Egyptian Black', had been made in Staffordshire for at least seventy-five years before Wedgwood's, but the market for it had been almost exclusively local. It was Wedgwood who saw the opportunity and discovered the means to make a refined body of such quality that it might be used for decorative vases, figures and medallions, some in imitation of Renaissance bronzes, which would attract the attention of collectors and connoisseurs. 'The Black is sterling, and will last for ever',[10] he told Bentley in 1774, and, although its popularity has been variable, it has been in almost continuous production ever since.

Having created the body and begun the production of a range of ornaments that were, themselves, enough to start a new fashion, he was quick to seize the moment to follow a fashion already created by the collectors of antique red-figure vases. It is significant that Wedgwood launched his 'Etruscan' ('encaustic'-painted) vases by showing them first to a select list of patrons – 'Sir Watkin Williams Wynn, Mrs Chetwynd, Lord Besborough, Earl of Stamford, Duke of Northumber-

*The Queen's Keeper of the Robes, who had been with the Queen from her infancy. Josiah refers to her as 'Mrs Shevelinberg'.

land, Duke of Marlborough, Lord Percy, Lord Carlisle, St James's Place, Earl of Dartmouth, Lord Clanbrazill, Lord Torrington, Mr Harbord Harbord'[11] – and the extensive use he made of the Hamilton collection for both shapes and painted decoration, brought him the priceless benefit of Sir William's friendly patronage and counsel for more than twenty-five years.

Hamilton was one of those whose advice and patronage was sought when Wedgwood & Bentley introduced their black basaltes bas-relief vases* in 1776. 'Sir William Hambleton,[12] our very good Friend is in Town,' Josiah wrote to Bentley on 12 September:

> Suppose you shew him some of the Vases, & a few other Connoisieurs, not only to have their advice but to have the advantage of their puffing them off against the next Spring, as they will, by being consulted, & flatter'd agreeably, as you know how, consider themselves as a sort of parties in the affair, & act accordingly.[13]

So anxious was he to have this advice before the vases were offered more widely that he took the unusual course of advising the Earl of Warwick, who saw them in the Etruria showrooms, against buying a set until the following spring, 'when we should have a greater variety'.[14]

The 'variegated' vases competed successfully with Boulton's ormolu-mounted 'Blue John' pieces and shared the existing market for metal-mounted ornaments made from real lapis lazuli, agate and other polished natural stones. Jasper, on the other hand, the most important invention of Wedgwood's lifetime, supplied a fashion that scarcely existed in English pottery or porcelain but that already dominated architecture and interior decoration and was rapidly assuming the dominance of silver design.

The key to Wedgwood's supremacy in pottery design between 1770 and 1790 was his pursuit of neoclassical form and decoration, a fashion which the manufacturers of porcelain found difficult to translate into their medium and which other potters failed to understand until Wedgwood had already taken the lead. It is generally assumed, though the evidence is not conclusive, that it was Bentley who steered Wedgwood away from the rococo, a dying fashion which was being discarded by the upper classes but was still favoured by the older generation and the 'middling' people. There is certainly no evidence of Wedgwood's interest in neoclassical design before his friendship with Bentley developed and, apart from Sir William Chambers, with whom he was

---

*Vases with applied relief ornament instead of cast decoration. See p. 85.

Josiah Wedgwood by George Stubbs. Ceramic colours on Wedgwood earthenware, 1780. *Wedgwood Museum*

Josiah Wedgwood by Sir Joshua Reynolds, 1782. *Wedgwood Museum*

Sarah Wedgwood by Sir Joshua Reynolds, 1782. *Wedgwood Museum*

Thomas Bentley attributed to Joseph Wright of Derby. *Wedgwood Museum*

Thomas Bentley and Josiah Wegwood. Jasper portrait medallions modelled by Joachim Smith, 1773-4. *Manchester City Art Gallery*

The Churchyard Works, Burslem, established by Josiah Wedgwood's great-grandfather. From an engraving, *c.*1864. *Photograph: Wedgwood*

The Ivy House Works. Drawn from memory by Aaron Wedgwood, *c.*1864. *Photograph: Wedgwood*

The Brick House ('Bell') Works. Drawn from memory by Aaron Wedgwood, *c.*1864. *Photograph: Wedgwood*

The Etruria factory from the canal. Drawing by Leonard G. Brammer, 1950. *Wedgwood Museum*

Rococo 'Cauliflower' teapot. Wedgwood, c.1763. *Wedgwood Museum*

Queen's ware 'feather-edge' dessert plate with pierced border, decorated by Sadler & Green with a transfer-print of 'Corinthian Ruins', c.1775. *Wedgwood Museum*

'Glacier' (ice-cream vase) from the 'Frog' service, decorated with views of Beau Desert, in Staffordshire, and Moor Park, Hertfordshire. *Photograph: Wedgwood*

Epergne (table centre) illustrated in Wedgwood's Queen's ware catalogue, c.1790. *Wedgwood Museum*

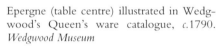

Black basaltes vase (shape no.1), c.1774. *Manchester Museum*

Black basaltes 'canopic' vase, painted in orange-red 'encaustic' colours, c.1773. *Wedgwood Museum*

Variegated ('surface agate') vase with gilded snake handles on white terracotta plinth, c.1780. *Wedgwood Museum*

Queen's ware plate with neo-classical centre and border in red and black, c.1790. *Wedgwood Museum*

Richard Wedgwood, Sarah Wedgwood's father, by George Stubbs, 1780. *Wedgwood Museum*

William Willet, Josiah's brother-in-law. Jasper portrait medallion modelled by William Hackwood, 1776. *Wedgwood Museum*

Thomas Byerley. Jasper portrait medallion modelled by William Theed, 1810. *Wedgwood Museum*

Etruria Hall, ceramic colours on Wedgwood earthenware attributed to Edward Stringer, 1773. *Wedgwood Museum*

The Wedgwood Family in the grounds of Etruria Hall by George Stubbs, 1780. *Right to left:* Josiah Wedgwood, his wife Sarah and their children, John, Josiah II, Susannah, Catherine, Thomas, Sarah and Mary Anne. *Wedgwood Museum*

Susannah Darwin, Josiah's eldest daughter and mother of Charles Darwin. From a portrait miniature by an unidentified artist. *Photograph: Wedgwood*

John Wedgwood, Josiah's eldest son. From a portrait miniature by an unidentified artist. *Wedgwood Museum*

Josiah Wedgwood II, Josiah's second son. From the portrait by William Owen, *c.*1805. *Wedgwood Museum*

Tom Wedgwood, Josiah's youngest son. From a chalk drawing by an unidentified artist, *c.*1805. *Wedgwood Museum*

Erasmus Darwin by George Stubbs, 1783. Ceramic colours on Wedgwood earthenware. *Wedgwood Museum*

R.L. Edgeworth, portrait minature on ivory by Horace Hone, 1785. *National Portrait Gallery*

Matthew Boulton. Portrait by an unidentified artist. *National Portrait Gallery*

Joseph Priestley. Jasper portrait medallion, modelled *c.*1779. *Wedgwood Museum*

George Stubbs, self-portrait, 1781. Ceramic colours on Wedgwood earthenware. *National Portrait Gallery*

Joseph Wright of Derby. Self-portrait *c*.1784. *National Portrait Gallery*

John Flaxman, detail from the portrait by George Romney, 1795. *National Portrait Gallery*

William Hackwood. Portrait by an unidentifed artist, *c*.1820. *City Museum and Art Gallery, Stoke-on-Trent*

Plate 31 from volume III of
Hamilton and d'Hancarville's
*Collection of Etruscan, Greek and
Roman Antiquities*, 1767, the
source of Flaxman's 'Apotheosis
of Homer' bas-relief.
Photograph: Wedgwood

Jasper 'Apotheosis of Homer'
tablet, modelled by John
Flaxman in 1787. *Wedgwood
Museum*

Jasper 'Apotheosis of Homer'
vase. *Wedgwood Museum*

Above: Lady Diana Beauclerk by Sir Joshua
Reynolds, 1764–5. *Iveagh Bequest, Kenwood*

Right: Elizabeth, Lady Templetown by
John Downman, 1790. *Private Collection*

Queen Charlotte. Transfer-printed portrait, after an engraving by Aliamet, on a Wedgwood creamware teapot, c.1761-2. *Mrs R.D. Chellis Collection*

William Eden. Wax portrait modelled by Eley George Mountstephen (the original model for Wedgwood's portrait medallion), 1789-90. *Private Collection*

Sir William Hamilton. Enamel on copper by William Hopkins Craft, 1802. *British Museum*

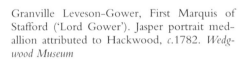

Granville Leveson-Gower, First Marquis of Stafford ('Lord Gower'). Jasper portrait medallion attributed to Hackwood, c.1782. *Wedgwood Museum*

'A Fox examining the Strong Box'. Unpublished cartoon by J. Sayers, undated but ascribed to February 1787. A complicated political cartoon containing allusions to events and European alliances during the previous fifteen months. The central group shows Lord Loughborough and the Duke of Portland presenting to Josiah Wedgwood their arguments against the French Commercial Treaty. On the mantelpiece stands a Wedgwood vase beside a figure of Mercury. Wedgwood's arms rest on a book labelled 'Chamber [of] Commerce Minu[te] Book', and the two volumes on the floor are labelled 'Wedgwood's Report' and 'Birmingham Case'. *British Museum*

Black and white jasper copy of the Portland Vase supplied to Thomas Hope, one of the original subscribers, in June 1793. *Wedgwood Museum*

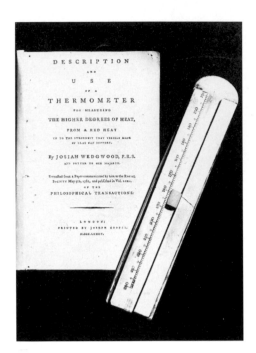

Wedgwood's pyrometer set, presented to George III in 1786. *Science Museum*

Gold-mounted black and white jasper Slave medallion, *c.*1790. *British Museum*

Base disc of the 'Hope' copy of the Portland Vase, 1793. *Wedgwood Museum*

never on terms of any intimacy, or Hamilton, with whom he had no contact before 1772, there is no one else to whom Josiah would have been likely to turn for advice on the subject. Wedgwood was the first earthenware potter to adopt the 'true style' for his wares, as he was also the first to use it for the design of his house and the front of his factory, and he was the first to make 'Egyptian' figures. Both styles appealed, at the time that he introduced them, to sophisticated taste, and the 'Egyptian' style did not become popular until the end of the century.

Wedgwood's decoration of his Queen's ware tablewares was hardly less innovative. Although a few rococo designs, such as bright green enamelled patterns of seaweed and shells which were probably personal favourites, lasted through the 1780s, the simple style of border decoration – admirably balanced running designs based on natural or architectural forms – was set in the first years of the 1770s and remained unchanged for about forty years. It was a style imitated almost everywhere from Staffordshire to Moscow[15] and repeated or adapted so regularly during the following two centuries that it has become part of the essential grammar of tableware design.

The imitation of his bodies, shapes, ornaments and designs was seldom a matter of serious concern for Wedgwood. He took it for granted that local manufacturers would lose no time in following his lead and he was confident that his ingenuity would enable him to maintain it. With the best of his competitors he was on terms of friendly rivalry. Boulton was a close friend, whose work and methods he admired sincerely, and they shared a number of models, notably from Sir William Chambers and John Flaxman senior, for reproduction in metal or stonewares. He exchanged portraits with William Tassie for reproduction in jasper or glass pastes. Among competing Staffordshire potters, he was on good terms with John Turner of Lane End and William Adams of Greengates, both of whom successfully imitated his jasper, producing similar stoneware bodies which some connoisseurs have preferred to Wedgwood's. He shared a journey into Cornwall with Turner in 1775, prospecting for clay, and they took joint leases on mines in St Austell and Redruth. He occasionally bought goods from other creamware manufacturers to supply deficiencies in production or stock, notably from William Greatbatch and from John Baddeley of Shelton, whose creamware he describes as 'the best ware perhaps of any of the Potter's here' – next, of course to his own. Even with Humphrey Palmer, the only one of Wedgwood's contemporaries to offer any genuine threat to the Wedgwood & Bentley 'Vase work' and the only competitor to challenge his patent for 'encaustic' decoration, Wedgwood's relations remained amicable.[16]

He was not by nature a quarrelsome man and in his rare disputes he showed a clear preference for reason, compromise and cooperation over bitter rivalry and confrontation; but the exceptional friendliness of his dealings with his competitors and imitators was founded on confidence in his ability to outrun them. Of Palmer he once wrote: 'We must proceed or they will tread upon our heels.'[17] It was a compliment that he paid to no other. Fair competition was never to be feared; the danger was always from spies and the theft of ideas, inventions or developments before they could be perfected and marketed.

Contrary to the most frequently repeated opinions,[18] Wedgwood's wares were never competitive in price with those of any of his contemporaries. In spite of advanced methods of production – especially in the use of machinery, division of labour and the efficient planning of quantity production – which should have reduced costs and therefore prices, his goods were always considered expensive, often unreasonably so, and the subject of uncomplimentary comparison with those of other potters.

The reasons for this are clear. First, his costs were never as low as they might have been if he had been content to lower his quality. His insistence on the highest standards obtainable resulted in the production of goods of a quality that few contemporary potters could hope or afford to emulate.[19] Most of those few who, like Turner, William Greatbatch and Humphrey Palmer, sometimes succeeded in doing so at lower prices, lost money and went out of business. Second, his costs were inflated by his heavy investment in land, buildings and machinery and by the high cost of his experiments. None of his contemporaries in the pottery industry incurred capital expenditure of such weight and only Boulton among his competitors spent as freely on his factory and private house.

Third, his marketing costs were exceptionally high. Few of his contemporaries bought or rented London showrooms, and several who attempted to do so did not last long. Spode, and much later Minton, succeeded; Boulton & Fothergill flirted with the idea for years but, in 1778, had still not found a situation that was both grand enough and affordable; the Chelsea and Bow porcelain factories had showrooms in the West End of London in the 1750s, and Longton Hall rented a warehouse in St Paul's Churchyard ten years before Wedgwood opened his first in London, but none survived for more than four years. Nor did any other pottery manufacturer open warehouses or showrooms in Bath or Dublin,[20] where Wedgwood opened establishments in 1772 and 1773.* Although most of his competitors, especially Boulton, paid attention to export markets, none invested in the adventurous marketing experiments which helped to spread the fame of Wedgwood & Bentley throughout Europe.

Last, probably at Bentley's insistence and in spite of their unprofitability, Wedgwood continued the Potteries custom of making what he called 'Uniques'[21]: single commissions, often requiring special modelling and decoration, for valued customers. This was common practice in small potteries, where little disruption to regular production was caused by individual orders, but in factories organised for long production runs of the same article such orders are costly to make and, because they can seldom be priced to take full account of true costs without defeating the object by offending the customer, are almost invariably sold at a loss. Accurate cost accounting would have shown a loss on the production of both Queen Charlotte's teaset and the Empress Catherine's 'Frog' service, though part of the modelling costs of the 'Catherine' service could have been applied to later sales of the same shape. As early as November 1769 Josiah warned Bentley about *'time loseing* with *Uniques* which keep ingenious Artists who are connected with Great Men of taste, poor & would make us so too if we did much in that way' and less than two months later he implored him, 'Defend me from particular orders.'[22] But reluctantly Josiah changed his mind, as he was obliged also to do about armorial services, and yielded to Bentley's argument that, although such orders might be trifling, 'we must please these great Friends who are warm Patrons of this Manufacture'.[23]

One of the most unprofitable of all such orders for 'Uniques' was probably one which Josiah acquired for himself little more than twelve months after he had cautioned Bentley against them. On a visit to Shugborough, the Staffordshire seat of Thomas Anson, in December 1770, he was shown an immense bronze tripod commissioned from Boulton to James 'Athenian' Stuart's design. This was an imaginative reconstruction of the tripod and bowl known as the Choragic Monument of Lysicrates, built in Athens in 334 BC. According to Josiah, the bronze legs alone weighed about 5 hundredweight and the workmen were 'stagger'd at the bowl, & did not know which way to set about it'. Seldom at a loss, Josiah suggested that one method of avoiding undue weight would be to make the bowl in black basaltes. He was startled to be taken seriously and, as he ruefully reported to Bentley,

*The Bath warehouse in Westgate Buildings was managed by William Ward and his wife Ann, the sister of Bentley's second wife, Mary Stamford. The Dublin warehouse, run by William Brock, was given up in 1778 and the business delegated to an agent.

'I have a fine jobb on my hands in consequence of a little harmless boasting.' He was, nevertheless, as good as his word: the bowl was made to a wooden prototype at the beginning of April 1771,* after an earlier model had been demolished by severe frost before it could be fired.[24] There was no further mention in Josiah's letters to Bentley of avoiding orders for 'Uniques'.

Wedgwood based the prices of his ornamental wares on estimated costs of production augmented by a subjective valuation of their worth to his customers: a 'great price' was at first necessary to make them 'esteemed *Ornaments* for *Palaces*' but the price might later be reduced for sales in greater quantity to 'the middling People'. He told Bentley, 'When I fix a price upon any new article, please to remember that I have more regard to the *expence of workmanship* than the *aparent & comparative* value with other things so you'l correct it by the latter, which is often most essential.'[25] Due allowance was also made in the price for improvements in quality for which Wedgwood paid higher wages. As he told Bentley:

> In my first essays upon Vases I had a great many things to learn myself, & everything to teach the workmen, who had not the least idea of beauty, or proportion in what they did, few, or none of our productions were what we should now deem tolerable, & the prices were fixed accordingly, but after so long practice from the best models, & drawings, such a long series of instruction, as our workmen have gone through, & so very expensive an apparatus, or rather a collection of Apparatus's as we are now masters of, & all to enable us to get up *good things*, I think we ought not, & I am sure we cannot without great loss return back again to make such things as we first started with. Besides this course would not be doing justice to *ourselves*, or our *manufacture* on many accounts. The same hands who at first finishd the serpent & other Vases . . . @ about 3/6 or 4/6 each were content with earning 7 or 8/- Per week, but they now are improv'd in their *wages*, as well as in their *workmanship*, to double that sum . . . I observe in the orders which have come from Paris, that no regard has been made to the *price*, but to the *goodness* only of the articles sent for . . .[26]

Production cost was a basis for pricing but it was seldom paramount. Wedgwood's prices were higher than those of his competitors

---

*It is not certain that Wedgwood's basaltes bowl was ever installed at Shugborough. It does not appear in Moses Griffith's drawing of the Lanthorn in 1780. The tripod and bowl now in place are fibre-glass reproductions made for the National Trust in 1963.

for two sensible reasons: his costs were higher and his profits greater. His inventiveness and the quality of his goods gave him the lead in Europe, and his superior marketing methods maintained that lead by making his goods recognisable and fashionable.

To complement his constant pursuit of patronage, Wedgwood used three forms of promotion: trade marks, catalogues and advertising. The first two were new to the pottery industry and the third little favoured before the last quarter of the century.

Until the eighteenth century was well advanced, the trade-marking of porcelain was generally confined to the largest and most influential of manufacturers. The crossed swords mark adopted for Meissen porcelain from about 1725 was imitated by a number of smaller German manufacturers and even at Vincennes. The first English factory regularly to mark its wares was the Chelsea porcelain factory about 1756, but marks were seldom used by other manufacturers before 1770. When makers of porcelain considered the identification of their wares as of so little account, it is not surprising that no potter of the humbler earthenware thought it worthwhile to have his own distinguishing trademark. Wedgwood changed both the attitude and the practice. The most crucial difference, however, lay in his choice of mark and the manner in which it was applied. Whereas, almost without exception, other potters chose signs and symbols or the name of the manufactory (usually its location) painted or printed on the base of the ware, Wedgwood used his own name, and had it impressed in the unfired clay. His work was thus far less vulnerable to forgery than that of other manufacturers and every piece advertised the name of its maker.

Wedgwood's earliest wares, like those of his contemporaries in the Potteries, were unmarked. The first evidence of his use of trademarks appears in a letter to Bentley dated 9 July 1771 in which he wrote: 'If we alter the large characters it must be by having new moulds. The letters are stamped with printers letters & we want a middle size betwixt those large ones & the least.' More primitive marks, incised or impressed with a separate stamp for each letter, had been in irregular use for some years, but it was not until the winter of 1772 that Josiah decided to extend the use of his improved trademark to everything, 'useful' and 'ornamental', made at Etruria.[27] Special stamps incorporating Bentley's name were made for ornamental wares and it is probable, though not certain, that the 'Wedgwood & Bentley' marks on those goods that were products of their partnership were in regular use before the plain 'Wedgwood' name that was used on all 'useful' wares. Indeed, it is possible that the suggestion of distinguishing their wares originated with Bentley but the innovatory decision to impress the mark in the clay is more likely to have been Wedgwood's. An impressed mark has been used by the firm ever since.

The first Wedgwood & Bentley catalogue was published in 1773. Josiah wrote to Bentley in the previous September suggesting a 'Printed Catalogue of the things we have'.[28] He was referring at the time only to cameos and medallions but by November 1773 he was considering a catalogue printed in French to send to agents and merchants abroad with sample boxes of nine tableware patterns. He proposed to send out '1 or 200 at least and have liberty to charge [for] them, as they will be useful'. The idea that the catalogue might be illustrated seems to have occurred to him even as he wrote:

> But this will not be complete without some copper plates of the princi-
> pal vessels which will give a much better idea of them than the names
> only. These may be slight Etchings, provided the drawings & perspec-
> tive are good.

He listed the pieces to be engraved, insisting that 'those Cover'd & water vessels should be drawn to show where the parts take off, & the internal disposition of the parts'.[29]

The catalogue, 'more extensive' than he expected, was issued in 1774, somewhat grandiosely entitled *A Catalogue of the different articles of Queen's Ware, which may be had either plain, gilt or embellished with Enamel Paintings, manufactured by Josiah Wedgwood, Potter to her Majesty*. Ten full-page engravings by John Pye* illustrated thirty-five shapes representative of the much larger range available. The accompanying letterpress was printed in English and French. This appears to be the earliest illustrated catalogue issued by an earthenware manufacturer and it is difficult to measure its success. While the Wedgwood & Bentley catalogue of ornamental wares, first published in 1773, ran to five editions in English, French, German and Dutch translations in six years, and was revised and enlarged for a new edition in 1787, the Queen's ware catalogue was not reprinted until about 1790, when a new and larger edition was prepared. This now exists, however, only in various proof forms and it is doubtful if it was ever issued.[30]

In contrast to his enthusiasm for these methods of publicising his wares, Josiah's attitude to advertising in the newspapers was ambiva-lent. He told Bentley in 1771, 'I would much rather not advertise at all if you think the sales are in such a way as to do without it.'[31] His

---

*John Pye (1745–after 1775) worked as an engraver for Sadler & Green, the Liverpool transfer-printers. He engraved landscapes for the London printseller John Boydell and supplied views for the 'Frog' service in 1773.

reluctance did not stem so much from a lack of regard for the efficiency of the medium, though he might well have objected to sharing a page with small traders, prostitutes, abortionists and quacks and seeing his advertisements beside others for women wrestlers, aphrodisiacs, mid-wives or 'a fine young breast of milk willing to enter a gentleman's household'.[32] Rather, he was wary of one who styled himself 'Great Bellows', who had published an article in the *St James's Chronicle* threat-ening to 'pay his respects occasionally to the Puffs, & Puffers in the Public papers'. A second critic, 'Antipuffado', had already chosen to criticise Wedgwood indirectly by attacking one of his agents. 'I think Antipuffado a clever sort of a fellow,' Josiah wrote on 11 February, '& would not say anything in reply that should anger or prevent his writing again, for I think he will do us more good than any *real puff* we could have contrived. I am well pleased too that I am not cut up & mangled by the hands of a dull rogue. He shews himself too plain (for his own credit I mean) by being so waspish & angry . . . but that is so much the better for me.'[33]

'Puffing' – the art of promoting goods, services or individuals in newspaper articles purporting to offer objective comment – had long been recognised in politics and rapidly became a conspicuous feature of the new consumer boom. Eight years after Wedgwood's encounter with Antipuffado, Sheridan introduced London audiences to Mr Puff in *The Critic*, 'a practitioner in panegyric', who described his work with precision: 'Yes, sir, puffing is of various sorts; the principal are, the puff direct, the puff preliminary, the puff collateral, the puff collusive, and the puff oblique, or puff by implication.'

As Josiah told Bentley, 'I should have no objection to the Public being acquainted *in some way or other* that I have not directly or indirectly been concerned in the publication of these or any other paragraphs on the subject. Except the advertisements with my name affixed to them.'[34] This was strictly accurate at the time but it represented a change of heart. Less than six months earlier he had urged Bentley to get an article 'into the next paper' to compete with a puff that had already appeared for Boulton's goods.[35] He asked his partner to reply to Anti-puffado, acknowledging the 'honor of being extravagantly praised & abused' and disavowing his 'having had any concern directly or indirectly in publishing either one or the other'. He added, 'I think the answer should be grave, too short to be dull, & as little pointed to any of Antipuffado's witticisms or particular expressions as possible.'[36]

Josiah was hopeful that the attack would do little damage: 'all things shall work together for good'. Bentley, however, had more sophistica-ted thoughts, ahead of his time, of turning the most obviously inflated

abuse to their favour. He and Josiah considered the possibility of pro-
voking Antipuffado to further extremes and using his malicious letters
'as a foundation for . . . advertiseing'. But 'How would you introduce
the mention of it into an advertisement?' Josiah asked, '& would not
that be giving it too much consequence, & seem something like a
bravado or puffing in the very face of our friend Anti – '.[37] The idea
was set aside, but the effect of his discussions with Bentley was to
persuade Josiah of the value of newspaper advertising. Just four days
later he disclosed the unwelcome information that the lack of sales in
November and December, insufficient even to pay the wages of his
work-force, 'seems to point out advertiseing, & if you think you can . . .
make an adequate shew, so that those who come in consequence of
the advertisement may not be disappointed & charge us with *puffing* I
will certainly do it. All trifleing objections vanish before a real necessity.'[38] Next day he sent Bentley a draft of a long and innovative advertisement.[39]

This was not the first time that Wedgwood had used the newspapers to advertise his goods, his factory or his London showrooms,[40]
but the draft sent to Bentley on 17 February was exceptional in three
respects: goods, already carried free to London, would in future be
delivered carriage-free, as far as the first carrier took them, to all parts
of the country; all deficiencies or breakages in delivery would be made
good or credited, provided that river navigation, notorious for theft and
careless handling, was not used; and, perhaps most significant of all,
satisfaction was guaranteed. This last offer to purchasers – that they
should 'be at liberty to return the whole, or any part of the goods they
order (paying the carriage back) if they do not find them agreeable
to their wishes'[41] – anticipates by nearly a century the 'satisfaction
guaranteed' policy usually said to have been invented by John Wana-
maker in America.[42]

However, while nationwide carriage-free delivery had been estimated three years earlier to add £500 to his costs,[43] a figure now greatly
inflated by increased sales and more widespread distribution, the other
two offers were, Josiah confessed, less generous than they appeared.
The new proposals would, indeed, make little difference, 'for at present
my Customers do return their goods if they do not like them, & they
are out of humour if the breakages are not made up in some way or
other'. But there were significant advantages to be gained by appearing
to be liberal: 'this advertisement will acquaint thousands who at present
know nothing of it, that they run no risque at all (except by paying a
little carriage of the goods back) by ordering goods from me, & I make

no doubt will induce numbers to order services who, without such intelligence would not think of doing so'.[44]

From 1771 Wedgwood advertised his wares freely, making the most of his royal appointments and patronage, the convenience and superiority of his showrooms and the generosity of his terms of business. By 1773 he was even preparing to advertise his trademark.[45]

Wedgwood could not be satisfied with the conquest of the British market. By the use of the most advanced methods of production he had succeeded in combining quality with quantity, and he was rapidly learning about cost accounting, but he had little understanding of the complications of forecasting or stock control. The result was too often production, sometimes of the wrong goods, running far ahead of orders and creating heavy stocks. Early in 1771, while Josiah was planning advertising to increase sales at home, he agreed with Bentley that 'nothing but a *foreign market*' would keep their stocks 'within any tolerable bounds'.[46]

Export markets became increasingly valuable until in the 1780s, it has been estimated, some 80 per cent of Wedgwood's output was being sold abroad.[47] This figure is in line with his own estimates in 1781 that five-sixths of the production of the Staffordshire Potteries was exported.[48] Wedgwood's interest in foreign markets was three-sided: they spread the fame and prestige of his name, his factory and his product; they increased sales and helped to diminish stocks; and they provided useful outlets for goods that were no longer fashionable at home.

As early as 1765 he told Sir William Meredith, 'The bulk of our particular manufacture you know is exported to foreign markets, for our home consumption is very trifleing in comparison to what is sent abroad'; and he added, 'the principal of these markets are the [American] Continent & islands of N. America'. North America was a strong market for saltglazed stoneware 'and some of the finer kinds' long before it took large quantities of creamware.[49] The islands – the Leewards, Barbados and Bermuda – were not considered ready for 'anything too rich and costly', but they were buyers of Wedgwood's greenglazed ware, helping to clear Wedgwood's stocks after it had ceased to be popular in England.[50]

Six years later, Arthur Young, passing through Staffordshire during his 'Eastern Tour', reported that large quantities of creamware were being exported to Germany and Ireland, Holland, Russia, Spain, the East Indies 'and much to America; some of the finest sorts to France'. In fact, exports of English pottery to France were severely hampered by excise duties and the numerous prohibitory edicts issued by Louis XV and Louis XVI to protect the Royal Manufactory from competition. Bentley, nevertheless, believed that a promising market existed there for Wedgwood. 'And do you really think', Josiah asked him in September 1769, 'we may make a *complete conquest* of France? Conquer France in Burslem? – My blood moves quicker, I feel my strength increase for the contest. We will . . . captivate them with the Elegance & simplicity of the Ancients. But do they love simplicity . . . *French & Frippery* have jingled together so long in my ideas, that I scarcely know how to separate them, & much of their work which I have seen *cover'd over with ornament*, had confirm'd me in the opinion.'[51]

Undeterred by such considerations as prohibitions, excise duties and the French preference for the rococo, and pursuing his own policy of courting 'noble introductions' and 'proper sponcers', Josiah made a direct approach to 'the Duke de Choiseul Minister & Secretary of France':

> Knowing the taste they have in France for every thing that comes from England, I thought your Excellency wou'd freely pardon the liberty I have taken to send you a box that contains a compleat apartment of Urns, & Vases in the antique taste, & after the Greek, Roman, & Etruscan models, & used for ornamenting apartments. This composition is the fruit of a manufacture lately established here under the immediate protection of the Queen, & for this reason called the Queen's Manufacture. The Apartment I take the liberty to address to your Excellency, is the same as one that hath been made here by order of the Empress of Russia, and hath been sent to the Kings of Denmark & Poland. The taste these different Princes have for these ornements made me imagine they wou'd not displease your Excellency.[52]

The description of the Etruria factory as 'under the immediate protection of the Queen' and 'called the Queen's Manufacture' was a calculated misrepresentation, intended to put Wedgwood's prestige on a footing with that of European porcelain factories under more direct royal patronage. It was, on the other hand, important to make it clear that Queen's ware offered no competition to French porcelain and might, perhaps, be excluded from the restrictions and heavy dues on imports. 'I know my Lord,' Josiah wrote with false humility, 'this composition is not comparable to those of France that are carried on at Sceaux, & Vincennes, & give it no other name than earthenware.'

His last paragraph was an ingenious but transparent attempt at persuasion:

I know my Lord, all this is counterband in France, but the liberty I have taken in sending these Merchandises to your Excellency is not with a desire to open trade between this country & France it is only to show my zeal & attention to your Excellency. I am not ignorant that with regard to curiosities the Nobility of France have the privilege of procuring for themselves what the rigeur of the law wou'd not permit to be sold publicly, & indeed it wou'd be a pity too literal & pharisaical an observation of the law shou'd deprive people of taste of what all the rest of Europe enjoy. It is only with this view My Lord, that I have taken the liberty to send you this parcel. I hope it will have the advantage of pleasing you & meriting your appreciation. If unfortunately it shou'd not, yur Excellency will have to goodness to order it to be return'd to the undertaker.[53]

It appears that nothing came of this effort but it is hard to imagine that Choiseul, if it reached him, could have read the letter without a smile. Some Wedgwood Queen's ware entered France, small quantities legally and much more smuggled, but nearly twenty years passed before Josiah was able to assist in the regulation of excise duties between the two countries.

The exercise was not, however, entirely useless. The experience of making up boxes of samples to attract the attention of such 'fine eyes' as the Empress of Russia, the Kings of Denmark and Poland and the duc de Choiseul, was not so disappointing as to dissuade Wedgwood from trying a similar experiment on a far grander scale.

In October 1771 Bentley put forward a plan, designed by his friend de Shoning, to broadcast Wedgwood wares throughout the smaller states of Europe, particularly those principalities, electorates, bishoprics and duchies whose ruling families were not accessible through diplomatic introduction. Josiah described the proposal as 'so very magnificent that it requires some time to take a very cursory view of it on every side so as to form any probable idea of the consequences of complying with it' and he wondered if 'such a Deluge of Earthenware coming down upon them all at once', particularly in those states where earthenware was manufactured, might not 'alarm the state & cause them to return the whole'.[54] The cost was likely to be enormous – 'say a thousand parcels @ £20 each Usefull & Ornamental is £20,000'* – and the consequent risk intimidating. Such a quantity of goods might pose production problems, for the bulk of it could not be found from stock, and there would be the additional burden of goods returned.[55] A pro-

*More than £2 million worth of goods at today's prices.

portion might be expected to be neither bought nor returned and these costs would have to be written off as bad debts. Nevertheless, the market was rich and, as Josiah told Bentley, it seemed 'almost the only mode in which our Goods can get into such Familys'.[56] To de Shoning he wrote: 'We know that nothing great can be done without some risque, nor is there any *absolute certainty* in trade.'[57]

In spite of his misgivings he agreed to make the attempt. The German states were chosen for the first trial. The precise number of parcels sent out is not known but eight months later Josiah was able to report to Bentley that they had received a promising response: 'If a few more should turn up with such letters as these & promises of farther *commissions* we may in the end have no great reason to repent what we have done.' Payments for these 'Voluntaries' and new orders connected with them continued to come in until finally only three debts remained outstanding.[58]

More conventional methods were employed to capture the most reliable and enduring market for Wedgwood in Europe, the Netherlands. Samuel Tabor,* an English merchant in Rotterdam, was one of the earliest recorded of Wedgwood's overseas agents. He wrote to Josiah on 22 April 1763, some three years before the name of Wedgwood was made famous by royal appointment, and remained a good customer for more than a quarter of a century.[59] Wedgwood's first agent in Amsterdam was John Du Burk but their association was never satisfactory. Du Burk was apathetic, sales were poor, stocks accumulated, invoices remained unpaid and Joseph Cooper, put in by Wedgwood & Bentley to protect their interests, found evidence of 'gross mistakes' in the accounts. Josiah began to suspect that the cause of the troubles might be more sinister than incompetence.[60]

Wedgwood persevered with Du Burk for seven years before he sent Ben Mather, whose personal experience of fraud might be considered to qualify him peculiarly well for the task, to Amsterdam to count the stock. By October 1766 enough evidence had been accumulated to condemn Du Burk as 'a bad Man, as well as a fool, & has a great deal of that sort of little craft & cunning about him which such characters are generally possessed of'. His lawyer advised him to deal with Du Burk, 'Sword in hand', and, after much unpleasantness, Du Burk was sent to prison. Nothing daunted, his wife, 'that Diable of a Woman' as Josiah called her, demanded that Wedgwood & Bentley pay her husband's debts. Suiting his language to the circumstances, Josiah replied that he would not pay 'a stiver'.[61]

---

*His father, Jonathan Tabor, was a merchant in Colchester, Essex.

The stock was quickly sold to a man of very different character, Lambertus van Veldhuysen, who was appointed sole agent for Wedgwood in the Netherlands. He and his heirs continued the business until 1820 and Lambertus II was responsible for the translation of the 1774 Wedgwood & Bentley Catalogue published in Amsterdam in 1778 as well as for many suggestions for production. None of Wedgwood's agents in Europe has been more trusted and few have been as successful. Veldhuysen shared Josiah's preference for 'noble introductions' and his list of customers amply justified his claim that he was 'in the Favour of the Nobility and Gentry'. But while he took orders from 'Their Highnesses the Oranges' and many about the Court, he admitted that he was unable to sell Wedgwood to 'the middle sort of people'. Wedgwood's prices were considered too high and, as Joseph Cooper told Josiah in 1773, 'the cautious Dutch . . . always look often at their money before they resign it'.[62]

Cautious spenders they may have been, but the Dutch were not slow to appreciate the quality of Wedgwood's wares. The popularity of lead-glazed Queen's ware had a disastrous effect upon the sale of local tin-glazed delft. Many of the delft potters, faced with bankruptcy, attempted to make Queen's ware, and van Veldhuysen made a particular point that every piece sent to him must be impress-marked with the Wedgwood name.[63] In 1785 he sent samples to Etruria of 'Queen's ware' (already accepted as the generic name of English creamware) made in Holland by a 'Mr Zwenck'. Josiah's response was as comforting to his agent as it would have been unwelcome to the manufacturer: 'Mr Zwenck has shewn a taste & attention . . . in respect of workmanship which does him great credit . . . [but] on the other hand truth obliges me to declare to you, that with regard to the quality of the body & glaze, they are both so bad that we could not sell such pieces at 1 shilling a dozen.' He could not, indeed, sell them at all, not even to 'those that hawk them about villages & at fairs & markets'.[64] No Dutch manufacturer successfully copied English creamware until the nineteenth century, and no great effort seems to have been made to imitate Wedgwood's stoneware bodies. The Dutch became, and have ever since remained, among Wedgwood's most valued customers.

During the eleven years of the Wedgwood & Bentley partnership the bulk of their overseas trade was conducted through Bentley & Boardman and Sadler & Green as exporters from the port of Liverpool or through Boulton & Fothergill in Birmingham. Boulton's part in Wedgwood's choice of export markets was significant and it may well have been the former's success in Paris that impelled the latter to solicit attention from Choiseul. 'One country is not a large enough markett',

Boulton told Lord Cathcart in October 1771, 'for commodities which can be bought only by persons of elegance and fortune.'[65] His own triumph in France was not won over prohibitions and excise duties but over the French metal-workers, who enjoyed a tacit monopoly of their home market and the domination of every market overseas. Although clear evidence is lacking, it has been authoritatively estimated that 'the greater part of the ormolu goods produced at Soho in the 1770s was exported' and this is supported by Wedgwood, who told Bentley as much in 1776.[66] One of Boulton's best markets was Russia, in spite of a 30 per cent tariff, and, like Wedgwood, he owed much to the patronage and active cooperation of the Cathcarts.

Like Wedgwood, too, he enlisted the services of British ambassadors abroad to promote his goods at the Courts to which they were accredited. Sir William Hamilton was one of the most enthusiastic of Wedgwood's champions and, after Jane Cathcart's death and her husband's return to England, Josiah profoundly wished that Hamilton could exchange Naples for St Petersburg. Otherwise, he feared, 'The Russians must have Etruscan, & Grecian vases about the 19th Century' for, without guidance such as Hamilton's, they would not be ready for them any sooner. Sir Robert Liston bought Wedgwood for use in his embassies in Lisbon and Stockholm, and later spread the word in Washington and Constantinople; Sir Robert Ainslie provided Wedgwood with models of tablewares suitable for the Turkish market, although Josiah was irritated to be told that Wedgwood & Bentley ornaments were not acceptable; Sir Robert Murray Keith helped to make Wedgwood better known in Vienna; Lord Macartney took Wedgwood vases to show to the Chinese Emperor.[67] Such introductions were worth much in immediate orders and much more in accumulated reputation. They opened the civilised world to Wedgwood's tablewares and ornaments so that it is no great surprise to find Faujas de St Fond remarking in 1797 that Wedgwood had created 'a commerce so active and so universal, that in Travelling from Paris to St Petersburg, from Amsterdam to the farthest point of Sweden, from Dunkirk to the southern extremity of France, one is served at every inn from English earthenware. The same fine article adorns the tables of Spain, Portugal & Italy, and it provides the cargoes of ships to the East Indies, the West Indies and America.'[68] In 1783 King Stanislaus Augustus of Poland went to the considerable expense of establishing a pottery at the Belvedere palace expressly in order to staunch the losses in currency caused by imports of English creamware.[69]

None of Wedgwood's contemporaries in the pottery industry made such an enormous range of articles, useful and ornamental, to furnish every room in the house from cellar to attic, from kitchen and dairy to drawing-room and library. None made such intelligent attempts to satisfy the unusual demands of his customers, wherever they might be. He made memorial urns and fonts for churches, medallions of the popes for Catholics, hookahs for 'Infidels', and royal portraits for most of Europe. He scanned Lady Mary Wortley Montagu's *Letters from the East*, which described her experiences in Constantinople in 1716–18 when her husband was ambassador there, for information about Turkish habits and customs and was gratified to discover that 'between the Windows in the Ladies Harams are little Arches to set *pots of Perfume* or *baskets of flowers* Alias Beaupots'. He greedily visualised 'double rows of windows in these rooms, & Arches between every window' and asked: 'what is a single chimney piece in our solitary rooms to twenty or thirty of these charming little Arches . . . Let who will take the Sultanas; if I could but get at those delightful little nitches, & furnish them'. He discovered further that, 'Thier Baths are all set round with the richest Vases' and decided approvingly, 'these people have the right notions of things'.[70] Nor was his pursuit of trade hampered by politics. He despised Lord North but sold his portrait, and his admiration for Fox did not prevent his commissioning a portrait of the Younger Pitt. In times of revolution he demonstrated a judicious impartiality by making portraits or commemorative objects for both sides.

Unlike Bentley, Josiah never travelled abroad and, although he journeyed extensively through England in search of materials and visited Sadler & Green, Boulton and other agents to discuss production and trade with them, there is little evidence that he involved himself in the business of selling to the public, except in the course of greeting illustrious visitors to the Etruria or London showrooms. Boulton's partner, John Fothergill, made a long tour of Northern Germany and Scandinavia in search of trade in 1766–8, and the partners employed salesmen to travel in Italy in 1767 and in Russia in 1774,[71] but this form of selling overseas was rare among British manufacturers. In the pottery industry, the employment of travelling salesmen did not become common until the end of the eighteenth century, although John and Thomas Wedgwood of the Big House, Burslem, may have employed 'riders' forty years earlier.[72] Josiah Wedgwood was certainly among the first to consider the idea, writing to Bentley in September 1771 to suggest that William Brock might be employed in this manner, 'continually among the Merchants *shewing them Patterns, bringing them to the Rooms, taking their orders, & receiving their money'*.[73] Brock, however, was sent to Dublin to manage the Wedgwood & Bentley showrooms there and the scheme was shelved. Josiah raised the subject again early in 1778, proposing that Joseph Brownbill might be equipped with a 'travelling machine' and take with him 'patterns of flower pots, & little bouquet pots, Tablets – Figures – Patterns – Ink pots & stands – Seals &c, & some pieces of usefull ware'. From personal experience he knew that 'without a variety of new & striking patterns . . . he may as well stay at home'.[74]

The following month this plan was put into effect and Brownbill was sent to call on some customers in the country, but succeeded only in involving himself in a series of ridiculous mishaps which Josiah described as 'like a dream, or one of Don Quixots adventures'. The carriage, or 'travelling machine', had not proved to be a success, over-turning at least once and adding to the undesirable impression that Wedgwood's goods were being hawked round the markets. Josiah was nevertheless determined to persevere with the scheme, which was, he was convinced, the only way in which his goal of supplying two retail shops in every considerable town – one a china shop and the other a jeweller's – could be achieved.[75]

Tom Byerley's first effort as a traveller, on his return journey from London after collecting Sukey from the Bentleys' at Turnham Green in April 1778, was sufficiently encouraging for Josiah to send him out again, 'into the tremendous North', in the following January. He carried with him a small stock of such easily portable pieces as portrait med-allions, seals and inkwells, as well as samples of tablewares, and, in thirty-six days on the road, he covered the large towns in the north-east from Warrington to Carlisle before crossing to Newcastle-upon-Tyne and returning through Yorkshire and Lancashire. His sales were modest, amounting to £125 16s. 7d., and his expenses unacceptably high, but he also collected debts totalling £162 9s. 4d., and the experi-ence was valuable. From that time onwards, Wedgwood employed travelling salesmen as a matter of policy, and their journeys gradually became regular to all parts of the country.[76] Tom Byerley was Wedg-wood's first regular traveller in Britain and became, a few years later with Jos, the first Wedgwood partner to make a selling trip abroad. Until his death in 1810 it was he who organised all travellers' journeys.

Among the Wedgwood manuscripts to have survived from the early nineteenth century is a traveller's pattern book. This little volume contains details of patterns and shapes of tableware and ornamental wares, meticulously drawn in watercolour, and it is likely that some-thing similar was carried by Byerley and all his immediate successors. Larger shape and pattern books, illustrating vase shapes and ornament and every tableware pattern available, were held in the showrooms in London and at Etruria.

Many of Wedgwood's marketing methods, some his own and some

suggested by Bentley, were innovative, and a few involved grave financial risk. He was always more ready to hazard money than reputation and his investment in the 'Voluntaries' venture in Germany, designed by de Shoning and supported by Bentley, was little short of reckless; but it was no more so than his purchase of the Ridgehouse estate and the building of Etruria. Of all the Staffordshire potters, Wedgwood was the boldest but he was also the best informed. His choice of an experienced and cultured merchant to be his partner was not inspired solely, or even primarily, by the warmth of their friendship. He recognised in Bentley qualities that were both in harmony with his own and complementary to them. As individuals they were both capable, as they had proved before they met, of successful enterprise. Together Wedgwood and Bentley formed one of the most active, original and effective entrepreneurial partnerships in history.

CHAPTER SIXTEEN

Dissent and Rebellion

The earnest, stubborn, rather dull twenty-one-year-old who had inherited the throne of England from his grandfather in October 1760, inherited also the prejudices of his father, the unlamented Frederick Louis, Prince of Wales, who had died in 1751. The first of the Hanoverian kings to consider himself British, George III had made his declaration of this belief in his speech from the throne in 1761: 'Born and educated in this country, I glory in the name of Britain.'[1] He cared little for Europe and even less for the Electorate of Hanover, which had been too often in the past forty-five years the axis around which British foreign policy had been determined. Contrary to his historical reputation, George III was neither stupid nor ill educated, and it is now understood that he was not, until the last few years of his life, insane.[2] That he was bluntly honest, courageous, tactless, often inept and, in his early years as King, disastrously advised, is seldom questioned.

Negotiations with France, concluded in March 1763, brought the Seven Years War to an end. Few foresaw the true danger arising from the conquest of Canada. The destruction of French power to the north of the New England colonies removed the one threat to their security which ensured their adherence to Britain. The most celebrated conquest of Pitt's administration, won in glory and applauded in public emotion, had laid the foundation for revolution and the loss of the American colonies.

Meanwhile, Britain enjoyed a welcome period of comparative peace in Europe blemished only by political disturbances at home. To avoid the necessity for unpopular taxation, ruthless reductions were made in the army and, a more serious blunder, in the maintenance of the navy. Warships were allowed to rot and the dockyards were run down. Having introduced the economies best designed to ensure that the British armed services would be in no condition to fight, the government led by Pitt's brother-in-law, George Grenville, then took the first unwitting steps towards creating a situation that must lead to war. The East India Company was self-financing, using the profits from trade to pay for its own civil administration and armed forces; and the great fortunes made by Englishmen in India generally returned to England with them when they retired. The American colonies, on the other hand, made no such sensible and useful contribution to national finances. Emigrants to America rarely returned to their home country and, when they did, it was more often because they had failed to settle than because they had prospered. The British treasury, and ultimately the British taxpayer, met the heavy costs of security and the maintenance of bases for trade.

Against these arguments might be set the American adverse trade balance – £9 million in 1760 – the severe shortage of bullion and the crippling burden imposed on the colonies by the regulation of their trade with other countries. Such regulation was, in effect, ignored: the duties on imported molasses were seldom paid and great fortunes were made out of goods smuggled to France and Spain, Britain's enemies in the Seven Years War. Grenville was determined that such taxes as might be imposed should be collected. He cut the duty on molasses by half and employed the navy to help enforce the collection of customs revenues. The manoeuvre was subtle. It would appear perverse to condemn the reduction of a tax or the enforcement of law more than thirty years old. Encouraged by the lack of opposition to these moderate measures, Grenville introduced, in March 1765, his Stamp Act imposing duty on all documents required for legal transactions and on newspapers.

On the face of it this form of taxation, already applied in Britain, was both logical and proper. It yielded valuable revenue with minimal costs of collection, it was difficult to evade, and it fell – fairly, it was thought – on those best able to pay. The revenue to be raised would amount to some £60,000, barely one-sixth of the cost of maintaining an adequate army in North America and about a shilling a year for every man, woman and child in the colonies. So moderate was the demand that Benjamin Franklin, after a token hesitation, not only accepted the Act but also secured the appointment of at least two of his friends as collectors at a salary of £300 a year.[3] To the colonists, however, this innovation of a direct tax appeared as the last, and worst, of a series of repressive measures which combined with commercial restrictions to endanger their prosperity and perpetuate their subservience. The dire economic state of the American colonies, for which there was ample evidence in the reports of the governors, the rising tide of private and commercial bankruptcies and the decline in real estate values, was either not appreciated or ignored in England.

The Stamp Tax injured principally the prosperous American middle class whose support was needed and who were best qualified to organ- ise revolution. By August it had become clear that the Act could not be implemented without the use of force. Grenville was dismissed and the Act repealed. A new ministry, under the Marquis of Rockingham, suffered a series of humiliating defeats, tottered and fell. Pitt, who accepted the task of forming a new government, accepted, also, the earldom of Chatham. In doing so he robbed his administration of its greatest political strength, his own voice in the House of Commons. Lord Chesterfield was not alone in finding incomprehensible Pitt's acceptance of a place in 'that Hospital for Incurables, the House of Lords'.[4]

Deprived of his authoritarian presence in the House of Commons, Chatham's government suffered a series of defeats. In Europe, his plans for realignment were rejected and Frederick the Great, for long an admirer of William Pitt, refused to risk conflict with Britain's enemies by allying himself with the Earl of Chatham.

In America Chatham's return to office was greeted with expressions of delight suitable to the long-awaited arrival of a liberator. Wedgwood, seldom slow to exploit an opportunity, greeted his return to office with a proposal to 'take advantage of the American prejudice in favour of that great man' by sending to the colonies Queen's ware jugs and teapots decorated with a transfer-printed portrait of him.[5] The colonists, however, confident of Chatham's favour, and encouraged by the ease of their victory over the Stamp Act, discovered another grievance. The Mutiny Act of 1766 gave British military commanders authority to demand from local inhabitants accommodation and food for their troops. Both Massachusetts and New York refused to comply with the Act.

Chatham's plans to reform the East India Company, bringing all Company territory under the sovereignty of the Crown and the regu- lation of Parliament, encountered opposition. As always, he was infuri- ated by obstruction or the questioning of his authority. Complaining of gout and 'the infelicity which ferments and sours the councils of His Majesty's servants', he withdrew to Bath to nurse his failing health and assaulted vanity.Chesterfield observed acidly, 'he has had a *fall upstairs* and has done himself so much hurt, that he will never be able to stand upon his legs again . . . he is now, certainly, only Earl of Chatham; and no longer Mr Pitt in any respect whatsoever'.[6] Rumours began to spread that Chatham was mad.

In his prolonged absence the government was committed to a solution for America, which it was claimed would raise revenue without creating unrest in the colonies. It consisted of new customs duties on a quantity of goods, including paper and tea, imported from Britain. This further regulation of legitimate trade, which would certainly have been rejected by any government actively led by Chatham, was approved by the King and a majority in both Houses of Parliament and yielded the predictable result: American opposition to direct taxation was extended to embrace all forms of tax imposed by the British Parliament. In October 1768 Chatham again resigned. The way had been cleared for the systematic mismanagement of colonial affairs which drove the Americans through resentment and resistance into rebellion and independence.

Opposition to the new taxes was led by Massachusetts, where the Assembly was suspended. The colonies rallied in support and signed non-importation agreements to exclude British goods from New England. On 1 May 1769 the Cabinet decided by five votes to four to remove all taxes imposed on the colonies except that applied to tea. This extraordinary manoeuvre must be assumed to have been intended to mollify the people of Massachusetts while simultaneously reassuring the British that their right to tax the Americans was unimpaired. The result was somewhat different: the people of Massachusetts, and indeed of all the American colonies, were made aware that taxation was to continue but that rebellion reduced it; the British were made to understand that the government was weak, vacillating and vulnerable to pressure. Seeking to retain the right to impose duties to produce revenue or control trade, the British government had succeeded only in maintaining an irrelevance.

As if such difficulties were not enough, even worse threatened: Chatham had recovered and was preparing to return to political life. To a government in trouble, no news could have been less reassuring.

On 9 January 1770 Chatham began the assault which brought the government to its knees in less than two weeks. Having brought about the resignation of the first minister, the Duke of Grafton, and seven of his Cabinet, Chatham was confident that his own return to power would quickly follow. But he had miscalculated: much as he respected Chatham's authority, patriotism and integrity, George III had come to detest him and he was not prepared to accept as his first minister any champion of Wilkes or electoral reform. He sent instead for Lord North.

Much has been written to North's discredit. It is true that the consequences of his long tenure of office were far from beneficial to Britain, but the portrayal of him as a fumbling incompetent is both false and unjust. He lacked the vision of the statesman but he possessed most of the qualities required in a political leader. He was shrewd, industrious, imperturbable, witty, well read, a master of language and repartee and impervious to defeat. His appearance was not engaging: leavy-lidded, protuberant eyes and bulging cheeks gave him, as Horace Walpole remarked, 'the air of a blind trumpeter'. Nathanial Wraxhall, who had plenty of opportunity to study him in Parliament, discerned in him one of the most valuable attributes of the complete parliamentarian: 'Lord North rarely rose to sublimity, though he possessed vast facility and command of language. If necessary he could speak for a long time, apparently with great pathos, and yet disclose no important fact.'[7]

For all his faults, North cannot be dismissed as a buffoon. He led the government for twelve years in a House of Commons* whose members had known Chatham in full vigour and against the formidable opposition of the Younger Pitt, Charles James Fox, Edmund Burke and Richard Brinsley Sheridan.

Chatham persevered in his attacks on the government, principally aimed against the excessive influence of the Crown and in favour of electoral reform, but, in accepting a peerage, he had sacrificed his voice in the Commons and his contact with the people. In the summer of 1771 he withdrew again to the country, attending Parliament only once the next three years.

Chatham's brief reappearance in the House of Lords was made in May 1772. Far from well and extremely lame, he returned to support a bill to relieve religious nonconformists from some of their disabilities under the law and to give them greater social freedom. To the charge that dissenters were men of close ambition, Chatham responded, 'They are so, and their ambition is to keep close to the college of Fishermen, not of cardinals, and to the doctrines of inspired apostles, not the decrees of interested and aspiring bishops.' His defence of dissent was in vain. Passed by the House of Commons, many of whose members owed their seats to dissenters' votes, the bill was, at the King's behest, thrown out by the Lords. It is unlikely that Bentley failed to pass on to Josiah a report of a political debate of such importance to them both, but the latter's interest in politics had not yet been inspired by events in America.

In June 1772 a British revenue cutter, run aground off Rhode Island, was burned by the local inhabitants. It was a minor incident, apparently isolated and of little significance. Fifteen months later another demon-

---

*North was the eldest son of the Earl of Guilford and thus eligible to sit in the House of Commons until his father's death in 1790.

stration of antagonism at Boston lighted the explosive train that had first been laid by Grenville in 1765.

New York broke the non-importation agreement in 1770. Other states followed suit and normal trade in British goods was resumed. For three years, while the duty on tea was reluctantly paid, hostility towards Britain festered beneath the surface and the colonies bickered among themselves. The immediate cause of more serious trouble was an ingenious scheme to help the East India Company out of financial difficulty. The large surplus stocks of the Company were to be permitted to be sent direct to America, without incurring either handling charges in England or British duties, enabling it to be sold at about half its previous price. Tea, regarded by Americans as the drink of traitors,* would thus, it was argued, become popular and satisfactory profits would accrue to the Company. The theory was logical but it lacked charm for Bostonians and for smugglers whose flourishing business was centred on New York and Philadelphia. The colonists might have agreed among themselves not to buy tea; instead, they chose to prevent its being landed. At the ports of New York and Philadelphia landing was refused and the ships loaded with tea were obliged to turn back to England; at Charleston it was dumped in damp cellars, where it was soon ruined; at Boston, on 16 December 1773, 340 of the Company's tea chests were thrown into the sea by parties of angry Bostonians unconvincingly disguised as 'Mohawk Indians'.

Reports of the 'Tea Party' reached London in January 1774. North's reaction, strongly approved by the King, was immediate and severe. Thomas Hutchinson was replaced as governor by General Thomas Gage; the port of Boston was closed until the ruined tea was paid for; changes were proposed for the Massachusetts constitution, replacing an Upper House elected by the House of Representatives by one whose members were nominated by the Crown; the new governor was empowered at will to transfer capital trials to England; and the quartering of troops in barracks was to be provided by the city. The colonies should be settled in prosperous tranquillity, if necessary by force.

American distrust and anger were aggravated by the passage of the Quebec Act to provide for the formal settlement of Canada after ten years of British rule. The Americans feared the creation of a new nation to the north, dominated by a Catholic majority supported by the British. It appeared to them as the re-creation of an old threat to their security which they had thought destroyed with the final expulsion of the

*In England, until the middle of the century, tea-drinking had been considered unmanly and an occupation suitable only for the ladies.

French in 1760. Even as Benjamin Franklin was advocating payment for the tea destroyed at Boston,[8] radicals were clamouring for a solemn league and covenant against Britain. The compromise, a congress in Philadelphia, was dominated by radical delegates. Resolutions were passed to restrict all trade with Britain to exports considered essential to the survival of the southern territories, to refuse all payment of taxes to Britain and to make preparations for defence.

North's government wavered between a desire to punish and the need to conciliate, between the determination to govern and an understanding of the impracticability of government at such a distance without consent. Chatham made appeals for the withdrawal of British troops from America and presented to the Lords a plan reasserting the legislative supremacy of Britain in all matters of trade and navigation but recognising Congress and freeing the colonies to assess and raise revenues by their own methods. In the Commons, Edmund Burke, in a speech of great eloquence, enunciated the principle of authority without the exercise of power. It was a cloak of compromise, never worn but already shop-soiled by frequent display to doubtful customers, from which he succeeded in drawing a thread of genuine policy. His insistence that freedom and prosperity were the essential ingredients of imperial unity and strength anticipated the ideals of commonwealth. North, like a fussy nurse, dispensed medicine with syrup. He proposed that the colonies should recognise British sovereignty and the right to levy taxes but devise their own means of raising revenue to contribute to common costs. Before this plan could be considered, the first shots of revolution were fired at Lexington.

Wedgwood, 'no Polititian', as he freely admitted, was uncomprehending: 'All the world are with the Minister [Lord North] & against the poor Americans', he wrote in dismay to Bentley in January. A month later he reported the arrival in Manchester of Dr Roe (a reference to Dr John Roebuck), 'exceeding hot & violent against the Americans . . . he quite froth'd at the mouth . . . & was so excessively rapid in his declamations, and exclamations, that nobody could put in a word'. Josiah believed that these 'harangues' had had 'a very considerable effect amongst many, Dissenters & others'.[9] His own sympathies were already plain. Some eight years earlier he had told Bentley of his conversation with Sir William Bagot, the Member of Parliament for Stafford:

we had a good chat upon political affairs, particularly American, in which I told him my sentiments very freely – That our Policy had a tendency to render the Americans independent a Century sooner than they would be in the common order of events, if treated agreeable to sound policy.[10]

These sentiments were not uncommon in London but they were not widely shared in the Midlands. 'I do not know how it happens,' Josiah wrote in February 1775, 'but a general infatuation seems to have gone forth, & the poor Americans are deemed Rebels, now the Minister has declared them so, by a very great majority wherever I go. Why should not the Americans be taxed as well as us? Do we not spend our money in defence of them? – These are the universal questions, & they will not have any answer to them.'[11]

The brief skirmish at Lexington, when a detachment of British troops sent to confiscate arms stored at Concord was fired on by the Massachusetts militia, resulted in about sixty American casualties; but 273 British soldiers were killed or wounded. This disproportion was sufficient to give the rebels cause for celebration and to alarm the government at home. Three major-generals – William Howe, John Burgoyne and Henry Clinton – were dispatched to serve under Gage. 'Howe', Horace Walpole wrote, 'was reckoned sensible, though so silent that nobody knew whether he was or not. Burgoyne . . . was a vain, very ambitious man, with a half understanding that was worse than none; Clinton had not that fault, for he had no sense at all.'[12] In the first major engagement of the war, at Bunker Hill on 17 June, British victory was bought at the cost of more than 1000 casualties. North's conciliatory proposals were rejected by the rebels and George Washington was appointed commander-in-chief of the American forces.

Sympathy for the colonists and an intelligent warning of the likely consequences of war in America were expressed in 'A FRIENDLY ADDRESS to Lord NORTH', published in the Gentleman's Magazine in July 1775. The anonymous author wrote:

Let me entreat thee if thou has any regard for trade, for the peace of thy own mind, and for the prosperity of Great Britain and the colonies, immediately to repeal all the repressive acts that have been passed, and to make such overtures as will secure a speedy accommodation. God knows, this is no time to quarrel with our best friends, and to give up three millions a year by suspending their trade, and contending for an unjust tax: for however pacific France and Spain may appear at present, be assured that, when we have ennervated ourselves by the unnatural contest, we shall be attacked by the united force of both.

The American invasion of Canada in August was a blunder that ended in failure at Quebec in December and hardened public opinion against the rebels. Wedgwood's opinion of the war was unchanged, but he was less free with it to any but his closest friends.

During the following eighteen months the war in America followed the generally negative course that Chatham had predicted. Gage had been replaced by Howe but, in spite of reinforcements of both British and hired Hessian troops, the army had failed to achieve conclusive victory. It was already clear that the country was too large to be conquered by any army that Britain could assemble and the time had passed when a few isolated defeats might have persuaded the loyalists into action or the less enthusiastic rebels to defect. Howe had captured Long Island and New York and Clinton had taken Rhode Island, and Washington's series of retreats to avoid defeat had done much to demoralise the Americans, but his surprise attack across the Delaware on 26 December, when nearly 1000 Hessians surrendered to him, had given the rebels new hope.

On 30 May 1777 Chatham appeared again in the House of Lords after an absence of two years, muffled to the neck in flannel and leaning heavily on a crutch. He made an eloquent appeal for the redress of American grievances, the repeal of vexatious laws, and for reconciliation, and he informed the House of his reasons for believing that the Americans were receiving financial help from France. French recognition of American independence must result in war with France and, as inevitably, with Spain. The defence of inalienable rights was not to be regarded as rebellion. By insisting on submission Britain would be casting away the greatest benefits of colonisation: trade in time of peace and support in time of war. His appeal elicited little support. The King told Lord North that the speech was 'highly unseasonable' and contained 'nothing but specious words and malevolence'.[13]

Even as Chatham spoke, the strategic plan to finish the rebellion by the conjunction of Howe's army from New York with Burgoyne's, moving south from the St Lawrence through the Hudson gap, provided the first disaster of the war. Howe diverted his force to take Philadelphia, leaving Burgoyne cornered and outnumbered by an American army under General Horatio Gates. He was obliged to surrender his entire army at Saratoga on 17 October. This news was received with jubilation by the French, who had been waiting for just such a sign that Britain would be wholly engaged in a long and wasting war 3000 miles away. In February 1778 France signed a treaty of friendship with the American revolutionary states and, as Chatham had predicted, Britain was again at war with France and Spain.

News from America was slow to reach England and slower to arrive in Staffordshire. More than a month after Saratoga the bells were being rung in the Potteries for 'the reported overthrow of Washington & destruction of the Rebels'. Josiah was doubtful of the truth of the reports but supposed, correctly, that Philadelphia had been taken. By the third week of December the shocking news of Burgoyne's disgrace had been confirmed. Bentley wrote asking if he would contribute to a fund for American prisoners in England and Josiah responded with caution: 'You may subscribe 10 or £20, or what you please for me towards alleviating the miseries of the poor captives. . . . Gratitude to their countrymen for their humanity to G. Burgoine & his army is no small motive for my mite.' He stipulated, however, that the contribution must be anonymous, 'under the signature of A B or C or what you please'. This was no time to be offending his most powerful customers by appearing to give comfort to the King's enemies.[14]

He was, in fact, already taking risks enough. Earlier in the year he had produced a quantity of intaglio seals engraved in the form of a coiled rattlesnake with the motto 'DON'T TREAD ON ME', adapted from the design chosen for the Union flag. This was intended for distribution to sympathisers with the American cause and Josiah warned Bentley that it would be prudent 'to keep such unchristian articles for *Private Trade*'.[15] Unlike the rest of the Wedgwood & Bentley seals of this period, which bore the impressed mark of the partnership (sometimes abbreviated to 'W & B'), the rattlesnake seal was unmarked. Josiah was also engaged in producing a portrait medallion of George Washington, modelled from a bronze medal designed by Voltaire and sent to him by Bentley, but he was doubtful about the wisdom of doing so. While others produced seals and the source of an unmarked rattlesnake seal might be disputed, there would be no disguising the manufacturer of a jasper portrait medallion which Josiah would, in any case, wish to bear his trademark. He wrote uneasily to Bentley: 'I may think [him] worthily employ'd, but many circumstances may make it highly improper *for me*, & *at this season*, to strike Medals in his honor.' Two days later he was still more anxious: 'My objections to striking medals from the Bronze you sent me rather increase. It would be doing no service to the cause of *Liberty in general*, at least so it appears to me, & might hurt us very much *individually*.' He was concerned to be seen as celebrating as the 'Patron of Liberty' a man 'at this time more absolute than any Despot in Europe' and added, 'Besides, if France should declare herself openly an Ally . . . I am from that moment an enemy to both . . . I may, as a subject of the British Empire, declare my self an enemy to all its enemies & their Allies though I may curse most bitterly those who have brought us into the dilemma of calling those our enemies, who were, & might have continued to be, our best friends.' He asked for Bentley's advice but warned him not to send it by the post.[16] Evidently he overcame his fears, for the portrait was produced in December as a companion portrait to one of Benjamin Franklin.[17] To restore the balance and counter possible criticism, he produced another, smaller and less distinguished portrait of Lord North.

By the end of the year even the 'Anti-Americans' in the country had lost their taste for war and Josiah reported them as thinking 'that the war would be ended in the best manner we could wish by granting the Americans all they have hitherto ask'd us for'. 'What fools must we have been then,' he wrote in disgust, 'to expend so much blood & treasure for something worse than nothing at all.'[18]

In January 1778 the King had warned Lord North of the immediate danger of a French declaration of war and had advised him, in this event, to withdraw the army from America to strengthen Canada, Nova Scotia and the Floridas. He also recommended attacks on French possessions in the West Indies and on New Orleans, while using the navy to wreck American trade. Sir Henry Clinton, who had succeeded Howe as commander-in-chief, was therefore ordered to concentrate on a naval war, blockading ports and destroying shipping, while his efforts on land should be devoted to drawing Washington and his army into a decisive action. North, rightly declaring the country 'totally unequal to a war with Spain, France and America' and that 'peace with America, and a change in the Ministry are the only steps which can save this country',[19] asked in vain to be permitted to resign. He made the same request at frequent intervals for the next five years.

Chatham was warned by the Duke of Richmond that he intended to introduce a motion granting the colonies independence. The old statesman could not stand aside and watch the liquidation of the empire he had shaped and, ignoring the protests of his physicians, he insisted on attending the debate. On 7 April the whole House rose to greet him as he entered the chamber, supported by his younger son William and his son-in-law, Lord Mahon. As soon as Richmond had spoken, Chatham rose to reply. He was scarcely able to stand, his voice was so weak that he was often inaudible and his mind wandered so that the thread of his argument was lost; and yet, amidst the confusion of thought, there were moments, all the more moving because of the memories they revived, of the old eloquence and authority. When he was master of his mind, he was still master of his audience. 'My Lords,' he reminded them, 'His Majesty succeeded to an Empire as great in extent as its reputation was unsullied. Shall we tarnish the lustre of this nation by an ignominious surrender of its rights and fairest possessions? Shall this great kingdom fall prostrate before the House of Bourbon? . . . Shall a people that fifteen years ago was the terror of the world now stoop so low as to tell its ancient inveterate enemy, "Take away all we have; only give us peace". It is impossible . . . in God's name . . . Let us make one effort; and if we must fall, let us fall like men.'[20]

It was his last heroic effort and the strain was too much for his enfeebled body. He fell back exhausted into the arms of his supporters. Richmond replied 'with great tenderness and respect'. When Chatham struggled to rise again, he collapsed and was carried, unconscious, into the adjoining Prince's Chamber, where he recovered sufficiently to be moved to a house in nearby Downing Street. Two days later he was taken to his own house at Hayes, in Kent. The Lords adjourned their debate as a mark of respect. Chatham had left the House for the last time.

From Etruria, Josiah wrote four days later to Bentley in London: 'Poor Lord Chatham! How are the mighty fallen! His body & mind seem to keep pace with each other. Methinks it was almost a pity to call him into life again he made his exit so much in his own way. He certainly will never die again so much to his own satisfaction.'[21] Chatham lingered for four weeks. When he died on 11 May, Sir Philip Francis, thought by some to have been the author of the Letters of Junius, which had pilloried many of the most celebrated politicians of the day, wrote of him: 'He is dead; and the sense of honour, and character, and understanding of the nation are dead with him.'[22]

Chatham's state funeral and burial in Westminster Abbey took place on Tuesday 9 June. Just twenty-two days later Josiah was arranging to obtain a cast from a relief portrait by John Flaxman junior to reproduce in jasper. Within twelve months he had added a fine black basaltes bust, about 2 feet high, after the original by Joseph Wilton. No comparable bust of any British politician was made during Josiah's lifetime.

A second great funeral procession wound its way to Westminster Abbey some six months after Chatham's: England's greatest actor, David Garrick, had died in January. Wedgwood, already provided with a portrait medallion, issued in jasper and basaltes in 1777, lost no time in producing a memorial bust of Garrick as well.

What Josiah described as 'the present most wicked & preposterous war with our brethren & best friends' was daily losing support in the country, and North was widely blamed for the 'absurdity, folly & wickedness of our whole proceedings with America'. Josiah reported that even 'some of the most violent tories here abuse him most heartily . . . D—n him, they say, could he not resign.'[23] Nothing would have pleased North more than to be allowed to oblige them, but the King would not permit it. In conversation with a guest at Etruria, a Mr Godwin of Gataker, who was loyal to the King and his ministers and was confident that 'a majority of the dissenters in Liverpool, Lancashire & Cheshire' shared his opinions, Josiah found to his surprise that he and Godwin could agree on a metaphor, if not a policy:

> In canvassing the relations of *parent* & *child* as applied to Britain, & America . . . we were both of us oblig'd to acknowledge the disagree-able facts that we had driven out the brat in his infancy, & expos'd him in an uncultivated forest to the mercy of wild beasts & savages, without any farther inquiries after him 'till we imagin'd he might be brought to render us some essential services. We then took him again under our parental protection; provided him with a straight waistcoat, & whenever he wriggled, or winch'd drew it up a hole tighter, & behav'd so like a step-mother to our son, now grown a very tall boy, that he determin'd to strip off his waistcoat, & put on the toga at once, & is now *actually carrying fire & water through the whole empire* wherever he pleases.[24]

On the subject of independence, they could agree on the end but not the means: 'it seems,' Josiah told Bentley, 'we must not acknow-ledge, or give it up to them – No, that it would be too mortifying for our high stomachs. We must sulkily clear the ground & let them take it. As much as to say – Go to the D—l in your own way.'[25]

In America, Clinton and Lord Cornwallis, who had become second-in-command in America, had moved the fulcrum of their operations to the south. Savannah was taken in December and by the end of January 1780 the whole of Georgia was in British hands. In May Charleston was surrendered by General Lincoln with more than 6500 soldiers and seamen, a belated revenge for Saratoga, and South Carolina was cleared. Three months later Cornwallis smashed an American army of 6000 men under General Gates, sent to defend North Carolina. The revised strategy was showing results and there were encouraging signs, in the increase in the numbers of loyalists joining the struggle and captured evidence that the French were dissatisfied with the progress and the heavy cost of the war, that the British army might, after all, be capable of winning the war in America.

These signs were misleading. The successes were too local and the country too large to permit Clinton to turn victory into conquest. The population was, on the whole, hostile, communications between armies and with the government at home were difficult and slow, and losses of men, as casualties or prisoners of the enemy, could not quickly be made good. Above all, there was a growing understanding in England that even a final victory which resulted in the colonists laying down their arms would not solve the problem of governing a resentful and remote population. Long before the Americans found their own solution Wedgwood suffered a loss that drove politics, war and American liberty from his mind.

CHAPTER SEVENTEEN

The Saddest Loss

In January 1780 Thomas Bentley celebrated his fiftieth birthday, as did Josiah Wedgwood his own six months later. 'It is an old adage', Josiah had written early in their friendship, 'that a Man is either a Fool, or a *Physician* at fifty, & considering the opportunitys I have with the Brindleys & Bentleys of the Age if I am not a very wise mortal before that Age I must be a blockhead in grain.'[1] Wedgwood and Bentley had been friends for nearly eighteen years and business partners for eleven, and only once had they had a disagreement serious enough to merit the description of a quarrel. On the contrary, their opinions diverged so seldom and so slightly, and each was so willing to accept the advice of the other, that they appeared almost as two halves of the same person, an impression confirmed by Josiah's avowal: 'I feel but like half of my self when we are separated.'[2] In one of many references to the similarity of their approach to all problems, Josiah wrote:

> I cannot help observing that the first part of your letter describes the situation of my mind so exactly, as well as your own, that I often think we shall spoil each other for ever acting separately again. I feel the same irresolution steal upon me in other matters, & nothing but the distance between us, & my natural aversion to writing prevents your being troubled with many a thing which only requires a moments thought & resolution to determine; for I can scarcely bring myself to think *anything determin'd* without haveing your opinion to guide my resolution upon it.[3]

And yet the qualities they brought to their friendship and partnership were very different. Bentley's education was formal and enlarged by foreign travel and a wide circle of cultivated friends. Wedgwood's formal education was slight but he was a voracious consumer of the tools of learning and his curiosity and appetite for knowledge were insatiable. The library of books that he acquired for himself and for the partnership was extensive and the varied subjects that he chose to study – chemistry, geology, shells, transport, the slave trade – were studied in depth. Wedgwood's admiration for Bentley's education and social accomplishments was matched by Bentley's delight in Josiah's enthusiasm and inventiveness.

In the early biographies of Wedgwood, Bentley is almost eclipsed by the titanic figure of his partner. In one later sketch of the relationship of the two men, the attempt to redress the balance has led to a facile division: 'Wedgwood, the inventor and technician', Bentley 'the sales-man and merchant';[4] Wedgwood the manufacturer and Bentley the sophisticated entrepreneur. The same author credits Bentley with having helped Wedgwood to 'win the patronage of the Queen, the nobility, the artists and the connoisseurs'[5] and for having made the first approach to Lord Cathcart. While there is no doubt that Bentley made regular visits to St James's Palace to show Queen Charlotte the latest vases and patterns, or that he played the diplomatic card admirably and made the most of his contacts among the nobility, it is also certain that Wedgwood won the patronage of the Queen, and of the King and Prince of Wales, without help from Bentley and that the first contact with Cathcart was Josiah's meeting with him in 1768.[6] Nor had Bentley anything to do with the powerful patronage of such local grandees as Lord Gower, the Duke of Bridgewater, the Ansons of Shugborough and the Bagots of Blithfield, or of the influential friends, such as the Marlboroughs, whom they introduced to Etruria.

The partnership was both more complex and more complete than such simple division allows. Wedgwood was, of course, the potter, with the essential help of 'Useful' Thomas directing all production at Etruria. As he put it to Bentley in 1769: 'My talents, which your friend-ship is so apt on all occasions to magnify, are very confin'd; they lie chiefly in *the Potter* – Such as they are, think of them as your own, inlarge, confine, or use them at your pleasure.' Ten years later he confirmed that 'in the distribution of our employments between us the manufacturing has fallen to my lot, and the sales to yours';[7] but this was a modest summary of his contribution. He could never be satisfied with a role that limited him to the factory and it is evident that he was the final arbiter in all things, the chief executive of the partnership. Bentley, on the other hand, whose prime concern was rightly described as 'sales' and who was necessarily involved in all aspects of marketing, nevertheless bore the final responsibility for all the work done in the Chelsea Decorating Studios, including the decorating of the 'Husk' and

'Frog' services for Catherine the Great, and carried out experiments of his own with lustre decoration in 1776. As early as May 1768 Bentley shared control of the Burslem factory with Cousin Thomas Wedgwood after the amputation of Josiah's leg and in the following November Wedgwood had again been content to leave the Burslem factory in Bentley's hands while he spent three weeks in London with Sally and Catherine Willet.[8] Both men brought skills to the partnership and they were satisfied to learn them from one another.

If Bentley had everything to learn about the business of pottery manufacturing, Wedgwood had less to learn from him about selling, of which he had already some valuable experience. But Bentley was a professional merchant, which Josiah was not, and he had superior knowledge of markets in Europe and America. He was also conversant with Court protocol and forms of address, unfamiliar territory to Josiah, and was comfortable in London society, where he easily acquired the understanding of fashion, so essential to the partnership. Josiah relied upon Bentley's advice in these matters and frequently asked him to write letters 'as only you know how' to patrons, 'princes and great folks'.[9] Josiah's spelling, always erratic, improved noticeably through his constant reading and re-reading of Bentley's letters and he was never too proud to ask if his use of French and Latin words or phrases was correct.

Josiah's appreciation of pottery form, an understanding almost instinctive to an experienced thrower, was second to none among contemporary potters, but fashion was an aspect of his business of which he was less informed. He relied on Bentley's guidance and on the advice of patrons, such as Sir William Hamilton, whose taste and knowledge he respected. His visits to Boulton's Soho factory were instructive, for Boulton's list of influential patrons was as formidable as Wedgwood's and he was making ornamental vases for many of the greatest houses in England, but much of his work was for export and designed to compete with the work of French craftsmen. Such designs were considered too 'shewy' for English taste.

Bentley's influence on design and production, his experience of marketing, his qualities as a man of business and ambassador for the firm were scarcely more important to Wedgwood than the strength and constancy of his friendship. There was no subject which Josiah felt unable to discuss with him, however private or personal. More remarkable is the extent to which the friendship was based on correspondence. The 'Good, long, affectionate & instructing letters', which Josiah described as 'my Magazines, Reviews, Chronicles, & I had allmost said my Bible', inspired in him 'taste, emulation & everything that is necessary for the production of fine things';[10] but they also gave him the encouragement and strength to persevere when his experiments were frustrating or unsuccessful, comfort when he was depressed or ill or anxious about Sally, and worldly advice on his personal affairs, from the conduct of his life to the preservation of his health and the education of his children.

The loss of all but a handful of Bentley's letters to Wedgwood gives a misleadingly one-sided appearance to the friendship. It is, however, plain from Wedgwood's letters that Bentley's were hardly less regular or less frequent than his own. Josiah wrote to express alarm at an interval of thirteen days between letters received from his friend in December 1778, evidently fearing that he was too ill to write. This may indeed have been the cause of Bentley's silence, for he was suffering from severe headaches or migraines, described by Josiah as 'the nervous complaint in your head', due partly, it seems, to the 'effrontery, accompanied with the basest ingratitude' of a 'vile and abandoned character' identified in Josiah's letters only as 'W'.[11] The circumstances of this incident, in which Bentley's name was slandered, are no longer known, but his letter of 18 December, one of the few to survive intact, is probably (with due allowance for his low spirits when it was written) a fair example of his style:

> Thanks to my dear Friend for the very affectionate & cheering letter of the 14th which I must reply to briefly tho' with a grateful heart. My Head is better & worse as I think more properly or weakly about the ill usage that I have met with, or may still meet with from a Man who sets no Bounds on his Malignity when it is once excited – or rather as my Head is better or worse I think more properly on the Subject. A full discussion, or one good conversation upon it with my dear Friend would probably do me more good than any application, for I have not any Friend here by whose side I have been accustomed to engage and conquer, and has the same energy that you constantly possess, when there is reason for it, either to promote the public good, assist your Friends, or support your own rights. I fancy I can do anything with your help, and I have been so much used to it, that when you are not with me upon these occasions I seem to have lost my right arm.
>
> Mrs Bentley & I are very much inclined to accept of your kind invitation: & I want very much to go & examine into & settle my affairs at Liverpool; but as you will have all your Infantry & Relations about you soon I am afraid the Time would be very inconvenient to you; otherwise we should be very glad to see all the Family happy together before the young Gentlemen return to School and we will keep the

Prospect of this Pleasure in our Thoughts 'till we hear from you what Time would be most convenient provided we should resolve to make a winter Flight. If we should undertake this Journey we must also pay our respects to our Friends in Derby & so make a sort of running Visit of it tho' the short winter Days will be very much against us.

Perhaps a few Days before your Sons return to School would answer all purposes the best & I might go to Liverpool when they return or you might perhaps like to return round by Liverpool or meet me at Warrington. But these are hasty Ideas subject to more mature Consideration & better arrangement.

If we should come, we hope that you & our good Mrs Wedgwood will return with Us, & favour Us with your Company as long as you can find in your Hearts at Turnham Green.

Mrs Bentley & Miss Stamford join in Love & respects to all the good Family with Yr truly affectionate & grateful Friend

Thos. Bentley

I had almost forgot to tell you the Sherry is excellent & very comforting to the Heart.[12]

The postscript refers to a gift of four dozen bottles sent by Josiah three weeks earlier. 'We have had it two years in the pipe,' he wrote. 'If it had not prov'd superb I should not have troubled you with any. As it is, if you like it do not spare the good creature, we have plenty at your service.'[13]

On 21 December Josiah wrote again, to reinforce his invitation and to give Bentley the comfort and support that he had so often received from him when his own spirits were low:

We have fought side by side in many a battle, & carried off our well earn'd laurels, but our objects have generally had that magnitude & meaning in them which the present occasion does not seem to furnish. A just contempt is the only weapon you can have occasion for, & when you sacrifice an hours rest or peace of mind to such a slanderer, you do your self & your friends injustice . . . Keep your mind at ease & your body out of his way, & defy him & all his malice.[14]

There is some suggestion in this that Bentley was more sensitive to criticism than Wedgwood and more vulnerable to personal attack. Josiah generally took a robust attitude to such troubles and there is little evidence in his letters that he was easily wounded. His own recurrent fits of depression were brought on by hypochondria, frustration and overwork. Bentley's loss of spirits, of which the evidence is less, was attributed by Josiah to an extravagant use of them: 'It is not, my Dear Friend, that I have more spirits to spend than you have, but they do not fly away so fast from me, as they do from you. – You exert yourself more than I do, & spend double the quantity of spirits in a given time – It is therefore no wonder if your stock be sooner exhausted.'[15]

Bentley's easy relationship with Josiah's Sally is illustrated in a few letters which have survived and especially those she wrote to him in Burslem during her stay in London in the winter of 1768. 'I will write a line tho I have nothing to say', she told him in a note appended to one from her sister-in-law, Catherine Willet, 'but to thank you for my share of your last letter and to assure you I take your advise in every thing I can. . . . I hope you take care of your self pray do call for every thing you want . . . we had a Gentleman here last Night that can fly. I wish I had thot of it in time I would have asked him to have lent you his wings that you might have come & chatted an hour or two without loss of time.' She signed herself 'Your Affectionate friend', a salutation which two weeks later had been improved to 'Your ever loving Friend till death'.[16]

There were times, no doubt, when Sally resented the time Josiah spent writing his long letters by candlelight, but there is little evidence that she ever complained. 'I have many things to say to you,' he wrote in June 1768, 'but Sally says "give over Joss, & tell our friend B. that I command it", so I have done.' On this occasion her concern was understandable: it was Josiah's first letter to his partner since the amputation of his leg at the end of May.[17]

Josiah's marriage had taken place only eighteen months after his first meeting with Bentley. Their friendship was therefore able to include Sally from the start and to grow with Josiah's family. Josiah had never known Bentley's first wife and was, in spite of his jocular references to Bentley's single state, accustomed to him as a bachelor friend whose time and company were much at his disposal. It was understood between them that it was Josiah's time that was the more valuable, that his was the more exacting task. 'We want nothing, my dear friend, just now but a little more time,' he wrote, '& in that article we find ourselves greatly limited, though we husband what little portion is allow'd us with tolerable economy, & pursue our experiments 'till supper calls us away, & sometimes after, & yet all is too little, much too little for the business before us.'[18]

In June 1772, after much teasing and heavy hints about his personal attributes and susceptibilities, Bentley married for the second time. His new wife was Mary Stamford, one of the four daughters of Thomas

Stamford of Derby, who had been known to both Wedgwood and Bentley since 1765.[19] Josiah had met Mary, who had helped Elizabeth Oates to entertain him when he visited Bentley's house in London in December 1770, and his pleasure in Bentley's marriage appears to have been warm and sincere.[20] Bentley's health was occasionally uncertain and his sister-in-law no longer wished to housekeep for him. Josiah must have felt some relief that his partner would have someone to care for him as well as someone to care for. Mary's health, however, was frail. She required the 'quietness & fine air of Eltham' to restore her in 1774[21] and was seriously ill again in January 1776, possibly a victim of the influenza epidemic in London at that time. 'I wish', Josiah wrote, 'Mrs Bentley could leave the Town for a while, but the time of year, the Snow, the bitter coldness of this Easterly wind, all seem to forbid that measure, & my reason for wishing it is that she might be out of the reach of business, for I know her active spirit will in some way or other be a partaker in the business of the Household, if she is within the reach, or hearing of it.'[22]

Mary Bentley visited Etruria with her husband in 1774 and 1779 and the Wedgwoods stayed with the Bentleys at Chelsea in July 1772. On no fewer than seven subsequent visits to Chelsea and to the Bentleys' new house at Turnham Green, Josiah travelled alone, but on at least one occasion Sally was too ill to accompany him and there is no reason to suppose that her absence was ever because she was either unwilling or unwelcome or that the relationship was ever less than cordial.[23] Josiah wrote after their visit in 1772: 'Mrs Wedgwood laments that Good Folks cannot live nearer together . . . but I am afraid we must submit to these things as they are at present, – love one another wherever we are, & meet together as often as we can.'[24] There is certainly no indication that the intimacy of his friendship with Bentley was in any way diminished by the latter's marriage. 'I often lament the necessity of our being so often, & so far seperated from each other & if wishes would avail we should not often smoke our pipes asunder,' Josiah wrote after his visit to Turnham Green in 1777,

I need not tell you how happy it would make us, & I believe it would be of no small advantage to us in respect of our business if we could manage to be a little more together – Besides I could teach you to bowl, & to love riding on horseback, – To think less & play more, all of which would be of great service to you, & of some use to my self. The very thoughts of them do me good & revive me, though I am afraid the *reality* is a little in the offing.[25]

In the third week of July 1776 Bentley went to Paris for five weeks, taking rooms at the Hôtel de Modena in the rue Jacob, visiting the Sèvres porcelain factory and carrying out several commissions. One of these was to present to Rousseau a copy of the Liturgy drawn up by his friend Dr David Williams, for use in the Margaret Street Chapel, which he attended in London. Others whose attendance was less regular included Sir Joseph Banks, Dr Daniel Solander and Benjamin Franklin, all also occasional guests at meetings of the Lunar Society. A second commission, but from Wedgwood, was to obtain samples of French porcelain and creamware, 'with any other specimens whose forms, texture or other qualitys' might strike him as of special quality or interest. Among the usable objects he succeeded in acquiring were more than thirty medals, most of them by an Amsterdam artist known only as 'Pesez', suitable as models for portrait medallions in the 'Illustrious Moderns' series.[26]

To his Liverpool partner, Bentley reported, 'it is startling and rather flattering to an Englishman to see how fond they are of making everything "à l'Anglaise" '. To Josiah he wrote that everything in Paris was either unfinished or 'going to decay'. Josiah replied accurately, 'It seems to indicate a great unsteadiness in the Nation.'[27]

During this journey abroad, and most severely after his return to London, Bentley suffered from a crippling attack of gout or rheumatism in the knee. Josiah was confident that this would soon yield to the combined effects of Mrs Bentley's nursing and 'Blue Flannel' and it was overshadowed, as Bentley's troubles with his eyes had been some six years earlier, by his own problems. In his partner's absence, Josiah had met with a serious accident while out in his chaise, 'occasion'd by a stupid *Man Animal* throwing a bundle of Weeds over an hedge into the Highway' in front of his horse, which shied violently, pitching Josiah to the ground, where he fell on the point of his right hip. 'I am very thankfull', he wrote to Bentley, 'that the joint is not dislocated, for my Surgeon tells me it could not have been reduc'd again, for want of a leg to pull by, & I should probably never have been able to put on my Artificial one again.'[28] He was, nevertheless, unable to move the joint without great pain and he was confined to the house for three weeks, at the end of which he was still able to walk only with crutches. Not until the second week of October was he well enough to visit Liverpool on business. Bentley's gout was as painful and as persistent.

Apart from brief references to some problem with his eyesight, which seems rapidly to have been cured, occasional severe headaches and attacks of gout, the letters between the two partners contain little evidence that Bentley's health was suspect. On the contrary, it was

Josiah's ailments and infirmities that gave them cause for concern. It came, therefore, as a particularly savage shock to Josiah to hear from his old friend Ralph Griffiths, a neighbour of the Bentleys at Turnham Green, that Bentley was dangerously ill. 'My Dear Sir,' Griffiths wrote in haste on 25 November 1780, 'Our poor friend yet breathes, but, alas, it is such breathing as promises but a short continuance. Almost every hope seems to have forsaken us! I dread the thought of what may be the contents of my next! á Dieu.'[29] Josiah set out at once for London, but Bentley died the following day, soon after the news of his collapse had reached Etruria.

The circumstances of Bentley's death are not known. Pleurisy, gout or apoplexy have been suggested as possible causes and it is alleged that his health had been declining steadily for five years,[30] but there is no evidence to suggest that Bentley's occasional colds were either exceptional or an indication of anything more serious. An interesting alternative theory is that his death was due to some unidentified infection picked up while he was living and working at Greek Street. Certainly there was a period when his staff there seemed to be unusually prone to illness. 'What is amiss with our young men that scarcely any of them preserve their health?' Josiah asked Bentley in October 1778.[31] Possible reasons for this might have been the old dissecting room, vacated ten years earlier but still unfumigated, or the proximity of the Manette Street workhouse.[32] In the absence of contemporary testimony, a simpler explanation may be found for Bentley's sudden collapse. He was overweight, fond of good living and his pipe, and unenthusiastic about any form of exercise. It seems most probable that the cause of his death was a fatal heart attack.

The blow was all the more terrible for having been struck without warning. No evidence has survived of the depth of Josiah's desolation. He was accustomed to death, to bereavement and to grief, but Bentley's death had robbed him simultaneously of his dearest friend, his most loyal and reliable supporter, his most honest critic and an incomparable partner. Bentley was irreplaceable and Josiah made no attempt to replace him, in his business concerns or in his heart.

If Josiah showed his grief to Sally or to any of his friends, he hid it in his letters. Only one substantial reference to Bentley's death has been found and it occurs in a formal letter written to William Ker, a business acquaintance in Liverpool: 'I have in common with all his friends & the public suffered a very great loss in the death of my most valued friend & partner, which I shall ever lament.'[33] He received letters of condolence from many friends, among them Erasmus Darwin, Joseph Priestley and Richard Lovell Edgeworth, and epitaphs were composed by Darwin, Priestley and James 'Athenian' Stuart. Bentley was buried in a new vault close to the west door of St Nicholas's church at Chiswick on 2 December 1780, and a memorial tablet by Thomas Scheemakers, inscribed with Stuart's epitaph, was placed in the church in 1781.

Josiah's grief is documented in his portrait, painted by Sir Joshua Reynolds in 1782. It shows a man prematurely aged. Allowing for the differences in style and medium, the alteration in Josiah's appearance since his portrait was painted by George Stubbs only two years earlier is remarkable. Overwork, stress, amputation, accident and minor illnesses during the previous twenty years had cumulatively overtaxed his strength, but the sudden deterioration between 1780 and 1782 must be attributed primarily to the effect of Bentley's death. This is confirmed by an equally sudden, but temporary, instability in his handwriting. The flame of ambition was not quenched but it burned with less intensity and it was several years before the spark which had kindled Josiah's invention could be struck again.

He is unlikely to have been much consoled by Darwin's well-intentioned but characteristically clumsy attempt to offer comfort. He wrote to Wedgwood three days after Bentley's death:

> Your letter communicating to me the death of your friend, and I beg I may call him mine, Mr Bentley, gives me very great concern; and a train of very melancholy ideas succeeds in my mind, unconnected indeed with your loss, but which still at times casts a shadow over me, which nothing but exertion in business or in acquiring knowledge can remove. This exertion I must recommend to you as it for a time disperses the disagreeable ideas of our loss; and gradually their impression or effect upon us becomes thus weakened, till the traces are scarcely perceptible, and a scar only is left, which reminds us of past pain.[34]

After recommending Sulpicius's letter to Cicero on the loss of his daughter – 'I think it contains everything which could be said upon the subject' – he added unhelpfully: 'I am rather in a situation to demand than to administer consolation.' Fat, forty-nine and far from handsome, Darwin's gloom was occasioned by fears that the current object of his affections, the newly widowed Elizabeth Pole, would attract the attentions of suitors who were both younger and more obviously eligible. To his abiding surprise, she became his second wife four months later and bore him seven children in nine years.

Bentley's death dealt a crushing blow to Josiah's spirits and threatened a hardly less serious one to his business. For the first time in eleven years he was without Bentley's advice and support. He was also without any adequate representative in London. If there was no one who could take Bentley's place as a friend, there was equally no one qualified to fill his shoes as manager of the London showrooms and offices, and this position could not be left unoccupied. When Bentley died, Tom Byerley was the only obvious choice to succeed him in London. At the age of thirty-three he became his uncle's most senior and most trusted manager.

His experience and organising ability were almost immediately tested by the dissolution of the Wedgwood & Bentley partnership. Bentley's share was bequeathed to his widow. In practical terms this necessitated the separation of all ornamental ware made after 26 November from earlier stock so that sales could be correctly apportioned between the old partnership and Wedgwood as sole proprietor. The quickest and fairest solution to this problem was found in an immediate and accurate count of all Wedgwood & Bentley stock and the disposal of it by auction. The alternatives would have involved Josiah in making an offer, which could scarcely have been at any figure above the cost of production, for half the stock, or the protracted disposal of it through sales to the public. This last would have continued, probably for several years, the complexities and likely errors of separate accounting, and would have been a fertile breeding ground for mutual distrust between Wedgwood and Mary Bentley.

The sale was held by Christie & Ansell, Pall Mall,* over a period of eleven days, with a break only for Sunday, from Monday 3 December 1781. The catalogue, which contains detailed and accurate descriptions of the 1200 lots preceded by a brief explanatory introduction, was undoubtedly written with considerable assistance from Josiah or Byerley. Many of the lots were large, consisting of twenty-four or more pieces, and the total sum realised by the sale, £2,182.6s.6d., now seems paltry for such a great quantity of fine ornaments. The sale appears, however, to have been considered a success.[35] Demonstrating how much he had learned from his close association with Bentley, Josiah seized the opportunity to combine gracious appreciation with advertisement. The *Morning Chronicle & Public Advertiser* for Tuesday 11 December carried an announcement worthy of Bentley in its composition:

Mr Wedgwood would feel himself greatly wanting in the gratitude

*Now Christie, Manson & Woods Ltd, King Street, London, who have preserved in their archives one of the rare surviving catalogues of the sale, annotated with prices and names of buyers.

which he owes to a generous public for long continued patronage, if he did not embrace every opportunity to express his unfeigned acknowledgements, and particularly for the last instance of their partiality to him, and to the memory of his late worthy and ingenious partner MR BENTLEY, in support of the sale in Pall Mall, where the appearance of so many of the first and most respectable personages of the Kingdom, has greatly flattered him, and cannot fail to excite his utmost endeavours to merit more the distinguished honour they have been pleased to confer upon him. He begs leave to add, that he derives no small part of his satisfaction from the consideration that, by this kind interposition, the property of the widow, Mrs Bentley, will be preserved from a considerable diminution, with which it was threatened at the beginning of the sale.

The sale will continue to the end of the week, and then be finally closed.

Bentley's brief will, made in July 1778, included bequests to his Liverpool partner, Samuel Boardman, and his first wife's sister, Elizabeth Oates, who had kept house for him until 1772. To Josiah he left part of his library and his share of their jointly owned books and engravings. The bulk of the estate, of which Bentley's share of his partnerships with Wedgwood and Boardman was a significant part, was left to Mary Bentley. Josiah maintained some connection with her for the rest of his life, supervising certain of her investments and mortgages. She left Turnham Green and lived out her last fifteen years in Gower Street, then, according to the actress Sarah Siddons who became her neighbour, 'most effectually in the country and delightfully pleasant'.[36] Mary Bentley died there in 1797.

Wedgwood's public expression of gratitude in December 1781 served an important and hidden purpose. For several years he had been experimenting with the production of vases in the jasper body. On 12 November 1780, in his last recorded letter to Bentley, he wrote: 'I am contriving some vases for bodies, and bodies for vases'[37] and there is good reason to believe that he had overcome most of his difficulties before Bentley died. After Bentley's death, there was speculation among some customers that, deprived of his taste and understanding of fashion, the quality of the firm's ornamental wares might decline. An ungenerous letter written twenty-seven years later by Tom Byerley describes the situation:

When Mr Bentley died, a great many discriminating people were so captivated by his intelligence and animated conversation that they believed & propagated the opinion that he was the origin of all the fine works of taste & all which they saw exhibited in our rooms – without reflecting that he could not be spending his day in social intercourse with them and at the same time sitting down at the Workmen's benches for days together directing them in the production of beautiful forms and inventing new modes of decoration. . . . He had some merit as a Culler and an index to works of antient art, but unfortunately less even in this way than has been imputed to him. It was however to be feared that this mistake would lead to a notion that with him would die away the whole of the art – and to counteract this it was determined to open the rooms after the public sale of W&B with works of original merit & quite dissimilar to anything before seen. At this period Jasper Vases were first introduced and answered the intention.[38]

It was no doubt this first exhibition of jasper vases that Josiah had in mind when he wrote his advertisement, a judicious reminder to London society of his continuing business.

If Wedgwood hoped, as he had once confided to Bentley, 'to amuse, & divert, & please, and astonish, nay & even ravish the ladies' and finally to gain the reputation of 'Vase maker General to the Universe',[39] it was the jasper vases that could realise his ambition. When, at last, they were offered to the public, they were an immediate success. Many of the shapes produced were variations of those already popular in black basaltes or variegated versions, but throughout his last active years Josiah continued to introduce new shapes and to experiment with colours, ornament and the decorative effects that could be obtained by skilful use of the engine-turning lathe. In particular, he commissioned new relief ornaments, some of them – especially those modelled by John Flaxman junior – of exceptional distinction, to sustain his reputation for quality and to demonstrate a continuing awareness of changing fashion. In his last ornamental ware catalogue, published in 1787, Wedgwood wrote of his vases: 'As these are my latest, I hope they may be found to be my most improved work.' His achievement as a potter was almost complete. In the years after Bentley's death, Josiah gave more and more of his time to other interests.

CHAPTER EIGHTEEN

Among the Politicians

During twenty-five years as a manufacturer Wedgwood had found little time for politics. He had enlisted the help of powerful patrons, especially Lord Gower, in his early struggles to improve communications by road and canal to the Potteries, and he had seldom lost an opportunity to commemorate leading political figures and national heroes, whenever he believed that their portraits, on teapots, jugs, mugs or medallions, had commercial value; but, while Bentley lived, he had been content to comment from a distance on political events and to leave active participation to others. This neglect was not for lack of often mordant and disrespectful interest. He sent Bentley a graphic, though secondhand, account of one of John Wilkes's several abortive elections, describing the popular slogan 'Wilkes and Liberty' as 'tagg'd together like Hobgoblins & darkness', and a more detailed and personal account of local politics during the general election of 1780 when he wrote: 'we all sit still saying the will of the lord be done & there is an end of our farce'.[1] In some of his opinions he was many years ahead of his contemporaries. He favoured universal suffrage, believing that *every member of the state* must either *have a vote* or *be a slave*', and he advocated annual parliaments, declaring that 'so long as we have septennial parliaments, 'tis of little consequence who is chosen into them'.[2]

In May 1780 Bentley sent Josiah a pamphlet, published a month earlier, describing the Society for Constitutional Information, one of the first 'Corresponding Societies' which spread through Britain at this period to agitate for parliamentary reform. The pamphlet, written by several contributors who included Richard Price, Dr John Jebb and Richard Brinsley Sheridan, affirmed the principal aims of the Society: the preservation of the Constitution; the separation of powers exercised by the Crown, the Lords and the Commons; and the reform of Parliament by the introduction of full and equal representation of the people. Thomas Day, one of Josiah's Lunatic friends, was a leading supporter of the Society. Although Josiah agreed with these aims, he was critical of the definition of representation, believing that an elected Member of Parliament should act as a delegate. 'I am for *particular representation* when I instruct my delegate,' he told Bentley. 'In all other cases he may consider himself in as *general* a capacity as he pleases, but when he is instructed by a majority of his constituents, if he is not to obey them, all idea of agency, delegation, or representation is at an end.'[3]

Four days later, after mature consideration of Dr Jebb's argument, he reinforced his opinion. Bentley was among those who agreed with it[4] and it is one that is still widely held:

> For what is the true idea of representation or agency? Is it not that the person so chosen to represent you in any assembly to transact any business for you at a distance where your other affairs will not permit you to attend should transact the business you so employ him in, in the way you would do it your self. And though in general you trust to his integrity & good sense, or if you please, to his superior knowledge & ability in the execution of the trust you have reposed in him, yet if you think proper to give him your positive instructions upon any particular point. – Suppose . . . in the house of commons it was to bring the minister to account for any particular expenditure though [it] . . . should appear to your representative to be against your interest. Yet if after telling you his opinion you insist upon his compliance & chuse to judge for your self in this instance, the agent in such case is, in my opinion to comply with his instructions.

To the suggestion that this might introduce unacceptable conflict between the opinion and conscience of the elected member and his constituents, Josiah replied:

> The instructed member has only to say – it is no matter what my private sentiments may be upon this bill – My constituents, who sent me here to transact *their business* & not *my own*, though they in general leave me at liberty to judge of their interests & act accordingly, they have in this instance chosen to think for themselves & have given me full instructions how I am to act as their agent and representative.[5]

Bentley joined the Society and, in spite of his reservations, Josiah pledged his support, 'either by my purse or my services'.[6] He had shown a keen and highly critical interest in the progress of affairs leading up to the American revolution and this continued until the end of the war in America, but the cause of parliamentary reform was the first purely national matter of politics which engaged his attention. This was the earliest indication of an active interest in politics which grew after the loss of Bentley made Josiah's personal involvement in affairs in London more necessary.

Barely two months after Bentley's death William Pitt the Younger took his seat in the House of Commons as Member of Parliament for Appleby, in Yorkshire. Others who came in to Parliament for the first time after the 1780 general election included Sheridan and William Wilberforce. Charles James Fox, who had previously represented Malmesbury, in Wiltshire, was returned for Westminster, which he held for the rest of his life. These were the young politicians with whom Josiah was to be most closely associated in his last active years.

In America, the encouraging successes in the south had not been consolidated and final victory looked as far away as ever. The Carolinas had been cleared and the army had moved into Virginia, but no sooner had British troops left an area of conquest than American rebellion took root there again. It was becoming obvious that the war could not be ended by military force alone and support for it at home was disintegrating. The appearance of a formidable French fleet in American waters threatened even the essential British command of the sea. In Europe, British isolation was, as Chatham had forecast, complete. Combined French and Spanish fleets commanded the Channel and the Mediterranean, and the Spanish had laid siege to Gibraltar. The fear that the Dutch would recognise the independence of the United States of America had persuaded the government to declare war on Holland. In India, the threat to British possessions from the Marathas and Hyder Ali, assisted by the French, was destroyed only by a brilliant combination of diplomacy, bribery, threats, force, audacity and resolution concocted and implemented by Warren Hastings, the first Governor-General. At home, the suppression of the Gordon riots* of 1780, a violent demonstration against Roman Catholics and the replacement, for military recruitment, of the oath of supremacy by a simple oath of allegiance, had required the use of 15,000 troops in London, and the danger of insurrection in Ireland had been averted at the last minute by economic concessions lifting restrictions on Irish trade.

Throughout this period of evident ministerial incompetence, when years of neglect had left the navy helpless against the fleets of France,

---

*Named after Lord George Gordon, the ambitious and mentally unstable leader of the anti-Catholic movement which became known as the Protestant Association.

Holland and Spain; when the army was engaged in a futile war in America; when every overseas possession was threatened; and when Britain had no ally in Europe or anywhere else, the opposition to the government in Parliament was, as Lord Hillsborough told William Eden, 'if not dead at least half asleep'.[7] Only one voice, that of the precocious twenty-two-year-old member for Appleby, was raised with Chathamite vigour to call for reform and to condemn the ministry's failures and the 'most accursed, wicked, barbarous, cruel, unnatural, unjust and diabolical war'. The news, received in London on 25 November 1781, that Cornwallis had surrendered his entire force of 7000 men to the Americans at Yorktown five weeks earlier was enough to divide North's supporters, and by the following March his majorities in the Commons had fallen to derisory figures. When the House passed a resolution to 'consider as enemies all who should advise or by any means attempt the further prosecution of offensive war on the continent of America', it was clear that he could no longer continue.

The King prudently agreed to Lord Rockingham's terms for accepting office in North's place. These included recognition of American independence. In the midst of negotiations for peace treaties with America, France, Spain and Holland, Rockingham died. He was succeeded by Lord Shelburne, the third prime minister in twelve months. Five weeks after his twenty-third birthday, William Pitt became Chancellor of the Exchequer.

The new ministry could not long survive. A cynical alliance was hatched between Fox and North with the sole purpose of bringing Shelburne down and, with him, his proposals for peace with America. Pitt looked beyond the immediate negotiations for peace to 'a revision of our whole trading system', abandoning the old mercantile policy of restrictions to open up a free trade between the United States of America and all British possessions. Trade agreements with America should be followed by commercial treaties with France and Spain.[8] Had he been permitted to implement his plans, the subsequent relationship of Britain with the United States would have been transformed and the seeds of another war, even more pointless and indecisive, in 1812 would not have been sown.

The Address on the Preliminaries of Peace was debated in both Houses on 17 February 1783. In the Lords the government scraped a majority of six; but in the Commons the efforts of Pitt, who was not at his best, seconded by Wilberforce, were not proof against the corrosive eloquence of Fox and Sheridan, and the government was defeated. A week later, Shelburne resigned, recommending to the King that he send for Pitt to succeed him. That afternoon George III summoned his youthful Chancellor and invited him to form a government. The temptation to become his country's prime minister at the age of twenty-three was considerable, but Pitt knew that so long as North and Fox continued in opposition – in what he had publicly described as a 'baneful alliance' and 'ill-omened marriage' – he was unlikely to succeed where Shelburne had failed. He declined. 'Nothing', the King told Shelburne later that evening, 'could get him to depart from the ground he took, that nothing less than a moral certainty of a majority in the House of Commons could make him undertake the task.'[9]

From 25 February until 2 April the country was without a government. The King was inflexibly resolved not to accept any administration formed by 'the most profligate and ungrateful coalition that was ever made in the Kingdom', but, in spite of declaring his willingness to accept even 'Mr Thomas Pitt or Mr Thomas anybody', he could find no one else prepared to form a government. For five weeks he explored every possibility, approaching Wedgwood's old friend Lord Gower, a frequent contender in the past, and even agreeing to accept the return of North without Fox. He summoned Pitt again and strove, once more, to overpersuade him. When Pitt refused again, the King rebuked him for not having sufficient regard for the Constitution to 'stand forth against the most daring and unprincipled faction that the annals of the Kingdom ever produced'.[10] He contemplated retiring to Hanover until Lord Chancellor Thurlow reminded him that English kings had found it easier to leave the country than to return to it. At last, when no alternative remained untried, he yielded. On 2 April the Duke of Portland took office as First Lord of the Treasury with North and Fox as Secretaries of State.

Peace treaties with America, France and Spain were signed at Versailles in September 1783 and with Holland in the following May. Pitt's resolution for the reform of parliament, strengthening the representation of the counties and larger cities and introducing measures to prevent corrupt electoral practices, was lost in spite of support from Fox and numerous petitions from constituencies. Before the end of the year, the government had been brought down. The apparent cause of its fall was Fox's Bill to reform the East India Company, but the true cause was the power of the King and his intelligent use of it. The contest and its consequences were of crucial importance because they determined the style of government in Britain for the remainder of the century.

While troops and money had been poured into America, where British armies surrendered and an empire was lost, Warren Hastings, with puny resources and without aid from Britain, had dismembered the alliances of powerful enemies and repulsed every assault on the territories for which he was responsible. In so doing he had secured British possessions, enhanced British prestige, and laid the foundations for the conquest, by a system of alliances and war, of a new empire. The task was Herculean and its achievement heroic.

There was general agreement on all sides of the House of Commons that the administration of British territory in India required to be reorganised. Although deep in debt, the East India Company remained a source of patronage and influence second only to the Crown. Burke, who fathered the bill presented by Fox, failed to understand its implications. Passionate and doctrinaire, he conducted his researches among those who shared his prejudices: the dissatisfied, the disappointed and the jealous; those, in short, who had returned without the rewards to which they felt themselves entitled. Hastings knew more about India and its peoples than any Englishman of his time and he had a remarkable record of success. Burke consulted only the Governor-General's enemies and his special study set him on a course of persecution – dedicated, malignant and occasionally hysterical – that threatened to destroy his own reputation with those of lesser men. Fox's bill was a genuine attempt to separate the political and commercial functions of the East India Company but it was a plain example of government intervention in a situation imperfectly understood. On 17 December, under heavy pressure from the King, who saw in Fox's bill the opportunity he sought to rid himself of the ministry he loathed, the Lords threw it out. George III waited twenty-four hours for North's resignation before sending him a note requiring him to give up the seals of his department. Two days later Pitt succeeded Portland as prime minister.

Wedgwood's political sympathies were generally Whig and he was among Fox's early admirers.[11] It was to Fox, then still engaged in negotiations expected to lead to commercial treaties with France and Spain, that he turned in April 1783 for help in reducing the duties on pottery exported to Europe. Writing on behalf of the earthenware manufacturers of Staffordshire, he complained that exports were 'greatly diminished in some states by high duties upon its importation there, & in others totally obstructed by prohibitions', while British ports were open to imports of a similar nature and duties were moderate.[12] Fox's dismissal from office before the end of the year removed him from the centre of negotiations and the matter was dropped. It was, however, of some significance that Wedgwood was chosen to act as spokesman for the industry.

For many years Josiah had been closely involved in attempts to obtain some consensus among potters in matters such as pricing, trans-port costs, taxes or import duties on materials and foreign restrictions on exports, which affected them all. In 1771 he had promoted dis-cussions to maintain prices when trade was 'going to ruin on the gallop' and many of the potters were 'quite in a pannick' and, two years later, he had attended 'a sort of General assembly', when he had stood out against an otherwise unanimous agreement to drop prices by a full 20 per cent.[13] In January 1784 he proposed to James Watt that the principle of joint agreement and action among the potters should be applied nationally, uniting the many local groups of manufacturers of all sorts of goods into a single 'Society formed out of the principle manufacturers in different parts of the island'.[14] This suggestion was aimed especially at preventing the emigration of skilled workers, and later in the year Josiah wrote a pamphlet on the subject in which he again called for concerted action. Nothing came of these proposals until the following year, when a situation arose which finally persuaded the manufacturers to use their united influence.

Pitt's appointment had been predicated on the assumption that there would be an early general election. Indeed, the King and his advisers had calculated that the new prime minister would be left at least sixty votes short of a majority in the Commons. Everyone expected an immediate dissolution of Parliament – everyone, that is, except Pitt himself. He believed that time would strengthen his following in the Commons and that nothing less than his own performance there could effect the necessary swing of political opinion in his favour and give the powerful forces working for him outside the House time to take effect. Mrs Crewe, the great Whig hostess, described the new govern-ment as a 'mince-pie administration', indicating that it would not last long beyond Christmas, and Edward Gibbon gave it as his opinion that 'Billy's painted wagon' would 'soon sink under Charlie's black collier'. This was the popular view, particularly when it became known that Pitt was finding it difficult to fill the places in his Cabinet. Once again, the faithful Lord Gower was one of those who offered to serve and Pitt gratefully appointed him Lord President of the Council. Pitt was the first commoner to be prime minister since his father twenty-six years earlier and, when his Cabinet was finally formed, he was the only member of it in the Lower House.

Facing an opposition that could rely on a majority, the government suffered a series of defeats in the New Year, but Pitt stolidly ignored the repeated demands for his resignation. By the third week of January, the Fox–North majority had fallen from 106 to eight, showing the grad-ual return of the independent members to their traditional support of the government and a general intention to renounce faction. Two months later, Pitt was ready for an election and he asked the King to dissolve Parliament.

The results of the 1784 general election exceeded both Pitt's most optimistic expectations and Fox's worst fears. No fewer than 160 members who voted with the opposition were unseated. Fox, publicly supported by the Prince of Wales and numbering three of England's most beautiful women – Georgiana, Duchess of Devonshire, Elizabeth, Countess of Derby, and Frances Crewe – among his canvassers in the streets, scored one of only two Opposition successes in the London area. Pitt was returned for Cambridge University and held the seat for the rest of his life. He was to be prime minister for the next seventeen years.

Pitt's was the fourth ministry in two years. Frequent changes of government and the failure, through incapacity or lack of parliamentary consent, of successive administrations to come to grips with the country's problems had created a shocking legacy of accumulated debt and overdue legislation. The most urgent issues were the regulation of the East India Company and the threat of national bankruptcy. Pitt's India Bill was passed in July. It was favoured partly because it was rational, practical and just, and partly because it was accepted, although with some lack of enthusiasm, by the East India Company. With minor changes, the system of regulation that it introduced lasted for more than seventy years.

The country's economic condition at first appeared to be bordering on catastrophe. At an unprecedented figure approaching £250 million, the national debt was almost twenty times the annual revenue from taxes. Interest on government borrowing automatically produced an annual deficit which was funded by further borrowing. This inexorable decline must be halted and then reversed. The printing by governments of devalued currency had not yet become an acceptable alternative for economic policy and Pitt was therefore left with three principal methods by which he might hope to master the situation: by increasing taxes; by cutting government expenditure; and by stimulating trade. He chose to employ all three. In the first eight years of his administration, Pitt raised the revenue by £6 millions, nearly fifty per cent of the total receipts in 1783, the greater part of which came from the increased yield on expanded trade, encouraged by reductions in indirect taxation. This increase was accompanied by a detailed but gradual reduction in government expenditure.

The national recovery could not have been achieved without a substantial increase in trade. Pitt had far-sighted plans for the expansion of trade with America and Ireland by the reduction or rationalisation of duties and restrictions, and negotiations were opened for commercial treaties with Spain, Portugal, France and Russia. Josiah Wedgwood played a leading part in the preliminary work towards two of these treaties.

The comprehensive expansion of trade planned by Pitt was associated with a problem that did not yield to logic: the settlement of Irish grievances. He was determined to right old wrongs and heal old wounds and his natural optimism and growing confidence allowed him sadly to underrate the ability of the Irish to reopen scars and nourish new abrasions. Bound to England by political and economic regulations designed to deny the population any hope of prosperity or those few rights enjoyed by the peoples of other Western European countries, Ireland was itself split into separately dissident factions, differing in their complaints and seldom united in their aims. Unsuccessful attempts had been made to reform the Dublin Parliament, little more than a debating chamber subservient in all but its right of taxation to the Westminster Parliament, but the majority of its members were nominated by Protestant landowners, who raised a storm of protest at any attempt to curtail their power. An equally angry storm had arisen, but on that occasion from manufacturers and merchants in England, when Lord North had proposed to remove some of the restrictions on Irish commerce.

The King's view was that all concessions should be resisted. He was convinced – as it proved rightly – that 'opening the door encourages a demand for more'.[15] He was implacably opposed to the repeal of the anti-Catholic laws, which he considered would endanger the Constitution, and this was the rock against which all possibility of a lasting Irish settlement foundered. The British government was nevertheless obliged to make concessions, including freedom to trade with the colonies and the right to export wool and glass. At the same time a modest gesture was made to the Catholics by allowing them to inherit property and to own long leaseholds. In 1782, the Rockingham government freed the Irish Parliament and courts from the jurisdiction of Westminster, but this only served to separate the freed legislature from the still fettered executive. The Irish understood that their legislative freedom was largely an illusion and their politicians accordingly adopted the attitude most natural to the national temperament: permanent opposition.

Pitt determined to remove the artificial restrictions that impoverished the Irish. His policy was unsentimental: a prosperous Ireland would provide an increasingly valuable outlet for English goods; and a settled Ireland would cease to be a magnet for Britain's enemies in any future European war. The freeing of trade was to be the first step in a logical progression that would eventually achieve the reform of the Dublin Parliament and the emancipation of the Catholic population. To prepare the ground for this transformation, Pitt sent his trusted friend the Duke of Rutland to Ireland as Lord-Lieutenant.

Rutland found Ireland in turmoil and Dublin in a state of riot. Sir Joshua Reynolds declined his invitation to visit the city and Sarah Siddons 'came away in a great fright'. Two years earlier, Fox had written of the Irish: 'My opinion is clear for giving them all that they ask, but for giving it to them so as to secure us from further demands.' Now Rutland echoed that opinion in his warning to Pitt: 'Whatever advantages Great Britain may be enabled and disposed to grant, let them be declared as *conclusive* . . . for as long as anything indefinite remains for expectation to feed on this country will never be at peace.'[16] It was the continuing and realistic misgiving haunting all British ministers that whatever might be granted, the Irish would demand more; and that whatever grievance was assuaged, the Irish would discover another that prohibited final agreement.

'*What is it*', Pitt asked, 'that in truth will give satisfaction and restore permanent tranquillity to Ireland?' He believed that 'the internal poverty and distress of the country' were the principal causes of unrest and he intended that 'the system of commerce should be so arranged as to extend the aggregate wealth of Great Britain and Ireland to its utmost limit, without partiality or preference to one part of the Empire or the other'.[17] Pitt devised what appeared to be a satisfactory scheme based on a linkage of the Irish contribution to defence costs to the increase or decrease in Irish revenues. In return for the reduction of duties on all manufactures and produce of both countries to the lower rate levied by either, and the freedom to import from and export into Britain the merchandise of other countries without increased duties, the Irish should make an agreed contribution, varied according to the rise and fall of the revenue. After much haggling, the Irish Parliament reluctantly passed the resolution. The apparent success of these delicate negotiations seemed to provide a permanent solution to the most urgent of Ireland's problems.

Pitt had assumed, with some justification, that Irish agreement to the terms would enable him to use his majority to obtain the assent of the House of Commons. He had taken the wise precaution of consulting British manufacturers, and their evidence, given to the Board of Trade in February, showed a general approval of his commercial proposals and confidence that, given conditions of equal competition, the British manufacturer would show himself 'equal, if not superior, to any other manufacturer of the world'.[18]

Evidence taken from manufacturers effectively disposed of the Opposition's most telling arguments. Josiah Wedgwood was among those called to give evidence and he stated on 19 February: 'I certainly apprehend that there might be a danger of competition in time, in their own [the Irish] and every foreign market. I should think it safer if earthenware was allowed to be imported free of all duties into both countries, because the Irish would not have then so much encouragement to begin to set up Potteries, or to establish them to any extent.'[19] Less than three weeks later he took the chair at the first executive committee of the newly formed General Chamber of the Manufacturers of Great Britain, pledged to oppose the Irish Resolutions. This volteface has laid Wedgwood open to charges of playing factional politics.

In February, immediately after his appearance to give evidence to the Committee of Trade, Wedgwood had decided, evidently at Boulton's suggestion, to go to Birmingham to consult Samuel Garbett and other manufacturers about the proposed commercial treaty. In weather so freezing that he could scarcely hold his pen, he wrote to Boulton:

> I mean to recommend them the measure of a Committee of Delegates from all the main factories and places in England and Scotland, to meet and sit in London all the time the Irish commercial affairs are pending. This strikes me as a measure which may be productive of many beneficial effects, principally informing and cementing a commercial band which may be great use upon others as well as the present occasion.[20]

The first committee of delegates, which included Garbett, Boulton, Watt and the ironmaster, John Wilkinson, met in London on 7 March, and on 1 May, the day before he appeared to give evidence on behalf of the manufacturers before the House of Commons select committee, Josiah wrote:

> For myself, I have only one plain, simple line of conduct to pursue. I have promised those who sent me hither to *do my best* for preventing the Irish resolutions from passing into law. . . . The Minister is using every engine to prevent the persons who are likely to be injured from coming forward. . . . The principal glover in this town has a contract under government, so he cannot come. The button maker makes buttons for his majesty, so he is tied fast to his Majestie's minister's button hole. In short the Minister has found so many buttons and loop holes

to fasten them to himself, that few of the principal manufacturers are left at liberty to serve their country.[21]

The attitude of the manufacturers requires some explanation. As Wedgwood complained in the same letter, the 'gentlemen of the iron trade' were convinced that they would be ruined if Pitt's proposals were passed, but none of them attended his meetings and even Boulton was frequently absent. Wedgwood had good reason also to complain of being 'left to *do alone*' the work of the manufacturers and he evidently resented being obliged to bear, on their behalf, the anger of the prime minister and the government. Wedgwood is the only non-political figure named in the *Rolliad* (a collection of satirical verses about Members of Parliament), singled out in an imaginary attack by Lord Chancellor Thurlow:

> Be Wedgwood damned,
> And double-damned his ware

These lines acknowledge the importance attached by the government to the opposition of the Chamber of Manufacturers under Wedgwood's leadership and Josiah told Priestley that the representations made by the Chamber had convinced Pitt of 'sixteen capital errors' in his detailed proposals and that they were now so altered that the Irish would be sure to reject them.[22]

His energetic opposition to the Irish commercial treaty appeared to be a total reversal of his earlier support for freer trade and he has been much criticised for the easy abandonment of his principles. His opinion and his behaviour were evidently influenced by his regular contacts at this time with two of the most formidable opponents of Pitt's plan, Lord Sheffield and William Eden, and by Fox, to whom he wrote in July after Fox had announced his opposition to the bill in the Commons. Sheffield and Eden had been the most active of canvassers, astutely basing their campaign on the threat to the Navigation Act and the organised opposition of British manufacturers. The Navigation Act, passed in 1651 and subsequently amended by a succession of subsidiary Acts, directed that all English imports and exports must be carried in English ships except for those imports carried in ships of the country from which the goods originated. This regulation applied also to all British territories overseas and effectively secured to Britain the greater part of the carrying trade of the world and an unrivalled merchant marine from whose ranks the seamen of the navy were drawn in time of war. Apart from their automatic involvement of the powerful West

Indian interest, no aspect of the Irish proposals was more likely to rouse the opposition of the independent Members of Parliament.

The cooperation of the manufacturers was essential and Sheffield and Eden obtained it by means that were at least ruthless and possibly discreditable. There is now no doubt that Wedgwood and his friends were misinformed, perhaps deliberately misled, by Sheffield. Pitt's declared intention was the equalisation of duties at the lower rate and not, as the manufacturers were encouraged by the Opposition to believe, equalisation by an increase in duties on British goods. That he was either deceived or had failed to grasp Pitt's true intention, is made clear in a letter from Josiah to Richard Lovell Edgeworth, then living in Ireland. Edgeworth was critical of the activities of the Chamber and Josiah was anxious to explain his views to a friend who, since Bentley's death, had become increasingly close. Josiah favoured full union with Ireland, for, as he wrote:

> the fundamental principals of political and commercial connection seem to me to require an equal participation of burthens as of benefits . . . In the present instance Ireland wishes to be admitted to all our markets and privileges, and to enjoy them in the same extent as they are enjoyed by ourselves – nay to bind us, never in any future time . . . to lay the smallest tax upon her staple manufacture, or even to lower our heavy imposts upon Russian or German linens, below the point which shall give effectual favour to Irish linens in the British market, and thus sacrifice, in this single article, our commerce and sale of our manufactures in two great empires, without having, in return, even the exemption of our staple manufacture from taxes in your market.[23]

He made clear his support for the removal of all duties: 'The whole system ought to be annihilated. . . . Excise laws are the bane of manufacturers'; but he could not condone the offer of conditions which he believed – as it happened mistakenly – would be damaging to British manufacturing.

Eden put forward another argument, more scrupulous than the information purveyed by his colleagues. 'It is', he wrote, 'idle and visionary to place on the same commercial ground two neighbouring nations, whom the one is highly taxed, and the other comparatively without taxes.'[24] He might justly have added that Irish labour was cheap. What Wedgwood failed to understand, or chose to ignore, was Ireland's lack of the natural resources required to support a pottery industry of any significance. The theoretical establishment of competitive potteries in Ireland at some unspecified date in the future played no part in the successful opposition to the Irish Resolutions but that Wedgwood's intervention, inspired primarily by self-interest, was material. The Chamber of Manufactures, founded at his instigation and sustained by his energy, commanded attention and respect. Although it was not able to attract the active support of many of its members, its sudden appearance in opposition was sufficient to raise doubts in the minds of Members of Parliament who were otherwise uncommitted, and some of Pitt's changes to the Resolutions – those amendments which made final rejection by the Irish inevitable – were clearly inspired by the complaints of the Chamber.

By the end of May, when the Resolutions were passed in the House of Commons, Pitt's original proposals, which had met with reluctant acceptance in Ireland, had been so mutilated that they had no chance of final approval by the Dublin Parliament. In August they were withdrawn. A far-sighted and liberal design had been thwarted by malice, prejudice, greed and ignorance. Whether he understood it or not, Wedgwood had been drawn into a shabby political conspiracy which resulted in the loss of a great opportunity. In spite of this failure, Irish finances benefited from the freedom, granted in 1780, to trade with the colonies, and this improvement, coinciding with a considerable advance in agricultural prosperity, provided a stimulus to manufactures. For a few years the Irish problem was muffled. It remained in ambush for the future.

In the summer of 1785, according to the *Morning Chronicle*, Lord Thurlow visited Etruria. Josiah greeted the Lord Chancellor personally and showed him around the factory, explaining the uses of the various machines and pointing out the large quantities of goods being made for export:

> 'You see, my Lord', said Mr Wedgwood, with something like a sneer, 'that the Irish have done more for us than your Lordships were willing to do, by rejecting the propositions.' To which the other emphatically retorted, 'But, by G—! Mr Wedgwood, the Irish would *not* have done so, if they had *believed* your evidence given *on oath* at our bar.'[25]

The story is unsubstantiated and the reported conversation is unlikely to be verbatim. It is, however, some measure of the damage done to Wedgwood's reputation for integrity. In British manufacturing towns, Fox was fêted as a hero for his opposition to the Resolutions, but the factory owners who had been glad to employ him as their spokesman showed no desire to champion his claims to be prime minister. Members of the Chamber of Manufacturers were happy to gather credit for the part played by their committee in this dubious victory, but the Chamber was no nearer to unity of opinion and action than it had ever been.

The consequence for Wedgwood's trade in Ireland was disastrous. His agent there was compelled to give up his business. 'He says', Josiah told Edgeworth in December 1786,

> I have offended the Irish & they will buy no more of Wedgwood's *double-damned* ware, a certain noble Lord told him that at a very numer-ous meeting of Nobility &c &c they had resolved that W—d was an enemy to Ireland, & his ware should not find a market there. Nay the noble Peer swore to my pot-seller that if the public suffer'd it to be landed, he would break it to pieces himself. So the poor man has actually given up the business & made a proposal to pay about half what he owes me.[26]

In his first venture among the politicians, Josiah had achieved his aims but the cost had been discouragingly high.

CHAPTER NINETEEN

Trade and Revolution

E arly in September 1785, after playing a leading part in the defeat of the government's plans for Ireland, William Eden wrote loftily to his brother: 'The Ministry wants Strength & Consistency & effect.'[1] Before the end of the month he was in correspondence with Pitt to solicit a government appointment. This sudden change of direction was not as disreputable as it now appears.

Fifteen years Pitt's senior, Eden was a shrewd and experienced politician, who had proved himself, as a Commissioner of Trade, Commissioner to America and Vice-Treasurer of Ireland in previous Whig administrations, an able administrator. He had been a determined opponent of the new government, particularly during the Irish negotiations, but personal ambition and hunger for recognition are often stronger than ties of friendship or party. His political patron, the Duke of Marlborough, had given him a clear indication of his own attitude: 'the more the late Members of Opposition keep together, the more the present Government will be embarrassed – But that does not seem to me to be a good reason for keeping together. I should hope that they would not keep together, but that some of the late Opposition who are Men of Business, would think it for the good of the country to offer their assistance and come over, or be Rats if you please.'[2] This was a respectable point of view among those who believed that they owed their first loyalty to the Crown and the elected government, and Eden's desire for advancement acted as a sharp spur to him in the recognition of his public duty.

Pitt favoured the employment of 'men of business' and he was keen to make the best use of Eden's talents. He could not, however, offer Eden a senior political post. Unlike independent Members of Parliament, who maintained their right to support or reject measures on their merits, Eden had been a politician of faction, a close associate of Fox and the friend of North. He was turning his coat and Pitt's colleagues in Cabinet looked upon such apostasy with mingled suspicion and contempt. After careful consideration, Pitt entrusted to him the negotiation of a trade treaty with France.

This was a proposal far more to Wedgwood's taste than the Irish treaty. When he wrote to Bentley in 1776, 'I should be asham'd to feel anything like a fear in having a free intercourse open'd between Great Britain & all the Potteries in the World', it was Europe, and most particularly France, that he had in mind, and he was adamant that 'a like liberty of exporting our manufactures to continental states' must be an essential condition.[3] In November 1784, the recently formed Earthenware Manufacturers Committee reported, 'the exportation of their manufacture into France is at present prohibited, though French manufactures of a like kind are admitted into this country upon a certain duty'.[4] Eden's appointment was welcome news to Josiah and he lost no time in writing to congratulate him, taking the opportunity to recommend to Eden the services of the General Chamber of Manufactures. 'If', he wrote,

> . . . applications can be made to you with propriety through the channel of the Chamber, rather than through individuals, it would doubtless have the best effect in giving consequence and stability to that institution.

Wedgwood was uncomfortably aware of the anger and distrust engendered by the Chamber's opposition to the Irish Resolutions:

> Two objections start in my mind, which may be only phantoms of my ignorance and inexperience in these matters. . . . One is that the Minister would expect these applications from a public body to be made to himself; and the other, that he might be displeased at your giving such sanction to an institution, against which he may harbour prejudices which I am persuaded in my own mind are unfounded.

He assured Eden that the Chamber was not opposed to any minister but was 'constituted and united' only to support and protect the 'manufacturing interest'.[5]

Eden, whose first duty was to the prime minister, passed Wedgwood's letter to him. Pitt's reply was cool. While he encouraged Eden to 'cultivate every channel of information . . . to collect, from all parts of the kingdom, a just representation of the interests of the various branches of trade and manufacture which can be affected by the French arrangement' and he was 'very glad' that Eden would have 'an opportunity of receiving his [Wedgwood's] suggestions', he reminded him 'that there are many reasons which make it desirable to give as little employment or encouragement as possible to the Chamber of Commerce'.[6] Such instructions made any reply to Wedgwood's letter an awkward exercise and Eden chose instead to ignore it.

Three weeks later, Josiah tried again, composing a letter of ingratiating flattery and requesting an interview with Eden before he left for France. He added, in a postscript and as if as an afterthought: 'With regard to our particular manufacture, we only wish for a fair and simple reciprocity, and I suppose (but I speak without any authority) that our Manchester and Birmingham friends would be willing to give and take in the same way.'[7] Evidently the reply was positive, for Wedgwood saw Eden at least three times before his departure at the end of March.

Josiah was in London in February to give evidence before the Lords' Committee of Trade and, when he did so, he gave them a brief and factual summary of the reciprocal trade in pottery and porcelain between England and France: the prohibition of imports of English earthenware into France, the fact that its bulk and small value relative to its carriage costs discouraged smuggling, and the lack of demand in England for French tin-glazed earthenware, together extinguished all possibility of any considerable trade in pottery; but quantities of the finer French porcelain were imported. He favoured unrestricted trade between the two countries, with duties equalised at 10–15 per cent, arguing that the French admiration for Queen's ware would give the advantage to Britain. He had several meetings with Lord Sheffield, at whose house he was introduced to Lord North and Lord Loughborough,* and visited the Duke of Portland, but none except Sheffield would talk freely of Eden, whom they regarded as a defector.

Early in March, shortly before Eden's departure, Wedgwood engagingly gave him permission to show his Queen's ware, jasper and cameo buttons 'to the whole french nation'.[8] Three months later he wrote to Eden at length, explaining, evidently at Eden's request, what he believed to be the difference between the French classifications of *poterie* and *fayence*, advocating 'much more conclusive calculations' of the different categories.

> . . . a trifling variation in many instances, constitutes the difference between *poterie* and *fayence*. A single line of colour put on, not by enamelling after the ware is finished as *poterie*, but while it is in the

---

*Formerly Attorney-General and Lord Chancellor from 1793 to 1801.

clay state, by a stroke upon the lathe . . . a little marbling or mixture of the clays, of which great quantities of our cheap wares are now made, and every variation of colour, however cheap and simple, constitutes *fayence*, though there is little difference in the prices of the goods themselves; for supposing one hundredweight of the plain ware to be worth 16s., the same weight of like articles in this cheap *fayence* would not be worth more than 20s, though the latter must pay a duty of 20 livres instead of 1 livre 8 sols, paid by the former.[9]

Josiah's (or, more probably, Tom Byerley's) knowledge of the French language was not, unfortunately, equal to the complex task of elucidating technical terms. His suggestion that the difference between *poterie* and *fayence* was 'trifling' and might be defined by the addition of a 'single line of colour' was misleading.* French *faïence*, like Dutch or English delft and Italian *maiolica*, is specifically tin-glazed earthenware, whereas *poterie* was reserved for common lead-glazed wares and was not used to describe either stonewares, such as English saltglazed wares or Wedgwood's jasper, or *faïence*. The word *poterie* was sometimes used for lead-glazed creamwares in the English style, but these were correctly known as *faïence-fine*, *faïence anglaise* or *terre-de-pipe anglaise*. Wedgwood never made tin-glazed earthenware, and by 1786 the manufacture of English creamware had all but extinguished the production of English delftware, while *faïence* was no longer imported from France. Any category of *faïence* for the calculation of duties between the two countries would have been irrelevant.

Negotiations regarding pottery and porcelain were already sufficiently complicated by the reintroduction in 1784 of former prohibitions against the production of porcelain anywhere in France but at Sèvres and by severe restrictions on the use of enamel decoration on *faïence*. These were, however, soon found to be unenforcable, and in 1787 they were replaced by the prohibition of any imitation of Sèvres without the King's permission. Wedgwood's argument, though apparently founded upon an erroneous assumption, probably persuaded the English Commissioners not to use the classification of pottery by type of body and decoration as the basis for the calculation of excise duties, but rather to impose a standard duty of 12 per cent *ad valorem*. This decision was well received by the Staffordshire potters[10] who were confident that English cream-coloured earthenware was superior to any other form of European earthenware in production. In fact, creamware

---

*Many modern French–English dictionaries offer *poterie* and *faïence* as interchangeable descriptions of earthenware.

of good quality, in imitation of the English creamware, was already being produced in France and this was soon providing competition for English imports.

The treaty was signed at Versailles on 26 September 1786. Although they failed to satisfy the combined opposition of Fox and Burke and their supporters in Parliament, and a powerful lobby of manufacturers, the terms negotiated by Eden were triumphantly favourable to Britain. The purpose of the treaty had been the settlement of duties to allow the principal products of each country to be exported, with the minimum of restriction, to the other. The apparent concessions obtained by France were illusory, and where reciprocal duties applied, it seemed certain that British manufacturers would gain the greater profits. Most important of all, the treaty opened to British manufacturers a market which, as Adam Smith had pointed out ten years earlier,[11] was eight times as populous as the American colonies and, because of its proximity to England, able to trade three times as fast.

Pitt congratulated Eden on an outcome 'far beyond our most sanguine wishes'. Even Lord Sheffield could not discover 'a single advantage the French have gained'.[12] Fox was reduced to arguing that France was 'the natural political enemy of Great Britain' and that trade between the two countries implied the subjection of Britain in foreign affairs.[13] Pitt expressed his continuing and realistic distrust of the French privately to Eden: 'Though in the Commercial business I think there are reasons for believing the French may be sincere, I cannot listen without suspicion to their professions of political friendship.'[14] He rejected with scorn Fox's repeated assertion that France was unalterably Britain's enemy, but he did not assume trade to be testimony of friendship.

Josiah, who had already written to Eden to congratulate him on the successful outcome of the negotiations, and to Garbett to express his opinion of the treaty, wrote at greater length on the subject to his friend Edgeworth:

> I think it the most fair, & liberal treaty we have with any nation, therefore the most likely to be lasting. The commercial advantages to both nations will probably be great . . . but sensible as I am to the interests of trade, manufactures & commerce, they all give way to a consideration much superiour in my mind to them all – I mean the probability that a friendly intercourse with so near & valuable a neighbour, may keep us in peace with her – may help to do away with prejudices as foolish as they are deep rooted, & may totally eradicate that most sottish, & wicked idea of our being *natural enemies*.[15]

There is no reason to doubt his sincerity but it is undeniable that he was both better informed and more concerned about the interests of the Staffordshire potters than about those of any other industry. His confidence in the treaty was not shared by all members of the Chamber of Manufacturers, some of whom openly accused Wedgwood of self-interest and treachery. It was not readily understood why he should have been so adamant in his opposition to the proposals for freer trade with Ireland but such a fervent supporter of apparently similar proposals for France unless it was that his own industry, and more particularly his own business, stood to lose from the first and to gain from the second. James Watt wrote to him in February 1787 to reassure him of the support of the Birmingham manufacturers:

> I am very sorry to see by the public papers that there are two opinions in the Chamber of Manufacturers about the Treaty with France. As your opinions on the subject seem to coincide with my own, I thought it might be some small support to you to inform you of it and also to assure you that Mr Boulton, Mr Garbett and I believe all the town of Birmingham are of the same sentiment.[16]

In their support for the treaty, the Birmingham metal workers were joined by the cotton spinners of Manchester and Derby, but there was a significant minority of the Chamber of Manufacturers who protested against the terms of the treaty and against the manner in which approval of it had been imposed on the Chamber by the Manchester, Birmingham and Staffordshire manufacturers, while a dissenting minority did not 'know where to communicate their thoughts, or how to collect the general sense and convey it with force to the minister'.[17] This minority was led by Thomas Walker, a Manchester manufacturer who had taken a leading part in opposition to the Irish proposals. At a meeting of the Chamber on 9 February, at which Walker took the chair in Wedgwood's absence, seven protectionist resolutions and an eighth calling for a petition to the House of Commons to postpone final ratification of the treaty were passed unanimously. Discussion in the House, which was to last five days, followed by three days of debate in the Lords, began on 12 February, and the treaty was given the formal approval of Parliament on 8 March.

Wedgwood's position was uncomfortable to the point of being untenable. Although, at a meeting which he chaired on 17 February, a resolution was passed offering him, as President, the thanks of the Chamber, another, also passed unanimously, reminded members that the first principles on which the organisation had been formed were to watch over the interests of all members and to furnish the government with impartial and true information 'for the want of which, or by relying upon the *information given by interested individuals*, the true interests of the WHOLE has often been unavoidably mistaken'.[18] A month later the Chamber was collapsing. As Wedgwood told James Caldwell, the partner of his Newcastle-under-Lyme attorney, John Sparrow, a disquieting number of the 'respectable members' had seceded, dissatisfied both with the business of the Chamber and the manner in which it was now being conducted by a dissaffected and unrepresentative minority, 'many of whose faces had scarcely been seen before'. He was undecided whether to follow the example of the 'respectable members' and risk being accused of 'a relinquishment of the trust reposed in him' or, in his view improperly, to continue to act 'with the *remaining few* under the character of a *Committee of the General Chamber of Manufacturers of Great Britain'*.[19]

In the meantime, the criticism of Wedgwood's actions, implied and specific, continued. While the Chamber was content to cloak the accusations in formal thanks to Thomas Walker and rehearsals of founding principles, with barbed references to abstention from 'selfish designs' and 'interested individuals',[20] the newspapers were less reticent. The *Gazetteer and New Daily News Advertiser* made scarcely veiled allegations of corruption against Wedgwood and the *Morning Chronicle* of 28 March carried a scurrilous attack on him which began:

> Mr. Wedgwood *was* united with men of principle and honor. – He *was* a principal informing the Chamber of Commerce. – He *was* the promoter of harmony and union among them. – He *was* the strenuous and indefatigable supporter of the *general*, and the reprobater of any *partial* interests of the manufacturing body. – He *was* the determined enemy of the *Irish Propositions*, in the fate of which he was *not* personally interested. – He *was* respected and revered by his fellow manufacturers. and esteemed by the whole nation.
>
> Mr Wedgwood *is* connected with, and become the tool of Administration. – He *is* their instrument in attempting to dissolve the Chamber of Commerce, so much dreaded by them . . .

Nothing could be more foolish than the last accusation. Wedgwood had always done his utmost to promote the status and reputation of the Chamber, which he had been instrumental in founding. His failure in this respect had been due totally to his misguided, but – among the manufacturers – widely popular opposition to the Irish treaty. Far from regarding the Chamber with dread, Pitt and his ministers dismissed it with contempt as a body attempting 'to take from Parliament the trouble of legislation'. While the manufacturers had been prepared to show some sign of unity in their demands, Pitt had admitted that they carried a 'most powerful weight'.[21] When, under the guidance of Walker, that unity was irretrievably lost, the Chamber was reduced to impotence.

That Wedgwood, as President of the Chamber, was sometimes high-handed in his neglect of minority opinion cannot be denied, and it would be unrealistic to suppose that he did not have his own industry constantly in mind when he was giving advice to William Eden. But it is significant that he was supported by some of the most active and inventive manufacturers of his time. The reform or removal of obstructive trade barriers acted as a stimulus to the young and expanding industries of the Midlands and northern counties. Older, less aggressive industries feared competition. Burdened by debt and discredited as much by its own sudden changes of policy as by government odium, the Chamber struggled on. Wedgwood was saddened and disappointed. He told Boulton, 'I am just wearied out with the nonsense of some & the pertness & abuse of others.' Without more support in the Chamber, he would feel obliged to resign. 'I have', he wrote, 'been buffeted & teased beyond human patience. Some of my friends say let the Chamber go to the Devil. I say no – we may want it hereafter. It should be new modelled . . . but not demolished.'[22] When Walker was finally rejected by the Manchester manufacturers there was little spirit left for quarrels about a treaty which had already been approved by Parliament. To Eden Wedgwood wrote: 'The Chamber of Manufacturers sleepeth for the present, but may be waked at any time when its services are called for.'[23] He was too optimistic: it had died of inanition.

Throughout these transactions, as in his opposition to the Irish Resolutions, Wedgwood had displayed a dangerous naïvety but he had learned some valuable lessons for the future. He now understood that a common cause was not enough to rouse manufacturers from their preoccupation with parochial interests; that political lobbying in the hands of the government and of astute 'men of business' was more potent than a rational or even a popular motive; and that self-interest operated even more strongly in politics than in business.

It is unlikely that Josiah mistook the condescension of such men as Eden and Sheffield for friendship. His letters to them, and to all members of the ruling classes, were never anything but deeply deferential. The true attitude of these patrons towards him is best illustrated by two letters which passed between Sheffield and Eden in February 1787. 'But to return to the manufacturers,' Sheffield wrote, 'it must be your education in France that has made such a change in your manners and politeness towards them; for I remember a time when with great liveliness you wondered how I could find time to talk with them, that *you* could not, and with difficulty suffered Mr. Wedgwood to be introduced to you . . .' To this Eden replied, 'When you menace me with the wavering and fickle disposition of the manufacturers, you remind me of what I well know. It is very certain that those who gain on such occasions, are shy and sly, and snug and silent; that those who do not gain are disengenuous, and sullen and suspicious; and those who either lose or think they may lose, are confoundedly noisy, and absurd, and mischievous.'[24] Wedgwood was seldom philanthropic: he used his contacts with the nobility to promote his business. In turn, the patronage he received was not disinterested. Friendship did not intrude upon these associations. Although it was later reported out of its true context, which referred to commerce between nations, Josiah had once declared that there was 'no such thing as friendship in trade'.[25] There was certainly little possibility of friendship between trade and politics.

Wedgwood lost no time in taking advantage of the new terms of trade with France. Apart from the popular (and already imitated) Queen's ware of which he might hope to sell substantial quantities, Wedgwood could offer jasper (also copied in France, notably at the Sèvres factory) in all its bewildering variety of objects from cameo buttons to vases, including some fine portrait medallions of French kings, statesmen and commanders, writers and artists. The treaty itself was celebrated by the production of his first important commemorative tablets, *Mercury Uniting the Hands of Britain and France* and *Peace Preventing Mars from Breaking Open the Gates of the Temple of Janus*, both designed by John Flaxman junior and produced in blue-and-white jasper. Of the first, Josiah told Flaxman:

> We must take care not to show that these representations were invented by an Englishman; as they are meant to be conciliatory, they should be scrupulously impartial. The figures for instance, which represent the two nations, should be equally magnificent and important in their dress, attitude, character and attributes, and Mercury should not perhaps seem more inclined to one than the other . . . you know upon this occasion expedition is of great consequence . . . [26]

Characteristically, Josiah commissioned these designs almost three months before the treaty was given final ratification by Parliament. The first pair was sent as a gift to William Eden the following year. Three years later, Josiah presented Eden and his wife with jasper portrait medallions by the Irish modeller Eley George Mountstephen.[27] The dates of these offerings controvert the suggestion[28] that they might have been inducements to Eden to favour Wedgwood's interests in the negotiation of the French Commercial Treaty.

By June 1787 Josiah had appointed agents to sell his wares in Paris, Rouen and Bordeaux and he wrote to Eden to inform him of these arrangements and also to congratulate him on his appointment to negotiate a commercial treaty with Spain.[29] His hopes for a rapid growth in trade with France were, however, not to be realised. On 21 July 1789 the *Morning Post* announced, with glowing approval, the fall of the Bastille and the start of 'one of the most IMPORTANT REVOLUTIONS the world has ever seen'. Fox hailed it as 'How much the greatest event . . . that ever happened in the world! And how much the best!'[30] Josiah's response was not much more restrained: 'I know you will rejoice with me in the glorious revolution which has taken place in France,' he wrote to Darwin. 'The politicians tell me that as a manufacturer I shall be ruined if France has her liberty, but I am willing to take my chance in that respect, nor do I yet see that the happiness of one nation includes in it the misery of its next neighbour.'[31]

Such confident predisposition to the Revolution was not uncommon. In 1789 the majority of people of education and enlightenment sympathised with the revolutionaries, who attracted support from all classes in Britain but particularly from the middling class of scientists and industrialists and from the poets. John Wilkinson, the ironmaster, and Thomas Telford, the engineer, were partisans, as were William Wordsworth, Samuel Taylor Coleridge, William Blake and Robert Burns. Even Pitt, understanding that the financial collapse of France dispelled any fears of renewed rivalry in India or anywhere else, and believing that there was little possibility that dangerous 'democratical' opinions would cross the Channel and take root in Britain, declared, with some satisfaction, that France must be seen as 'an object of compassion'.[32]

Wedgwood's delight in the Revolution, which he proclaimed with two medallions commemorating the fall of the Bastille, was shared by most of his friends in the Lunar Society. Priestley, in particular, made his opinion public in his *Letters to the Right Honourable Edmund Burke*, published in 1791 in response to Burke's *Reflections on the Revolution in France*. Darwin celebrated the Revolution in eighteen lines of Canto II of 'The Economy of Vegetation' (Part I of *The Botanic Garden*, 1791) and wrote to Watt in January 1790: 'Do you not congratulate your grandchildren on the dawn of universal liberty? I feel myself becoming all french both in chemistry and politics.'[33] Even James Keir, perhaps the most moderate among them, was a supporter. Wedgwood considered the Revolution 'a very sudden and momentous event' whose consequences would be 'extensive beyond anything perhaps we can at present imagine' and he forecast that these consequences were unlikely to be contained within the frontiers of France. 'When', he wrote, 'the rights of men are ascertained with such precision and laid down from such authority as the National assembly of France, other nations will begin to consider whether they are not men, and if men whether these rights do not belong to them.'[34] He told Darwin of a visitor to Etruria, lately arrived from the Continent, who had spoken of 'the same spirit of liberty . . . developing all over Germany, & all over Europe'. He added, however, that his informant had also spent twelve months in Turkey but did not 'say anything about the spirit of liberty breaking forth there'.[35]

Much intellectual support for the French Revolution was based on a false comparison with the Glorious Revolution of 1688. But the revolution in England had been the work of the aristocracy in defence of the Constitution and it had achieved its aims without creating any pattern for revolution elsewhere. The French Revolution began as an attempt by the aristocracy to regain control of the state and developed, through a series of terrifying convulsions, into a rebellion, led by the middle class, that overthrew the state and formulated a constitution. The freedom of the individual declared in the revolutionary slogan 'Liberty, Equality and Fraternity' would have shocked Englishmen in 1688. It was to be dispelled by Napoleon but the vision remained as the inspiration of all revolution. It was in France, not in England, that the vocabulary of revolution was invented; and it was France that discovered the concept of mobilisation.

Sympathy for the Revolution in France sprang as much from the hope that it would transform French attitudes and policies as from true accord with its aims. Hostility to France had been the dominant influence in English foreign policy since the Middle Ages, and in the eighteenth century it was the most consistent thread running through English thought. As the abbé le Blanc wrote in 1747, 'the bulk of the English nation bear an inveterate hatred of the French, which they do not always take the pains to conceal from us'.[36] France was Britain's most dangerous rival in commerce, in colonial expansion and in the struggle for command of the sea; and she was also the greatest Catholic power, the repository of the hopes of the Pretenders to the English throne and the centre of the Bourbon family alliance. French intervention in the American Revolution had further embittered British sentiment. By helping to bankrupt France it had also led more directly to revolution there than had the comparatively paltry extravagances of Louis XVI's court, which amounted to little more than 6 per cent of government expenditure.

British foreign policy had long been founded on an attempt to maintain the balance of power in Europe by forming natural alliances between the Protestant powers – the United Provinces, Prussia and the German States, the Scandinavian countries – against France, Spain, Austria and Italy. This had been combined successfully with Chatham's strategy of containing France in Europe by the use of liberal subsidies to Britain's allies while he used superior sea power, in which the Dutch alliance was particularly relevant, to mop up the French colonial empire. This policy called forth Choiseul's accusation that Britain was 'pretending to protect the balance on land which no one threatens, [while] destroying the balance at sea which no one defends'.[37] Through the Commercial Treaty of 1786, the Younger Pitt had sought a lasting peace by lessening the effects of economic rivalry. As long as Britain and Prussia remained aloof and the Bourbons did not intervene, the Revolution appeared to offer Britain further time for economic revival without threatening immediately to destabilise Europe. In Parliament in February 1790, while Burke warned against the contagion of democratic principles, Pitt declared, 'The present conditions in France must, sooner or later, terminate in general harmony and regular order; and though the fortunate arrangements of such a situation may make her more formidable, it may also render her less obnoxious as a neighbour.'[38]

In January 1790 Tom Paine had written to Burke: 'The Revolution in France is certainly a Forerunner to other Revolutions in Europe.'[39] It was this, above all, that Burke feared, and the winter and spring of 1791–2 brought disturbing signs of unrest in Britain. The London Society for promoting Constitutional Information was revived in December and the following month the London Corresponding Society for the Reform of Parliamentary Representation was formed. At the same time an association in Sheffield reprinted and distributed 1600 copies of the first part of Paine's Rights of Man. In February 1792 Paine published the second part, advocating republican and egalitarian doctrines that went far beyond his first thesis and created an even greater sensation. It was no longer so certain that 'democratical ideas' could be restricted to the French.

These first tremors were matched by occasional disturbances by loyalist mobs. The most serious of these took place in Birmingham in 1791. The pretext for it was provided by a meeting of the Revolutionary Society, founded to commemorate the Revolution of 1688, and held, perhaps provocatively, on 14 July to celebrate Bastille Day. James Keir agreed to be chairman but Priestley, who had played a leading part in founding the Society, was not present. Riots, suspected to have been organised and led by agents of the government or local authorities, began that evening and lasted for three days. The violence was directed at dissenters, radicals and known supporters of the Revolution. While fourteen houses, including Priestley's, William Hutton's, and the Old and New Meeting Houses were destroyed, and Withering's was ransacked, magistrates refused to act until the danger to people and property became more general. Boulton and Watt armed their workers to repel any attack on the Soho factory, and Watt went armed to the next meeting of the Lunar Society at Galton's house, 4 miles from the city, on 24 September. The extent of the damage may be measured by the compensation paid to the principal victims: £5390 to Hutton and £2502 to Priestley.[40]

Wedgwood, who was in Weymouth, received a secondhand but instructive account of the riot from his younger son. Jos wrote on 20 July:

> Watt says that he firmly believes the inhabitants of Birm. would easily have quelled the riots in the beginning if they had associated & armed with firearms, or even if they had armed the constables with firelocks instead of mop staves. But it appears that the magistrates possessed neither acivity nor resolution, or that they were not heartily desirous to put a stop to their excesses. Mr Carles is known for a bigot & he is said even to have hinted to the mob that they ought not to contain themselves with breaking the windows at the Hotel, for he happened to be dining there that day, & came out to the door saying 'My lads it is no use breaking the windows here, the gentlemen are all gone & you might be better employed elsewhere.' Where are they gone said the mob? 'To the new meeting [house] to be sure.'

'But', Jos added with a touch of his father's irony, 'I should think this was not to be believed of a magistrate.'[41]

Priestley's losses were devastating: the whole of his library, his papers, his laboratory and scientific apparatus were destroyed with his house, his furniture and even his clothing. Josiah wrote immediately to offer him whatever help he might require, including sanctuary at Etruria Hall: 'Can I be of any use or service to you upon the present occasion? Assure yourself, my good friend, that I most earnestly wish it. Believe this of me – act accordingly, instruct me in the means of doing it & I shall esteem it as one of the strongest instances of your friendship.'[42] At Darwin's instigation, the Derby Philosophical Society sent Priestley a 'sympathetic address' congratulating him on his escape from 'the sacrilegious hands of the savages at Birmingham' and lamenting the loss, both to Priestley and to the scientific world, of his library, experimental apparatus and 'more valuable' manuscripts: 'Almost all great minds in all ages of the world, who have endeavoured to benefit mankind, have been persecuted by them. . . . Your enemies, unable to conquer your arguments by reason, have had recourse to violence; they have halloo'd upon you the dogs of unfeeling ignorance, and of frantic fanaticism.'[43] The style is roundly Darwinian. Galton offered Priestley and his wife his protection. Watt counselled caution: 'There are duties you owe to your family, to your friends, and to humanity in general, that should direct you not to risk a life so valuable to them all.'[44] Boulton, more cautious still, was silent.

Priestley settled for a time in London, where he re-established his laboratory and continued his experimental work. Wedgwood, Galton and Withering sent him money, Keir supplied chemicals, Wedgwood and Watt contributed apparatus. All his Lunar friends advised Priestley to postpone or abandon publication of his 'Appeal to the Public on the Subject of the Riots in Birmingham' but several offered to support his claims for damages and, although it was never again thought safe for him to return to Birmingham to attend their meetings, he maintained his correspondence with the Society and continued to send papers describing his experiments for discussion. He found, however, that prejudice against his name was too strong and too widespread to allow him or his sons to prosper. Three years after the Birmingham riots, Priestley left England with his family and emigrated to the United States. He set up his laboratory in Pennsylvania but the quality of his scientific work declined. He missed the regular discussion and exchange of ideas with other 'Lunatics'. Correspondence was not enough. As he was later to remark: 'I consider my settlement at Birmingham as the happiest event in my life, being highly favourable to every object I had in view, philosophical or theological.'[45] The Lunar Society, which had meant so much to him, gradually withered and there is no record of any meeting of the remaining members after March 1798.[46]

Although Priestley had been driven from the country by bigotry, the growth of associations declaring their sympathy for democratic principles continued. The society known as the Friends of the People, founded in April 1792, boasted a number of distinguished Whig politicians among its members, although Fox prudently refused to join. The professed aim of the society was the reform of the Constitution by the correction of old abuses but it soon became identified with the republican views of the Corresponding Societies, regarded as the British equivalent of the Jacobin Clubs of France (the most radical group of revolutionaries, led by Robespierre).

To Pitt, coolly indifferent to the effects of the Revolution upon the people of France, the threat of serious unrest or even revolution at home was enough to induce him to abandon one of his most cherished ambitions: the reform of parliamentary representation. On 30 April Charles Grey, Fox's closest friend in the House of Commons, gave notice of a motion for reform to be introduced in the next Parliament. Pitt knew that the motion would include a demand for universal suffrage, the acknowledged aim of the Societies following principles enunciated by Paine, and he attacked the proposal as an invitation to anarchy. Universal suffrage had never been part of his own plans and he was resolutely opposed to it. His anxiety for the preservation of order now persuaded him to abandon even the most moderate reforms. He had joined the ranks of those who looked upon all change with suspicion and on all reformers as party to the conspiracy of the Societies to subvert the Constitution.

Josiah's views were made plain in a letter to young Jos:

> Speaking politically, I believe you know my sentiments that so long as we have septennial parliaments, 'tis of little consequence who is chosen into them. . . . A real parliamentary reform is therefore what we most stand in need of; and for this I would willingly devote my time the most precious thing I have to bestow, or any thing else by which I could serve so truly noble a cause.[47]

The cause was already lost. When Louis XVI and his family were arrested in June 1791, after their ill-judged flight to Varennes, and when, ten months later, France declared defensive war on Austria, many of those in Britain who had supported the Revolution began to doubt its virtues. Reform was no longer expedient. By the summer of 1792, the fear of insurrection had persuaded Pitt to impose peace at home as a precaution against war in Europe.

On 21 May a royal proclamation solemnly warned the King's subjects against 'divers wicked and seditious writings'. It instructed magistrates to discover and prosecute authors, printers and distributors of such material and to take all necessary steps for the preservation of order and a 'due submission to the laws'. This proclamation has since been condemned as an overreaction against largely imaginary dangers, an incitement to violence, and the first in a series of reactionary and repressive measures dictated by ministerial panic. In retrospect this judgement may be justified. At the time, however, the spread of the

Constitutional Societies, whose avowed object was to unite in 'a radical Reform of the country . . . consistent with the Rights of Man',[48] to number several hundred throughout the country, was menacingly like the development of the Jacobin Clubs in France and it is ingenuous to suppose that the reforming ambitions of the British Societies were confined to the ballot box. They had absorbed and approved both parts of Paine's *Rights of Man*, the second of which advocated action that could only be regarded as revolutionary. If Pitt overreacted, it was because he chose not to distinguish between the aspirations of moderate reformers and the demands of extremists, and because the threat of European war made peace at home his first concern.

In opposition to the Constitutional Societies, various associations were founded 'for protecting liberty and property against republicans and levellers'. Josiah wanted nothing to do with them. As he told his nephew, Tom Byerley, at the end of the year:

> I do not know their object, but so far as I can judge, I think them useless, to speak in the most moderate terms, but if they should unhappily set one part of the nation against the other they would be some thing worse than useless. It will not be expected that I should upon this occasion make profession of my Loyalty or attachment to our constitution. I shall let my actions speak for me, & continue to perform what appears to me to be my duty to all around me. I shall certainly love my friends, & if I cannot arrive at the perfection of loving my enemies likewise, I will not injure them unless in my defence.[49]

The voice has the tone of a man wearied of politics.

CHAPTER TWENTY

Call It Trade

One other political cause, and one in which he had no commercial interest, had already engaged Wedgwood's sympathies and support. It was Wilberforce's campaign for the abolition of the slave trade.

Negro slaves from the west coast of Africa were sold for the first time in Lisbon in 1444. Sixty years later, to supply labour for the new settlements in America, the Portuguese started what soon became regular shipments across the Atlantic. For 200 years the English took little part in the trade. Indeed, Queen Elizabeth severely reprimanded Sir John Hawkins for his two slaving adventures, warning him that the forcible abduction of black Africans would 'call down the vengeance of Heaven'. By the treaty of Utrecht, however, Britain acquired sole rights to the slave trade with the Spanish colonies, and conquests in Africa during the Seven Years War increased her share of the trade.* Although an Act of Parliament passed in 1750 forbade the abduction of blacks, none but the Society of Friends paid much regard to the law and Liverpool overtook Bristol and London as the most prosperous slaving port in the world.

In 1772, Lord Mansfield overturned previous legal opinions by his reluctant judgement in the case of a runaway Negro slave, James Somerset, whose owner claimed title under Virginian law. Mansfield declared that such a claim to property had never been in use or acknowledged by the laws of England and that 'the claim of slavery can never be supported'. This, *de jure*, freed some 14,000 slaves in Britain, but it had no effect on the slave trade and jurisdiction was not extended to foreign ships carrying slaves in British ports or waters.

*Estimates vary widely but it appears that Britain shipped a little over half the total number of slaves, France less than a third, and the remaining trade was shared between the Dutch and the Danes.

Fifteen years after Mansfield's judgment, the Committee for the Abolition of the Slave Trade was founded. The first Chairman, Granville Sharp, and Thomas Clarkson, one of the committee, were the heart and brain of the movement; in William Wilberforce they found their voice. Intensely religious, compassionate, idealistic and politically experienced, Wilberforce was also the friend of the prime minister and one of the most persuasive speakers in the House of Commons.

The formal title of the Committee was carefully chosen. It recognised a clear distinction between slavery and the slave trade. A campaign against the first, which would be interpreted as an attack on property, would provoke powerful opposition even from among those without any personal interest to protect, but its success would automatically destroy the trade. The abolition of the trade alone, on the other hand, could be expected to excite the animosity of the West Indian interest without inviting the hostility of any other group, and it would bring slavery to a gradual end. In the meantime, the inevitability of this consequence might encourage planters to treat their slaves with greater humanity. Clarkson and Wilberforce agreed to aim their campaign at the trade. They were alert to the danger of suddenly granting to thousands of slaves the freedom to turn on their masters and subsequent events in St Domingue* emphasised the wisdom of their decision.

Wilberforce was seriously ill in the spring of 1788 and Dr Richard Warren warned him that he would be dead within twelve months. Although, in common with others of Dr Warren's patients, Wilberforce did not oblige him by confirming his prognosis, he was unable to open the campaign in Parliament and Pitt offered to take his place. His formal motion for a debate was carried without a division on 8 May. Sir William Dolben's bill to limit the number of slaves to be carried in proportion to ships' tonnage was passed also by an overwhelming majority in the Commons, only to be returned, mangled, by the Lords. Pitt let it be known that opponents of the Bill would not be allowed to remain in government and the amended Bill was finally passed by both Houses.

Opposition to abolition of the slave trade centred upon three objections: the ruin of the West Indian islands' commerce, which depended on slave labour; the injury to the navy, which benefited from the trade as a considerable nursery for seamen; and the futility of renouncing a profitable trade which would be appropriated immediately by the French. It was contended also that accounts of the slaves' sufferings

*The western half of the island, now Haiti, discovered by Columbus in 1492. Wilberforce, and most of his English contemporaries, used 'St Domingo' for both the Spanish colony of that name occupying the eastern half of the island and the French colony of St Domingue.

were grossly exaggerated. When Wilberforce was able to introduce the motion for abolition in May 1789, he produced evidence to refute each of these objections. Debate was delayed by the King's illness and the Regency crisis and the vote was further postponed by a decision to hear evidence. The hearing was not completed until April 1790.

By then the campaign was attracting public support. Thomas Day's epic poem, *The Dying Negro*, published seventeen years earlier, may have been responsible for arousing Josiah Wedgwood's practical opposition to the slave trade, and both his own and Bentley's close associations with Liverpool and its commerce kept him better informed of the trade than many of his contemporaries. Darwin was certainly affected by the poem: his verses condemning slavery are the most forceful political statement in *The Loves of the Plants*, published in 1789. Two years later, in 'The Economy of Vegetation', he returned to the subject with renewed vigour, demanding that Britannia take note of the British trade in slaves:

> How AFRIC's coasts thy craftier sons invade
> With murder, rapine, theft, – and call it TRADE!
> – The SLAVE, in chains, on supplicating knee,
> Spreads his wide arms, and lifts his eyes to Thee;
> With hunger pale, with wounds and toil oppress'd,
> 'ARE WE NOT BRETHREN?' sorrow choaks the rest; –

These verses echo two lines which occur earlier in the same poem:

> . . . poor fetter'd SLAVE on bended knee
> From Britain's sons imploring to be free.[1]

They serve as a description of Wedgwood's contribution to the cause of the Society for the Abolition of the Slave Trade, of which Josiah had become a committee member. This was a cameo depicting a kneeling slave in chains, the outer edge moulded with the words 'AM I NOT A MAN AND A BROTHER?' This was modelled in 1787 from the seal of the Society in black jasper on a white ground and Wedgwood distributed it free to those closely concerned with the movement. Clarkson described how the cameos became fashionable: 'Some had them inlaid in gold on the lid of their snuff-boxes. Of the ladies, several wore them in bracelets, and others had them fitted up in an ornamental manner as pins for their hair. At length the taste for wearing them became general, and thus a fashion . . . was seen for once in the honourable office of promoting the cause of justice, humanity and freedom.'[2]

At the end of February 1788 Josiah sent a quantity of cameos to Benjamin Franklin, President of the Pennsylvanian Society for the Abolition of Slavery. 'I embrace the opportunity', he wrote in a covering letter, 'to inclose for the use of your Excellency and friends, a few Cameos on a subject which I am happy to acquaint you is daily more and more taking possession of men's minds on this side of the Atlantic as well as with you. It gives me great pleasure to be embarked on this occasion in the same great and good cause with you, Sir, and I ardently hope for the final completion of our wishes.'[3] While expressing 'the highest veneration for your virtue and gratitude for the benefits you have bestowed on Society', Josiah surprisingly makes no reference to their previous acquaintance. Franklin's reply, acknowledging receipt of the cameos, is equally reticent;[4] and yet it is almost incredible that they should not have met while Franklin was in England between 1757 and 1762, or during his longer stay from 1764 to 1775. He was certainly known to Bentley; Matthew Boulton met him in 1758; and Erasmus Darwin's friendship with him, probably begun in the same year and recorded in their correspondence, lasted throughout their lives. Wedgwood's and Franklin's mutual friends included Priestley, Whitehurst and the Quaker physician John Fothergill and it is unlikely that Josiah would willingly have missed Franklin's visit as a guest to the Lunar Society.[5]

Boulton, Priestley, Galton and Garbett were among Wedgwood's friends who supported the work of Wilberforce and Clarkson, and Josiah's own efforts were not limited to the production of a few hundred cameos. He was active in promoting publications, meetings and petitions, and in canvassing the support of anyone whose voice might command respect. One such was the author and poet, Anna Seward, 'The Swan of Lichfield', to whom he wrote at length, discussing the opposing arguments for abolition or regulation of the trade, 'for I do not know any', he told her, 'who say there is no necessity for either'.[6] Fox had already settled this debate to the satisfaction of all Wilberforce's supporters in the Commons by declaring that he 'knew of no such thing as regulation of robbery or a restriction of murder: the legislature must either abolish the trade or avow their own criminality'.[7]

Anna Seward was an anti-abolitionist whom Josiah was especially anxious to enrol. As a member of the committee of the Society, he was well informed of the arguments to counter her objections that abolition would lead to the loss of 'the West India commerce' and that, as the trade was taken up by other countries, the slaves would only 'change their masters, without being able to shake off their bondage'. 'How Mortifying is it', he wrote, to be assured that even . . . a mere change of masters, would be a blessing of no small magnitude to those poor wretches! Turn them over to a Spanish master, and a ray of hope, unknown to our West India slaves, breaks in upon their poor benighted minds; for here you put them within the sight, within the reach, and even within the probability of liberty.

He went on to explain that Spanish slaves started with two days of the week to themselves and were permitted, by their work, progressively to buy their freedom:

What labour will not hopes like these enable them to endure, when every exertion brings them nearer and nearer to that state which they must so earnestly be looking after. . . . Contrast this chearing state . . . with the absolute despair of a West Indian slave, wearing out by immoderate & incessant labour, with *known* & *calculated* certainty, in the course of a few years, and we cannot but confess that a change of masters would, in this instance, be to him a blessing most devoutly to be wished for.[8]

Pitt was later to employ a stronger argument for abolition: if the British Parliament voted against it, other nations might say, 'Great Britain has not only not abolished, but has refused to abolish, the Slave Trade. She has investigated it well. Her senate has deliberated on it. It is plain then, she finds no guilt in it.' Britain would be held responsible for the crimes of Europe.[9]

Wilberforce moved the abolition of the slave trade in the House of Commons on 18 April 1791. In spite of the powerful support of both Pitt and Fox, who made one of the great speeches of his life, the motion was lost by 88 votes to 163.

The explanation for this reverse lay in the progress of the French Revolution and the growth of radical societies in Britain. The connection between these circumstances and the slave trade appears obscure but it was not so to opponents of the Bill. Their conviction that 'democratical' ideas and revolution were the natural consequence of increased freedom was, in their view, justified by later events in St Domingue, the most prosperous of the French sugar islands. A rising by the mulatto community against the white colonists had been ruthlessly suppressed at the beginning of 1790. On 15 May 1791, by decree of the National Assembly, all slaves in the French colonies were freed and granted rights of citizenship. Three months later the slaves rose in rebellion and butchered their masters. When accounts of the worst atrocities committed on the island were received in England, the cause of abolition was gravely damaged. Wilberforce, who had been preparing to introduce his Bill again, told Thomas Babington, 'people here are all panic struck with the transactions of St Domingo, and the apprehension, or pretended apprehension of the like in Jamaica, and other of our islands'.[10] He was advised to defer the reintroduction of his motion until the climate of opinion was more favourable. In November he visited Wedgwood at Etruria and they 'discussed all evening'. Neither left any account of their conversation, Wilberforce merely mentioning dinner with Wedgwood, 'three sons and three daughters and Mrs W. – a fine, sensible spirited family, intelligent and manly in behaviour'. Etruria Hall is succinctly described as 'situation good, house rather grand. Pictures &c'.[11]

Foremost among those who advised postponement was Pitt, whose accurate appraisal of the feeling of the House of Commons and understanding of the damaging effect of a second defeat led to accusations of a lack of genuine sympathy for the Bill. Nor was Wilberforce's cause helped by Clarkson's all too public enthusiasm for the French Revolution, which served irrationally to identify abolitionists with Jacobins. In spite of advice and warnings, Wilberforce determined to continue the struggle. There was no party division on the issue and he knew that all the most persuasive orators in the House would speak in his support.

As late as January 1792 Josiah was corresponding with Clarkson about the distribution of pamphlets, proposing to pay the profit of the hawkers who would deliver them and suggesting improvements to their appearance. One of these was the addition of 'a wooden cut of the negro kneeling with the motto "Am I not a man and a brother" in place of the advertisement in the title page' of William Cowper's popular poem *The Negro's Complaint*. To the last he was active in obtaining petitions for abolition from the Potteries and nearby towns in Staffordshire and Derbyshire.[12]

The motion was reintroduced on 2 April 1792 and, in spite of a speech by Pitt that came to be regarded as the greatest ever heard in the House, it was defeated by 230 votes to 85. An amendment calling for gradual abolition in the hope that this would lead to the end of hereditary slavery, a proposal likened by Fox to a declaration that there might be moderation in murder, was passed by a majority of 68. A bill for abolition was not finally passed until 1807. Of the Lunatics who had most actively supported the movement – Wedgwood, Darwin, Boulton, Day and Priestley – Boulton alone lived to see it succeed.

CHAPTER TWENTY-ONE

Arts and Manufactures

So great was the admiration for Wedgwood's work in his own time and so enduring has been his personal reputation ever since that historians and, more particularly, biographers have been inclined to claim for him qualities that he did not possess. A near contemporary, the German poet and philosopher Freidrich von Hardenberg, known as 'Novalis', compared Wedgwood's work to that of Goethe. A distinguished modern historian of the Industrial Revolution has drawn another false comparison: 'Boulton, the friend of art and science, was, above all, a manufacturer. But in Wedgwood we have an artist, and, some would maintain, a great one.'[1]

Although some examples of Wedgwood's work have survived to attest to his competence as a modeller, and he was a trained thrower, with the thrower's instinct for satisfying form, the drawings that appear occasionally among his letters and memoranda are childish and there is no evidence that he was able to produce detailed designs. There is, indeed, scarcely anything in the production of the Wedgwood factory during Josiah's lifetime that may be truly described as original. By far the greater number of Wedgwood designs for tableware patterns or for relief ornament were copied or adapted, by artists who were either employed or commissioned by Wedgwood, from earlier work by others. Both Wedgwood and Boulton were, above all, manufacturers and they shared several of the same sources, notably the Flaxmans and Sir William Chambers. Wedgwood was the more inventive and his knowledge of the chemistry of his trade was probably greater than Boulton's, but he was not an artist, except in the obsolete sense of a practitioner of a manual art.

It is clear from his letters that Wedgwood's knowledge of art history or artistic techniques was slight but his interest in artists was not confined to those whom he could commission or employ. He had aspirations also to be regarded as a patron. There is an early hint of these in his proposal to make 'a Colony of Artists, Modelers, carvers &c.' in his London studios,[2] but he was content for many years to copy models bought from the London makers of plaster casts and to hire the best modellers he could afford.

The first professional modeller to be employed by Wedgwood was John Voyez. In 1768, when Josiah first engaged him, Voyez was working in London and he was 'paid by the piece' until he moved to Staffordshire. He had spent two or three years with Robert Adam and was reputed to be the best modeller in London and 'a perfect Master of the Antique stile in ornaments, Vases &c.'. He was hired for three years and Josiah sent the considerable sum of £20 to London, 'enough besides to bring them here in the Coach'. Since Voyez was unmarried, the plural reference was probably to Voyez and what Josiah was later pleased to called 'his Doxy', whom Sally more tactfully, or in innocence, called 'Mrs Voyez'. After demands, to which Josiah oddly yielded, for more money to buy himself a feather-bed, Voyez arrived in Burslem in the middle of July 1768. Within four months Sally was expressing the wish, evidently shared with Josiah and Bentley, that Voyez would either 'mind his business or go his ways'.[3]

He did not immediately do so. Although his later signed work for Humphrey Palmer is evidence that his reputation was not wholly unfounded, Voyez was a sad disappointment to Wedgwood. A vase-candlestick of his modelling was described in March 1769 as 'that Solomangundy'* but poor modelling was the least of his faults. At the end of January he had been found guilty of stealing '11 Models of Clay val[ue] 5£. 15 Moulds of Clay val. 50s and 15 moulds of Plaister val. 50s Goods of Josiah Wedgwood at the par[ish] of Burslem'. He was sentenced to transportation for seven years.[4] It appears that he may have suffered a whipping and five months' imprisonment instead for he was certainly in the employment of Palmer before the end of the year. Josiah agreed with Bentley that he should not have 'anything further to do with him on any account'.[5]

This was a decision more easily made than acted upon. Whatever the faults of Voyez as an employee, Josiah was anxious to keep him out of the hands of competitors. As senior modeller, he had been given access to too many secrets and, while Voyez was still serving his sentence, Josiah proposed to Bentley that they should pay him a retainer of thirty-six shillings a week 'for doing nothing at all' when he was

---

*A corruption of 'Salmagundy', 'a dish composed of chopped meat, anchovies, eggs and onions, with oil and condiments' (*Oxford English Dictionary*): commonly used to describe an incongruent mixture or 'dog's breakfast'.

released: 'The selling a single V[ase]: say a Medallion less per week through such competition would be a greater loss to us than paying him his wages for nothing! . . . Suppose we should lose the sale of 20 or twice that No. pr week & lower the price of others!'[6] This remarkable suggestion shows how seriously Josiah was concerned that the knowledge of clay compositions and production processes gained by Voyez during his brief period at the Brick House factory should not be made available to Palmer or to any other substantial potter. His failure to prevent this is unexplained.

Voyez worked for Palmer in 1769 and turned up again in 1773, selling black intaglio seals in imitation of Wedgwood's. Although these were dismissed by Josiah as 'sad trash', several of the Birmingham jewellers were happy to buy them cheaply for mounting in silver. Worse was to come a year later, when Josiah obtained proof that Voyez was forging the Wedgwood & Bentley mark on his seals. Josiah drafted an advertisement entitled 'An Imposition Detected', warning dealers of the fraud, but in February 1776, when he contemplated more strenuous action, he was warned by his lawyer that the outcome of litigation was uncertain, even with a London jury. With a country jury there was 'no chance of punishing the Invader as they would not understand the nature, or consequence of his offence'. Next month he told Bentley that he had received 'an impudent penetential letter' from Voyez, admitting his offence, but added: 'I have not given any answer & nor do I intend it, as I neither like the letter, nor the writer.'[7] Four years later, Josiah was happy to report that Voyez had 'done our country the favour of turning his back upon it'.

This experience was no encouragement to Josiah to employ professional modellers. It was, however, his invariable policy to train craftsmen to his own ways and on 20 September 1769, just eight months after Voyez had been sentenced for theft, Josiah told Bentley:

I hired an ingenious Boy last night for Etruria as a Modeler. He had modeled at nights in his way for three years past, has never had the least instructions, which circumstance considered he does things amazingly & will be a valuable acquisition. I have hired him for five years. . . . Palmer, & several others would fain have hired the Boy but he chose to come to me.[8]

The boy was William Hackwood and he chose to stay with Wedgwood for sixty-three years.

During the next five years Hackwood made himself indispensable, restoring plaster busts and remodelling figures obtained from London and repairing gems. Josiah wrote that he was 'of the greatest value & consequence in finishing fine small work' and that he could do with 'half a dozen more Hackwoods'.[9] It was probably inevitable that the young modeller, not yet twenty, should have acquired a high opinion of himself. In 1777 Josiah complained that he was 'growing very extravagant in his prices', an indication that he was being paid by the piece instead of a weekly wage, and a further problem arose when it was discovered that he was signing the portrait medallions he modelled for Wedgwood. Josiah preferred, and it appears that Bentley agreed with him, that no name but their own Wedgwood & Bentley trademark should appear on their ornamental wares, but they did not wish to offend Hackwood by denying him the right to sign his work. Apparently they came to an agreement that permitted him to put his signature to original work but not to pieces remodelled from other artists' originals.[10]

Little of Hackwood's work was essentially his own. He was employed primarily in 'mending' (amending and repairing) or remodelling the work of others and for this reason his style is not easily identified. Two portraits of outstanding quality show his mastery of the difficult art of portrait modelling in relief. The first, a faithful likeness of Josiah's brother-in-law William Willet, was modelled in 1776. Of the second, a portrait of Edward Bourne, an old bricklayer at Etruria, Josiah wrote: 'Old Bourne's is the man himself with every wrinkle crink & cranny in the whole visage.'[11] It was Hackwood who was given the task of modelling the medallion for the campaign for the abolition of the slave trade and he worked on the relief ornament for many of Wedgwood's most impressive vases and tablets.

Hackwood's modelling lacked the sophistication of a professional sculptor's, but his talent was exceptional and his output, during his long years of service, enormous. In 1802, when he had already served the Wedgwoods for more than thirty years and his reputation was well known throughout the Potteries, it was rumoured that he was being courted by Josiah Spode II to join his factory at Stoke-on-Trent.[12] Hackwood was not to be tempted. Unquestionably the most important resident modeller ever to be employed by Wedgwood, he remained at Etruria for a further thirty years.

Of the commissioned artists, most of whom lived in London, by far the most gifted and distinguished was the younger John Flaxman. His work for Wedgwood was of the first importance in the development of jasper, bringing to it the technical excellence and originality of a professional sculptor and creative artist of the first rank. Without Flaxman, Wedgwood's jasper would have lacked much of its most sensitive and stylish neoclassical ornament.

Born in 1755 in York, John Flaxman junior was the second son of a modeller and maker of plaster casts who, early the following year, moved to London and set up his studio at New Street, Covent Garden. The family was poor and the young Flaxman was a sickly child, suffering from congenital curvature of the spine. 'So unhappily formed by nature',[13] he was none the less cheerful and intelligent and spent much of his time in his father's shop, where he showed a precocious talent for drawing and modelling. At the age of eleven he won a premium from the Society of Arts and three years later was enrolled as one of the first students of the newly founded Royal Academy Schools. Among his fellow artists there was James Tassie, later to be Wedgwood's rival in the gems business. Flaxman exhibited at the Royal Academy for the first time at the age of fifteen and forty years later became its first professor of sculpture.

John Flaxman's name was known to Wedgwood as early as 1771, when he entertained at Etruria Sir George and Lady Strickland, and her father, a Mr Freeman of Schute Lodge. Freeman was, so Josiah informed Bentley, 'a man of Taste as you will be convinced when I tell you that *he admires our works exceedingly* but says our materials are so fine & we execute so well we should to be complete spare no expence in having the finest things abroad model'd for us . . . He is a great admirer of young Flaxman & has advised his Father to send him to Rome which he has promised to do. Mr Freeman says he knows young Flaxman is a Coxcomb, but does not think him a bit the worse for it *or the less likely to be a great Artist.'*[14]

Although this information may have sown important seeds for later cultivation, it does not appear to have been sufficient recommendation for Josiah, who took no further action for more than three years. By then he and Bentley were having trouble with Joachim Smith,[15] the first professional portrait modeller to supply them with wax portrait models, who was reported to have formed an association with the Derby porcelain factory. 'Pray try to obtain another modeller,' Josiah wrote on New Year's Day 1775. Less than two weeks later Bentley replied that he had met Flaxman and Josiah immediately suggested that he model 'a good Tablet for a chimneypiece'.[16] By the middle of April both Flaxmans, father and son, had supplied a quantity of bas-reliefs and other models.

This was the beginning of a business relationship which developed into friendship and lasted for the rest of Josiah's life. At this early stage, the greater part of the models supplied by the Flaxmans were casts from the elder John Flaxman's stock-in-trade. No certain evidence exists of original work by the younger Flaxman for Wedgwood before August 1775 when Josiah wrote to ask Bentley to urge him to finish portraits of Joseph Banks and the Swedish naturalist Dr Daniel Solander. Flaxman's style developed from a modified baroque to a spare classicism that identifies him, more than any other artist, with the neoclassical period in England. As a modeller, his style is recognisably that of a sculptor. His portraits and other bas-reliefs, modelled in a hard greyish-white wax composition on to grounds of glass or slate, showed marked variations in the depth of the relief, the darker ground being used to give the impression of shading. Although this effect might be considered desirable in the finished jasper medallion, it was, as Josiah complained,[17] almost impossible to make satisfactory casts from reliefs that were so thinly modelled. Flaxman amended his technique to suit reproduction and nearly fifty portrait medallions of the 'Illustrious Moderns' series are documented as his work or attributed to his hand on grounds of style or long tradition.[18] He continued to model portraits for Wedgwood at least until 1788, and probably as late as 1796.

Flaxman's work on bas-reliefs for the decoration of vases and tablets was no less important. His model of 'A Victorious Citharist', a subject copied with only slight alteration from an engraving of a vase from the Hamilton collection,[19] was used for one of Wedgwood's finest tablets. Sir William Hamilton, to whom Josiah presented one of the first to be made, at once identified the 'Delightful Bas-relief' as illustrating 'the Apotheose of Homer, or some celebrated Poet',[20] helpfully providing Josiah with a more popular title, and a companion piece, *The Apotheosis of Virgil*, was later commissioned from Flaxman. Both subjects were adapted for vases and the Minutes of the General Meeting of the Trustees of the British Museum briefly record Josiah Wedgwood's presentation of a vase 'of his own manufacture', an 18-inch blue-and-white jasper vase ornamented with Flaxman's *Apotheosis of Homer* reliefs, in May 1787. Josiah described it in a letter to Sir William Hamilton as 'the finest & most perfect I have ever made'.[21]

On 16 June 1787 Josiah wrote to Sir William that Flaxman was preparing to go to Italy for two years.[22] This is the first hint of Wedgwood's intention to set up a modelling studio in Rome to supply him with casts and copies of antique bas-reliefs for reproduction in jasper. These would be, in a sense, 'originals', which would not be available, through the London makers of plaster casts, to other manufacturers who sought to imitate his ornaments. Henry Webber, a sculptor and modeller recommended to Wedgwood by Sir Joshua Reynolds and Sir William Chambers in 1782, who had become head of the ornamental department at Etruria, was also to go to Rome to take charge of the new studio. He would journey by way of Switzerland and Paris with Josiah's eldest son John, who would thus enjoy a miniature Grand Tour and gain useful experience of travel abroad and of working with artists employed by Wedgwood. Flaxman, who had promised, as Josiah told Hamilton, 'to employ for me all the time he can spare in Rome', was also to superintend the work of a third modeller, John de Vaere, hired especially to travel with him and to work full time for Wedgwood in Rome.

These three modellers formed the nucleus of Wedgwood's studio in Rome. There they employed at various times seven Italian modellers, notably Camillo Pacetti, 'a proud imperious fellow'[23] but an excellent artist, Giuseppe Angelini and Angelo Dalmazzoni, who also assisted Webber with administration and took charge of the studio when the latter returned to England in 1789.

Flaxman found little time to spend on Wedgwood's behalf and, reproved by Josiah for the infrequency of his letters, gave as his excuse 'the Laberinth of fine things by which I am surrounded'. He added: 'My Good Sir, my situation is somewhat similar to that of Brutus who declared he did not kill Caesar because he loved him less, but because he loved Rome more.'[24] There is evidence of only two pieces of work completed by him for Wedgwood during this period, a large bas-relief in wax of *The Birth of Bacchus* and a small portrait of King Victor Amadeus III modelled at the request of John Wedgwood.[25]

Webber seems to have been even less productive than Flaxman on Wedgwood's behalf although he was paid the high salary of £250 per annum and all expenses expressly 'for the purpose of making Models, Drawings and other improvements in the Arts of Modelling and designing for the benefit and advantage of the said Josiah Wedgwood'.[26] No evidence has been found of any work he did in Rome and it is plain that he delegated much of it to Dalmazzoni as well as a good part of the active management of the studio.[27] This was, no doubt, a practical arrangement which reflected Webber's ignorance of the country and its language, and Dalmazzoni's knowledge of local artists and their work, but it may have owed as much to Webber's responsibility for the young John Wedgwood until his return home in 1789.

The Italian modellers and John de Vaere were more industrious and produced a good number of fine and large bas-relief models in wax, several of which have survived.[28] The addition of these to Wedgwood's list of tablets and plaques again put him far ahead of his few competitors.

Some of these bas-reliefs and many of those reproduced earlier from moulds supplied by the London plaster cast-makers, were in part 'repaired' or even invented by the modellers. Few of the carvings which they used as sources were in anything approaching original condition, and the replacement of missing heads, limbs, figures or groups was at the discretion of the modellers or 'repairers'. Some of the source material was deliberately 'improved' in the model: Pacetti's series of groups, the 'whole life of Achilles', for example, is a beautifully classicised version of some rather dumpy late Roman carving. Such models cannot accurately be described as 'copies' from the antique: some are more classical in composition and technique than their sources; in others the adaptation is so clearly neoclassical as to seem entirely eighteenth-century in execution and classical only in theme.

The preservation of classical themes was important, for the foundation of the fashion for neoclassical art – indeed, one of the essential elements of the style itself – was an education that made allusions to classical history and mythology instantly recognisable to all but the illiterate. During the last ten years of Josiah's life, however, he again followed fashion to the extent of commissioning work in the Romantic style, much of it showing a marked sentimentality. In the latter part of the eighteenth century there was a reaction against what was seen as the distant austerity of classical design in favour of more emotional and modern domestic subjects. Among Wedgwood's contributions to this fashion were subjects from Goethe's best-selling romance, *The Sorrows of the Young Werther*, published in 1774, and Laurence Sterne's *Sentimental Journey* of 1768. These bas-reliefs, all modelled by Hackwood from cut paper designs by Charles Fox's friend, Lady Templetown, first appeared about 1785. Altogether fourteen subjects were taken from Lady Templetown's designs, and at least three more were provided by Frances Crewe's daughter, Emma. Lady Diana Beauclerk, another amateur but more accomplished artist and also a friend of Fox's, supplied drawings of attractively vigorous and unsentimental groups of 'bacchanalian boys' and they, too, were translated into jasper bas-relief ornaments. Unlike the models sent from Rome, these were original designs and of a size suitable for cameos and small decorative pieces which could be made by other manufacturers. Their popularity made them immediately vulnerable to imitators.

Almost everything that Wedgwood made was copied or imitated by competitors in England or elsewhere in Europe during his lifetime, and much of it continued to be imitated after his death. A small number of pieces, each unique, escaped. This was the group of plaques painted by George Stubbs between 1778 and 1795. They were ignored by other manufacturers for good reasons: they were not fashionable, or even

saleable, and they posed almost insurmountable problems in production. They were, in fact, a commercial disappointment for both the
artist and the manufacturer, a flop which no one cared to imitate. And
yet, more than 200 years later, they are valued more highly than any
English pottery of the period. The explanation for this reversal lies in
the reappraisal of the work of George Stubbs rather than in any mature
understanding of Wedgwood's achievement in making the plaques.

Josiah's earliest contact with Stubbs occurred in 1775, when the
artist asked if Wedgwood could produce plain white earthenware plaques or tablets measuring about 4 by 3 feet, or 3 by 2 feet, suitable for
use as supports for his paintings. Josiah was already complaining that
tea-trays half the size that Stubbs wanted were 'very hazardous things
to make & I cannot promise success',[29] but this was the sort of technical
challenge that he found irresistible.

In November 1777 he told Bentley, 'He shall be gratified, but large
tablets are not the work of a day.'[30] For Stubbs, who had already waited
nearly two years for a favourable reply, this was not reassuring, but
Wedgwood, after his hectic and frustrating pursuit of the fugitive jasper
body, was at last able to give some attention to Stubbs's request. At
the end of the month he fired two plaques but they measured only
about 22 by 17 inches and both cracked or warped in the oven. Two
more were fired in December. One was successful and may have been
the oval, 17 by 23½ inches, used by Stubbs for his painting *Lion Attacking a Stag*, which is the only example known to be signed and dated
1778.

Eleven months later, Wedgwood had still not solved the problem
of firing large, flat, earthenware slabs without cracks or distortion. His
experiments and trials had to take second place to general production
and he was unable to give them either the time or the oven space that
was needed for success. He wrote to Bentley in some exasperation:

> When you see Mr Stubs pray tell him how hard I have been labouring
> to furnish him with the means of adding immortality to his excellent
> pencil. I mean only to arrogate to myself the honor of being his *canvas
> maker*. But alass this honor is at present denied to my endeavours,
> though you may be sure that I will succeed . . . [31]

At last, at the end of May 1779, fully three-and-a-half years after
Stubbs's first inquiry, Josiah was confident that he could make the
tablets 'with certainty and success', but only in sizes up to 30 inches,
'perhaps ultimately up to 36 inches by 24, but that is at present in the
offing'. The costs had been formidable: special kilns had been built and

later altered, and losses in firing had been heavy. It had been found necessary to develop a new earthenware composition with a form of thin glaze to offset its porosity and provide a suitable surface for paint; and the proper firing temperature had been found only after prolonged trials. Josiah hoped that Stubbs would pay something towards these expenses but he was prepared to accept paintings instead of cash for 'the next £100 or £150' of tablets.[32] A compromise was reached and Stubbs paid in work for most of the tablets delivered to him. He continued to receive them at least as late as 1786, and his last paintings, *Haycarting* and *Reapers** were completed in 1795. The tablet for *Reapers*, measuring 30½ by 41½ inches, was the largest ever delivered to Stubbs and more than justified Josiah's earlier expectations.

In 1779, when Wedgwood was at last satisfied that he could produce these large tablets, he wrote confidently to Bentley: 'If Mr Stubbs succeeds he will be followed by others to which he does not seem to have the least objection, but rather wishes for it; and if the oil painters too should use them they may become a considerable object.'[33]

Josiah's hopes were not realised. Stubbs did succeed but his success was technical. Although paintings on Continental and English porcelain plaques, particularly the reproduction in miniature of popular paintings in the great collections, became fashionable in the nineteenth century, and Josiah's descendants both commissioned and employed artists to paint Queen's ware plaques on a smaller scale, there were no followers of Stubbs in this experiment.

Whatever Josiah had hoped to gain from this speculative and costly endeavour, it was certainly not, as has been asserted,[34] either financial profit or prestige from his association with Stubbs's name. It was clear, almost at the outset, that Stubbs would not be able to pay for development costs and even payment for the tablets delivered was made in paintings. By 1775, when Stubbs first approached Wedgwood & Bentley, their name was already established in Court circles throughout Europe, whereas Stubbs, a 'horse-painter', had little social or artistic standing. Nor is it true that Stubbs profited from the association, either in reputation or through sales of his 'enamel' paintings on Wedgwood supports. When they were exhibited at the Royal Academy in 1791–2, they were received with almost unanimous disapproval, and twenty-six out of a total of thirty-seven 'enamels' on ceramic or metal supports remained unsold at Stubbs's death, when they were bought for derisory prices. The *Gentleman's Magazine* of 1791 was not alone in hoping that Stubbs, 'mounted upon his proper Pegasus', would never again

---

*Both now in the Lady Lever Art Gallery, Port Sunlight.

'experience the disgrace . . . attendant on mounting his *hobby horse* of enamel portrait painting'.

The portraits were certainly the least successful of the Stubbs paintings. The most effective are the two equestrian portraits of himself and of Warren Hastings,* both splendidly mounted, and these are as much paintings of horses as of men. The pictures of animals, which include one of a panther, are as vigorous and expressive as one might hope from the hand of Britain's greatest animal painter, and the country scenes with figures of labourers have a realism that lifts them above painting in this genre by most of his contemporaries. 'Nobody suspects Mr Stubs of painting anything but horses & lions, or dogs & tigers,' Josiah told Bentley in September 1780, 'and I can scarcely make anybody believe that he ever attempted a human figure.' Stubbs himself, according to Josiah, regretted his reputation as a 'horse painter' and wished 'to be considered as an history, a portrait painter', but there was some doubt how far he could succeed in bringing about the change at the age of fifty-six.[35]

Josiah had already suggested to Stubbs that part of what he owed for earthenware 'canvasses' should be paid in 'enamel' portraits of himself and Sally and perhaps of Bentley and his wife. He had precise ideas also for two family groups of the children:

> Sukey playing upon her harpsicord, with Kitty singing to her which she often does, & Sally & Mary Ann upon the carpet in some employment suitable to their ages. This to be one picture. The pendant to be Jack standing at a table making fixable air with the glass apparatus &c.; & his two brothers accompanying him. Tom jumping up & clapping his hands in joy & surprise at seeing a stream of bubbles rise up just as Jack has put a little chalk to the acid. Joss with the chemical dictionary before him in a thoughtful mood, which actions will be exactly descriptive of their respective natures.[36]

He had at first thought of commissioning these from Joseph Wright of Derby, a neighbour of Darwin's who had painted his portrait in 1770, but decided to add them to the list for Stubbs and instead 'mention'd a fire piece to Mr Wright', whom he invited, evidently by mistake, to Etruria in June 1779 when he was already expecting Stubbs. 'But what', he asked Bentley, 'shall I do about having Mr. S and Mr. W here at the

---

*The self-portrait, for many years erroneously described as a portrait of Josiah Wedgwood, is in the Lady Lever Art Gallery, Port Sunlight; the portrait of Warren Hastings, now in a private collection, was bought for £2.5s. at the sale of Stubbs's effects in 1807.

same time, will they draw kindly together think you.'[37] The problem did not arise. Wright, who had been ill with a cold and nervous fever and had not touched a pencil since April, did not reply to the invitation for seven weeks and Josiah had no further contact with him until 1782.

Stubbs visited Etruria in July 1780 and appears to have stayed for several months. Bentley was there to see Stubbs making his first sketches for his painting of the Wedgwood family but the work was delayed by difficulty in obtaining a suitable wood panel, which Stubbs preferred to canvas. Josiah, meanwhile, suggested that he might be employed in painting 'some large jarrs . . . the present idea is to cover them over with painting, with ground – figures, trees & sky without any borders or divisions, in short to consider the whole surface as one piece of canvas'.[38] Nine of these 'Cream Culler large jarrs', each more than 21 inches high with its domed cover, were successfully fired in August 1780 and at least one has survived,* elegantly innocent of decoration, but no evidence has been found to prove that Stubbs ever painted any of them.

Stubbs was, nevertheless, kept well occupied. He had been briefly a drawing master at Heath Academy, teaching perspective, which he believed to be 'just as rational a method of drawing as learning the letters first in acquiring the art of reading', and Josiah lost no time in enrolling him to instruct his boys.[39] Later in the month he took Stubbs to Trentham, where they spent the morning viewing 'the finest scenes, Mr Stubs says, he ever saw'. Lord Gower, Josiah told Bentley, 'was polite enough to ride with us thro' the park & grounds & shew us their beauties, but there was too much variety to fix a single sketch upon paper though that was Mr Stub's original design'. The rest of the day was agreeably spent in 'feasting the body & mind in his Lordships mansion', dining with Gower and his family and a number of guests. 'We had a great deal of conversation, & chat upon various subjects,' Josiah reported, 'but not a single word upon politics. They are not talk'd at Trentham this season.'[40]

Stubbs was already working, at his suggestion, on a bas-relief model of The Lion and the Horse from his own engraving. Josiah was not pleased with the choice of subject but, finding Stubbs deaf to his arguments, allowed him to proceed with it. He was evidently surprised to observe that Stubbs was almost as much master of his modelling tools as of his pencil and by 21 August the new tablet of The Frightened Horse was finished.[41] Josiah's earlier objections to the subject were overcome by

*Now in the Birmingham Museum of Art, Alabama.

the excellence of the finished model and he made immediate arrangements to have it reproduced and a copy sent to Bentley.[42]

The family portrait proved to be the subject of some dissatisfaction and disagreement. Having persuaded Josiah against his original design of two groups of the children, Stubbs had produced his own sketches of the whole family in the park at Etruria: Josiah and Sally seated beneath a great oak, while Sukey and the boys are mounted on well-groomed ponies and the youngest children play nearby. In August, when the picture was in an early stage of development, Josiah was pleased with it: 'Our little lasses & their coach are just put into colours, & the characters of the children are hit off very well,' he told Bentley. 'I have given him [Stubbs] one sitting, & this is all we have done with the picture. The stable is preparing, & the horses are to *sit* this week.'[43] By the middle of September he was already expressing doubts:

> I think the likenesses promise to be strong but I do not know what to say upon this subject because the likeness in those that approach towards being finished grows weaker as the painting increases. Mr Stubs says the likeness will come & go off many times before finishing.[44]

Stubbs worked on the picture for a further five weeks, at the end of which he declared it close to completion. Josiah was less sure and far less satisfied. 'I think', he told Bentley, 'he is not quite so near a finish as he seems to apprehend':

> He thinks he has finish'd six of the children, the horses & little carriage. The children are most of them strong, but not very delicate likenesses – Some parts are either a little caricatur'd, or my own eyes & those of many of my friends are much deciev'd . . . but I will not say any more upon this subject at present, & *this is only to your self*, as it would be hardly fair 'till the picture is turned out of his hands as completely finished, & besides he has promised me to compare the originals & copies carefully together & give any last touches which may be found wanting as soon as he has brought my wife, my daughter Susan & my self up with the rest. I think he has not been so happy in hitting off the likenesses of the two former as he has in the others.[45]

Some hint of his exasperation appears in his final comments: 'Time & patience in large doses, are absolutely necessary in these cases, & methinks I would not be a portrait painter upon any condition whatsoever. We are all heartily tired of the business, & I think the painter has more reason than any of us to be so.'

A week later, when Stubbs believed that he was finally finished with the picture, Josiah was still demanding changes, although he admitted that, having 'plagued him a good deal in these finishing strokes', his final demands on Stubbs, who had borne his 'impertinence' with commendable patience, could be made only 'by degrees'.[46] As late as 12 November, Stubbs was still in Staffordshire, still making changes to the Wedgwood family group. Josiah was not yet satisfied with the portraits: 'My wife I think very deficient – Mary Ann more so, & Susan is not hit off well at all. I say nothing of my self, but upon the whole agree with Mr Edgeworth that there is much to praise, & a little to blame.' He added: 'As soon as I *think* the picture is finish'd I will hie away to kiss your hand at Turnham Green.'[47] It was not to be. Two weeks later Bentley was dead.

Stubbs's 'enamel' portraits of Josiah and Sally, painted on oval earthenware tablets, were finished some weeks earlier, and he painted a more conventional study in oil colours, also on panel, of Sally's father, Richard, which Josiah judged 'a very strong likeness'. The superiority of this portrait over those of Josiah and Sally underlines the restrictions imposed by the use of the limited ceramic palette. By the time Stubbs finished his last paintings on ceramic supports, between 1791 and 1795, he had overcome some of these limitations but he never found it possible to obtain the same freedom of effect that he gave to his canvases and there is a noticeable lack of depth in all his painting on ceramic grounds.

While he was at Etruria Stubbs made one more significant contribution to Wedgwood's list of tablets. This was a bas-relief adapted from his painting in enamel on copper, *The Fall of the Phaeton*. At the end of October 1780, Josiah wrote that Stubbs wished to 'employ some of his evenings in modelling a companion to his frighten'd horse' and had chosen 'one of his Phaetons for that purpose'. He required an engraving of the subject to be sent to him from London. Josiah objected to this subject on the grounds that the frightened horse was 'a piece of natural history' while Phaeton was 'a piece of un-natural fiction'. Stubbs was not impressed by this argument and persisted with his choice, working 'hard at it every night almost 'till bedtime'.[48] The finished tablet in jasper is not in shape or design a companion piece for *The Frightened Horse*, and is quite unlike any other produced by Wedgwood in the eighteenth century, but the modelling shows a strength and vigour that amply justify Stubbs's steadfast defence of his subject.

Wedgwood's regular reports to Bentley reveal much about his relationships with commissioned artists. They were necessarily different from the more restrictive and authoritarian attitude that he adopted towards those he employed but, in all his dealings with artists and craftsmen, he remained a perfectionist and he was never able entirely to curb his propensity for interference when he believed that improvement was possible.

This tendency was particularly evident in his correspondence with Joseph Wright. It is possible that Bentley had met Wright in Liverpool, where both knew Dr Matthew Turner, who had first introduced Bentley to Wedgwood; and it is more than likely that Wedgwood made Wright's acquaintance as a mutual friend of Erasmus Darwin's in 1770. It is certain that Wedgwood met Sir William Meredith at Wright's studio in Derby in March 1773, when Josiah went there with his father-in-law in an ineffectual attempt to resolve the latter's dispute with Meredith.[49] This first meeting with the artist was not forgotten by Wedgwood and he wrote to Bentley some five years later that he would like to have an example of Wright's work. It appears that Bentley was regularly in touch with Wright in London and Josiah asked him to speak to the artist about a commission. He knew what he wanted: 'Mr Wright once began a piece in which our Vases might be introduced with the greatest propriety. I mean the hand writing upon the Wall in the Palace of Nebucadnazer.' A suggested alternative was 'Debutade's daughter',[50] Josiah's first name for the painting later called the Corinthian Maid.* Four months later he met Wright himself at Derby and 'had some little talk upon the subject of a picture'. Josiah told Bentley: 'He does not meet with the encouragement his superior talents ought to command, & would starve as a painter if the Empress of Russia had not more taste & sense than the English, to buy these pictures now, which we may wish the next century to purchase again at treble the price she now pays for them.'[51] This was far from accurate. Wright's English commissions were more than adequate and, by 1778, Catherine had bought only one picture from him. His deliberate exaggeration was no doubt intended to impress the manufacturer of the 'Husk' and 'Frog' services.

Wedgwood's decision to employ Stubbs to paint the family group, a composition much changed from the pair of children's groups that he had intended to offer to Wright, postponed the development of their association. It was renewed in February 1782 when Wright told Wedgwood that he had been working on a painting of the 'maid of Corinth', which, he wrote, 'will certainly, make the best Candlelight picture I have painted . . . I take the liberty of mentioning it to you, as

---

*Pliny relates the legend of the daughter of Dibutade, a Corinthian potter, who traced the outline of her lover's shadow so accurately upon the wall of her room that her father was able to take a clay impression of the figure outlined and bake it in his pottery kiln.

you sometime ago had thought of having that Subject painted. If you still continue in that intention I should wish to have your thoughts upon it.' His own intention was to keep the composition as uncluttered as possible, with 'some elegant vases upon a shelf, others on the ground' to 'mark her father's profession . . . but I think I would not introduce a Furnace'.[52]

Wedgwood had evidently expressed his wish to have some of his own vases displayed in the picture and was probably also the author of the suggestion that a potter's oven or 'furnace' should be shown. Wright consulted his friend, the poet William Hayley, whose 'lines upon the Corinthian Maid' had inspired his interest in the subject, about every detail of the composition. He sought advice also from Darwin, who contrarily advised against the inclusion of any vases. At the end of February 1782 Wright sent Hayley a 'rude sketch' to illustrate his intentions and, at his request, this was passed on to Wedgwood, with whom he raised his own questions as well as the opinions he had received from others. So much comment, suggestion and criticism was, as Wright admitted, confusing: 'When I ask other people's opinion, 'tis to profit by them,' he wrote to Hayley early in 1783, 'if they happen to coincide with my own I am happy, if otherwise, they stagger my opinion, & leave me undetermined whether I shall go on with the picture.'[53] By April, however, he had made sufficient progress to encourage him to ride over to Etruria to settle with Wedgwood such details as the 'forms of the long irons which stand about the Oven' (which he had decided, after all, to show in an adjoining room) and the shapes of the vases to be supplied to him for copying.[54]

Meanwhile, in March, Wedgwood's eldest daughter, Susannah (Sukey) had paid a visit to Wright's studio. 'The servant shew'd us two rooms of excellent pictures which ought to have satisfied anybody,' she told her father, 'but we were not content having heard a good deal of two pictures, The Story of Hero and Leander, which he is now painting upon. How to contrive to see them we did not know.' Lacking none of her father's determination, she was not slow to find a way to persuade Wright to invite her into his 'painting room', where she was enchanted by the pair of pictures, of which she gives a detailed description,* one praised as 'a beautiful piece' and the other 'quite sublime'.[55] Josiah was apparently not tempted by Sukey's enthusiastic report of these pictures, the existence of which Wright was anxious to keep secret until he was ready to exhibit them, or by her suggestion that he should see them

---

*Since neither picture has been traced, Susannah Wedgwood's account is all that survives of them.

for himself in Derby, but he was interested in acquiring more work from Wright, especially a suitable companion painting to the *Corinthian Maid*. The subject agreed upon was *Penelope Unravelling her Web*. By his candid painting of lightly draped or nude figures, Wright was to encounter problems with both paintings and they became the subject of detailed and sometimes unintentionally comic correspondence between Wright, Hayley and Wedgwood.

In December 1783 Wright sent Wedgwood a sketch of his proposed composition for *Penelope*. Josiah's comments have not survived but they may be deduced from Wright's reply written on the last day of the year. 'I am glad you like the disposition of the Groups & composition of the light & shadow,' he wrote. 'As it was customary among the Antients to make their Statues naked I had designed Ulisses to be so, but being seen nearly in profile, the private parts become too conspicuous, for the chamber of the *chaste* Penelope, I therefore made him rest on his bow, & put the Quiver in the other hand so as to cross the body & conceal that part which might give offence to our delicate Ladies.' This chaste expedient was derisively rejected by Hayley: 'I am afraid', he told Wright, 'the Quiver crossing the bottom of the Hero's Belly, may to some saucy imaginations produce a ludicrous effect, & make some prophane Wag exclaim "Happy is the man that hath his Quiver full".' Hayley recommended 'a light drapery' but Wright 'cou'd scarce do little enough it so injured the outline of the figure *which alone is seen*' he anxiously assured Wedgwood, 'when a figure is in dark Shadow'. Josiah had recommended 'a firmer action', a more active stance for the figure, but Wright explained that the proportions in his sketch were inaccurate and would be corrected in the painting.[56]

Four months later Josiah visited him at his house in Derby to see the two paintings. On his return to Etruria he wrote to repeat doubts which he had already expressed to Darwin

> I could not speak to you when I was with the ladies at your house about the particular part of the drapery of the Corinthian Maid which I liked the least; but finding afterwards that some of the ladies had seen that part of the drapery in the same light with myself, and not being able to wait upon you again I begged Dr Darwin to mention it to you.
>
> My objections were the divisions of the posteriors appearing too plain thro' the drapery, & its sticking so close, the truly Grecian, as you justly observe gave that part a heavy hanging like (if I may use a new term) appearance, as if it wanted a little shove up, which [he added hastily, aware of the possibility of misunderstanding] I only

mention in illustration of the term hanging as used above.

He was plainly embarrassed by this criticism and anxious not to offend the artist by ignorant or apparently prudish complaints:

> I do not say that I am *satisfied* with the lover, but that I think it is excellent, I had almost said inimitable, and I should quake for every touch of your pencil there. It is unfortunate in my opinion that the maid shows so much of her back, but I give it as my *opinion* only . . . Make her to please yourself.[57]

Wright, in reply, thanked Wedgwood for his 'friendly & polite letter', promising to 'do everything in my power to make the picture agreeable to you in every respect'. He agreed to 'cast a fuller drapery upon the Corinthian Maid, which will conceal the Nudity' but could not alter her position.[58]

In April 1785 Wright showed twenty-five pictures in a one-man exhibition at Robins's Rooms in Covent Garden. Fourteen were already reserved for patrons, three of them – the *Corinthian Maid, Penelope Unravelling her Web* and *The Lady in Milton's 'Comus'* – for Josiah Wedgwood. Josiah had admired also a self-portrait painted for Wright's friend Jacob More and he persuaded Wright to let him have it at the huge price of £300. In seven years he had become one of Wright's most enthusiastic and valuable champions but it is none the less surprising to find him prepared to pay for a Wright self-portrait double the figure charged by Sir Joshua Reynolds in 1782 for a full-length portrait. In spite of Wedgwood's criticisms and his requests for changes to the artist's original design, he and Joseph Wright remained on the most amicable terms, and Wright acknowledged his generous patronage by presenting him with a painting of Dovedale,* in Derbyshire, which he inscribed on the reverse: 'The gift of Joseph Wright of Derby to his friend Jos. Wedgwood Esq., the patron and encourager of living artists, 1787'. Josiah responded in 1789 with a 'table service green shell edge, for his own use, gratis, about 10 guineas value to be looked out very good'.[59]

Josiah's criticisms of the *Corinthian Maid* and *Penelope* have often been quoted to support assertions that he was *bourgeois* and prudish in his attitudes to art, and especially towards nudity in sculpture. There was nothing prudish about his humour, and his letters to Bentley often show a frank bawdiness which was both typical of his period and evidently natural to him. His attitude to nudity was conditioned by his

*Now in the Wedgwood Museum, Barlaston.

desire to avoid giving offence to his family and his customers and this was a concern that Bentley shared. It was Bentley who thought the bas-relief subjects of Jupiter and Leda, and Jupiter and Danaë, 'too warm' for their 'climate'.[60] The censorious middle-class attitude to nudity is well illustrated by Jonathan Spilsbury, an engraver and modeller employed by Wedgwood & Bentley in 1770-1, who complained of being asked to model nude figures. 'I cannot', he wrote to Bentley, 'be recon-cil'd to those Figures which are *quite* naked. Whether there be any immodesty in making such Representations I can't say, but to *Me* such an Employment wou'd be at least exceedingly disagreeable.'[61]

Josiah's acceptance or rejection of nudity was governed by his knowledge of his market. If the price of an object was such that it was likely to be bought only by collectors and the aristocracy, all accustomed to classical nudity, it could be confidently assumed that the addition of tactfully arranged drapery was superfluous. It was the prosperous middle class, always less tolerant than any other stratum of society, who might be offended. The point is argued in Josiah's letter to Flaxman in Rome in 1790:

> . . . the last model, the discovery of Achilles, I admire very much, for the spirited action and beauty of the figures . . . but there is one objection which I am afraid is insurmountable, & that is the nakedness of the figures. To clothe them would not only be a great increase of labour, but would require the hand of an experienced master in the art, & besides, the piece would not then be a copy from the antique. I know the nudities might be covered with leaves, but that is not enough.
>
> The same objection applies to the [model of] the Judgement of Paris & other pieces; & indeed the nude is so general in the works of the ancients, that it will be very difficult to avoid the introduction of naked figures. On the other hand it is absolutely necessary to do so, or to keep the pieces for our own use, for none either male or female, of the present generation will take them as furniture if the figures are naked.[62]

Although Flaxman's reply has been lost, it was surely he who per-suaded Wedgwood that he was wrong: that nudity, in copies of classical sculpture, was entirely respectable, where modern nakedness might not be. Certainly, many of the finest reproductions modelled in the studio at Rome, and a number of those taken from earlier casts supplied from London, include male and female nudes in the compositions. It is clear, too, that usage played a part in Josiah's decisions. Some of his earliest black basaltes figures – those of Morpheus, Ganymede and

Bacchus, for example – are nudes, but these were obviously intended, in the way that small Renaissance bronzes were displayed, as ornaments for libraries, generally the preserve of gentlemen, not for drawing-rooms, where their ladies spent much of their time. Although minimal fig leaves were added to some of the subjects sent from Rome, it was not until the latter part of the nineteenth century that Josiah's descendants were obliged by a largely middle-class Victorian market to drape the figures in these compositions to hide their nakedness.

No such difficulties arose in Josiah's relationship with Sir Joshua Reynolds. This was essentially one of a prosperous patron commissioning the most eminent portrait painter of his day. Both were already famous: Reynolds had been President of the Royal Academy since its foundation in 1768 and knighted in the following year: Wedgwood's reputation as Britain's greatest potter had spread throughout Europe. There is no record of their first meeting and they appear to have had few friends in common before 1782, when Reynolds painted his portrait of Josiah. It is possible that they were first introduced by Sir William Hamilton or Sir William Chambers, whose portraits had been painted by Reynolds, or even by Flaxman, but a more likely intermediary is Sir Watkin Williams Wynn, an exceptionally munificent patron to both the painter and the potter.

Reynolds seldom made preliminary drawings or sketches of his subjects, preferring to paint directly on to the canvas during sittings, at least three of about an hour and a half each, which might start as early as eight o'clock in the morning but more often took place between the hours of eleven and four. Sitters, even junior members of the royal family, were generally expected to come to Reynolds's painting room in his house in Leicester Fields (now Leicester Square), although occasionally he would paint portraits during visits to the owners of great country houses such as Blenheim Palace or Saltram. The portraits of Josiah and Sally, painted in 1782, are simple bust portraits without hands, the heads of which might have been painted by Reynolds in a single sitting, leaving the rest to be completed by pupils. The fugitive quality of his colours and his use of personal concoctions of varnish, wax, eggs and, most disastrously, bituminous pigments, gave an impermanency to his work which was captured in an epigram composed by Sir Walter Blackett, who sat to Reynolds in 1766–9:

> Painting of old was surely well designed
> To keep the features of the dead in mind,
> But this great rascal has reversed the plan,
> And made his pictures die before the man.[63]

The portraits of Josiah and Sarah Wedgwood have lasted far better than Blackett suggests. In the long catalogue of Reynolds's work they are relatively insignificant but the heads are lively and painted (except for the omission of Josiah's smallpox scars) without flattery. The pigments have not faded, as they have in so many of Reynolds's portraits, and Josiah's high colour, which may be evidence of his fondness for red meat, porter and fortified wines, contrasts with his wife's fashionably more delicate complexion. Their dress is unostentatious. Sarah's dress is simple and she wears no jewellery or ornament. Josiah owned a fine coat of scarlet cloth with gold lace, which he wore on the grandest occasions, but for his portrait he chose a plum-coloured coat of the plain style he favoured and a powdered toupée, parted in the centre and curled over the ears, which replaced the long, light brown wig of his younger days. His is the portrait of a confident and successful man, one whose convictions would be defended with strength. The features, except for the eyes, are undistinguished, neither fine nor especially coarse, but blurred by age. Only the eyes, a cool and faded grey-blue, speak of the years of experience and achievement, the resolution, the humour and the exertion.

CHAPTER TWENTY-TWO

Last Experiments

A key factor in Wedgwood's success had always been his enthusiasm for experiment. As he told his young cousin Ralph, 'Useful' Thomas's eldest son, 'Everything gives way to experiment.'[1]

In 1774, the Staffordshire potters, led by Wedgwood and with considerable help from Lord Gower, successfully contested Richard Champion's application to extend the patent granted to William Cookworthy for the exclusive use of Cornish china clay and china stone. The result of their opposition was to limit Champion's patent to the production of translucent porcelain, and even then only to his own patented specification, leaving other potters free to use the materials for any other purpose. In the following year, Josiah, accompanied by a friendly competitor, John Turner, and Thomas Griffiths, who had obtained a quantity of Cherokee clay for Wedgwood from South Carolina in 1768, made an expedition into Cornwall, searching for clay on behalf of their fellow potters. As a consequence of their findings it was decided not to grant exclusive rights in the clay to any company, which 'would soon degenerate into a pernicious monopoly', but instead to create a 'Public experimental work' under the direction of a joint-stock company composed of 'potters and subscribers to the opposition to Champions porcelain bill, and the journey into Cornwall'. This would be primarily concerned with trials of Cornish materials for the benefit of all the company's members.[2]

On 2 December, after much discussion among the potters, a committee was elected and agreement was reached 'to establish an Experimental Work for the purpose of trying the materials lately brought from Cornwall as well as those which may in the future come from that County or any other place in order to improve our present manufacture, and make an USEFUL WHITE PORCELAIN BODY, with a colorless glaze for the same and a blue paint under the glaze'. The specification is especially significant in two respects: first, that it refers to all materials from any source, and not only to those already obtained from Cornwall; and second, that it applies only to the production of porcelain. The intention was, at first, to use the knowledge gained from experiments with Cornish china clay and stone to improve the quality of Staffordshire creamwares and to create a new porcelain body to compete with the underglaze blue-painted porcelains of Worcester and Liverpool, in particular. Further developments were left for discussion in the future.[3]

The scheme failed because, as Josiah discovered during negotiations for the Irish and French trade treaties, it was never easy to obtain the simplest agreement from any number of Staffordshire potters. On this occasion the project foundered on the matter of the subscription, or deposit, of £25 to be paid by members. Josiah told Bentley at the end of 1775:

> Our Experimental work expir'd in Embrio last night – We could not settle the question whether the Partners in [the] Company should pay seperately, or jointly. . . . I consented to agree to either plan, being determin'd it should not fail on my account. . . . I heartily wish a general improvement to the Manufacture – But it seems it cannot be in this way, & haveing done my duty I am contented, & shall take my own course quietly by myself as well as I can, & may perhaps have it in my power to serve the trade some other way.[4]

His own course included the invention of jasper, on which he was already engaged. His service to the Staffordshire pottery trade in general was most conspicuous in his involvement in the drafting of the French Commercial Treaty (see Chapter 19).

The end of the proposal for an experimental factory put an end also to the last of Josiah's lingering doubts about manufacturing porcelain. To one Matthew Horne of Lambeth, who wrote to him claiming to be able to make porcelain figures 'four or five feet high without supports or props' and offering himself for employment, Josiah replied, 'our experemental work is over, & for my own particular, it does not suit with my business to begin upon Porcelain at present'.[5] After the success of his experiments with jasper and its subsequent development, Josiah was content to leave the production of porcelain to others.

Although he was prematurely aged by continuous overwork, Josiah's passion for experiment remained undiminished for a decade after Bentley's death. It was almost as if the loss of his partner had made Wedgwood the more determined to busy himself with experiments and with adventures in politics and patronage. On the other hand, there seems to have been a tacit acceptance that his most creative work was done; that his last efforts would be towards improving what he had already developed. His extraordinary energy still enabled him simultaneously to conduct his business, to involve himself in political affairs and to engage in a series of experiments which culminated in an invention of undisputed technical importance.

Before 1782, no method existed for measuring accurately the heat of a pottery oven beyond a temperature of about 360° C. When Wedgwood began his career as an independent manufacturer, the only way in which a kiln master could judge the temperature inside his oven was by removing a small plug set in the kiln wall and observing the colour of the fire. In the making of pottery or porcelain, success or failure of the entire concern depended largely on the skill and experience of the kiln master, for his errors of judgement were likely to be more costly than those of any other craftsman. In August 1768 Josiah complained that every vase in one of his kilns had been ruined by such a slight variation in temperature that the Queen's ware fired with them had been unharmed.[6] Such complaints were not rare and the consequent losses could overwhelm a small manufacturer. He wrote in his Commonplace Book: 'In a long course of experiments for the improvement of the manufacture I am engaged in, the greatest difficulties I have met with have arisen from my not being able to ascertain the degrees of heat to which the experiments have been exposed.'[7]

It is not surprising that Wedgwood should have turned his mind to finding a solution to this problem as soon as he could spare time for it. The spur to this new set of experiments was probably his wish to produce larger ornamental jasper pieces, especially vases, which were suffering heavy losses in firing. Over the years he had already recorded the variations in firing of different ceramic bodies and in 1780 he began a series of experiments with a clay that burned to a red colour in firing, withdrawing trial pieces from the oven at two-hourly intervals while the temperature was rising and noting the gradual change of colour.[8] These colour changes suggested the possibility of constructing a thermoscope which matched clay cylinders of a standard composition against a set of cylinders fired at known temperatures, ranging in colour from low-temperature buff to high-temperature red.

This method was primitive and unreliable. Through Priestley, Josiah sought the opinion of Sir Joseph Banks, President of the Royal Society since 1778, whose help he had requested in the past. Banks expressed doubts about the validity of the method of calculation,[9] and it was also feared that kiln masters might have difficulty in matching colours with the necessary accuracy and consistency. Josiah altered the basis of his experiments, calculating instead the rate of shrinkage of clay cylinders during firing, and tests were carried out for him at the Tower Mint to discover the melting points of various precious and base metals.[10]

Josiah's first sketch for a pyrometer, which he preferred always to call a thermometer, consisted of two straight-edged wooden rulers mounted at an angle – ½ inch apart at the top and ⅓ inch apart at the bottom – on a baseboard. One of the rulers was marked with a scale graduated in 'degrees Wedgwood', which ran from 0 to 240.* Small clay cylinders, ⅖ inch high and ½ inch in diameter were prepared. A cylinder was fired and allowed to cool, shrinking as it did so by an amount proportionate to the temperature to which it had been subjected. It was then placed between the rulers and pushed along until it would go no farther, when the temperature at this point could be read off the scale.

This pyrometer soon became widely known, and since it was the first instrument to provide anything like an accurate estimate of temperature it was in great demand for many scientific purposes, apart from potters' ovens. The first pyrometers were made in brass but this was an expensive metal in the eighteenth century and by the autumn of 1783 Wedgwood was experimenting with pyrometers made of stoneware and porcelain. From 1784 an instruction booklet was available. One thousand copies of a French translation were printed in 1785 and 500 copies in German followed next year. In 1786 Wedgwood presented a boxed set of two stoneware gauges (graduated from 0 to 120 and from 120 to 240) and a stock of clay cylinders to George III for his collection of scientific instruments at the King's Observatory, Richmond, Surrey.

A further use for the pyrometer was found in determining the 'heats by which many porcelains of the distant nations and different ages have been fired. For as burnt clay and compositions in which clay is a prevailing ingredient, suffer no diminution in their bulk by being repassed through degrees of heat which they have already undergone, but are diminished by any additional heat . . . if a fragment of them be made to fit into any part of the gage, and then fired along with a thermometer piece, the division at which the fragment begins to diminish will point out the degree of heat which it had before undergone'.[11] By this means Josiah discovered the temperatures at which examples of Roman and Etruscan pottery had been fired as well as acquiring useful information about the porcelains of Worcester, Derby, Chelsea, Bow and Bristol.[12]

A paper entitled *An Attempt to make a Thermometer measuring the*

---

*60° Wedgwood was equivalent to 1100° C.

higher Degrees of Heat from a red Heat up to the strongest that Vessels made of Clay can support, communicated by Josiah Wedgwood to Sir Joseph Banks, was read to the Royal Society on 9 May 1782.[13] Three weeks later, James 'Athenian' Stuart put forward Wedgwood's name for election and he was formally elected Fellow of the Royal Society on 16 January 1783.[14] In March 1876 he was elected Fellow of the Antiquarian Society, and in October of the same year Fellow of the Society for the Encouragement of Arts, Manufactures and Commerce.* Josiah presented further papers to the Royal Society in 1783, 1784 and 1786, the last two concerned with the development of his thermometer.[15]

In this work and in his experiments towards the production of mortarware and laboratory apparatus, quantities of which were supplied freely to Priestley and other experimental scientists, Josiah was assisted, from 1781, by Alexander Chisholm. Formerly assistant to Dr William Lewis, practical chemist to the Society of Arts, Chisholm became Josiah's secretary and general assistant, as well as tutor in chemistry to his children. Later he became chief chemist at the Etruria factory, and there can be no doubt that his practical knowledge of chemistry was of great value to Wedgwood in his later experimental work. Many of the entries in Josiah's Commonplace Books are in his handwriting.

On 5 February 1784 John Flaxman wrote a letter to Josiah which was to have extraordinary and lasting consequences and which, some two years later, set him off on another train of experiments. 'I wish', Flaxman wrote from London, 'you may soon come to town to see William Hamilton's Vase, it is the finest production of Art that has been brought to England and seems to be the very apex of perfection to which you are endeavouring to bring your bisque & jasper; it is of a kind called "Murrina" by Pliny, made of dark glass with white enamel figures. The Vase is about a foot high† & the figures between 5 & 6 inches, engraved in the same manner as a Cameo & of the grandest & most perfect Greek Sculpture.'[16] It is notable that at a time when the composition of the vase was not widely understood and it was a common misapprehension that the figures were of some form of enamel, Flaxman was well informed about its true nature. Josiah was too busy immediately to take advantage of Flaxman's suggestion and the date on which he first saw the vase is uncertain. When he did so, he was sufficiently impressed by it, and by Flaxman's hint that it might be reproduced in jasper, to study the illustration of the vase in his copy

*Now, respectively, the Society of Antiquarians of London and (informally abbreviated) the Royal Society of Arts.
†In fact 9¾ inches (24.5 cm) high and maximum diameter 7 inches (17.7 cm).

of Montfaucon's *L'Antiquité expliquée* and to consider the possibility of copying it.

Like many others who have seen the vase during the past four centuries, Josiah was fascinated by its history and the significance of the enigmatic cameo-cut figures which are its ornament. Although the vase is probably the most famous of all surviving Roman works of art, nothing is known about its history before 1600. The story current in the eighteenth century, when it was a familiar object to art historians through the wide distribution of more or less accurate engraved illustrations, that it was the cinerary urn of the Emperor Alexander Severus and his mother, Mammea, recovered from a sarcophagus during the excavation of the Monte del Grano in 1582, is now known to be based on inaccurate supposition.

The vase is made of glass in two fused layers: the body, or foundation, in a deep blue, overlaid with almost opaque white. The bas-relief design was carved out of the white by *diatretarii*, or gem engravers, and its meaning is still the subject of controversy. Most modern authorities are agreed that it represents the myth of Peleus and Thetis, but the precise identification of episodes from the myth with the decoration on the two sides of the vase is less sure. All are agreed that it is a masterpiece of cameo-cutting and it is believed to have been made at Rome, perhaps by Alexandrians or by craftsmen trained in Alexandria, centre of glass-making in the ancient world, about 27 BC – AD 14, during the reign of Augustus.

The shape of the vase is not now, nor was it in the eighteenth century, as it was made, and it lacks the grace and balance of the amphora, probably tapering to a point, that was its orginal form. The flat disc on which the vase stands* is a later piece of cameo glass of paler colour, cut from a larger composition and presumed to have been attached when, at some unknown date, the foot of the amphora was broken. The cameo-cut decoration of the disc is thought to represent the head of Paris, son of King Priam, who awarded the golden apple to Aphrodite at the wedding of Peleus and Thetis. The coincidence of themes of decoration on the body of the vase and the disc is unlikely to be accidental.[17]

The date of the disc is believed to be about fifty years later than that of the vase, but a repair could have been effected at any time between the first century and the end of the sixteenth century. The vase is first recorded as seen by Nicolas de Pieresc, the Provençal scholar and antiquarian, at the Palazzo Madama in the winter of 1600,

*Now displayed separately from the body of the vase in the British Museum

when it was in the collection of Cardinal Francesco Maria del Monte. Correspondence between de Peiresc and Peter Paul Rubens[18] shows that the disc was already fitted to the foot by 1600 and additional proof of this repair is provided by a drawing by Cassiano dal Pozzo now in the collection of Her Majesty the Queen.[19] In 1627, on the death of Cardinal del Monte, the vase was bought by Cardinal Barberini and it remained in the possession of the family until 1780, when it was sold to settle the gambling debts of Donna Cornelia Barberini-Colonna, Princess of Palestrina and last of the Barberini family.

The purchaser was James Byres, a Scottish architect of marked entrepreneurial ability living in Rome, who had turned antiquarian and dealer. His first major acquisition had been a *Picture of the Assumption* by Poussin* for Lord Exeter, and his crowning achievement the illegal export from Italy of the same artist's *Seven Sacraments*, which he sold to the Duke of Rutland. Some three years after his purchase of the Barberini vase, as it was now known, and after commissioning sixty plaster casts to be made by Wedgwood's old rival James Tassie, Byres sold the vase on to Sir William Hamilton for £1000.

The delighted Hamilton, presumably misinformed by Byres, had 'no doubt of this [vase] being a work of the time of Alexander the Great, and was probably brought out of Asia by Alexander, whose ashes were deposited therein after his death'. He told Wedgwood: 'Except the Apollo Belvedere, the Niobes, and two or three others of the first-class marbles, I do not believe that there are any monuments of antiquity existing that were executed by so great an artist.' This hugely costly purchase was 'concluded in a moment', although Hamilton admitted that 'God knows it was not very convenient for me'.[20]

On this occasion, Hamilton's zeal as a collector outstripped his discretion and available means, and he was relieved to be able to sell the vase secretly to the eccentric Duchess of Portland, 'a simple woman', according to Horace Walpole, 'and interested only by *empty* vases'.[21] She did not live long to enjoy it, dying on 17 July 1785. The vase was Lot 4155 on the final day of the sale by auction of her extraordinary collection between 24 April and 7 June 1786. It was bought by Charles Tomlinson, thought to be bidding on behalf of the Duke of Marlborough, for 980 guineas. Tomlinson was, in fact, acting for the 3rd Duke of Portland, son and heir of the previous owner. Three days later the vase was in the hands of Josiah Wedgwood,[22] on loan from the Duke, who had given his permission – in return, it is said, for Josiah's agree-

*Now in the National Gallery, Washington, DC.

ment not to bid against his representative at the auction – for it to be copied in jasper.

Two weeks later, when he had given himself and his modellers time to examine the vase in detail, Josiah wrote at length to Sir William Hamilton for advice:

> You will be pleased, I am sure, to hear what a treasure is just now put into my hands. I mean the exquisite Barberini vase with which you enriched this island, & which now that we may call it the Portland vase, I hope will never depart from it. His Grace the Duke of Portland . . . has generously lent it to me to copy. . . . I stand in much need of your advice & directions in several particulars. . . . I stand more in need of them than ever, being engaged in an undertaking which appears more & more formidable upon every review of the charming original.[23]

As he explained, the illustration of the vase in Montfaucon's *Antiquité expliquée* had encouraged him to believe that an imitation in jasper could be made without much difficulty.

> I proceeded with spirit, & sufficient assurance that I should be able to equal, or excel if permitted, that copy of the vase; but now that I can indulge myself with full and repeated examinations of the original work itself my crest is much fallen & I should scarcely muster sufficient resolution to proceed if I had not, too precipitately perhaps, pledged myself to many of my friends to attempt it.[24]

Josiah was confident that his best throwers could fashion the shape of the vase and that his best modellers – Henry Webber, assisted by William Hackwood and William Wood* – were sufficiently skilled to make accurate copies of the relief figures. His sudden loss of confidence was caused by the colour of the Portland vase and the exquisite quality of the cameo-cutting. He had already developed a black jasper that was perfectly satisfactory for vases, tablets and smaller ornaments, but its manganese base yielded a brown-black hue quite unlike the rich blue-black of the Portland vase glass. A new colour must be created, mixed with cobalt, that would more closely resemble that of the original. He was anxious, too, about the effect of light and shade achieved by the cameo-cutter:

*Eldest son of Aaron Wood (see p. 20) and brother of Enoch Wood, sometimes styled 'Father of the Potteries', William was apprenticed to Wedgwood in 1767 and remained with the firm until his death in 1808.

It is apparent, that the artist has availed himself very ably by the dark ground, in producing the perspective and distance required, by cutting the white away, nearer to the ground as the shades were wanted deeper, so that the white is often cut to the thinness of paper, & in some instances quite away, & the ground itself makes part of the bas-relief; by which he has given his work the impression of painting as well as sculpture.[25]

He doubted that jasper bas-relief could ever be applied thinly enough to emulate this effect and feared that his ornaments would display a 'disgusting flatness' in consequence. He did not, in fact, ever succeed in applying the figures so thinly that the ground colour, showing through the relief, provided sufficient light and shade, and the loss of transparency and 'perspective' had to be remedied by the application of a thin black wash over the white as a form of shading.[26]

The most serious of all obstacles was Josiah's personal dissatisfaction with the form of the vase. Although capable occasionally of producing combinations of shapes and ornament that were at best eclectic and at worst bizarre, Josiah had made a closer study of form – and especially of classical vase form – than all but a select few of his contemporaries. He had acquired, partly from his early experience as a thrower and partly from years of observation and study, a perceptive understanding of clay form and of the proper disposition and balance of decoration. He felt instinctively that the squat shape of the Portland vase was ungraceful and inappropriate and he was honest enough in his opinions not to be overawed by its antiquity and fame.

Expressing such irreverent thoughts to Sir William Hamilton required some delicacy. 'I suppose,' he wrote, 'it is admitted that the form of this vase is not so elegant as it might be made if the artist had not been possessed of some very good reason for contenting himself with the present form.' He had evidently not seen an article in the *General Advertiser* of 26 April stating that the base of the vase had been broken and repaired. He therefore continued to try to find excuses for its lack of formal beauty, supposing that 'the material made use of . . . that is, the body being made of one colour, & the surface covered over to a due thickness with another, was not capable of taking a form with those delicate parts on which its beauty as a simple vase would in great measure depend'. 'I suppose', he wrote reluctantly, 'you would still advise me to copy the form of the vase as well as the figures.'[27]

The beauty of the figures was not questioned, although their identities and significance were uncertain. Josiah believed that they represented death and the entrance of the soul into Elysium.[28] He was anxious to know whether he could properly use them 'in other works & forms, in which [he added persuasively] they might perhaps serve the arts, & diffuse the seeds of good taste, more extensively than by confining them to the vase only. For instance, many a young artist, who could not purchase any edition of the vase, would be glad to buy impressions of the heads of the figures, or the whole figures, in a durable material for his studies.'[29] This somewhat contrived appeal to Hamilton's desire to be esteemed as an antiquarian, was followed by a frankly commercial proposal to exploit the figures by producing 'intaglios of the heads for seals, & cameos of two colours & polished grounds for rings, or the whole figures in separate pieces or groupes, finished to any degree for cabinet pieces or pictures. In tablets for chimney pieces, & many other purposes, I have some reason to believe they will be acceptable. . . . I should be glad to know if you see any objections to these proposed extensions & applications.'[30]

Josiah had plans, also, to make the best commercial use of the vase by issuing several editions of it at varied prices. He thought that 'the working artist would be content with a true & simple copy, a cast in one colour'; others would want a painted blue ground; a third might want the ground colour in the same material as the vase; and a fourth might pay for the ground to be lapidary polished. Only the last two would be customers for jasper copies of the Portland vase. As always with new projects, ideas poured from him; and, as it often happened, his enthusiasm was allowed to override his understanding of what was suitable. Hamilton, surprisingly, had nothing but praise for these ideas, applauding the proposal to copy the single figures and heads and even approving 'the most simple copies' of the vase, though he seems to have misunderstood their purpose, believing that they would be used only as a step on the way to the production of more perfect copies in jasper. He approved, too, of Wedgwood's intention to restore, in his copies, 'surfaces partially decayed by time' and proposed that Flaxman be employed in that task.[31]

By the middle of June 1787, after just twelve months' work on the vase, Josiah wrote to Hamilton to inform him of Flaxman's and Webber's impending departures for Rome. By then he had finished 'a third & last edition of the figures, the two first being suppressed in hopes of making the third still more perfect' and he had made some trials in applying the figures, probably at this early stage to jasper tablets.[32] He had reached a stage in the development of the vase when he no longer needed Flaxman's help and could allow his most senior modeller to accompany John to Rome and to establish his studio of artists there.

Three problems remained, all technical. The first, the difficulty in giving 'those beautiful shades to the thin & distant parts of the figures, for which the original artist availed himself of the semitransparency of the white glass, cutting it down and nearer & nearer to the blue ground in proportion as he wished to increase the depth of shade', was resolved by applied shading. The second was the old and constant trouble with firing. 'I must', Wedgwood explained, 'depend upon an agent, whose effects are neither at my command, nor to be perceived at the time they are produced, viz. the action of fire on my compositions.'[33] In the solution of this he was greatly helped by the perfecting of his pyrometer. The third was the invention of a new jasper colour that would satisfy his desire to match the colour of the Portland vase and yet stand the intense heat of the oven without blistering, distortion or collapse. This proved to be the most intractable of the three and Josiah worked on it tirelessly with his second son, Jos.

These technical difficulties proved to be greater than Josiah had anticipated. Always the most stubborn and frustrating of compositions, Wedgwood's jasper was still capable of trying the patience of its inventor to the limit. In spite of years of trials and experiment, in spite of Josiah's final conquest in 1778 of the problem of making large jasper ornaments,[34] and in spite even of several years of experience in the making of jasper vases, the copying of the Portland vase proved to be as laborious and infuriating a task as any that he attempted. The long struggle exhausted him. In April 1788 he consulted Dr William Heberden,* the distinguished London physician, about a pain in his head and 'a general weakness'. Heberden prescribed a blister, which proved effective in curing the headache, rest and a holiday. Josiah agreed to follow the second part of the prescription 'as soon as the Portland Vase is complete'.[35] He had told Hamilton, 'my great work is the Portland Vase'[36] and he was determined to finish the task of reproducing it in jasper to the best of his ability, regardless of the cost in time, materials and labour, or the damage to his health. Like his invention of jasper, it had become for him a matter of pride, a challenge to his endurance and ability that must be conquered.

It had become also a matter of reputation. He had been encouraged by several of his most valued patrons to make copies of the vase by subscription and he had agreed to this arrangement on condition that the subscribers should be free, when they saw their vases, to accept or refuse them, and on the understanding that orders would be completed,

---

*William Heberden FRS, FRCP, physician to Samuel Johnson and the poet William Cowper, among others, was the first to describe *angina pectoris*. His son, also William, was physician in ordinary to King George III and Queen Charlotte.

without time limit, in rotation.[37] By 9 May 1790 he had received subscriptions for twenty vases.

In July 1789 Josiah wrote to William Eden, who had recently been
rewarded for his services by being raised to the peerage as Baron
Auckland:

> You will perhaps wonder at your not having heard something of the
> Barberini Vase. I was always very sensible of the difficulty of attempt-
> ing to copy so exquisite a piece of workmanship, but in the progress of
> the undertaking difficulties have occurred which nothing but practice
> would have discovered to me. The prospect however brightens before
> me, and, after having made several defective copies, I think I see my
> way to the final completion of it.[38]

The letter was written with an eye to future benefit: not only did he
hope for Auckland's name to appear among the subscribers, but also
he confidently expected Auckland to be in a diplomatic post abroad
where he might, if he were so inclined, materially affect sales of the
vase in Europe.

Two months later Josiah sent the first perfect vase to his friend and
'favourite Aesculapius', Erasmus Darwin, with a caution not to show
it to anyone except his family. Darwin, who could be relied upon to
ignore all instructions but his own, replied in October: 'I have disobeyed
you and shown our vase to two or three; but they were philosophers,
not cogniscenti. How can I possess a jewel, and not communicate the
pleasure to a few Derby philosophers?'[39] Later, he was to include a
description of the vase, which he chose to regard as a 'mystic urn'
whose decoration was symbolic rather than mythological, in *The Botanic
Garden*, accompanied by engraved illustrations attributed to William
Blake.

Darwin's poetry, reflecting its author, was a strange mixture of
high-flown, turgid rhetoric, original thought and genuine humour. The
last quality, often shown in self-parody, has seldom been appreciated
since *The Botanic Garden* first delighted a large reading public and even
the most austere of literary critics. It is a massive poem: the second
part, *The Loves of the Plants*, in 968 decasyllabic rhyming couplets, was
published first; Part I, 'The Economy of Vegetation', in 1224 couplets
and considered less accessible to the general public, followed two years
later. It brought Darwin fame as a poet, a result that he had not sought,
believing that it might injure his reputation as a physician, but which
nevertheless delighted him. In *The Economy of Vegetation*, which was
concerned with the whole spectrum of natural philosophy, Darwin

called on several of his fellow Lunatics for information and there are, in the poem or its abundant notes,* tributes to Priestley, Whitehurst, Keir, Edgeworth and 'immortal Franklin', as well as lavish praise of Wedgwood:

> Etruria! next beneath thy magic hands
> Glides the quick wheel, the plastic clay expands,
> Nerved with fine touch, thy fingers (as it turns)
> Mark the nice bounds of vases, ewers and urns;
>
> . . .
>
> And pleased on WEDGWOOD ray your partial smile
> A new Etruria decks Britannia's isle,
> Charmed by your touch, the kneaded clay refines,
> The biscuit hardens, the enamel shines,
> Each nicer mould a softer feature drinks,
> The bold Cameo speaks, the soft Intaglio thinks.
>
>
> Whither, O Friend of Art! you gems derive
> Fine forms from Greece, and fabled Gods revive;
> Or bid from modern life the Portrait breathe,
> And bind round Honour's brow the laurel wreath;
> Buoyant shall sail, with Fame's historic page,
> Each fair medallion o'er the wrecks of age.[40]

As if this were not enough, there was a footnote describing Wedgwood's industry and inventiveness, a long Additional Note on the Portland vase and engravings of some Wedgwood cameos to illustrate the poem.

It is not to be wondered at that such a detailed encomium pleased Wedgwood, and his Lunatic friends were hardly less enthusiastic in their opinions of Darwin's work. James Watt had responded playfully in November 1789 to Darwin's request for information about steam-engines: 'I know not how steam-engines come among the plants; I cannot find them in the Systema Naturae, by which I should conclude that they are neither plants, animals nor fossils, otherwise they would not have escaped the attention of Linnaeus. However, if they belong to *your* system, no matter about the Swede.'[41] More seriously, he sent

---

*The footnotes are even longer than the poem and the Additional Notes cover 120 densely printed pages. Horace Walpole pertinently questioned the purpose of 'describing in verse what nobody can understand without a long prosaic explanation'.

Darwin a long account of his work which was used in the poem as well as for a short, prophetic footnote about Watt's achievements in the use of steam. After predicting that steam power would be used for the propulsion of boats and carriages, Darwin continued:

> As the specific levity of air is too great for the support of great burthens by balloons, there seems no probable method of flying conveniently but by the power of steam, or some other explosive material; which another half century may probably discover.[42]

The illustrious reputation of Darwin's great poem, for so it was considered, was short-lived. It ran through seven editions, including one American, in as many years, but it died with the Enlightenment, a victim of the reaction against the Terror,* and the rejection of reason in favour of romanticism. While it lasted, Josiah was highly delighted by the advertisement for his work, describing Darwin as 'a powerful *magician*, who can work wonders, – who can liquefy the granite, and still harder flint, into the softest poetic numbers'. He wrote gratefully: 'I need not say how proud I am of the very honorable mention you make of me and my works. . . . Whether', he added, 'your prophecies respecting the productions of modern Etruria be as true as your poetry is excellent, when you assure us that

> "Nor Time shall mar, nor Steel, nor Fire, nor Rust,
> "Touch the hard polish of the immortal bust,"

it will take some time to discover.'[43]

Darwin's approval of the first perfect copy confirmed Josiah in his opinion that he was ready to show the jasper Portland vase to his most influential patron, the Queen. She was given a private view of the vase on 1 May 1790,[44] and later that day another private exhibition was held at the house of Sir Joseph Banks, conveniently no more than a few yards from Wedgwood's showrooms. This was recorded in the *General Evening Post* and rather more fancifully described in the *Gazetteer and New Daily Advertiser* four days later:

> On Saturday night last there was a numerous *converzationi* at Sir Joseph Banks's, Soho-square, when Mr Wedgwood produced the *great vase*, manufactured by himself, in imitation of that superb one about four

---

*A contributory and related factor may have been the witty and savagely accurate parody that appeared in the *Anti-Jacobin* in April and May 1798.

years ago exhibited in the Museum of her Grace the Duchess Dowager of Portland. This vase is as large as the original; the ground colour that of an emerald, embossed with white. It is most exquisitely finished, and allowed by all present, *in point of look* to be at least equal to the original, which was valued at *two thousand five hundred pounds*. The whole of the above vase is a composition of the most beautiful transparency, and does infinite credit to the artist. He has not yet, however, arrived at the *certainty* of *casting* them, as several cracked in the experiment. Beside Sir Joseph and a numerous company who attended on the above occasion, there were present Sir Joshua Reynolds, Mr Locke,* the Hon. Horace Walpole and several members of the Royal and Antiquarian Societies.[45]

Two weeks later, Sir Joshua Reynolds, President of the Royal Academy, signed a certificate of approval, declaring Wedgwood's copy of the Portland vase to be 'a correct and faithful imitation both in regard to general effort, and the most minute detail of the parts'.[46]

Sir William Hamilton, perhaps the best judge of Wedgwood's vase, was unable to see it until the following summer but then declared himself 'much pleased with it'. He wrote to Josiah on 23 July, a few days after a visit to Etruria, to congratulate him:

I have accomplished one of my great objects which was the seeing of your wonderful Copy of the Portland Vase. I that am so well acquainted with the Original and the difficulties you must have met with, really think it so. The sublime character of the Original is wonderfully preserved in your Copy & little more is wanting than the sort of transparency which your materials could not imitate . . . in short I am wonderfully pleased with it, and give you the greatest credit for having arrived so near the imitation of what I believe to be the first specimen of the excellence of the Arts of the Ancients existing . . . [47]

The favourable reception given to his vase by the Queen, the Presidents of the Royal Society and the Royal Academy, and the distinguished and knowledgeable gathering at Sir Joseph's house at the beginning of May, was sufficient to encourage Josiah to show the vase in Europe. Twenty years earlier he had written to Bentley about the need for 'a *proper* & *noble* introduction' for new ornaments; now he repeated to his son the policy which he had always tried to implement: 'begin at the Head first, & then proceed to the inferior members'.[48] He

*William Locke (1732–1810), art amateur and collector.

had never been slow to take advantage of the goodwill of his patrons and he was happy to learn that Lord Auckland had succeeded Lord Malmesbury, another of Pitt's invaluable 'men of business', as Ambassador Extraordinary to the Court at The Hague. This was clearly too good an opportunity to miss and by the end of June 1790 the younger Josiah and Tom Byerley were on their way to Rotterdam at the start of a promotional tour of Europe that was to last until December.

The vase was shown to Lord and Lady Auckland on 3 July and Auckland arranged for it to be seen privately by the Prince and Princess of Orange* at their summer 'house in the wood' next day. 'The prince and princess', Josiah II told his father, 'both spoke very highly of the vase though I believe the latter only had much feeling for it. . . . The princess has the look of a very clever woman & I believe she is so.'[49] This was somewhat short of the truth: the Anglophile grandson of George II,† William V was weak and vacillating; his Prussian Princess, on the other hand, the niece of Frederick the Great (and sister to 'my booby of a nephew' as Frederick called him), was capable, devious and domineering. If the Stadholder were to order a Wedgwood Portland vase, it would be the Princess Wilhelmina who would make the decision to do so.

On 5 July a more public exhibition was held at Auckland's residence at The Hague. Josiah II described it in breathless detail:

> About half after 10 Mr B[yerley] & myself went over to Lord Aucklands and disposed all our chaise seat full upon 4 tables, one of which the collection of cameos filled. In this room there were upon the chimney piece seven jasper vases belonging to Lord Auckland so that altogether we cut a very respectable figure. We had some few cameos mounted very handsomely in necklaces, bracelets & ear drops which we also displayed. We had a thermometer [pyrometer] also which was much looked at & people seemed very inquisitive about it. In another room was the Vase by itself & in the third & 4th the company breakfasted.[50]

The Princess examined the vase, she admired it, but she did not buy it. In spite of the number of distinguished guests assembled by Auckland (no fewer than fifty, according to the Princess), the immediate commercial benefits were slight. Princess Wilhelmina bought a pair of bracelets[51] for 14 guineas, and some mounted cameos were sold to the

---

*William V, Stadholder from 1751 to 1795, and his wife, Princess Frederica Sophia Wilhelmina of Prussia. They fled to England in 1795 when the revolutionary party set up the Batavian Republic, which lasted until 1806.
†William IV, 6th Stadholder, married Anne, daughter of George II.

ladies present, but there is no record of any sales of vases or tablets and no subscription order was taken for Wedgwood's Portland vase.

Josiah was concerned that the high costs of making the vase might have priced it beyond any accessible market and he asked Byerley if Auckland had made any comment on the price.[52] Auckland's name appears on the list of subscribers,[53] though there is no record that the order was ever completed, as does that of the author, designer, collector and patron of contemporary artists, Thomas Hope, who probably saw the vase in Amsterdam a few days after it was shown to the Stadholder.

Two months later the price was still not settled. Josiah wrote to Jos in Frankfurt that he had not yet succeeded in making another perfect copy, although five more had been fired, and a price of £50 would not cover production costs. 'Perhaps,' he suggested, 'it would not be amiss to say this to some of the noblesse . . . What encouragement is there for the moderns to attempt the production of such works if their patrons refuse to pay ¹⁄₂₀ of what the ancients paid to their artists.'[54] The Wedgwood Portland vase continued to be costly in production and the problems of blistering and cracking were never entirely solved in Josiah's lifetime. Between May 1791 and the end of December 1796, forty-three black and white jasper Portland vases were fired at Etruria. Of these, eleven were broken; the number of faulty vases is not recorded.[55]

The later history of the original Barberini vase is not wholly edifying. Broken at least twice before it reached the hands of Josiah Wedgwood[56] – once by the notoriously rowdy Duchess of Gordon – it was deposited on loan to the British Museum by the 4th Duke of Portland in 1810. There, in the Hamiltonian Ante-Room on 7 February 1845, a young Irishman, who subsequently gave his name as William Lloyd, smashed it more thoroughly, using for the purpose a handy exhibit variously described as 'a Persepolitan monument of basalt' and 'a curiosity of sculpture'.[57] The culprit admitted the offence, claiming that he had been 'indulging in intemperence for a week before' and was consequently suffering from 'nervous excitement'. By one of those freaks of English law which encourage applause for Mr Bumble's apothegm, the wording of the Wilful Damage Act made it unlikely that any action for damage to an article valued at more than £5 could succeed. 'Lloyd' (the name was probably borrowed for the occasion) was therefore found guilty of breaking the glass display case in which the vase had been standing. After three days in gaol he was released, on payment by a friend of a fine of £3.[58] The vase was restored in 1848, when more than 200 fragments were patiently pieced together over six months. Purchased by the British Museum in 1945, it has been restored twice since that date, incorporating some missing chips of glass and using modern colourless and soluble adhesives to replace old discoloured glues.

There can be no doubt that, whatever his disappointment at its commercial failure, Josiah considered his jasper Portland vase to be a technical triumph, and the few near-perfect copies that survive[59] from the so-called 'first edition'* are ranked among the greatest technical achievements of the English potter's craft. Their quality as works of art is more doubtful. However fine the quality of workmanship, there must be more to creation than copying, and an excellent craftsman's *tour de force* is rarely also a work of art. Wedgwood's Portland vases are copies in the wrong material, reproduced by entirely different techniques, of a vase which, as a result of serious damage and not altogether sympathetic repair, had already lost much of its original grace. What is left derives its beauty from the colour and nature of its material – glass – and the exquisite artistry of the Alexandrian cameo-cutter. Neither of these qualities could be reproduced in stoneware. Hamilton had noted the lack of 'the sort of transparency which your materials could not imitate', and Josiah had always been uneasy about the shape of the vase and his inability satisfactorily to reproduce the effect of shading in the figures. In spite of the praise of Reynolds, Banks, Hamilton, Darwin and many others, it is doubtful that Josiah was ever wholly satisfied with his Portland vase and it was left to his son to present a Wedgwood copy to the British Museum.[60]

It might be argued that the Wedgwood Portland vase was a great labour that should not have been attempted, because true success was unattainable: a wasted effort that was, moreover, a costly commercial failure. From the incomplete evidence available it appears unlikely that more than thirty-one vases of the first edition were ever produced to a standard of quality high enough for them to be sold to subscribers, and Josiah II, writing about forty-five years later, stated his belief that his father never sold as many as ten copies. It is most improbable that sales of the vase repaid the development and production costs. There were, however, other less tangible benefits. The most evident of these was the lustre that the vase added to the name of Wedgwood and the reputation of the Etruria factory. Nothing of such technical difficulty had ever before been attempted by a British pottery and its fame spread quickly and has lasted ever since. The vase was the recognised hallmark of the firm's excellence long before it was used regularly as part of its trademark.[61] Benjamin West chose the Portland vase as one of the

---

*'First edition' vases are those potted (if not finished and fired) between September 1789 and January 1795.

objects illustrating his theme in 'Etruria', a sketch for his painting of *Genius calling forth the Fine Arts to adorn Manufactures and Commerce, and recording the names of eminent men in these pursuits.** Since the 'Frog' service for Catherine the Great fifteen years earlier, nothing had gained Wedgwood and his factory such prestige.

Josiah had one more brief set of experiments to complete and, although he undertook it gladly, it was not one that he sought. On 26 January 1788 eleven ships, carrying some 850 convicts and 200 officers and men, commanded by Captain Arthur Phillip, who was appointed first governor of New South Wales, dropped anchor in Sydney Cove. Ten months later, Phillip wrote to Sir Joseph Banks to give him details of quantities of white clay found in the area. This was used by the natives for personal decoration but Phillip had been told by the Abbé Monges, a naturalist on the French scientific expedition led by Jean-François, Comte de la Perouse, to Botany Bay early in the year, that it would be suitable for the manufacture of porcelain. Perouse's two ships were shortly afterwards wrecked north of the New Hebrides and there is no evidence that this information was ever sent back to France. Phillip, however, sent a sample of the clay to Banks, who passed it on at once to Wedgwood for testing.[62]

Josiah reported on 12 March 1790 that the Sydney Cove clay was 'an excellent material for pottery, and may certainly be made the basis of a valuable manufacture of our infant colony there' and enclosed some medallions made from it for Sir Joseph's inspection. In his Commonplace Book he added that the clay lacked whiteness, made an ugly colour when mixed with cobalt and contracted excessively in firing – defects which made it unsuitable for use in either porcelain or jasper. Its strength and construction, however, made it suitable for cameos and medallions, 'where extreme fine impressions' were necessary or where reduction in size was required.[63]

A commemorative medallion representing 'Hope encouraging Art and Labour under the influence of Peace' was designed by Henry Webber to celebrate the founding of the settlement. This was modelled by Hackwood and the first consignment of medallions, made from Sydney Cove clay, was sent out to Botany Bay with the 'Second Fleet', which sailed on 19 January 1790. Webber's design was copied for the title-page of John Stockdale's *The Voyage of Governor Philip to Botany Bay,* published in November, and Erasmus Darwin, who had been supplied with a medallion, composed some verses to go with it. If not to be applauded for his style, Darwin compels admiration for his vision of

*Now in the Cleveland Museum of Art.

the Sydney of the future, complete with harbour bridge. It is described, in his poem, by Hope:

> *There* shall broad streets their stately walls extend,
> The circus widen and the crescent bend;
> *There* ray'd from cities o'er the cultur'd land,
> Shall bright canals and solid roads expand. —
> *There* the proud arch, Colossus-like, bestride
> Yon glittering streams, and bound the chafing tide;
> Embellish'd villas crown the landscape-scene.
> Farms wave with gold, and orchards blush between. —
> *There* shall tall spires, and dome-capt towers ascend,
> And piers and quays their massy structures blend . . .

He proposed to add two lines:

> Here future Newtons shall explore the skies,
> Here future Priestleys, future Wedgwoods rise.

But this was too much even for Wedgwood, who demanded that 'Wedgwoods' be replaced by 'Darwins'.[64] The couplet was deleted.

The testing of clay from Sydney Cove was the last significant set of experiments in which Wedgwood was personally involved. Before they were completed, he had made the decision to hand over the firm to his sons, the 'future Wedgwoods' of his own vision.

CHAPTER TWENTY-THREE

Handing Over

In 1788 Josiah suffered a second loss of partner. On 10 October his cousin Thomas Wedgwood – reliable, loyal and always 'useful' Thomas – was accidentally drowned. He was buried in the churchyard at Burslem. On this occasion the loss of a friend was a greater shock to Josiah than the loss of a partner. He had known for more than six months, having been warned of it by Jos,[1] that Thomas was planning to leave and set up his own pottery. After twenty-two years of patient and devoted service to the 'useful' partnership with his cousin, and almost thirty in his employment, Thomas had decided to take over the Hill Works in Burslem, owned by his father-in-law John Taylor.

There is little evidence that Thomas's work was ever either properly appreciated or adequately rewarded. The partnership he shared had been deprived not only of such benefits as there may have been from the 'Frog' service but – far more damaging – of the substantial profits from stoneware tablewares (teasets and coffeesets in black basaltes, jasper and the two other coloured bodies, 'rosso antico' and 'cane'), and the whole range of decorated terracotta flowerpots, all of which might fairly have been classed as 'useful' and to the development of which he had made some contribution. Apart from a slight hint of dissatisfaction with the favourable treatment given to the Wedgwood & Bentley partnership when black basaltes teapots were first allotted to it, he seems never to have complained of the manner in which his interests were so evidently subordinated to Bentley's. That he was content to stay with his cousin so long is evidence of their friendship, his loyalty and his lack of ambition. When finally he decided to make a change, he was already fifty-four years old. He did not live to profit by his decision. His partnership agreement ended on 11 November 1788, just one month after his death. The true consequences of his loss were not apparent for another ten years.

From the end of 1788, therefore, Josiah was the sole surviving partner in both the 'useful' and ornamental businesses, and sole owner of the Etruria factory. After a little more than a year of bearing the whole burden, he decided to shed part of it. On 31 January 1790 he wrote to Lord Auckland: 'You will not be displeased that I am endeavouring to provide a little more quiet for my self by taking my three sons and Mr Byerley into partnership with me. By this division of the burden I hope it will become light to each of us, at least a little less attention to the minute arrangements of a manufactory will I hope fall to my share.'[2] The partnership dated from 16 January and allocated shares in the business in portions of one-quarter each to John, Jos and Tom, and one eighth each to Tom Byerley and himself.

Naturally anxious that news of this reconstruction of the firm should not leak out to be misconstrued as an indication of his final retirement, Josiah composed an emollient statement, which he signed personally, for distribution to customers:

AFTER an unremitting attention of nearly forty years to a manufactory which I have had the happiness to establish, and to see flourish even beyond my most sanguine expectations, a wish to enjoy that ease and relaxation from the severity of business, so necessary in advanced years, might perhaps meet with your indulgence: But a stronger motive urges me to the new arrangement which I have now the honour to acquaint you with – I have sons grown up, and prepared to enter into the active scenes of life; and a nephew, who has long conducted the business of my warehouse in London to my entire satisfaction. They have chearfully undertaken to unite their best endeavours in carrying on the various branches of this manufactory and promise to pursue, with alacrity and diligence, the improvements which I have begun. I have therefore associated them with me in business, under the firm of Josiah Wedgwood, Sons, *and* Byerley.

Permit me to take this opportunity of returning you my sincere thanks for the favours you have been pleased to confer upon me, and to entreat the continuance, to this new establishment, of that goodness which I have so long experienced, assuring yourself of our utmost endeavours to merit your friendship and esteem.

I have the honour to be, with the greatest regard,
Your much obliged, and most obedient humble Servant.[3]

Although not yet sixty, Josiah was, by the standards of his time, already an old man. The rate of child mortality was so high that it distorted averages of life expectancy, and a child who survived to become an adult had a fair chance of living for thirty or forty years more; but few reached the age of seventy and those who did were considered very old. Sixty years later the average age at death of professional men and gentry in the northern industrial cities was forty-three and of labourers twenty-two.[4]

Except in his work, Josiah had always been moderate in his habits: he enjoyed the occasional pipe of tobacco, had a taste for oysters and wines, particularly a good sherry, and took regular exercise in riding and games of bowls;[5] but his body, weakened by the amputation of his leg in 1768, had been subjected to a punishing course of over-exertion, often to the limit of endurance, for more than twenty years. The effect of this is apparent in the deterioration of his handwriting, which now became cramped and shaky, and in his acceptance of his need to withdraw from active management, tacit recognition of the decline in his health and vigour.

He had never lived ostentatiously and his domestic establishment was modest compared with the opulence of Boulton, who entertained sumptuously at Soho House. Etruria Hall, substantially enlarged in 1780,[6] was spacious and comfortable and enhanced by mouldings designed by Flaxman. Wilberforce had remarked on the fine situation of the house, its walls hung with pictures by Reynolds, Stubbs and Wright of Derby, its carved chimneypieces inset with fine jasper tablets, and the ceiling of the saloon painted with an allegorical subject from sketches by Flaxman.[7] No full list of servants survives for this period, but a male staff of seven – butler, under-butler, footman, groom, coachman, postilion and gardener – was employed at the Hall in 1794, no doubt assisted by a much larger number of female servants and extra labourers for the estate. In July 1773 Josiah was already able to afford a 'Genteel carriage' and horses, preferring black for the paintwork of his carriage, but he never kept a large stable and in 1778 his 'whole stand' consisted of 'old Will of 22 years standing – George runaway & the little poney'.[8] This poor state of affairs was not, however, normal, and in 1794 he owned ten horses and three carriages, the third a two-wheeler for his daughters.[9]

In his statement to his customers, Josiah had assured them of the fitness of his sons to take up executive roles in the business. It was true that they were 'prepared', in the sense that they had been trained for the job. All had been given a thorough grounding in the management of the business and had spent time in all production departments of the factory. They lacked lengthy practical experience but they were supported by Byerley and an able team of managers and foremen and there was no suggestion that Josiah intended to retire altogether from participation in the management of the firm. That Josiah's sons were prepared, in the sense of being willing, was less certain.

As long ago as 1777, Bentley had warned Josiah against the dangers of spoiling his sons, and some effort had been made to educate them to 'a life of drudgery . . . & application to business'.[10] In December 1779 Josiah had planned John's future as a 'gentleman farmer in some desirable situation' but this had not prevented him from giving his eldest son the factory training that he had designed for Jos and Tom, both of whom he expected to succeed him in the firm. During his time at Warrington Academy and Edinburgh University, John had worked intermittently at Etruria and in the London showrooms and by 1786 he was considered capable of taking charge of the Works in his father's absence.[11]

Towards the end of the year John went to Paris, accompanied by Byerley, to take advantage of the recently negotiated Trade Treaty and appoint agents to handle Wedgwood in France. The voyage across the Channel lasted five hours, the ship pitched and rolled and most of the passengers were sick, particularly, as John reported, Matthew Boulton and his son, who were also on board with James Watt. Tom Byerley was 'so light headed that he rolled about in the cabin'.[12] From Paris John wrote to his father: 'a great commerce may be carried on in this kingdom though perhaps not so much just in Paris, except in the second order of people for the first order have either plate or porcelain'. He found the cost of living in Paris as high as in London and was obliged to ask for more money. 'We have,' he wrote in explanation, 'spent a great deal, Mr Byerley and I, in purchasing Porcelaine & some other things.'[13] It is clear that 'some other things' included the costs of mixing with members of the Court, with whom he had become acquainted, especially two 'Gentlemen ordinary' to the King, the Comte de la Motte and Comte de Choisimon, with whom he was engaged to spend Christmas. Through their influence he was able to visit Versailles, where he saw the Dauphin, 'a little tender lad of 8 years old' supervised by '3 or 4 Duchesses', and Louis XVI, 'very fat & awkward & waddles terribly in his gait'. Queen Marie Antoinette he described as 'handsome but not pretty'.[14]

John Wedgwood's cultivation of influential friends was a calculated attempt to gain access to the royal family and the Court for Wedgwood's products. He and Tom Byerley were also engaged in finding suitable agents for their wares in Paris and finally appointed Dominique Daguerre, a *marchand privilégié de la cour*, who supplied fine furniture to the French Court, and a Mr Sykes.

Trade with France, begun in optimism after the conclusion of the Trade Treaty, was soon ruined by the collapse of the French economy.

The plight of Wedgwood's agents is illustrated by a piteous letter from Verlingen & Son of Boulogne, who owed Wedgwood £380 in July 1789:

> We are Sir in very unfortunate circumstances, the crisis that France & of consequence Commerce, suffers at present, the horrid misery which ravages all the provinces & which influences all conditions, has totally suppressed circulation and sale. . . . We beg you to consider our situation in the payment of what we owe you & be persuaded that as soon as sales are renewed we will exert ourselves to the utmost to satisfy you; trust our probity & the delicacy of our sentiments . . . [15]

Conditions did not improve, and Wedgwood's business in France was destroyed by revolution and war. Daguerre retired to England in 1793.

In 1787, accompanied by Henry Webber, John set off on a version of the Grand Tour, an extended visit to Italy via Germany and Switzerland which, Josiah hoped, would achieve the dual results of broadening his eldest son's education and enabling him to 'fix ultimately upon some plan of life'. By the end of April 1788 he appeared to have made up his mind to stand for Parliament, 'unconnected with any Party'. 'By this means', he suggested, 'I shall not be prevented from following the business but shall rather add credit to it.'[16] To Josiah, for whom the pottery business was a passion which had consumed his life, this suggestion that it could be a part-time occupation is unlikely to have been welcome.

John returned home in 1789, and it was soon plain that the tour had done little to improve his disposition. Josiah was unusually patient with his sons, anxiously hoping that they would choose to follow him in the business but wishing them to 'judge for themselves before they engaged in it'.[17] He was especially indulgent towards his eldest son: 'you in particular', he wrote to him, 'I desired to take some time to consider your own inclination before you gave your final determination'. John's 'aversion to the business' had not passed unnoticed, but Josiah wrote to him: 'as I believed the ideas upon which that aversion was founded were taken up in your travels, I thought you might probably drop them again by a change of place & Company'. He reminded John sharply that, by accepting a partnership, he had engaged to take his share in the work of the business as well as the profits.[18]

Jos and Tom, taken into partnership at the same time, 'to ease myself of increasing care in the decline of life', as Josiah put it,[19] were no more drawn to the pottery industry than was their eldest brother. Jos made a show of interest in it but, like John, he privately despised the business, and there were occasions when he aired his true feelings.

He was disappointed that he was never offered the sort of extended tour that John had enjoyed and he found little consolation in his journeys with Byerley in Holland and Germany, as superior travelling salesmen, to show the Portland vase. He had intended that his friend William Sneyd of Belmont should accompany them, a proposal that had not met with the approval of Josiah, who believed that young Sneyd's influence might be more conducive to social activity and entertainment than to business. To this, Jos replied angrily, 'I have no more desire myself to make our journey, a journey of pleasure, than you have that it should be so, and I am very sensible of the strong distinction kept up on the continent & especially in Germany, between those engaged in business & gentlemen.'[20]

In the following April, when Byerley fell ill and was temporarily unable to manage the Greek Street showrooms, Jos's offer to stand in for him was conditional. 'What I mean', he told his father, 'is that I would live in the house and take care of the correspondence while Mr B is unfit for it, and do what other business I could, except attending in the rooms any farther than waiting upon some particular people, for I have been too long in the habit of looking upon myself as the equal of everybody to bear the haughty manners of those who come into the shop.'[21] Such arrogance was no more designed to please his father than John's even more evident distaste for industry.

Jos's interest in the business was slight. Like his brothers, he was well trained in the techniques of pottery manufacture, but he regarded the work as his duty, an act of filial responsibility, undertaken without enthusiasm and to be ended, in due course, without regret.

Tom, the youngest and always regarded as the cleverest of the brothers, suffered from continuous ill-health, real or imagined, the cause of which might, 200 years later, be diagnosed as endogenous depression. At Edinburgh, where he had followed his brothers, he had formed a close friendship with John Leslie, a scientist and mathematician five years his senior, whom he invited to Etruria to help him with his own scientific studies. Tom proposed to set up house with Leslie, away from Etruria Hall, and enlisted the help of Jos in trying to persuade Josiah to agree to this arrangement. 'I know', he wrote in April 1790, 'my father is afraid of my secluding myself too much from the world & becoming too hermetical. I can only say that I think it would be greatly to the advantage of most young people to pass three or four most important years of their life, in a calm retired manner. The Business of Education is to teach the mind to *think*. . . . What an insignificant set of puppies or fools are the generality of *young gentlemen*. At our universitys, schoolboys assume prematurely the habit & customs of men & indulge in all the pleasures of society – & of consequence they leave the place with less real learning, but more conceit.'[22]

Jos showed this letter to his father as evidence of Tom's serious intentions and Josiah, who was in London, replied sympathetically, though he was not convinced by Tom's argument. He agreed with Tom that 'a too early mixture with the world and its rounds of dissipation are the bane of the young people (generally speaking) of the present age' and applauded his plans for serious study. 'Dear boy', he wrote, '. . . if you will hearken to me as a friend when I apprehend my knowledge of experience may be of use to you, I will thank you and gladly waive any other claim upon your attention.' While he was prepared to accept that there might be advantages in 'an uninterupted intercourse & conversation with a man of Mr L's extensive knowledge', he did not agree that they should be gained by giving up altogether the comforts and advantages of family life. It was possible to purchase almost anything at too great a price and 'Even knowledge itself, if received in exchange for the blessings of society & the family charities would be dearly bought.'[23]

Josiah may have consulted some of his scientific friends about Leslie's qualifications.* Certainly he appears to have recognised the ability that lay beneath Leslie's rather sententious manner. A satisfactory compromise was reached. Leslie was invited to stay with the family at Etruria Hall, where he remained until 1793. It was during this period of over two years, when Leslie was, in Josiah's words, 'a part of Mr Wedgwood's family . . . bringing his sons to a more intimate acquaintance with some branches of philosophy than the time that they were at Edinburgh would allow them to acquire',[24] that Tom made his first experiments with the chemical action of light. He wrote two papers on the 'Production of Light from Different Bodies', both of which were read before the Royal Society and published in the Society's *Philosophical Transactions* for 1792. He was then just twenty-one.

He was, perhaps, freer with his opinions than was welcome from so young a partner in the business, and his criticism of the appearance and displays in the London showrooms are unlikely to have endeared him to Tom Byerley, who had managed them since Bentley's death ten years earlier, but Josiah was prepared to accept them as welcome signs of his interest in the business.

Of Josiah's relationship with his younger daughters – Catherine,

*Leslie was later professor of mathematics at Edinburgh University, then professor of natural philosophy, and was knighted in 1832. He invented a differential thermometer, a hygrometer, the pyroscope atmometer and aethriscope, and published, in 1804, *Inquiry into Heat.*

Sarah and the pathetic Mary Anne – the little that is known comes from scattered references to them in his own letters and a few affectionate letters from young Sarah, written when she was eight years old. Of all his children, none was so dear to him as his eldest, his daughter Sukey. Her letters to him display an ease and affection that is absent from those written by his sons and she often teased him gently about his politics or public reputation, quoting scurrilous rumours about him from the newspapers and repeating comment that she had heard during her ventures into London society. Lady Clive, her hostess in London, was, she reported in 1787, critical not only of his politics but also of his religious principles, which 'cannot be right or you would not be acquainted with such a man as – as – Dr Darwin – as for her Ladyship she would rather die than have his advice if there was not another physician in the world'. It was a sure sign of Josiah's increasing infirmity that Sukey wrote, in April 1794, of sparing him the trouble of writing, 'which I know you are not very fond of'.[25] The years when no day was so short or so full that he was not eager to write at length to Bentley were long past. The fits of depression to which Sukey had been prone in earlier life seemed to have lifted as she grew into a sociable and vivacious young woman, but there was a strain of melancholia in the family that affected all the boys and would be inherited by later generations.

In 1792, Tom visited Paris in time for the third anniversary of the fall of the Bastille. 'It is entirely impossible', he wrote to his father, 'for me to give any just account of French politics – they are as mutable as the wind.' The younger James Watt, who was with him, predicted that there must inevitably be another revolution soon and that it would prove fatal to the King, Lafayette and 'some hundred others'. Tom was disgusted by the state of the French capital: 'The streets of Paris stink more than the dirtiest hole in London.'[26] He returned restless, depressed and in poor health. In April of the following year, both he and John resigned their partnerships.

This double defection was a sad blow to Josiah's plans for the future of his firm but John's resignation was not unexpected. Josiah cheerfully advanced the money to buy him a partnership in the newly founded banking house of Alexander Davison & Co in London,[27] advising him only that he should serve out the first seven years of his Etruria partnership while he settled in at the bank. 'By that time', Josiah wrote, 'you will know better how the bank is likely to answer, & if that should not turn out to your satisfaction & you should determine to relinquish that & take your share of the business along with him, Jos says, & I doubt not very truly, that he had much rather have the assistance necessary for him from a brother than from any other person.'[28] Jos generously declined his brother's offer to forgo part of his share in the profits, adding, in a footnote that must further have saddened his father, 'I did not wish that he should consider himself as obliged to pay any attention to the business which I knew he disliked very much.'[29] It was decided that John and Tom should have a fixed sum annually from the business as long as it continued to make a certain profit. If profits should fall, their share would fall in proportion.

Josiah was disappointed, hurt and displeased, but he was true to the principle on which he had founded his relationships with his children. He had never tried to force his beliefs or opinions on them: 'I do not desire you to adopt them merely because they have been mine,' he had written to Jos when the latter was only nine years old. 'Examine them for yourself, & then act according to your honest conviction, in this & in every other instance, & your conduct, whether it is the same as my own would have been in like circumstances, or the contrary, will nevertheless have my approbation.'[30]

All Josiah's hopes for the succession now rested in his second son alone. He made his will on 2 November 1793,[31] leaving the Etruria factory to him. Three years earlier, he had written to him: 'You can do anything you attempt.'[32] Believing this to be true, he had little to fear for the future of Etruria.

In December 1792, after a brief and determined courtship, Jos married the lovely Elizabeth ('Bessie') Allen of Cresselly, Pembrokeshire, and two years later John married her sister, Lousia Jane ('Jenny'). Sarah Elizabeth Wedgwood, the eldest child of Jos and Bessie, and Josiah's and Sally's first grandchild, was born in 1793. The new generations gradually succeeded the old. All Josiah's brothers had died and, of his sisters, only Catherine Willet and Tom Byerley's mother, Margaret, still lived. Some friends remained: Darwin, the most intimate, but gone from Lichfield to live in Derby; Matthew Boulton and James Watt; Priestley, living far away in America; and Edgeworth, who had become an increasingly regular correspondent, in Ireland. The Lunar Society, described by Edgeworth as 'such a society as few men have had the good fortune to live with: such an assemblage of friends as fewer still have had the happiness to possess and keep through life',[33] no longer met.

In 1794, feeling tired and unwell, and worried by palpitations of the heart and an irregular pulse, Josiah spent several weeks away from the Potteries, leaving the management of the factory to Jos. On 20 November Darwin prescribed a mixture of alum and nutmeg to be taken with a 'decoction of bark' and powdered rhubarb,[34] but, after a short visit to the spa at Buxton, Josiah was sufficiently recovered for Darwin to advise him to 'leave off the bark and to take no medicine at present'.[35] A few days later, however, Josiah's face began to swell and he was suffering acute pain in the jaw, which he attributed to a decayed tooth. Summoned to extract it, James Bent, his surgeon, discovered signs of 'mortification' and immediately sent for Darwin, who hastened from Derby to his friend's bedside. There was, he saw, nothing to be done. Josiah's condition deteriorated rapidly, with inflammation in the throat and intermittent high fever. The family assembled at Etruria Hall, where Josiah was nursed by Sally and their three daughters, and Tom Byerley arrived from London. On 3 January, after ten days of pain and fever, during the last two of which he was unconscious, Josiah Wedgwood died.[36] It was Sukey's thirtieth birthday.

CHAPTER TWENTY-FOUR

The Wedgwood Legacy

Within four months of Josiah's death, and two months before his will was proved, Jos and his family moved from Staffordshire to Surrey. John, meanwhile, sold the house that Josiah had bought for him in London and acquired a large house and estate in Wiltshire. Tom, seldom free from headaches, intestinal disorders and depression, set off on a five-month walking tour in Germany with John Leslie. In the spring of 1796, Sukey fulfilled one of her father's dearest wishes by marrying Erasmus Darwin's third son,* Robert. Etruria Hall was occupied only by the grieving Sally and her two unmarried daughters. Saddened by his friend's death, 'a public as well as a private loss', as he told Edgeworth, and sickened by the repressive measures of the government, Darwin thought of emigrating to America, 'the only place of safety . . . America untax'd by Kings and priests'.[1]

Josiah had disposed of a substantial part of his estate during his lifetime. He had made large gifts to his children, including the capital for John's partnership in the bank, and gifts and settlements to John and Jos on their marriages.[2] Under the terms of his will, Etruria Hall, with part of the land, all personal papers and listed household goods, were left to Sally, who also received £3000. A further sum of £10,000 was entrusted to the executors for her benefit. John and Tom received £30,000 and £29,110 respectively, Tom having also twenty shares in the Monmouth Canal; each of Josiah's three daughters received £25,000; and the rest of the land, the Etruria factory and all the models, moulds and equipment became the property of Jos. After a few personal bequests, among them an annuity of £20 to Alexander Chisholm, accompanied by an instruction to Jos that he should 'give him any

---

*Darwin's eldest son, Charles, had died of blood-poisoning in 1778; the second son, Erasmus, an unmarried lawyer, drowned himself in the River Derwent during a thunderstorm on 29 December 1799.

further assistance that he may stand in need of to make the remainder of his life easy and comfortable', the residue of the estate was to be divided among Josiah's six children in proportion to their legacies. The total approached half a million pounds.

In the absence of all the brothers, including Jos, who had inherited responsibility for the business, the daunting task of managing both the Etruria factory and the London showrooms fell to Tom Byerley. It was one which Josiah had found taxing, even with his nephew's competent assistance in London, and it is not surprising that Byerley was unequal to it.

The consequences of Josiah's death now became apparent. Throughout his life, he had been aware of his importance to his own firm. He was not only its founder but also its power-house: the driving, innovative force which had given it the lead in Europe, and which had maintained that lead while many of the more prestigious porcelain factories, and even more of his imitators among the pottery manufacturers, had fallen behind or failed. He was a complete manufacturer, and whatever he had lacked in entrepreneurial skills he had learned from Bentley during the years of their partnership. From the end of 1780 until he took his sons into partnership in 1790, he alone had controlled the twin functions of production and marketing of one of the most successful business enterprises in Europe. And yet he had never believed that he was indispensable to the continuance of his firm. His experience of working with Jos had apparently convinced him that he was a credible successor. As matters turned out, he was not proved entirely mistaken.

For several years the young Wedgwoods appear to have been unaware of any difficulty. Towards the end of 1799, with the threatened collapse of Davison's bank and the consequent loss of John's invested capital, it was suggested that he might return to active management, but there was no suggestion that either he or Jos might give up his country estate or otherwise alter his way of life. John imagined that the business could be satisfactorily managed by his spending three months a year in London.[3] He visited Etruria for a few months each year, but spent most of his time at Cote House, his estate at Eastbury, where he pursued his interest in botany and horticulture, building greenhouses, employing a retinue of gardeners and cultivating exotic plants and tropical fruit. He was to be responsible for founding the Society for the Improvement of Horticulture, later the Royal Horticultural Society. Not until 1806, a full ten years after Josiah's death, did Jos return with his family to Staffordshire, to take control of a business that was foundering.

But it was not only Josiah who was sorely missed. He had often left the factory in the hands of others while he visited London or went exploring for materials, but on those occasions he had been able to leave Bentley, Byerley, John or Jos in charge of his business affairs and supervising the Ornamental Works while 'Useful' Thomas saw to the production of Queen's ware. After Josiah's death, it was the 'Useful' Works which declined the more quickly. Manufacturing standards were allowed to deteriorate and discipline became slack, and these faults were matched by failure in design. Wedgwood was no longer the leader of fashion in pottery, and might be said to be producing for a market that was rapidly disappearing. Intermittent appearances at Etruria by John merely confused the situation, making it all the easier for idle or incompetent managers to ignore Byerley's instructions in John's absence.

Tom Wedgwood had all but lost interest in the family firm. Although he was still entitled to a share of the profits and occasionally wrote to his brothers with ideas for new shapes for production,[4] his self-absorption, so characteristic of depressive illness, allowed him little time for the contemplation of anything but his own unhappiness. 'I must remind you', he told Jos, 'that all the livelong day, I neither do nor can think of anything else than my own difficulties.'[5] Dr Matthew Baillie, a London physician whom he consulted, diagnosed his complaint as 'hypochondriasis'. 'His attention is almost entirely absorbed in watching his health & minutely scrutinising every feeling of the body,' he told Robert Darwin; and he added, without elaboration, 'he does in some measure lack the usual propensity towards the other sex'.[6] Tom poured out descriptions of his symptoms and feelings of misery in his letters to his brothers and his friends, and in retrospect it is not easy to discern what charm he exercised over them. Nevertheless it was powerful. Coleridge, Wordsworth, Southey, Thomas Poole and, most particularly, Jos loved him, and not only for his generosity with his money.

Tom's inventive ability cannot be doubted. In 1802 Humphry Davy published in the *Journal* of the Royal Institution, of which he was then assistant editor, an essay entitled 'An Account of a Method of Copying Paintings upon Glass and of making Profiles by the Agency of Light upon Nitrate of Silver, invented by T. Wedgwood Esq., with observations by H. Davy'. This described a method of obtaining an image of an object by projecting its shadow on to a piece of paper or leather sensitised by moistening with nitrate of silver. This, and other more dubious evidence published by Eliza Meteyard,[7] has since been hailed as the earliest record of photography in England, and Tom Wedgwood's reputation was briefly established as 'the discoverer of modern photography',[8] but he was unable to discover any method of fixing the images he obtained and his experiments were abandoned before they were fully exploited.

Tom's natural gifts were wasted. He travelled, he bought country houses only to sell them as quickly, he was unable to settle his mind or his body for more than a few weeks at a time. He contemplated suicide: 'the final scheme which would bring immediate ease to my mind'.[9] In spite of some understanding of the dangers of addiction, Erasmus Darwin recommended opium in quantities varying between half a grain a day to 'very large doses' for the treatment of such disparate ailments as anorexia, impotency, gallstones and tetanus.[10] In August 1794, while Tom was staying in Devonshire, close to the Coleridges, Darwin wrote to recommend treatments for his several complaints. These included '¾ of a grain of opium, or a grain, of opium, taken every night for many months'.[11] Coleridge's opium habit is believed to have started at about that time and it is likely that Darwin was indirectly responsible for it, as he was directly for Tom's addiction.

Ten years later Tom admitted to Jos that all his efforts to reduce his use of opium had failed: 'I cannot do it,' he wrote in despair, 'my spirits become dreadful & I am now resolved to maintain a constant intoxication. The dullness of my life is absolutely insupportable without it.'[12] His behaviour became more irrational as his body became more emaciated. He died on 10 July 1805 at the age of thirty-four. Jos, who had written to him in 1800, 'I did not know till now how dearly I love you',[13] was grief-stricken, but he had prepared himself for the end. 'I had long ceased to look on him with any hope', he wrote, 'and I may be said to have seen him die for two years.'[14]

Because Tom, in failing health, was at Eastbury House, an estate adjoining that of Gunville Hall, Jos's home since August 1799, Jos had delayed his necessary return to Etruria. Tom's death released him from any obligation to remain in Dorset, but the sale of the Gunville estate occupied much of his time during the following fourteen months and he did not return to anything like full-time control of the factory until the winter of 1806.

Meanwhile, Byerley struggled on with an increasingly impossible job. He was not devoid of ideas. It was at his suggestion that power, generated by a steam-engine designed by Boulton & Watt, was introduced to drive some of the factory machinery, and he was responsible for a number of new products. John, too, was full of plans, all of them costly, for the enlargement of the factory, the extension of production to include underglaze blue printing, which had not previously been attempted at Etruria, and the introduction of a whole range of patterns for which expensive engravings must be commissioned. Meanwhile, the lease of the Greek Street premises had run out and more spacious London showrooms in York Street had been acquired and redecorated at great cost.[15]

In spite of Byerley's limitations, and the magnitude of his task; in spite of the neglect of the Wedgwood brothers and a serious decline in the standards of production; and in spite of generally unfavourable trade conditions in part of Europe, sales and orders continued to be buoyant and the business made profits.[16] In 1810, the year in which Byerley died, sales reached a total of £43,474, a figure that does not appear to have been bettered for nearly a century.[17] The foundations of the firm were so secure that even a lengthy period of neglect by the owners could not undermine them. Nevertheless, the two brothers decided that they must take a more active part in the direction of the firm and, by the end of 1806, John was spending more time at Etruria and Jos had sold his estates and returned to Staffordshire to take control of the business. The faithful and uncomplaining Byerley was relieved of all responsibility for the factory and installed with his family in London.

The most serious danger, to the family as much as to the firm, was the mismanagement of the partners' finances. John was irresponsibly and incurably extravagant, drawing far more than his share from the partnership. Jos admitted that he had 'a very heavy load of debt . . . incurred in making purchases quite disproportionate to my means'.[18] He had been appointed Sheriff of Dorset in 1803, a costly sinecure, and had enjoyed all the pleasures and the heavy expenses of assuming his new social status. Among other ruinous indulgences, he had planted 65,000 trees, many of them types rarely seen in England, on his estate.[19] Both brothers were in debt to the firm as well as to their brother-in-law, Robert Darwin.

No one was better aware of failings of the business than Tom Byerley and, because he was the partner most intimately concerned with the partnership accounts, he was the best informed of the potential threat to the firm's survival posed by the prodigality of the two senior brothers. His own private finances were, however, in no better shape. He had borrowed against his partnership share to support his large family. Eight of his children were living at home, his wife was not strong, and his two eldest sons were the cause of frequent anxiety on account of their repeated, but unspecified, indiscretions. The full horror of his own financial situation, and of the firm's accounts, was revealed when he died. His own partnership account showed a deficit of more than £2000. John's stood at the shocking figure of £11,091.[20] Worse still, the firm's bills to outstanding debtors had been allowed to accumulate to the staggering sum of £48,679, a figure nearly double the estimated value of the entire business, and the whole of it incurred during the past ten years.[21] Far from being reformed by the more active direction of the Wedgwood brothers, the firm had, under their direction, plunged towards bankruptcy.

It was saved by the ruthless application of radical reforms and the personal application of Jos to the task that he was expected to undertake when his father died in 1795. Byerley's partnership share was paid off by his debts to the firm. John, who had sunk from self-pity and lack of resolve into the lethargy of despair, was persuaded to relinquish his share of the business, and a series of family trusts was put together to enable him and his family to live decently, but dependent on others to manage his affairs. His interest in the business was not renewed by any of his seven children or their descendants. The partnership was dissolved and for the next twelve years, until he was joined in a new partnership by his eldest son, Jos ruled alone at Etruria.

Josiah's legacy to his sons had been a famous and flourishing business, one that made substantial profits and that had acquired, over a period of thirty-five years, an international reputation for innovation, high quality in design and production, and integrity. Less than twelve years after his death, the son to whom he had left control of it was writing: 'The business is now not worth carrying on, and if I could withdraw my capital from it, I would tomorrow.' It is, however, notable that the reason he gave for this attitude was not falling sales and profits but 'the Partners having drawn too much'. Byerley's loyal and untiring efforts had kept the business going. It was Jos's personal inheritance and trust, the factory itself, with its collapsing discipline and falling standards of production, that was dying of neglect. Awakened at last to his responsibilities and to the urgency of the problem, Jos reluctantly accepted the burden. 'I must,' he wrote, 'continue it, if it be only to pay the interest of the money borrowed.'[22]

It was not all gloom. John, for all his evident failings, had introduced some blue-printed patterns that are acknowledged to be among the finest ever produced in Staffordshire; there was still a strong core of craftsmen who needed little more than proper management to perform well; and, although the technique for making large pieces of jasper, including vases, had been mysteriously lost,[23] there was an enviable list of ceramic compositions and shapes to draw upon as a firm foundation for future development.

Jos was an unwilling potter but he was not incapable. Under his direction the firm survived, to be handed on to his reluctant descend-ants. All were high principled, serious minded and conscientious; none, before the twentieth century, was especially gifted or whole-hearted in his enthusiasm for the task. In 1844 the factory, Etruria Hall and the entire estate were put up for auction, but the factory failed to reach its reserve and the Wedgwoods were, once more, obliged to carry on with the business. Not until 1930, when the fifth Josiah Wedgwood was appointed managing director of the company which had been incorpor-ated in 1895, was there a worthy successor to the founder at Etruria, and he, like his great-great-great-grandfather, built a new factory. The intervening years were not without brief periods of distinction but, having lost the lead in the production of the highest quality of pottery in Europe, Wedgwood did not regain its place until some fifty years after the regular manufacture of porcelain, in the form of bone china, had been introduced at Etruria.

What was most clearly lacking among Josiah's descendants in the nineteenth century was any genuine commitment to a life in industry. It is a paradox of the British character that, since the eighteenth century, those who have owned and directed British industry have seldom been comfortable with industrialisation. Industry in Britain has never acquired the status that it has achieved in other European countries, let alone in the United States of America or Japan, and it has been the almost invariable aim of those who have been successful in it to remove themselves as soon as possible from the 'profitable smoke' to the countryside, from the 'dark satanic mills' to the pastoral vision of a 'green and pleasant land'. Josiah Wedgwood's sons were among the earliest examples of this flight from industry, the distaste for commercial activity or the industrial scene. It seems that no sooner had British invention produced the Industrial Revolution than those who inherited its greatest financial benefits were anxious to distance themselves from it. It is not an attitude for which Josiah would have felt much sympathy.

Nor is it one which would have been likely to find favour with Sally Wedgwood. She had been brought up with commerce and married to manufacturing, and she had been both accustomed and willing to take her share in whatever there was to be done. After Josiah's death she remained for some years at Etruria Hall, moving in 1802 to Parkfields, a substantial cottage at Tittensor, where, increasingly rheumatic and cantankerous, she lived out her life. She died there in April 1815, at eighty the last of her generation in the family. She left an estate of £7000, a further indication that the bulk of her fortune had been in her husband's name. A little more than two years later, her eldest child

Sukey Darwin died, probably of peritonitis.[24] She was the mother of six children, including Caroline, who married Jos's eldest son (Josiah III) and Charles, who married Jos's youngest daughter Emma.

Jos finally achieved his brother's ambition, being elected, after the passage of the Reform Bill, to one of the two parliamentary seats newly allocated to the borough of Stoke-on-Trent in 1832. His experience of the House of Commons evidently did not encourage a belief that his future lay in public life, for he neither spoke in the House nor offered himself for re-election in 1835. In 1841 he retired from the Wedgwood partnership, in which he had been joined by two of his sons, and he died two years later. Bessie, bedridden and senile, survived him by three years in a condition that was described as 'sadder than death'.[25] Her sister, Jane, had already died in 1836. John, rather to the surprise of his family, who had noticed how aged and enfeebled he had become in his late sixties, lived on for another eight years. Josiah's youngest daughters, Catherine and Sarah, remained with their mother until her death and both died unmarried: Catherine in 1823, and Sarah, the youngest and, at eighty, the most venerable, in 1856.

Of all Josiah Wedgwood's children, none inherited his energy or tenacity and none but Tom inherited more than a small fraction of his inventiveness. With few exceptions, the nineteenth-century Wedgwoods were a dullish lot, whose lethargy, hypochondria and lack of humour or inspiration tended to overshadow upright and honourable behaviour and earnest endeavour. As one of their number wrote in 1887: 'We have enough dullness in the family & plenty of virtue – a little vice would make a pleasant variety.'[26] Josiah had, nevertheless, founded a dynasty. Only one grandchild, Charles Darwin, could boast of achievements more notable than those of his grandfather, but Josiah's descendants in the twentieth century have included a number of scientists of the first rank, a great composer, Ralph Vaughan Williams OM, and Dame Cicely Veronica Wedgwood OM, the distinguished historian.

In 1769, at the beginning of their partnership, Josiah had suggested to Bentley that their days should be spent in the pursuit of *Fortune Fame & the Public Good*.[27] It was not an unworthy ambition. He made a great fortune. He achieved abiding fame: when he died, Wedgwood's pottery was known all over the world, even in China, where examples of his vases had been presented to the Emperor by Lord Macartney in 1793.[28] And it may fairly be claimed that he made a lasting contribution to public good. Wedgwood's principal legacy was far greater in its application than anything he bequeathed to his descendants. By marrying art to industry and applying the principles of formal beauty to things of everyday use, he set standards that made the appreciation, and even the ownership, of articles of fine quality and design open to all.

If Josiah Wedgwood's domination of the pottery industry were to be denied, if the great firm that he founded were to be destroyed and all his inventions and developments forgotten, his name would still be remembered for his influence on industrial design, of which he was one of the founders. It is a memorial which might have surprised him but one with which he would have been well satisfied.

NOTES AND REFERENCES

Unless otherwise specified, all manuscript references are to the Wedgwood collection of manuscripts deposited at Keele University or held at the Wedgwood Museum at Barlaston, in Staffordshire. These are designated as 'WMS' except for those already prefixed 'W/M', 'LHP' or 'E'. The prefix W/M refers to manuscript material in the Mosley collection; the prefix LHP refers to uncatalogued manuscripts in the Leith Hill Place collection; the prefixes E and L, used in the past to distinguish between the manuscripts from the Etruria and Liverpool collections, have been retained only for the Wedgwood Letters and where the box numbers alone might be insufficient for identification.

CHAPTER ONE
An Uncertain Start in Life

1. W/M 1131 n.d. Unpublished notes for a biography of Josiah Wedgwood.
2. Even this is uncertain. It follows the information given by Josiah Wedgwood IV (*Staffordshire Pottery*, London, 1947, p. 48), Dame C. V. Wedgwood (*The Last of the Radicals*, London, 1974, p. 15), and John Ward (*The Borough of Stoke-on-Trent*, London, 1843, pp. 200 and 428). Recent research among the parish records by Wedgwood's museum staff, however, has failed to discover evidence of more than eleven older brothers and sisters.
3. Mayer MSS quoted by Eliza Meteyard, *The Life of Josiah Wedgwood*, 2 vols., London, 1865–6, I, p. 193, n. 1.
4. W. A. Pitt, *A Topographical History of Staffordshire*, Newcastle-under-Lyme, 1817, p. 380.
5. A brief biography of Josiah Wedgwood was attempted by the mathematician and physicist, John Leslie, for some years tutor to the Wedgwood children and a close friend of the youngest son Tom (see pp. 336–7). Part of this has survived (MS E29–21439), but the first sixteen pages, which might have cast some light on Josiah's early life, are missing.
6. Meteyard, *op. cit.*, I, p. 218, n. 1, quotes receipts signed by Josiah's sisters, Margaret (Byerley) and Catherine (Willet), dated 1776. These appear to have been paid by Josiah acting as his brother's executor, but, although the sums are identical, there is no certain evidence that they are the unpaid legacies from their father's will. If they were indeed those legacies, the reason for their remaining unpaid for so long is not clear, but it is notable that it was only the surviving daughters that were so treated.

7. There is no documentary evidence for this story, which depends on the recollections of Blunt's grandson, a retail chemist in Shrewsbury, who was known to Miss Meteyard (*op. cit.*, I, p. 208, n. 1).

8. Lorna Weatherill, *The Pottery Trade and North Staffordshire 1660–1760*, Manchester, 1971, pp. 96–7. Mrs Weatherill points out, however, that the tax on registration evidently caused many apprenticeships to go unrecorded.

9. Meteyard, *op. cit.*, I, p. 220.

10. Quoted by Josiah C. Wedgwood and Joshua G. E. Wedgwood, *Wedgwood Pedigrees*, Kendal, 1925, p. 100, n. 2.

11. See Ward, *op. cit.*, pp. 229–30, 356 and 530; Simeon Shaw, *History of the Staffordshire Potteries*, Hanley, 1829, p. 136.

12. E25–18755 7 May 1777.

13. Meteyard, *op. cit.*, I, p. 233. This imaginative account has been followed, more or less, by almost all later authors.

CHAPTER TWO

The Search for White Gold

1. Macaulay, T. B. (Lord), *History of England* (4 vols., 1848–55), Folio Society edition, 5 vols., 1985, III, p. 43.

2. Much of the collection wrongly described as Chinese is identifiable from objects still preserved at Burghley House.

3. WMS 39–28408.

4. See Otto Walcha, *Meissen Porcelain*, London, 1973, p. 17, n. 10.

5. Werkarchiv of the VEB Staatliche Porzellan-Manufaktur, Meissen, IA f2/169. Quoted by Walcha, *op. cit.*, p. 441, n. 12.

6. Quoted by T. Compton, *William Cookworthy*, London, 1895, pp. 40–1.

7. J. H. Plumb, *In the Light of History*, London, 1972, p. 57.

8. For information about this little-known factory see Paul Bemrose, 'The Pomona Potworks, Newcastle, Staffs.', in English Ceramic Circle *Transactions*, vol. 9, pt. I, 1973, pp. 1–18. In 1970 Mr Bemrose excavated the base of a porcelain bowl dated '25th July 1746' from this site.

9. John Dwight's actions against six Staffordshire potters (including Josiah Wedgwood's kinsmen, the brothers Aaron, Richard and Thomas Wedgwood) for infringement of his patent were heard between 1694 and 1697.

CHAPTER THREE

Wedgwood with Whieldon

1. The discovery of the Fenton Vivian site was made by Arnold Mountford and from the subsequent excavation of it comes most of our knowledge, fragmentary as it is, of Thomas Whieldon's work (see Arnold Mountford, 'Thomas Whieldon's Manufactory at Fenton Vivian', in English Ceramic

Circle *Transactions*, vol. 8, pt. 2, 1972, pp. 164–82. The most recent research on this subject is published by Mrs P. Halfpenny, Keeper of Ceramics at the City Museum and Art Gallery, Stoke-on-Trent, 1992.

2.   WMS 29–19121. Josiah Wedgwood's *Experiment Book* was written, after 1781, by Alexander Chisholm, as a fair copy of the original. The introduction was probably added at the same time, but a partial draft of it in Josiah's hand, possibly contemporary with the original account of the experiments, exists in an earlier record.

3.   Preserved in the City Museum and Art Gallery, Stoke-on-Trent. Quoted by Mountford, *op. cit.*, pp. 172–3.

4.   Simeon Shaw, *History of the Staffordshire Potteries*, Hanley, 1829, p. 182.

5.   *Ibid.*, pp. 153–4; manuscript note signed by Enoch Wood and attached to a portrait of his father, Aaron Wood, painted by W. Caddick (see F. Falkner, *The Wood Family of Burslem*, London, 1912, p. 21).

6.   The first record of Spode's hiring by Whieldon is dated 9 April 1749 but, as Leonard Whiter has pointed out (*Spode*, London, 1970, pp. 3–4) the terms of his employment are not precise and it is almost certain that he started work with Whieldon, or with someone else, at least two years earlier. By 1754, when the Whieldon–Wedgwood partnership began, Spode had graduated to journeyman.

7.   For an authoritative account of William Greatbatch and his work see D. Barker, *William Greatbatch. A Staffordshire Potter*, London, 1990.

8.   See Mountford, *op. cit.*, pp. 171–2.

9.   Plot, R., *The Natural History of Staffordshire*, Oxford, 1686, p. 124.

10.   John Wedgwood's Account Book, City Museum and Art Gallery, Stoke-on-Trent, uncatalogued; J. Mallet, 'John Baddeley of Shelton', English Ceramic Circle *Transactions*, 1966, vol. 6, pp. 126–7.

11.   *Gentleman's Magazine*, 1752, vol. XXII, p. 553.

12.   Arthur Young, *Tour of the North of England*, 4 vols., London, 1770, III, p. 433.

13.   Shaw, *op. cit.*, p. 124.

14.   Young, *op. cit.*, IV, p. 581.

15.   Meteyard, *op. cit.*, I, pp. 246–7.

16.   *Ibid.*

17.   Barbara and Hensleigh Wedgwood, *The Wedgwood Circle*, London, 1980, p. 11.

18.   Anna Seward, *Memoirs of the Life of Dr Darwin*, London, 1804, pp. 8–9.

19.   British Museum Add. MSS. 6815.

20.   Warde MSS., Brigadier-General James Wolfe to Mrs Henrietta Wolfe, 11 August 1758; quoted by Robin Reilly, *The Rest to Fortune. The Life of Major-General James Wolfe*, London, 1960, pp. 196–7.

21.   Mrs H. Paget Toynbee, *The Letters of Horace Walpole*, 16 vols., Oxford, 1903, vol. 4, p. 314, H. Walpole to George Montagu, 21 October 1759.

CHAPTER FOUR
Useful Partners

1. WMS 27–19281 30 December 1758, 'Memorandum of an agreement between Josiah Wedgwood . . . and Thos Wedgwood Journeyman'.
2. John Wedgwood's Account Book, City Museum and Art Gallery, Stoke-on-Trent, p. 30.
3. *Ibid.*
4. *Ibid.*
5. Simeon Shaw, *History of the Staffordshire Potteries*, Hanley, 1829, pp. 182–3.
6. Recollections of 'Mr Aaron Wedgwood of Burslem', quoted by Eliza Meteyard, *The Life of Josiah Wedgwood*, 2 vols., London, 1865–6, I, p. 251.
7. WMS 29–19121, Josiah Wedgwood's Experiment Book, 10 March 1760, Experiment 93; Experiment 100, n.d.
8. See Robin Reilly, *Wedgwood*, 2 vols., London, 1989, I, pp. 44–6 and 179.
9. W/M 1431 11 October 1763, J. Sadler to Wedgwood.
10. E25–18129 25 September 1766.
11. WMS 55–31115 11 March 1763, D. Rhodes to Wedgwood; quoted by Donald C. Towner, *The Leeds Pottery*, London, 1963, p. 164.
12. This event is reported by Meteyard, *op. cit.*, I, p. 300, as an accident on the road, but no evidence has been found to support this story, which lacks detail or any source.
13. Turner delivered a number of lectures to the Academy on the subjects of anatomy and the theory of forms. See Historic Society of Leicestershire and Cheshire, *Transactions*, V, p. 140; VI, pp. 71–2.
14. E25–18048 15 May 1762.
15. E25–18651 6 February 1776, Wedgwood to Bentley: 'I am now reviewing your good letters of the 18th, 20th, 24th, 28th and 31st past.'
16. E25–18264 1 October 1769, Wedgwood to Bentley.
17. The collection was restored to Wedgwood in 1887, when Mayer's vast accumulation of Wedgwood manuscript material was sold by Sotheby, Wilkinson & Hodge in the Strand. It was bought by Godfrey Wedgwood for £20 on behalf of the firm and is now housed at Keele University. See Reilly, *op. cit.*, II, p. 151.
18. E25–18049 26 October 1762.
19. E25–18256 [September 1769].
20. E25–18049 26 October 1762.
21. *Ibid.*
22. E25–18053 12 April 1763.
23. Josiah C. Wedgwood and Joshua G. E. Wedgwood, *Wedgwood Pedigrees*, Kendal, 1925, p. 174.
24. WMS 32–24293.
25. E25–18055 9 January 1764.
26. Llewellyn Jewitt, *The Wedgwoods*, London, 1865, p. 157, and *The Ceramic Art of Great Britain*, 2nd rev. edn., London, 1883, p. 512.

27. E25–18056 23 January 1764.
28. Julia Wedgwood, *The Personal Life of Josiah Wedgwood*, London, 1915, p. 61.
29. E25–18057 28 May 1764.
30. J. C. Wedgwood and J. G. E. Wedgwood, *op. cit.*, p. 174, n. 3.
31. Jewitt, *op. cit.*, p. 157.
32. E25–18070 6 March 1765.
33. E25–18183 n.d. [January?] 1768 and see Reilly, *op. cit.*, II, p. 760, n. 62.
34. E25–18059 1 February 1765.
35. E25–18845 19 August 1778.
36. E25–18230 15 February 1769.
37. E25–18054 16 June 1763, to Bentley.
38. E25–18057 28 May 1764.
39. E25–18070 6 March 1765.
40. E25–18072 3 April 1765.
41. E25–18139 2 March 1767.
42. E25–18199 June 1768.
43. E25–18204 6 July 1768.
44. E25–18529 April 1774, to T. Byerley; E25–18559 19 September 1774, to Bentley; E25–18603 postmarked 23 June [1775], to Bentley.
45. E25–18603 postmarked 23 June 1775, to Bentley.
46. *Kent's Directory*, London, 1763 (but not in 1766 edn.); *Baldwin's Directory*, London, 1765.
47. See E25–18059 1 February 1765.
48. E25–18071 11 March 1765, to John Wedgwood.
49. E25–18078 29 May [1765]. As this letter indicates, the surviving correspondence is far from complete.
50. E25–18072 3 April 1765.
51. E25–18078 November 1764–May 1765, 'Mr Josiah Wedgwood his account currt with Mr Jno Wedgwood'; E25–18087 2 August 1765; E25–18080 6 July 1765; E25–18083 n.d. [July 1765]. All to John Wedgwood.
52. E25–18073 postmarked 17 June [1765].
53. *Ibid.*
54. E26–18898 19 June 1779.
55. Aris's *Birmingham Gazette*, 9 June 1766.
56. E25–18167 n.d. [about 15 September] 1767.
57. E25–18084 n.d. [July 1765], to Sir William Meredith, enclosed with a letter to John Wedgwood.
58. E25–18087 2 August 1765, to John Wedgwood.
59. E25–18089 7 August 1765, to John Wedgwood.
60. E25–18095 15 October 1765; E25–18096 2 November 1765.
61. E25–18127 15 September 1766; E25–18128 19 September 1766. For much of the information about Wedgwood's London showrooms in this and later chapters, I am indebted to Una des Fontaines, 'Wedgwood's London Showrooms', in Wedgwood Society *Proceedings*, no. 8, 1970, pp. 193–223.
62. E25–18080 6 July 1765, to John Wedgwood.

63.   E15–18322 29 August 1770; E25–18324 3 September 1770.

CHAPTER FIVE
Commercial Communications

1.   E25–18070 6 March 1765, to John Wedgwood.
2.   City Museum and Art Gallery, Stoke-on-Trent: John Wedgwood's Account Book, p. 30.
3.   E25–18123 18 July 1766.
4.   William Hodgson, Wedgwood's agent for this purchase; probably a member of the firm Ashton, Hodgson & Co., Wedgwood's bankers from 1764, (E25–18117 n.d. [4 June?] 1766).
5.   E25–18160 6 July 1767.
6.   Journal of the House of Commons, 16 February 1763.
7.   Ibid.
8.   Josiah Wedgwood's Commonplace Book, WMS 39–28408.
9.   E25–18059 1 February 1765.
10.   E25–18070 6 March 1765.
11.   24 George II, c. 25 (1751).
12.   H.Homer, An Inquiry into the Means of Preserving and Improving the Public Highroads of the Kingdom, Oxford, 1767, p. 8.
13.   Andrew Yarranton, England's Improvement by Sea and Land . . . , London, 1677, pp. 7, 181 and 191.
14.   E25–18071 11 March 1765.
15.   LHP 3 April 1765, Wedgwood to E. Darwin.
16.   Ibid.
17.   E25–18072 3 April 1765, to John Wedgwood.
18.   LHP 5 June 1765, Wedgwood to E. Darwin.
19.   E25–18091 26 September 1765.
20.   E25–18092 27 September 1765.
21.   LHP n.d. [October 1765], E. Darwin to Bentley.
22.   LHP 22 October 1765, Bentley to E. Darwin.
23.   E25–18096 2 November 1765.
24.   E25–18093 7 October 1765.
25.   LHP 11 October 1765, Bentley to E. Darwin.
26.   LHP 22 October 1765, Bentley to E. Darwin.
27.   Ibid.
28.   LHP 9 November 1765, Bentley to E. Darwin.
29.   E25–18095 15 October 1765.
30.   E25–18096 2 November 1765.
31.   E25–18099 18 November 1765.
32.   E25–18102 n.d. [25 November or 2 December 1765].
33.   Ibid.; E25–18105 12 December 1765.
34.   E25–18102 n.d. [25 November or 2 December 1765].

35. E25–18106 [14?] December 1765.

36. E25–18107 23 November 1765.

37. E25–18058 dated 2 January 1765 in error for 1766 and reprinted out of order in K. E. Farrer (ed.), *Letters of Josiah Wedgwood*, 3 vols., Manchester, 1903–6, I, pp. 19–24.

38. E25–18113 11 January 1766, to John Tarleton.

39. E25–18117 dated 4 May 1766 in error for 4 June 1766 to John Wedgwood, and enclosure, 'At a general assembly of the proprietors of the Navigation from the Trent to the Mersey. 3rd June 1766'.

40. Quoted by Roy Porter, *English Society in the Eighteenth Century*, London, 1982, p. 224.

41. E25–18139 2 March 1767.

42. E25–18141 2 April 1767; E25–18166 8 September 1767.

43. E25–18408 26 September 1772.

44. E25–18409 28 September 1772.

45. Adam Smith, *An Inquiry into the Nature and the Causes of the Wealth of Nations*, 4 vols., London, 1776, I, ch. III.

46. Those of Bentley's letters that have survived do not show any inclination towards extreme brevity.

47. W/M 16 12 February 1786, to R. L. Edgeworth.

48. E25–18058 dated 2 January 1765 in error for 1766.

49. E43–28632 n.d. [? February 1768].

50. E25–18116 26 May 1766; E25–18122 endorsed by Bentley 'Recd July 4 1766'.

51. E25–18049 26 October 1762.

52. James Thomson, *The Seasons (Autumn)*, London, 1730.

53. Nicholas Goodison states that the two men met for the first time in May 1767 (*Ormolu: The Work of Matthew Boulton*, London, 1974, p. 7), but Boulton's election to the Committee of Proprietors on 3 June 1766 strongly suggests earlier meetings in 1765–6, and the introduction is likely to have been made by Samuel Garbett or Erasmus Darwin. Goodison's date is based on the first mention of Boulton in Wedgwood's letters to Bentley (E25–18147 23 May 1767) but nothing in this letter indicates that it describes their first encounter. Goodison's admirable study is the standard work on Boulton's Soho factory and production and I have drawn gratefully on his research.

54. Matthew Boulton to J. H. Ebbinghaus, 18 November 1767 and 2 March 1768, quoted by Goodison, *op. cit.*, p. 14.

55. *Ibid.*, p. 10.

56. William Hutton, *History of Birmingham*, Birmingham, 1782, p. 63.

57. E25–18147 23 May 1767.

CHAPTER SIX
The New Etruria

1. E25–18120 26 June 1766.
2. E25–18132 8 November 1766. This letter appears in K. E. Farrer (ed.), *Letters of Josiah Wedgwood*, 3 vols., Manchester, 1903–6, I, 1762–70, out of sequence and postdated by one year. See Robin Reilly, *Wedgwood*, 2 vols., London, 1989, I, p. 701, n. 78.
3. *Ibid.*
4. *Ibid.*
5. *Ibid.*
6. *Ibid.*
7. E25–18232 [12 or 16] February 1769.
8. E25–18080 6 July 1765.
9. E25–18186 n.d. [February 1767].
10. W/M 1826 'Warrington Novr 15 1767', Bentley's memorandum.
11. E25–18127 15 September 1766.
12. E25–18132 8 November 1766 (see n. 2 above).
13. E25–18160 6 July 1767; E25–18161 5 August 1767.
14. E25–18176 [?11 December] 1767.
15. *Ibid.*
16. E25–18177 17 December 1767.
17. E25–18181 24 December 1767.
18. E25–18182 31 December 1767.
19. E25–18184 16 January 1768.
20. E25–18186 n.d. [?29 January] 1768.
21. E25–18188 n.d. [February 1768].
22. E25–18191 3 March 1768 and cf. WMS 43–28632 n.d. [February 1768].
23. *Ibid.*
24. E25–19198 10 April 1768.
25. WMS 96–17760 30 April 1768.
26. The invoice is dated 28 May. Josiah himself mistakenly referred to 31 May as 'St Amputation Day' (E25–18305 31 May 1770).
27. No evidence has been found to substantiate the graphic accounts of the amputation given by Eliza Meteyard, *The Life of Josiah Wedgwood*, 2 vols., London, 1865–6, II, pp. 40–1, largely repeated by later authors, including Barbara and Hensleigh Wedgwood, *The Wedgwood Circle*, London, 1980, pp. 37–8.
28. Peter Swift to William Cox, 4 June 1768, quoted by Meteyard, *op. cit.*, II, p. 41.
29. See WMS 96–17666 13 June 1768, written by Bentley except for the last few lines.
30. E25–18199 n.d. [about 17 June 1768].
31. *Ibid.*; E25–18200 20 June 1768; E25–18204 6 July 1768.
32. E25–18204 6 July 1768.

33. E25–18201 25 June 1768; E25–18210 15 September 1768; and see E25–18191 3 March 1768.
34. E25–18213 6 November 1768.
35. E25–18215 21 November 1768.
36. WMS 96–17661 4 May 1768.
37. E25–18269 19 November 1769.
38. Erasmus Darwin to Peter Templeman, 4 February 1769, quoted by Desmond King-Hele, *Doctor of Revolution*, 1977, p. 80.
39. E25–18193 15 March 1768.
40. E25–18191 3 March 1768.
41. Darwin Correspondence, quoted by Meteyard, *op. cit.*, II, p. 31.
42. E25–18951 30 July 1779.
43. E25–18453 3 April 1773.
44. For a full account of these machines see John Thomas, *The Rise of the Staffordshire Potteries*, Bath, 1971, pp. 46–50.
45. E25–18772 19 July 1777.
46. For examples of early turned teapots, see Reilly, *op. cit.*, I, Plates 230, 231 and 234.
47. See *ibid.*, p. 691.
48. E25–18057 28 May 1764.
49. E25–18061 11 February 1765, Wedgwood to T. Byerley; E25–18080 6 July 1765, Wedgwood to John Wedgwood.
50. E25–18147 23 May 1767; E25–18170 24 October 1767; E25–18187 22 February 1768; E25–18269 19 November 1769.
51. E25–18237 9 April 1769.
52. E25–18269 19 November 1769.
53. E25–18212 31 October 1768.

CHAPTER SEVEN
Vase-maker General

1. Wedgwood to William Constable of Burton Constable, 13 October 1783. Quoted by George Savage and Ann Finer (eds.), *The Selected Letters of Josiah Wedgwood*, London, 1965, pp. 271–3.
2. WMS 22149–21–30.
3. Wedgwood to Constable, 13 October 1783 (see n. 1).
4. See Robin Reilly, *Wedgwood*, 2 vols., London, 1989, I, p. 249.
5. E25–18252 13 September 1769.
6. E25–18124 August 1766 (erroneously) printed in K. E. Farrer (ed.), *Letters of Josiah Wedgwood*, 3 vols., Manchester, 1903–6, as part of letter of 18 July.
7. E25–18198 April 1768.
8. E25–18160 6 July 1767.
9. Wedgwood & Bentley Ornamental Ware Catalogue, 1773.
10. E25–18167 [about 15] September 1767.

11. E25–18208 August 1768.
12. WMS 96–17668 14 September 1768, Wedgwood to W. Cox.
13. WMS 96–17667 31 August 1768, Wedgwood to W. Cox.
14. E25–18196 24 March 1768. In 'Josiah Wedgwood and Thomas Bentley: An Inventor–Entrepreneur Partnership in the Industrial Revolution', *Transactions of the Royal Historical Society*, Fifth Series, XIV, p. 20, Neil McKendrick states that it was Bentley who first made this contact, but there is no evidence to support this.
15. WMS 96–17665 13 July 1768, Wedgwood to W. Cox.
16. WMS 53–31201 'Books belonging to W & B the 10th of Aug 1770'.
17. Wedgwood & Bentley Catalogue, 1779, Class XIX, 'Vases, Ewers, &c., Ornamented with Encaustic Paintings'.
18. WMS 96–17667 21 August 1768.
19. E25–18266 9 October 1769.
20. E25–18238 25 October 1770.
21. LHP 13 June 1771; E25–18346 n.d. [? 16 June 1771].
22. E25–18261 27 September 1769.
23. E25–18334 24 December 1770. No example of an encaustic-painted basaltes tea-urn has survived and it is uncertain that such a piece was ever made.
24. WMS 29–19121, Josiah Wedgwood's Experiment Book.
25. P. J. Wendler, Venice to Matthew Boulton 4 July 1767, quoted by Nicholas Goodison, *Ormolu: The Work of Matthew Boulton*, London, 1974, p. 27.
26. E25–18193 15 March 1768.
27. *Ibid.*
28. Matthew Boulton's Notebook, 1768–75, p. 1, quoted by Goodison, *op. cit.*, p. 30.
29. E25–18215 21 November 1768.
30. M. Boulton to Wedgwood, 20 December 1768, quoted by Goodison, *op. cit.*, p. 28.
31. M. Boulton to Wedgwood, 17 January 1769, quoted by Goodison, *op. cit.*, p. 28.
32. E25–18261 postmarked 27 September 1769.
33. *Ibid.*
34. *Ibid.*
35. See Reilly, *op. cit.*, I, Chapters 7 and 8. Wedgwood's terracotta body was unidentified for more than 100 years and was only rediscovered in 1985. Publication of its description has made necessary the recataloguing of public and private collections.
36. E25–18150 6 June 1767; LHP n.d. [late November–early December 1768], Sarah Wedgwood to Bentley.
37. E25–18215 21 November 1768.
38. For example, E25–18328 25 October 1770, Lord March's Sèvres vases; E25–18322 29 August 1770, Lord Bessborough's porphyry vase.
39. E25–19216 [January] 1769; E25–18269 19 November 1769; E25–18314 2 August 1770.

40. E25–18392 23 August 1772.
41. Tassie's invoice dated 11 November 1769.
42. R. E. Raspe, *Catalogue raisonné d'une collection générale de pierres gravées antique et modernes*, London, 1791.
43. E25–18500 postmarked 22 November 1773.
44. E25–18502 27 November 1773.
45. E25–18504 2 December 1773.
46. E25–18263 30 September 1769.
47. E25–18755 7 May 1777.
48. E25–18212 31 October 1768; WMS 1–56 21 January 1769.
49. E25–18582 8 January 1775.
50. E25–18269 19 November 1769; E25–18232 [11 or 16 February] 1769; E25–18256 16 September 1769.
51. E25–18302 23 May 1770.
52. Frederick Norden, *Travels in Egypt and Nubia*, London, 1743, II, p. xxiii.
53. British Architectural Library.
54. LHP 16 February 1771.
55. LHP 12 February 1771.
56. This bust of George II was for many years identified as a portrait of the 1st Duke of Marlborough.
57. It has been authoritatively stated that Wedgwood's quality was 'easily reproduced' (Neil McKendrick, John Brewer and J. H. Plumb, *The Birth of a Consumer Society: The Commercialization of Eighteenth-century England*, London, 1982, p. 104). If this was so, it is difficult to understand why so few potters of the period came anywhere near reproducing it, either in Britain or the rest of Europe. Quality of form, design and production are never easy to create or to reproduce and Wedgwood's methods of production, unlike those of most of his contemporaries, were not regulated by a requirement to keep prices, and therefore costs, competitively low.

CHAPTER EIGHT
Elegance and Truth

1. E25–17852 10 August 1769.
2. E25–18141 31 May 1767.
3. *Ibid.*
4. *Ibid.*
5. E25–18152 14 June 1767.
6. E25–18154 n.d. [June 1767].
7. E25–18152 14 June 1767.
8. E25–18153 dated 14 June (in error for 13 June) 1767.
9. E25–18157 4 July 1767, Wedgwood to R. Griffiths.
10. E25–18155 27 June 1767; E25–18159 n.d. [early July 1767].

11.   E25–18160 6 July 1767.

12.   E25–18196 n.d. postmarked 24 March 1768 and also written on that date.

13.   E25–18197 31 March 1768.

14.   96–17660 30 April 1768, Wedgwood to W. Cox.

15.   96–17666 13 June 1768, Wedgwood to W. Cox.

16.   E25–18200 20 June 1768.

17.   E25–18375 2 June 1772 and see Una des Fontaines, 'Wedgwood's London Showrooms', Wedgwood Society *Proceedings*, no. 8, 1970, p. 198.

18.   E25–18246 17 July 1769.

19.   See E25–18215 21 November 1768; E25–18216 n.d. [late November 1768]; LHP postmarked 29 November 1768.

20.   E25–18251 9 September 1769.

21.   See, for example, E25–18285 22 January 1770; LHP 13 March 1771; 96–17693, D. Rhodes expenses 10–12 May 1775; E25–18606 6 July 1775.

22.   See Robin Reilly, *Wedgwood*, 2 vols., London, 1989, I, pp. 436–8.

23.   E25–18279 30 December 1769.

24.   *Ibid.*

25.   E25–18328 25 October 1770.

26.   E25–18245 25 June 1769.

27.   E25–18301 19 May 1770.

28.   E25–18273 6 December 1769.

29.   E25–18302 23 May 1771.

30.   E25–18304 18 May 1770.

31.   E25–18301 19–21 May 1770.

32.   E25–18281 3 January 1770.

33.   The 'Queen's shape' is generally believed to have been modelled especially for Queen Charlotte in 1765 but there is some evidence that it may have existed before that date. See Reilly, *op. cit.*, I, p. 202.

34.   E25–18258 20 September 1769.

35.   E25–18250 4 September 1769; W/M 1442 19 March 1771, Jane, Lady Cathcart from St Petersburg to Wedgwood; E25–18487 14 August 1773.

36.   W/M 1445 28 January [O.S] /8 February [N.S.] 1770, Lady Cathcart to Wedgwood.

37.   E25–18297 29 April 1770.

38.   E25–18300 19 May 1770; E25–18310 December 1770.

39.   E25–18302 23 May 1770.

40.   *Ibid.*

41.   *Ibid.*

42.   E25–18297 29 April 1770.

43.   E25–18298 4 May 1770.

44.   E25–18295 23 April 1770.

45.   E25–18311 19 June 1770; and see Reilly, *op. cit.*, I, p. 107.

CHAPTER NINE
Crises of Management

1. E25–18309 13 June 1770.
2. E25–18322 29 August 1770.
3. E25–18324 3 September 1770.
4. *Ibid.*
5. *Ibid.*
6. *Ibid.*
7. *Ibid.*
8. *Ibid.*
9. W/M 1713 'Messrs Wedgwood & Bentley Goods in Co' (10 August 1769 to 3 December 1775).
10. E25–18324 3 September 1770; Bentley's comment is added in his own hand at the foot of the letter. See Robin Reilly, *Wedgwood*, 2 vols., London, 1989, I, pp. 427 and 715, n. 30.
11. E25–18280 1 January 1770; E25–18277 postmarked 29 December 1769.
12. *Ibid.*
13. E25–18282 6 January 1770; E25–18284 15 January 1770; E25–18286 24 January 1770.
14. E25–18287 3 February 1770.
15. E25–18289 10 February 1770.
16. LHP 5 March 1770.
17. E25–18324 3 September 1770.
18. E25–18269 19 November 1769; E25–18281 2 June 1770; E25–18271 1 December 1769.
19. E25–18301 19 May 1770; E25–18302 23 May 1770.
20. LHP 16 February 1771.
21. E25–18384 5 August 1772; E25–183992 23 August 1772.
22. E25–18384 5 August 1772; W/M 1780 n.d. [August 1772].
23. LHP 10 April 1771.
24. E25–18392 23 August 1772.
25. E25–18396 1 September 1772.
26. E25–18397 dated 1 September 1772 but probably written 2 September 1772.
27. E25–18412 12 October 1772.
28. E25–18409 28 September 1772; E25–18411 4 October 1772.
29. LHP 13 August 1780.
30. E25–18407 20 September 1772.
31. E25–18397 dated 1 September 1772 but probably written 2 September 1772.
32. *Ibid.*
33. E25–18334 24 December 1770.
34. See Nicholas Goodison, *Ormolu: The Work of Matthew Boulton*, London 1974, pp. 37–40 and 87–95 for a full account of Boulton's auction sales in London and his proposals for London showrooms.
35. E25–18365 11 April 1772.

36. *Ibid.*; E25–18371 3 May 1772; E25–18394 30 August 1772; E25–18421 23 November 1772.
37. Quoted by Geoffrey Beard, *The Work of Robert Adam*, Edinburgh, 1978, p. 15.
38. E25–18426 3 December 1772; E25–18427 7 December 1772; E25–18452 29 March 1773; E25–18518 25 February 1774. See also Una des Fontaines, 'Wedgwood's London Showrooms', Wedgwood Society *Proceedings*, no. 8, 1970, pp. 193–207.
39. E25–18421 23 November 1773.
40. W/M 1724 16 June 1774; WMS 59–10517 17 April 1779. See also Una des Fontaines, 'Portland House, Wedgwood's London Showrooms (1774–95)', Wedgwood Society *Proceedings*, no. 11, 1982, pp. 136–47.

CHAPTER TEN
Landscapes with Frogs

1. Horace Walpole to Sir Horace Mann, 11 February 1779. Mrs Paget Toynbee (ed.), *Letters of Horace Walpole*, 16 vols., Oxford, 1905, vol. 10, p. 377.
2. Lord Cathcart to Matthew Boulton, 21 February 1772, quoted by Nicholas Goodison, *Ormolu: The Work of Matthew Boulton*, London, 1974, p. 97.
3 *Ibid.*, p. 48.
4 E25–18450 postmarked 23 March 1773.
5. E25–18314 2 August 1770; E25–18321 28 August 1770.
6. E25–18450 postmarked 23 March 1773.
7. *Ibid.*
8. WMS 32–24197 [n.d.] 1774. This shows the cost of the Table service as £36. 6s. and that of the Dessert service as £15. 2s. 4d.
9. In spite of Josiah's recent exercise in cost accounting, no allowance was made for this in the accounts of the 'Frog' service.
10. E25–18451 [27 March 1773]
11. *Ibid.*
12. E25–18484 30 July 1773.
13. Buck's *Antiquities* was not published until 1774. In order to have use of this, Bentley must have had access to some of the plates, or to proofs from them, before publication.
14. The frog emblem does not, however, appear on the duplicate pieces made for Wedgwood, nor on the polychrome-enamelled examples (see Robin Reilly, *Wedgwood*, 2 vols., London, 1989, I, p. 282 and Plates 337 and C53.
15. WMS 1–65/70, bill for 7 February to 2 April 1774.
16. E25–18500 22 November 1773; E25–18508 12 December 1773. See Alison Kelly, 'Wedgwood Catherine Services', *Burlington Magazine*, August 1980, p. 557.
17. The identity of 'young Stringer' is uncertain and it is possible that he was in fact the Daniel Stringer, who is listed, with Samuel Stringer of Knuts-

ford ('lately dead'), in the Catalogue of the Exhibition of the Society for Promoting Painting and Design in Liverpool, September 1784.

18. E25–18297 29 April 1770.
19. E25–18486 12 August 1773.
20. E25–18510 25 December 1773. See also E25–18494 28 October 1773; E25–18496 6 November 1773; E25–18503 1 December 1773. The Etruria Hall sketch was done at the end of October or the beginning of November; see E25–18495 4 November 1773.
21. Bentley's Introduction to the *Description of Views*, quoted by G. C. Williamson, *The Imperial Russian Dinner Service*, London, 1909, p. 61.
22. E25–18498 14 November 1773.
23. E25–18455 9 April 1773.
24. WMS 32–24190, Wage sheets prepared by B. Mather.
25. E25–18533 n.d. [late May 1774]; Josiah Wedgwood to Richard Wedgwood, 31 May 1774, quoted by George Savage and Ann Finer (eds.), *The Selected Letters of Josiah Wedgwood*, London, 1965, p. 160.
26. Mary Granville (Mrs Delany), *Autobiography and Correspondence*, London, 2 vols., 1862, I, p.593.
27. E25–18547 15–16 July 1774.
28. Two conflicting and incomplete accounts have survived. See Williamson, *op. cit*, pp. 47–9. The apparently definitive figure for the price was published by L. N. Voronizhina in *The Service with the Green Frog*, Leningrad, 1962.
29. E25–18546 8 July 1774.
30. *Diaries and Correspondence of Sir James Harris, First Earl of Malmesbury*, ed. 3rd Earl of Malmesbury, 4 vols., London, 1884, I, pp. 230–1.

CHAPTER ELEVEN
Management and Security

1. E25–18367 18 April 1772. The last rent for the Red Workhouses was paid in arrears in April 1772. This date is usually given as 1773 (for example, Eliza Meteyard, *The Life of Josiah Wedgwood*, 2 vols., London 1865–6, I, p. 329), but it is unlikely that the move, begun in April 1772, would have taken so long to complete, and Wedgwood's letter of 6 February 1773 (E25–18443) may be taken to indicate that 'many months' had passed since the departure from Burslem.
2. E25–18089 7 August 1765, Josiah Wedgwood to John Wedgwood.
3. E25–18269 19 November 1769.
4. E25–18248 29 July 1769.
5. E25–18788 postmarked 25 October 1777; E25–18269 19 November 1769.
6. E25–18356 7 March 1772.
7. E25–18407 19 September 1772.
8. E25–18271 1 December 1769.

9. WMS 39–28409, Josiah Wedgwood's Commonplace Book.

10. E25–18265 9 September 1769.

11. E25–18788 postmarked 25 October 1777.

12. E25–18321 28 August 1770; LHP 5 December 1771; E25–18785 4 October 1777; E25–18273 6 December 1769.

13. E25–18269 19 November 1769.

14. E25–18443 6 February 1773.

15. E25–18745 8 April 1777.

16. LHP 25 May 1789 and 29 May 1789, Josiah II to Josiah I.

17. E25–18726 15 December 1776.

18. E25–18287 3 February 1770; Wedgwood to Bentley, 6 December 1767, quoted by John Thomas, *The Rise of the Staffordshire Potteries*, Somerset, 1971, pp. 175–6 (original MS letter now missing); E25–18321 28 August 1770; E25–18381 postmarked 22 July 1772; E25–18414 27 October 1772.

19. E25–18782 6 October 1777.

20. Godfrey Wedgwood, Private Letter Book, 1897–1906, letter to Etruria Workpeople, 17 October 1890; E25–18489 [July] 1773; E25–18453 3 April 1773; E25–18913 2 August 1779.

21. WMS 39–28409 Josiah Wedgwood's Commonplace Book.

22. *Ibid.*

23. E26–19114 'Josiah Wedgwood's Experiments, Potters Instructions &c.', 1780.

24. WMS 5–4045 'Regulations and rules made for this manufactory more than 30 years back. Mfy. 1810', MS by R. Rhead.

25. *Ibid.*

26. See Peter Mathias, *The First Industrial Nation: An Economic History of Britain 1700–1914*, 2nd edn, London, 1983, p. 138; T. S. Ashton, *An Economic History of England: The 18th Century*, London, 1955, pp. 212–14.

27. E26–19114 and see E25–18271 1 December 1769.

28. *Ibid.*

29. E25–18261 postmarked 27 September 1769.

30. E25–18263 30 September 1769.

31. Quoted by V. W. Bladen, 'The Association of the Manufacturers of Earthenware (1784–6)', in *Economic History*, no.3, 1928, p. 366.

32. *An Address to the Workmen in the Pottery on the Subject of Entering into the Service of Foreign Manufacturers* by J. W., Newcastle-under-Lyme, 1783.

33. *Ibid.*

34. *Ibid.*

35. (J. Wedgwood), *An Address to the Young Inhabitants of the Pottery*, Etruria, 27 March 1783.

36. W/M 12 11 March 1783, Tom Wedgwood to Josiah Wedgwood.

37. *Essai sur les maladies des artisans par Ramazzini. Traduit du Latin avec des notes et des additions par M. de Fourcroy*, 1834, p. 36n. Quoted by Bevis Hillier, *Pottery and Porcelain 1700–1914*, London, 1968, p. 20.

38. *Local Notes and Queries* (Birmingham Free Reference Library), 1885–8,

quoted by P. Mantoux, *The Industrial Revolution in the Eighteenth Century*, London, 1947, p. 390, n.4; E. Posner, 'Eighteenth-Century Health and Social Service in the Pottery Industry of North Staffordshire', *Medical History*, vol. 18, no. 2, 2 April 1974.

39. C. Maxwell (ed.), *Travels in France during the Years 1787, 1788 and 1789 by Arthur Young*, Cambridge, 1950, pp. 117–9 and 310.

40. Thomas Oakey (ed.), *Travels in France during the Years 1787, 1788 and 1789 by Arthur Young*, London, 1934, p. 249.

41. WMS 30–22321 8 March 1784, endorsed 'Emigration, the 8th March 1784, Samuel Jones, Painter'.

42. E25–18147 23 May 1767; E25–18186 [? January 1768]. This letter is printed in part in K. E. Farrer, (ed.), *Letters of Josiah Wedgwood*, 3 vols., Manchester, 1903–6, I, pp. 115–17, dated '[Feb. 1767]' but the context suggests a date nearly a year later.

43. WMS 26–19115, uncatalogued MS in the handwriting of Alexander Chisholm inserted into Josiah Wedgwood's first Experiment Book (WMS 26–19115).

44. E26–18912 1 August 1779.

45. E26–18968 25 October 1785, Josiah Wedgwood to Mr Nicholson, Secretary to the General Chamber of Manufacturers.

46. For information on L.-V. Gerverot, I am indebted to Bevis Hillier's admirable *Master Potters of the Industrial Revolution*, London, 1965, pp. 40–6, and 'An Arcanist at Etruria', in Wedgwood Society *Proceedings*, no. 6, 1966, pp. 91–5. These are based on Heinrich Steegman's *Die fürstlich Braunschweigische Porzellanfabrik zu Fürstenburg* (1893) and articles in *Sprechsaal für Keramik, Glas und Emil*, Coburg, 1883, nos. 14 and 15.

47. H. Steegman, *Sprechsaal fur Keramik, Glas und Emil*; translation by J. K. des Fontaines in Wedgwood Society Proceedings, no. 6., 1966, pp. 93–5.

48. *Ibid.*

49. E26–19009 20 October 1789, Josiah Wedgwood to Sir John Dalrymple.

50. E25–18245 25 June 1769.

51. W/M 1529 12 December 1790, Josiah Wedgwood to Thomas Byerley.

CHAPTER TWELVE
The Great Invention

1. E25–18432 31 December 1772.

2. *Ibid.*

3. E25–18412 12 December 1772.

4. E25–18443 6 February 1773.

5. E25–18521 7 March 1774.

6. WMS 27–19437 5 August 1822, Ralph Wedgwood to Josiah Wedgwood II.

7. E25–18548 21 July 1774; E25–18645 21 January 1776.

8. *Ibid.*

9. E25–18555 30 August 1774.

10. E25–18556 3 September 1774; E25–18557 5 September 1774.

11. E25–18562 6 November 1774.

12. This remarkable piece was presented by Carlo Ginori to the Accademia Etrusca di Cortona at the time of his nomination as President of the Academy. See Alessandra Mottola Molfino, *L'Arte della porcellana in Italia*, 2 vols., Busto Arsizio, 1976–7, Plate 477.

13. E25–18562 6 November 1774.

14. *Ibid.*; E25–18567 21 November 1774.

15. E25–18573 12 December 1774; E25–18575 18 December 1774.

16. *Ibid.*; E25–18576 26 December 1774.

17. E25–18581 5 January 1775.

18. E25–18584 15 January 1775.

19. *Ibid.*

20. See A. G. Toppin, 'Nicholas Crisp, Jeweller and Potter', English Ceramic Circle *Transactions*, I, 1933, and Wedgwood's account of his 'Journey into Cornwall in company with Mr Turner in search of Growan Stone and Clay', ed. Geoffrey Wills, published in Wedgwood Society *Proceedings*, vols. 1 and 2, 1956–7.

21. E25–18612 23 July 1775; E25–18614 6 August 1775.

22. E25–18640 4 January 1776; E25–18641 6 January 1776; E25–18642 14 January 1776; E25–18643 18 January 1776.

23. E25–18650 3 February 1776; E25–18660 10 March 1776; E25–18671 21 May 1776.

24. E25–18673 6 June 1776.

25. E25–18671 postmarked 29 May 1776.

26. *Ibid.*; E25–18672 29 May 1776; E25–18687 8 August 1776; E25–18717 16 November 1776.

27. E25–18683 10 July 1776.

28. E25–18746 13 April 1777.

29. E25–18796 24 November 1777; LHP 24 December, Josiah Wedgwood to R. L. Edgeworth; E25–18740 19 March 1777.

30. E25–18734 25 January 1777; E25–18753 28 April 1777; E25–18771 17 July 1777; E25–18790 3 November 1777.

31. E25–18803 17 December 1777.

32. E25–18853 6 October 1778.

33. The manuscript (W/M 1455 'Memorandum Novr 23 1777 Jasper Composition', a later copy in the hand of Alexander Chisholm), describing the process was found by the author in 1986 and published for the first time in Robin Reilly, *Wedgwood*, 2 vols., London, 1989, I, pp. 535–6.

34. See Reilly, *op. cit.*, II, pp. 505 and 509–10.

35. E25–18802 15 December 1777.

36. WMS 60–32823 1824–5.

37. *A Catalogue of cameos, intaglios, medals, busts, small statues, and bas-reliefs;*

with a general account of vases and other ornaments, after the antique, made by *Wedgwood & Bentley*, 5th edn., London, 1779.

38. *Ibid.*

39. *Ibid.*

40. Horace Walpole, *The Last Journals*, 2 vols., London, 1910, II, pp. 247–8; Pretyman MSS T108/39.

41. E26–18878 25 February 1779; E26–18880 1 March 1779; WMS 96–17696 4 March 1779, Wedgwood to W. Brock; E26–18882 8 March 1779; Oven Book 13 March 1779; E26–18884 14 March 1779; E26–188891 26 May 1779.

42. E25–18772 19 July 1777.

43. Huntington Library MO 50256, Mrs Montagu to Leonard Smelt.

44. E26–18860 8 November 1778.

45. D. Watkin, *Athenian Stuart*, London, 1982, p. 51.

46. E26–18863 22 November 1778.

47. E25–18394 30 August 1772.

48. E25–18404 14 September 1772.

49. E25–18849 1 September 1778.

50. E26–18855 16 October 1778.

51. E26–18951 30 July 1779.

52. E25–18803 17 December 1777. The Longton Hall chimneypieces are now in the Lady Lever Art Gallery, Port Sunlight.

53. E26–18911 19 July 1779.

54. Alison Kelly, *Decorative Wedgwood*, London, 1965, p. 12.

55. *A Catalogue of cameos, intaglios, medals . . . made by Wedgwood & Bentley*, 5th edn., London, 1779; Wedgwood & Bentley, *A Catalogue of cameos, intaglios, bas-reliefs, medallions, busts, vases, statues . . . now in joint property of Mr Wedgwood & Mrs Bentley*, Christie & Ansell, London, 1781.

56. For example, Eliza Meteyard, *The Life of Josiah Wedgwood*, 2 vols., London, 1865–6, II. p. 378; David Buten, *18th-Century Wedgwood*, New York. 1980, p. 146; and especially Neil McKendrick, John Brewer and J. H. Plumb, *The Birth of a Consumer Society: the Commercialization of Eighteenth-Century England*, London, 1982, p. 116. See Reilly, *op. cit.*, I, pp. 580–1.

57. E25–18700 28 September 1779.

CHAPTER THIRTEEN
Time for the Family

1. LHP 8 October 1780.

2. E25–18563 10 November 1774; E25–18564 16 November 1774; E25–18565 19 November 1774.

3. E25–18570 30 November 1774.

4. E25–18574 17 December 1774.

5. E25–18372 9 May 1772.

6. E26–18936 8 November 1779; E26–18937 17 November 1779; LHP 2 July 1780.

7. E26–18943 12 December 1779; LHP 5 May 1784, Sarah Wedgwood (daughter) to Josiah Wedgwood.

8. E25–18059 1 February 1765; E25–18087 2 August 1765; E25–18078 29 May 1765.

9. E25–18473 postmarked 21 June [1773].

10. E25–18689 30 January 1775.

11. E25–18819 26 March 1778; E25–18821 30 March 1778.

12. E25–18806 29 December 1777.

13. E26–18939 23 November 1779.

14. E26–18940 28 November 1779.

15. E26–18935 1 November 1779.

16. E26–18940 28 November 1779.

17. E26–18946 19 December 1779; quoted by Desmond King-Hele, *Doctor of Revolution*, London, 1977, p. 131.

18. E26–18945 18 December 1779; E26–18946 18 December 1779; E26–18948 27 December 1779.

19. E26–18946 19 December 1779.

20. E25–18894 30 May 1779.

21. E26–18946 19 December 1779.

22. E26–18948 27 December 1779.

23. E26–18947 27 December 1779, Wedgwood to Erasmus Darwin.

24. LHP 'Feb. abt 19' 1780; LHP 27 February 1780.

25. LHP 27 February 1780.

26. E25–18663 17 March 1776; E26–18854 9 October 1778; E25–18842 17 July 1778.

27. See Judy Egerton, Introduction, *George Stubbs 1724–1806*, Tate Gallery, London, 1984, p. 14.

28. See King-Hele, *op. cit.*, p. 78.

29. E25–18138 18 February 1767; E25–18139 2 March 1767; E25–18176 [December 1767].

30. E25–18132 8 November 1766.

31. E25–18442 3 February 1773; E25–18443 6 February 1773; E25–18445 1 March 1773.

32. E25–18442 3 February 1773.

33. E25–18465 30 May 1773.

34. E25–18755 7 May 1777.

35. E25–18827 16 April 1778.

36. LHP 27 May 1780.

37. E25–18059 1 February 1765.

38. LHP n.d. Mrs Catherine Willet to Thomas Bentley [November/December 1768].

39. LHP 'Feb abt 19' 1780; LHP 5 October 1780.

40. E25–18680 5 July 1776.

41. E25–18833 '2nd of May I think but sunday morng certainly' [in fact, 3 May 1778].
42. E25–18837 12 May 1778.
43. This date, which is that given in Josiah C. Wedgwood and Joshua G. E. Wedgwood, *Wedgwood Pedigrees*, Kendal, 1925, p. 174, is contradicted by Barbara and Hensleigh Wedgwood, *The Wedgwood Circle 1730–1897*, London, 1980, p. 79, who give the date of Richard's death as 'early 1780'. This latter date seems unlikely since the Stubbs portrait of Richard, which he was working on in October 1780 (LHP 8 October 1780), is believed to have been painted from life (indeed it is difficult to imagine what other model might have been available to the artist since no second portrait of this subject is known). It is also almost inconceivable that Wedgwood should have failed to mention Richard's death in any of his letters to Bentley.
44. E26–18937 17 November 1779.
45. For example, E25–18392 23 August 1772; E25–18399 7 September 1772; E25–18402 10 September 1772.

CHAPTER FOURTEEN
Lunatics and Other Enlightened Friends

1. The principal authority for all references to the work of the Lunar Society is R. E. Schofield's *The Lunar Society of Birmingham*, Oxford, 1963, to which I acknowledge a heavy debt. In 1966 the Birmingham Museum and Art Gallery mounted an excellent small exhibition celebrating the bicentenary of the Society's foundation (as the less formal Lunar circle) and the achievements of its members. The informative catalogue, which corrects some of Schofield's rare errors, was published by the Museum in 1966.
2. R. L. Edgeworth and Maria Edgeworth, *Memoirs of Richard Lovell Edgeworth*, 2 vols., London, 1820 (reprinted Shannon, 1969), p. 188.
3. Quoted by Herbert Ganter, 'William Small, Jefferson's Beloved Teacher', *William and Mary College Quarterly*, IV, third series, 1947, p. 505.
4. Quoted by Desmond King-Hele, *Doctor of Revolution*, London, 1977, p. 61.
5. Edgeworth, *op. cit.*, I, p. 63.
6. *Ibid.*, p. 164.
7. MS at the Birmingham Library, quoted by King-Hele, *op. cit.*, p. 66.
8. Anna Seward, *Memoirs of the Life of Dr Darwin, Chiefly During his Residence at Lichfield*, London, 1804, p. 17.
9. Edgeworth, *op. cit.*, I, p. 197.
10. *Ibid.*, p. 180.
11. *Ibid.*, p. 183.
12. Eliza Meteyard, *The Life of Josiah Wedgwood*, 2 vols., London, 1865–6, II, p. 207.
13. James Watt to Dr Lind, 22 October 1768. Quoted by J. P. Muirhead, *The*

Origins and Progress of the Mechanical Inventions of James Watt, 3 vols., London, 1854, I. p. 32.

14. Correspondence between William Small and James Watt, 5 July–5 November 1769, quoted by Schofield, *op. cit.*, pp. 77–8; *Journals of the House of Commons*, XXXVII, p. 915.

15. Cf. 'An Exhibition to Commemorate the Bicentenary of the Lunar Society of Birmingham', Birmingham, 1966, p. 65.

16. Edgeworth, *op. cit.*, I, p. 184.

17. Matthew Boulton to James Watt, 7 February 1769, quoted by Schofield, *op. cit.*, p. 69.

18. E25–18136 16 February 1767; E25–18168 27 September 1767; E25–18237 9 April 1769.

19. E25–18714 9 November 1776; E25–18857 24 October 1778; E25–18859 4 November 1778.

20. Meteyard, *op. cit.*, II, pp. 557–8 and 558, n. 1.

21. *Memoirs of Joseph Priestley Written by Himself (to the year 1795) &c.*, 2 vols., London, 1806, I, p. 97.

22. Muirhead, *op. cit.*, II, p. clix.

23. Edgeworth, *op. cit.*, I, p. 185.

24. See Schofield, *op. cit.*, *passim*, and King-Hele, *op. cit.*, *passim*.

25. [James Keir], *An Account of the Life and Writings of Thomas Day Esq*, London, 1791, pp. 29–30.

26. Muirhead, *op. cit.*, II, pp. 81–2.

27. *Ibid.*, p. 82.

28. E25–18846 24 August 1778.

29. E. Darwin to W. Withering 25 February 1775, quoted by King-Hele, *op. cit.*, pp. 101–2.

30. Darwin papers, Downe House, quoted by Schofield, *op. cit.*, p. 125.

31. Dr John Hope to M. Boulton, 21 September 1776, quoted by Schofield, *op. cit.*, p. 126; E25–18851 15 September 1778; R. L. Edgeworth to M. Boulton, 14 September 1777, quoted by Schofield, *op. cit.*, p. 126.

32. Hesketh Pearson, *Doctor Darwin*, London, 1930, p. 131.

33. M. Boulton to James Keir, 1 March 1776(?), quoted by Schofield, *op. cit.*, pp. 141–2.

34. E25–18139 2 March 1767; E25–18411 4 October 1772.

35. E25–18367 18 April 1777.

36. LHP 31 August 1880.

37. Commonplace Book 39–28408 p. 33. Extract from a letter from Dr M. Turner, Liverpool, to Wedgwood, 11 December 1762.

38. *Ibid.*, p. 58.

39. *Catalogue of cameos, intaglios, medals, bas-reliefs . . .* , 6th edn. (107 pp.), Etruria, 1787.

40. J. T. Rutt (ed.), *The Theological and Miscellaneous Works of Joseph Priestley*, 25 vols., London, 1817–31, III, p. 204.

41. Roy Porter and Mikulás Teich (eds.), *The Enlightenment in National Context*, Cambridge, 1981, p. 6.

42. Christiana C. Hankin (ed.), *The Life of Mary Anne Schimmelpenninck*, London, 1860, pp. 30–3.

43. *Ibid*.

44. A. M. Broadley and L. Melville (eds.), *The Beautiful Lady Craven, the Original Memoirs of Elizabeth, Baroness Craven afterwards Margravine of Anspach &c*, 2 vols., London, 1913, I, p. 46.

45. Joseph Priestley, 'Additional Experiments and Observations . . . with letters to him on the subject by Dr Withering and James Keir', *Philosophical Transactions*, LXXVIII, London, 1788, p. 327.

46. John Whitehurst, *An Inquiry into the Original State and Formation of the Earth*, London, 1778, p. 28.

CHAPTER FIFTEEN
Competition and the Market

1. For opposing arguments see Eliza Meteyard, *The Life of Josiah Wedgwood*, 2 vols., London, 1865–6, II, *passim*, and Neil McKendrick, 'Josiah Wedgwood and Thomas Bentley: An Inventor–Entrepreneur Partnership in the Industrial Revolution', Royal Historical Society *Transactions*, Fifth Series, XIV, 1964, pp. 1–33.

2. Earl of Ilchester (ed.), *Lord Hervey and His Friends*, London, 1950, p. 71.

3. Horace Walpole, *The Last Journals*, 2 vols., London, 1910, I, p. 7.

4. James Boswell, *London Journal*, Yale, 1950, p. 320.

5. E26–18895 19 June 1779.

6. E25–18811 9 February 1778.

7. See McKendrick, *op. cit.*, *passim*.

8. LHP 8 July 1771.

9. LHP 21–22 April 1771.

10. E25–18521 [7 March] 1774.

11. E25–18274 9 December 1769.

12. Josiah's continuing difficulty with the spelling of Hamilton's name has led to the invention of another patron, 'Sir William Hambleton' (see especially McKendrick, *op. cit.*, p. 24, where he is mentioned in the same sentence as Hamilton). For evidence that the confusion is due to Josiah, see E25–18263 30 September 1769; E25–18296 28 April 1770; E25–18300 19 May 1770; LHP 23 June 1770 and others. The 'Hambleton', who died in 1774 (E25–18554 22 August 1774) was Captain Edward Hamilton, a close friend of Sir Watkin Williams Wynn's, whose portrait was modelled by Joachim Smith and copied by Wedgwood, *c.* 1772–4. 'Sir William Hambleton, our very good friend', on the other hand, is reported in London in 1776 (E25–18690 12 September 1776).

13. E25–18693 12 September 1776.

14. *Ibid.*

15. See, for example Robin Reilly, *Wedgwood*, 2 vols., London, 1989, I, Plate 342 (Rörstrand) and II, pp. 76–8 (Russian creamware).

16. See E25–18215 21 November 1768; Nicholas Goodison, *Ormolu: The Work of Matthew Boulton*, London, 1974, pp. 57–8; Reilly, *op. cit*, I, pp. 461, 463 and 474 and Plates 678–80; Wolf Mankowitz and Reginal Haggar, *The Concise Encyclopedia of English Pottery and Porcelain*, London, 1957, p. 226; Geoffrey Wills (ed.), 'Josiah Wedgwood's Journey into Cornwall', Wedgwood Society *Proceedings*, no. 1. 1956, pp. 34–57 and no. 2, 1957, pp. 80–103; LHP 21 January 1771.

17. E25–18266 9 October 1769.

18. See Neil McKendrick, John Brewer and J. H. Plumb, *The Birth of a Consumer Society; The Commercialization of Eighteenth-century England*, London, 1982, p. 105.

19. Cf. *ibid.*, p. 104, where it is erroneously stated that 'his quality [was] easily reproduced'. If this were so, it is remarkable how few of Wedgwood's contemporaries succeeded in their endeavours to reproduce it.

20. McKendrick's inclusion of Liverpool among the warehouses and showrooms set up by Wedgwood (*ibid.*, p. 120) is incorrect. The Liverpool warehouse was the property of Bentley & Boardman and, apart from doing a considerable trade with Wedgwood, was nothing to do with him.

21. McKendrick (*ibid.*, p. 110) assumes that 'Other potters fought shy of such projects', but this is the reverse of the truth. In the eighteenth century, as today, the smaller the pottery the less the disruption to the daily production line caused by small commissions. Josiah was among the first to understand the almost certain loss incurred by accepting them.

22. E25–18269 19 November 1769; E25–18283 10 January 1770.

23. WMS 1–622 Bentley to Wedgwood, 21 June 1769.

24. E25–18334 24 December 1770; LHP 24 January 1771, James Stuart to Wedgwood; E25–18339 February 1771, Wedgwood to James Stuart; LHP 3 April 1771.

25. E25–18307 4 June [1770]

26. E25–18283 10 January 1770.

27. LHP 9 July 1771; 25–18420 15 November 1772.

28. E25–18404 13 September 1772.

29. E25–18501 21 November 1773.

30. See Reilly, *op. cit.*, II, p. 785.

31. *Ibid.*, I, p. 328.

32. Quoted in McKendrick, Brewer and Plumb, *op. cit.*, p. 150.

33. LHP 9 February 1771; LHP 11 February 1771.

34. LHP 11 February 1771.

35. E25–18325 13 October 1770.

36. LHP 11 February 1771.

37. LHP 12 February 1771.

38. LHP 16 February 1771.

39. E25–18341 17 February [1771].
40. See, for example, E25–18230 [February 1769], Josiah Wedgwood to Sarah Wedgwood.
41. Ralph M. Hower, 'The Wedgwoods – Ten Generations of Potters', *Journal of Economic and Business History*. vol. 4, no. 2, 1932, p. 305.
43. E25–18191 3 March 1768.
44. E25–18341 17 February [1771].
45. E25–18489 7 June 1773.
46. LHP [? 11 March 1771], dated 11 February 1771 but postmarked 14 March 1771.
47. McKendrick, Brewer and Plumb, *op. cit.*, p. 135.
48. Aubrey Toppin, 'The China Trade and Some London Chinamen', English Ceramic Circle *Transactions*, I, Part 3, p. 43.
49. E25–18067 2 March 1765, Wedgwood to Sir William Meredith. The letter is ambiguous and has been frequently misinterpreted as referring to the continent of Europe and the West Indies. For the argument correcting this and the equally erroneous assumption that the continent of America was not considered ready for anything but 'cheap goods and seconds', see Reilly, *op. cit.*, I, p. 95.
50. E25–18124 18 July 1766, Josiah Wedgwood to John Wedgwood.
51. E25–18252 13 September 1769.
52. E26–19047 October 1770, Wedgwood to Choiseul.
53. *Ibid.*
54. LHP 26 October 1771.
55. *Ibid.*
56. LHP 2 November 1771.
57. LHP [?11] November 1771; Wedgwood to de Shoning.
58. E25–18383 29 July 1772; see McKendrick, Brewer and Plumb, *op. cit.*, p. 130, n. 222.
59. See WMS 132–26381 15 March 1791, Samuel Tabor to Wedgwood.
60. WMS 93–17173 7 January 1774, Joseph Cooper to Wedgwood; LHP 10 August 1775; E25–18529 4 December 1773.
61. E25–18703 8 October 1776; E25–18706 9 October 1776; E26–18859 4 November 1778; E25–18746 13 April 1777 ('stiver' from the Dutch *stuiver*).
62. See WMS 44–28767–28858 25 February 1780 to 19 March 1790, L. v. Veldhuysen to Wedgwood; WMS 30–30317 30 July 1773, Joseph Cooper to Wedgwood; *mededelingenblad nederlandse vereniging van vrienden van de ceramiek*, Dordrecht, 1982, p. 112 and n. 62.
63. WMS 44–28785 11 May 1781, L. v. Veldhuysen to Wedgwood.
64. WMS 44–2817 23 September 1785, L. v. Veldhuysen to Wedgwood. 'Mr Zwenck' has been identified as the Dutch pottery manufacturer J. Zwancke (*mededelingenblad nederlandse vereniging van vrienden van de ceramiek*, p. 53 n. 151); WMS 44–28819 19 November 1785, L. v. Veldhuysen to Wedgwood.

65. M. Boulton to Lord·Cathcart, 30 October 1771, quoted by Goodison, *op. cit.*, p. 95.

66. Goodison, *op. cit.*, p. 95; E25–18684 14 July 1776.

67. E25–18367 18 April 1772; McKendrick, Brewer and Plumb, *op. cit.*, p. 129, nn. 214–15; Sir G. Stanton, *Embassy of Lord Macartney to the Emperor of China 1792–3*, London, 1797, p. 42.

68. B. Faujas de St Fond, *Voyage en Angleterre, en Ecosse et aux Iles Hébrides*, 2 vols., Paris, 1797, I. p. 112.

69. See McKendrick, Brewer and Plumb, *op cit.*, p. 137, n. 251.

70. E25–18407 19 September 1772.

71. Goodison, *op. cit.*, p. 100.

72. Josiah Clement Wedgwood, *A History of the Wedgwood Family*, London, 1908, p. 154, and *Victoria History of the County of Stafford*, VIII, p. 134.

73. LHP 9 September 1771.

74. E25–18807 1 February 1778; E25–18810 7 February 1778; E25–18812 13 February 1778.

75. E25–18827 16 April 1778.

76. WMS 121–23376 18 January 1779, T. Byerley to W. Brock; WMS 13–12428 22 January 1779, T. Byerley to P. Swift; 13–12431 11 March 1779, T. Byerley to P. Swift; 121–23382 17 May 1779, T. Byerley to P. Swift; 121–23397 12 September 1783, T. Byerley to Josiah Wedgwood II.

CHAPTER SIXTEEN
Dissent and Rebellion

1. British Museum, Add. MSS 32684, f. 121.

2. See especially Ida Macalpine and Richard Hunter, *George III and the Mad Business*, London, 1969.

3. John Hughes for Pennsylvania and Jared Ingersoll for Connecticut.

4. Lord Chesterfield, *Letters to His Son* (4th edn.), 2 vols., London, 1912, II, p. 353.

5. E25–18213 18 July 1766, Josiah Wedgwood to John Wedgwood. See Robin Reilly, *Wedgwood*, 2 vols., London, 1989, I, p. 95, and Appendix B, p. 688.

6. Chesterfield, *op. cit.*, p. 353.

7. Henry B. Wheatley (ed.), Sir Nathaniel Wraxhall, *The Historical and Post-humous Memoirs 1772–1784*, 5 vols., London, 1884, I. p. 366.

8. *Virginia Gazette*, 5 May 1774.

9. E25–18582 8 January 1775; E25–18590 6 February 1775.

10. E25–18148 27 May 1767.

11. E25–18590 6 February 1775.

12. A. F. Steuart, *The Last Journals of Horace Walpole*, 2 vols., London, 1910, I, p. 433.

13. Hon. George Pellew, *The Life and Correspondence of the Rt. Hon. Henry Addington, First Viscount Sidmouth*, 3 vols., London, 1847, I, p. 6.

14. E25–18795 20 November 1777; E25–18805 22 December 1777.
15. E25–18776 8 August 1777.
16. E25–18771 17 July 1777; E25–18772 19 July 1777.
17. E25–18797 26 November 1777; E25–18803 17 December 1777.
18. E25–18806 29 December 1777.
19. Sir J. W. Fortescue, *Correspondence of George III from 1760 to December 1783*, 6 vols., London, 1927–8, IV, p. 59.
20. John Almon, *Anecdotes of the Life of the Right Honourable William Pitt, Earl of Chatham*, 3 vols., London, 1793, II, pp. 511–2.
21. E25–18826 11 April 1778.
22. Quoted by Pellew, *op cit.*, I, p. 8.
23. E25–18815 3 March 1778.
24. E26–18890 9 May 1779.
25. *Ibid.*

CHAPTER SEVENTEEN
The Saddest Loss

1. E25–18187 22 February 1768.
2. E25–18486 12 August 1773.
3. LHL 20 February 1770.
4. Neil McKendrick, 'Josiah Wedgwood and Thomas Bentley: An Inventor-Entrepreneur Partnership in the Industrial Revolution', *Transactions of the Royal Historical Society*, fifth series, XIV, 1964, p. 14.
5. *Ibid.*, pp. 22 and 20.
6. E25–18196 24 March 1768.
7. E25–18925 20 September 1779; E25–18264 1 October 1769.
8. WMS London Experiment Book, Experiment No. 280 and see Robin Reilly, *Wedgwood*, 2 vols., London, 1989, II, p. 569–709; E25–18215 21 November 1768.
9. LHP 17 April 1771; E25–18476 26 June 1773.
10. E25–18256 [September 1769].
11. E25–18867 14 December 1778.
12. WMS 1–1281 T. Bentley to Josiah Wedgwood, 18 December 1778.
13. E26–18865 29 November 1778.
14. E26–18869 21 December 1778.
15. E25–18557 5 September 1774.
16. LHP [late November – early December 1768]; LHP 8 December 1768.
17. E25–18199 about 17 June 1768. This is quoted by McKendrick, *op. cit.*, p. 12, n. 1, misdated '2 [June 1768]'. Josiah had his leg amputated on 28 May and Bentley, at Burslem, dealt with all his correspondence until at least 13 June.
18. E25–18881 7 March 1779.
19. E25–18094 10 October 1765; E25–18124 1 August 1766.

20. E25–18332 21 December 1770; E25–18376 6 June 1772; E25–18377 13 June 1772; E25–18379 24 June 1772.
21. E25–18554 22 August 1774.
22. E25–18647 27 January 1776.
23. E25–18560 31 October 1774; E25–18876 14 February 1779; E25–18380 13 July 1772;. E25–18445 1 March 1773; E25–18460 14 May 1773; E25–18515 14 February 1774; E25–18781 4 October 1777; E25–18808 2 February 1778; E26–18888 8 May 1779; LHP 'Feby abt 19 1780'.
24. E25–18380 13 July 1772.
25. E25–18781 4 October 1777.
26 Papers of the Reverend David Williams, National Library, Cardiff, quoted by Richard Bentley, *Thomas Bentley 1730–1780*, Guildford, 1927, pp. 64–5; E25–18687 8 August 1776; E25–18688 7 September 1776.
27. Quoted by George Savage and Ann Finer (eds.), *The Selected Letters of Josiah Wedgwood*, London 1965, p. 196; E25–18687 8 August 1776.
28. E25–18688 7 September 1776.
29. Ralph Griffiths to Josiah Wedgwood, 25 November 1780, quoted by Savage and Finer, *op. cit.*, p. 262.
30. Eliza Meteyard, *The Life of Josiah Wedgwood*, 2 vols., London, 1865–6, II, p. 459; Barbara and Hensleigh Wedgwood, *The Wedgwood Circle*, London 1980, p. 76.
31. E26–18561 27 October 1778.
32. See Una des Fontaines, 'Portland House, Wedgwood's London Showrooms 1774–85', Wedgwood Society *Proceedings*, no. 11, 1982, pp. 139–40.
33. Josiah Wedgwood to William Ker, January 1781, quoted by Savage and Finer, *op. cit.*, p. 262.
34. Charles Darwin, *Life of Erasmus Darwin*, London, 1879, pp. 31–3.
35. See Reilly, *op. cit.*, I, p. 704, n. 29, where the arguments put forward by Meteyard and others that the sale was a disastrous failure are discussed.
36. H. B. Wheatley and P. Cunningham, *London Past and Present*, 2 vols., London, 1891, II, p. 134.
37. LHP 12 November 1780.
38. W/M 1503 1 October 1807, Tom Byerley to Josiah Wedgwood II.
39. E25–18614 6 August 1775; E25–18232 [12 or 16] February 1769.

CHAPTER EIGHTEEN
Among the Politicians

1. E25–18194 16 March 1768; LHP 9 September 1780.
2. LHP 1 June 1780; LHP 20 May 1780; E26–18994 17 May 1790, Josiah Wedgwood to Mr Fletcher.
3. LHP n.d. [16 My 1780].
4. LHP 1 June 1780.
5. LHP 20 May 1780.

6. LHP 1 June 1780 and 5 June 1780.

7. British Museum Add. MSS 34419, ff. 325–6.

8. *Considerations on the Provisional Treaty with America, and the Preliminary Articles of Peace with France and Spain*, London, 1783.

9. J. Holland Rose, *Pitt and the National Revival*, London, 1911, p. 126.

10. Bathurst MSS, Historical Manuscripts Commission, London 1923; Lord E. Fitzmaurice, *Life of William Earl of Shelburne*, 3 vols., London, 1875–6, III, p. 375; Earl of Stanhope, *Life of The Right Honourable William Pitt*, 4 vols., London, 1861–2, I, Appendix, p. iv.

11. E25–18571 [5] March 1774, endorsed by T. Bentley, 'Rec'd March 7th 1774'.

12. E26–18957 April 1783, Josiah Wedgwood to C. J. Fox.

13. LHP 21 and 22 April 1771; E25–18457 14 April 1773.

14. Birmingham Reference Library, Boulton & Watt MSS., Josiah Wedgwood to J. Watt, 30 January 1784.

15. Sir J. W. Fortescue (ed.), *Correspondence of George III from 1760 to December 1783*, 6 vols., London, 1927–8, IV, p. 244.

16. Lord John Russell (ed.), *Memorials and Correspondence of Charles James Fox*, 4 vols., London, 1853–7, I, p. 412, Fox to Richard Fitzpatrick, April 1782; Lord Ashbourne, *Pitt: Some Chapters of his Life and Times*, London, 1898, p. 72.

17. Bolton MSS, quoted by Ashbourne, *op. cit.*, pp. 85–90.

18. Evidence given to the Committee of Trade by the Manchester Cotton Delegation. Quoted by Vincent T. Harlow, *The Founding of the Second British Empire 1763–93*, 2 vols., London, 1952, I, p. 595.

19. Josiah Wedgwood's evidence given before the Committee of Trade in the Council Chamber, Whitehall, 19 February 1785.

20. E26–19098 21 February 1785, Josiah Wedgwood to Matthew Boulton (MS copy).

21. WMS. 4–3244 1 May 1785, Josiah Wedgwood to Matthew Boulton.

22. Josiah Wedgwood to Joseph Priestley n.d. [? June 1785], Royal Society MSS, Priestley 25.

23. W/M 16 3 October 1785, Josiah Wedgwood to R. L. Edgeworth.

24. Eden to Wedgwood 16 April 1785, quoted by Eliza Meteyard, *The Life of Josiah Wedgwood*, 2 vols., London, 1865–6, II, p. 544.

25. Quoted by Julia Wedgwood, *The Personal Life of Josiah Wedgwood*, London, 1915, p. 236.

26. W/M 16 23 December 1786, Josiah Wedgwood to R. L. Edgeworth.

CHAPTER NINETEEN
Trade and Revolution

1. Auckland Papers. British Museum Add. MSS 34420, f. 106v.

2. *Ibid.*, Add. MSS 34419, f. 385.

3. E25–18650 3 February 1776.

4. Quoted by V. W. Bladen, 'The Association of the Manufacturers of Earthenware (1784–6)', *Economic History* (supplement to the *Economic Journal*), no. 3, 1928, pp. 356–7.

5. Auckland Papers. British Museum Add. MSS 34420, f. 253–4.

6. Robert J. Auckland, 3rd Baron, Bishop of Bath and Wells (ed.), *The Journal and Correspondence of William, Lord Auckland*, 4 vols., London, 1862, I, pp. 90–1, William Pitt to William Eden, 16 December 1785.

7. *Ibid.*, pp. 92–3, Josiah Wedgwood to William Eden, 5 January 1786.

8. Josiah Wedgwood to William Eden, 7 March 1786, MS copy of draft, WMS uncatalogued, quoted by George Savage and Ann Finer (eds.), *The Selected Letters of Josiah Wedgwood*, London, 1965, p. 291, n. 7, but dated in error 1785.

9. Auckland, *op. cit.*, I, p. 133, Josiah Wedgwood to William Eden, 30 June 1786.

10. See Staffordshire Potters to H. M. Commissioners of Customs, 19 October 1786, British Museum, Add. MSS 34422, f. 481.

11. Adam Smith, *An Inquiry into the Nature and Causes of the Wealth of Nations*, 4 vols., London, 1776, IV, Ch. 3.

12. Auckland, *op. cit.*, I, pp. 163–5; Melville MSS, Eskbank, quoted by Holden Furber, *Henry Dundas, Viscount Melville 1742–1811*, Oxford, 1931, p. 68.

13. C. J. Fox, *Speeches of the Right Honourable Charles James Fox in the House of Commons*, 6 vols., London, 1815, III, p. 273.

14. Auckland, *op. cit.*, I, p. 127.

15. WMS 26–19041 19 October 1786, Josiah Wedgwood to Samuel Garbett; British Museum Add. MSS 34422, f. 482, 20 October 1786, Josiah Wedgwood to William Eden; W/M 16 23 December 1786, Josiah Wedgwood to R. L. Edgeworth.

16. James Watt to Josiah Wedgwood, 26 February 1787, Soho MSS, quoted by P. Mantoux, *The Industrial Revolution in the Eighteenth Century*, London, 1947, p. 401, n. 2.

17. *Gazeteer and New Daily News Advertiser*, 12 January 1787.

18. *Public Proceedings of the General Chamber of the Manufacturers of Great Britain in the French Treaty*, London, 1787, pp. 44–7, quoted by Terence A. Lockett, 'Wedgwood and the Politicians', Wedgwood Society *Proceedings*, no. 7, 1968, p. 126. This important article questions the generally accepted view of Wedgwood's part in the negotiations and his dealings with the Chamber of Manufacturers.

19. W/M 1515 20 March 1787, Josiah Wedgwood to James Caldwell.

20. See Lockett, *op. cit.*, pp. 128–9.

21. Quoted by Mantoux, *op cit.*, p. 407.

22. Josiah Wedgwood to Matthew Boulton, 23 February 1787, Soho MSS, quoted by Eliza Meteyard, *The Life of Josiah Wedgwood*, 2 vols., 1865–6, II, p. 562.

23. Auckland, *op cit.*, I, p. 427, Josiah Wedgwood to William Eden, 16 June 1787.

24. Auckland, *op cit.*, I, pp. 399–403, Lord Sheffield to William Eden, 11 February 1787; Eden to Sheffield, Paris, February 1787.

25. E26–18973 20 February 1786, Josiah Wedgwood to Archdeacon Clive.

26. WMS 2–30193 23 December 1786, Josiah Wedgwood to John Flaxman junior.

27. Auckland, *op. cit.*, I, p. 427; II, p. 372–3.

28. Lockett, *op. cit.*, p 128.

29. As n. 27.

30. Russell, Lord John (ed.), *Memorials and Correspondence of Charles James Fox*, 4 vols., London 1853–7, II, p. 361.

31. E26–19003 July 1789, Josiah Wedgwood to Erasmus Darwin.

32. Stanhope, Earl, *Life of the Right Honourable William Pitt*, 4 vols., London, 1861–2, II, p. 38.

33. MS in the Birmingham Reference Library, quoted by Desmond King-Hele, *Doctor of Revolution*, London, 1977, p. 205.

34. Josiah Wedgwood to J. Barker, Geneva, 29 August 1789, quoted by George Savage and Ann Finer (eds.), *Selected Letters of Josiah Wedgwood*, London, 1965, p. 319.

35. E26–19003 July 1789, Josiah Wedgwood to Erasmus Darwin.

36. Quoted by D. B. Horn, *Great Britain and Europe in the Eighteenth Century*, Oxford, 1967, p. 25.

37. Quoted by George Rudé, *Europe in the Eighteenth Century*, London, 1972, p. 268.

38. The debate is reported in *Parliamentary History*, XXVIII, pp. 334–72.

39. Thomas Paine to Edmund Burke, 17 January 1790. Northumberland Record Office A IV 73a (copy). Printed in *The Durham University Journal*, 1951, XLIII, pp. 50–4.

40. Llewellyn Jewitt (ed.), *The Life of William Hutton*, London, 1872, p. 255.

41. LHP 20 July 1791, Josiah Wedgwood II to Josiah Wedgwood.

42. Josiah Wedgwood to Joseph Priestley, July 1791, quoted by H. C. Bolton, *The Scientific Correspondence of Joseph Priestley*, New York (privately printed), 1891, p. 112.

43. King-Hele, *op. cit.*, pp. 212–13.

44. J. P. Muirhead, *The Origins and Progress of the Mechanical Inventions of James Watt*, 3 vols., London, 1854, II, pp. 243–4.

45. (Priestley), *Memoirs of Dr Joseph Priestley Written by Himself (to the year 1795)*, 2 vols., London, 1806, I, p. 97.

46. See R. E. Schofield, *The Lunar Society of Birmingham*, Oxford, 1963, p. 370.

47. E26–18994 17 May 1790, Josiah Wedgwood to Josiah Wedgwood II.

48. Declaration by the Sheffield Society, May 1792.

49. E26–18986 14 December 1792, Josiah Wedgwood to Thomas Byerley.

CHAPTER TWENTY
Call It Trade

1. Erasmus Darwin, *The Botanic Garden, Part I, 'The Economy of Vegetation'*, London, 1791, II, pp. 423–30 and 315–6.
2. T. Clarkson, *History of . . . the Abolition of the African Slave Trade*, 2 vols. London, 1808, II, pp. 191–2.
3. American Philosophical Society Library, Franklin Papers, XXXVI, 28, Josiah Wedgwood to Benjamin Franklin, 29 February 1788. See Robin Reilly, *Wedgwood*, 2 vols., London, 1989, I, p. 705, n. 44.
4. Yale University Library, Benjamin Franklin to Josiah Wedgwood, 15 May 1788.
5. Both Bentley and Franklin were members of the Club for Honest Whigs, which met regularly in London, and news of the death of 'our old friend Mr Bentley' was sent to Franklin by another member, William Hodgson, on 4 December 1780 (American Philosophical Society Library, Franklin Papers, XX, 105). I am indebted for this reference to a well-researched article, 'Josiah Wedgwood, Benjamin Franklin and their Mutual Friends' by Whitfield J. Bell in Wedgwood International Seminar *Proceedings*, vol. 15, 1970, p. 60; Desmond King-Hele, *Doctor of Revolution*, London, 1977, p. 137 and see also Nicholas Goodison, *Ormolu: The Work of Matthew Boulton*, London, 1974, p. 8; Darwin's meeting with Franklin in 1758 is not recorded but it is likely that they would have met during Franklin's tour of the Midlands during that year when he first met Boulton. The latter introduced him to a number of his friends, Darwin surely among them.
6. E26–18978 February 1788 (draft), Josiah Wedgwood to Anna Seward.
7. C. J. Fox, *Speeches of the Right Honourable Charles James Fox in the House of Commons*, 6 vols., London, 1815, IV, p. 16.
8. As n. 6.
9. An incomplete account of the debate appears in *Parliamentary History*, XXIX, pp. 1133–58.
10. Robert and Samuel Wilberforce, *The Life of William Wilberforce*, 5 vols., London, 1838, V, pp. 340–4.
11. Wilberforce's Journal, quoted by Julia Wedgwood, *The Personal Life of Josiah Wedgwood*, London, 1915, p. 256.
12. E26–18990 18 January 1792, Josiah Wedgwood to the Reverend T. Clarkson.

CHAPTER TWENTY-ONE
Arts and Manufactures

1. W. E. Gladstone, 'Wedgwood. An Address delivered at the Burslem

Institute, 26 October 1863'; P. Mantoux, *The Industrial Revolution in the Eighteenth Century*, rev. edn., London, 1947, p. 391.

2. E25–18196 24 March 1768.

3. WMS 96–17661 4 May 1768, Wedgwood to W. Cox; E25–18197 31 March 1768; 95–17572 18 May 1768, T. Bentley to W. Cox; 96–17666 13 June 1768, Wedgwood to W. Cox; 96–17668 30 June 1768, Wedgwood to W. Cox; E25–18653 13 February 1776; LHP [November–December] 1768, Sarah Wedgwood to T. Bentley; 96–17664 29 June 1768, Wedgwood to W. Cox; E25–18205 14 July 1768; LHP 29 November 1768, Sarah Wedgwood to T. Bentley.

4. E25–18234 2 March 1768; *Crown Book* of the Oxford Circuit quoted by R. J. Charleston, 'John Voyez – Fact or Fiction', in *Antiques Magazine*, January 1961, p. 100.

5. E25–18234 2 March 1769; E25–18237 9 April 1769.

6. E25–18237 9 April 1769.

7. E25–18500 postmarked 22 November 1773; E25–18571 4 December 1774; E25–18655 21 February 1776; E25–18659 3 March 1776.

8. E25–18258 20 September 1769.

9. LHP 30 November 1771; E25–18520 2 March 1774; E25–18558 11 September 1774; E25–18641 6 January 1776; E25–18679 2 July 1776.

10. See Robin Reilly, *Wedgwood*, 2 vols., London, 1989, I, pp. 558–9.

11. E26–18862 endorsed 'Rec'd November 21 1778'.

12. WMS 121–23483 20 August 1802, T. Byerley to Josiah Wedgwood II.

13. The architect Charles Cockerell's description quoted by David Watkin, *C. R. Cockerell*, London, 1974, p. 100.

14. LHP 7 September 1771.

15. See Reilly, *op. cit.*, pp. 524–5.

16. E25–18579 1 January (second part); E25–18583 14 January 1775; E25–18584 15 January 1775.

17. E25–18682 postmarked 9 July 1776.

18. See Reilly, *op. cit.*, II, Appendix H.

19. Sir William Hamilton and P. H. d'Hancarville, *Antiquités étrusques, grecques et romaines*, 4 vols., Naples, 1767. III, Plate 31.

20. WMS 32–5365 22 June 1779, Sir W. Hamilton to Josiah Wedgwood.

21. E26–18976 24 June 1786, Josiah Wedgwood to Sir W. Hamilton.

22. E26–19090 16 June 1787, Josiah Wedgwood to Sir W. Hamilton.

23. W/M 1526 'Account of the Letters from and to M. Angelo Dalmazzoni at Rome 1788–90'.

24. WMS 2–1342 24 December 1788, John Flaxman junior to Josiah Wedgwood.

25. *Ibid*.

26. WMS 1–148 16 July 1787.

27. As n.23.

28. See Reilly, *op cit.*, I, Plates 874, 876–8, 884, 885A, 886A, 887–8.

29. E25–18635 23 December 1775.

30. E25–18791 4 November 1777.
31. E26–18856 17 October 1778.
32. E26–18894 30 May 1779.
33. *Ibid.*
34. Neil McKendrick, 'Josiah Wedgwood and George Stubbs', in *History Today*, VII, No. 8, August 1957, pp. 508–9. Dr McKendrick's assumptions about the relationship between Wedgwood and Stubbs are at variance with the evidence, much of which he has apparently not examined or chosen to ignore.
35. LHP 25 September 1780.
36. E26–18894 30 May 1779.
37. *Ibid.*
38. LHP 7 August 1780.
39. *Ibid.*
40. LHP 21 August 1780.
41. *Ibid.*
42. *Ibid.*
43. LHP 13 August 1780; LHP 21 August 1780.
44. LHP 14 September 1780.
45. LHP 21 October 1780.
46. LHP 28 October 1780.
47. LHP 12 November 1780.
48. LHP 28 October 1780; LHP 12 November 1780.
49. E25–18451 27 March 1773.
50. E25–18834 5 May 1778.
51. E25–18850 10 September 1778.
52. WMS 1–670 11 February 1782, Joseph Wright to Josiah Wedgwood.
53. WMS 1–671 March 1782, Joseph Wright to Josiah Wedgwood; Ingleby MSS, Joseph Wright to William Hayley, n.d. [? February 1783].
54. WMS 1–672 29 April 1783 and 23 October 1783, Joseph Wright to Josiah Wedgwood.
55. Susannah Wedgwood to Josiah Wedgwood, quoted by Julia Wedgwood, *The Personal Life of Josiah Wedgwood*, London, 1915, pp. 356–7.
56. WMS 1–672 31 December 1783, Joseph Wright to Josiah Wedgwood.
57. E26–18966 29 April 1784, Josiah Wedgwood to Joseph Wright.
58. WMS 1–673 3 May 1784, Joseph Wright to Josiah Wedgwood.
59. WMS 1–677 1789.
60. E25–18278 28 December 1769.
61. W/M 1570 24 May [1770?], J. Spilsbury to T. Bentley.
62. E26–19008 11 February 1790, Josiah Wedgwood to John Flaxman.
63. R. and S. Redgrave, *A Century of British Painters*, London, 1981, p. 55.

CHAPTER TWENTY-TWO
Last Experiments

1. WMS 27–19437 5 August 1822, Ralph Wedgwood to Josiah Wedgwood II.
2. E25–18602 18 June 1775; E25–18603 postmarked 23 June [1775]; WMS 39–28408, Commonplace Book.
3. E25–18628 'Heads of Agreement', enclosed with E25–18627 2 December 1775. This specification has been misconstrued, most notably by Dr McKendrick (*Times Literary Supplement*, 16 August 1990), who asserts that what he calls the 'proposed cooperative research scheme' was 'to be devoted solely' to the making of blue-and-white earthenwares, a form of decoration deliberately shunned by Wedgwood because he wished to avoid any direct comparison with porcelain decoration. McKendrick's erroneous and misleading interpretation of the 'Heads of Agreement' manuscript, which he does not appear to have consulted in the original, betrays a failure to understand the basic problems of design and marketing faced by the manufacturers of creamwares.
4. E25–18638 n.d. [December 1775].
5. WMS 25–18628 n.d. [November/December 1775].
6. E25–18208 30 August 1768.
7. WMS 39–28408, Commonplace Book.
8. See WMS 26–19117, Experiment Book, pp. 374–5, Trial No. 3526.
9. Royal Society MSS V, no. 22; E25–18367 18 April 1772; WMS 39–18408 2 December 1781, criticism by Sir Joseph Banks.
10. WMS 26–19117, Experiment Book, pp. 378–9, Trial Nos. 3557–3586; WMS 39–28408, Commonplace Book.
11. WMS 39–28408, Commonplace Book.
12. *Ibid.*
13. *Philosophical Transactions*, LXXII, 1782, pp. 305 ff.
14. Royal Society Certifications, vol. 4, no. 101; Royal Society *Journal*, vol. 31, p. 164.
15. Antiquarians' Society Minute Book, vol. 21, pp. 168–9; Royal Society of Arts Minute Book, vol. 32, pp. 8–9; *Philosophical Transactions*, LXXIV, 1784, pp. 358 ff. and LXXVI, 1786, pp. 390 ff.
16. WMS 2–30188 5 February 1784, John Flaxman junior to Josiah Wedgwood.
17. D. E. L Haynes, whose *The Portland Vase* (2nd rev. edn., London, 1975) is among the most respected descriptions and interpretations of the Portland vase, takes the view (p. 26) that the relationship of the themes 'must have been a coincidence'; but if the themes have been correctly identified, this seems unlikely. Even in Roman times, and certainly by the sixteenth century, this vase would have been prized as a superb example of the cameo-cutter's arts, and it is sensible to suppose that great trouble would have been taken to match any repair, as nearly as possible, in colour, style and theme.
18. For a discussion of this correspondence, see Nancy T. de Grummond,

'Rubens, Pieresc and the Portland Vase', *Southern College Art Conference Review*, III, no. 1, 1974.

19. This is reproduced in Aileen Dawson's *Masterpieces of Wedgwood in the British Museum*, London, 1984, p. 114.

20. Sir William Hamilton to Josiah Wedgwood, July 1786. This letter, quoted at length by Wolf Mankowitz, *The Portland Vase and the Wedgwood Copies*, London, 1952, pp. 28–30, and then in the manuscript collection at Barlaston (prior to its removal to the archives at Keele University) has since disappeared.

21. Horace Walpole to the Countess of Upper Ossory, 19 August 1785. Mrs Paget Toynbee (ed.), *Letters of Horace Walpole*, 16 vols., London, 1905, XIII, p. 308.

22. WMS 33–24859, receipt dated 10 June 1786 signed by Josiah Wedgwood and witnessed by Tom Byerley.

23. E26–18976 24 June 1786, Josiah Wedgwood to Sir W. Hamilton.

24. *Ibid.*

25. *Ibid.*

26. For a description of this technique, see W/M 1460 12 April 1791, Josiah Wedgwood II to Josiah Wedgwood.

27. E26–18976 24 June 1786, Josiah Wedgwood to Sir W. Hamilton.

28. An excellent brief account of the various interpretations is given by Haynes, *op. cit.*, Appendix, pp. 27–32. Josiah's own is in a long letter (E26–19004) to Erasmus Darwin endorsed 'Oct 1789'. See also Josiah's *Account of the Barberini now Portland Vase. With various explications of its bas-reliefs that have been given by different authors*, London [1788?]. It is probable that he was familiar with the interpretations of Bartoli, *Gli antichi sepolchri*, Rome, 1697. p. xxi, Plates 84–6; Montfaucon, *L'Antiquité expliquée*, 5 vols. and supplement 5 vols., Paris, 1719, V. Plate 19; and perhaps also with P. H. d'Hancarville, *Recherches sur l'origine, l'esprit et les progrès des arts de la Grèce*, London, 1785, II, pp. 142–60, Plates 9–11.

29. E26–18976 24 June 1786, Josiah Wedgwood to Sir W. Hamilton.

30. *Ibid.*

31. As n. 20.

32. E26–18976 24 June 1786, Josiah Wedgwood to Sir W. Hamilton.

33. *Ibid.*

34. See Robin Reilly, *Wedgwood*, 2 vols., London, 1989, I, pp. 535–7.

35. Uncatalogued letter (copy in the hand of Chrisholm), 25 April 1788, Josiah Wedgwood to Dr W. Heberden.

36. E26–18976 24 June 1786, Josiah Wedgwood to Sir W. Hamilton.

37. *Ibid.*

38. Josiah Wedgwood to Lord Auckland, 5 July 1789. Eden MSS printed in *Athenaeum Journal*, no. 1694, 17 April 1860.

39. E. Darwin to Josiah Wedgwood, October 1789, Darwin MSS quoted by Eliza Meteyard, *The Life of Josiah Wedgwood*, 2 vols., London, 1865–6, II, p. 581.

40. E. Darwin, *The Economy of Vegetation*, I, pp. 281–8; *ibid.*, I, pp. 271–8.

41. Quoted by J. P. Muirhead, *The Origins and Progress of the Mechanical Inventions of James Watt*, 3 vols., London, 1854, II, p. 232, J. Watt to E. Darwin, 24 December 1789.

42. E. Darwin, *The Economy of Vegetation*, I, p. 254.

43. E26–19002 July 1789, Josiah Wedgwood to E. Darwin.

44. M. de Luc, the Queen's private secretary, wrote to Wedgwood on 5 June (E82–14607) apologising for not being able to accompany Her Majesty when she viewed the vase and asking if he might see it at a later date. Since the viewing at Sir Joseph Banks's house was held on the evening of Saturday 1 May, and it is unlikely that this could have taken place prior to the vase being shown to the Queen, it is almost certain that it was displayed for her approval earlier that same day.

45. *The General Evening Post* was published between 1 and 4 May, and the *Gazetteer and Daily News Advertiser* on Wednesday 5 May. Both references were researched by Ann Eatwell of the Victoria and Albert Museum and quoted in Dawson, *op. cit.*, p. 122.

46. This document, quoted in Mankowitz, *op. cit.*, p. 35, is dated 15 June 1790. Originally in the Wedgwood manuscript collection at Barlaston, it cannot now be found.

47. W/M 1460 20 July 1791, Josiah Wedgwood II to Josiah Wedgwood; E30–22498 23 July 1791, Sir W. Hamilton to Josiah Wedgwood.

48. E25–18314 2 August 1770; E26–18993 9 June 1790, Josiah Wedgwood to Josiah Wedgwood II.

49. W/M 1529 4 July 1790, Josiah Wedgwood II to Josiah Wedgwood.

50. W/M 1529 5 July 1790, Josiah Wedgwood II to Josiah Wedgwood.

51. *Ibid*.

52. W/M 1529 13 July 1790, Josiah Wedgwood to Josiah Wedgwood II.

53. E33–24860 T. Byerley's Notebook. List of Subscribers.

54. W/M 1529 postmarked 14 September 1790, Josiah Wedgwood to Josiah Wedgwood II.

55. WMS Oven Book records, 27 May 1791–31 December 1796.

56. In an article in the *General Advertiser* for 26 April 1786, an anonymous author describes the vase as being broken 'at least into three pieces and its original bottom was most certainly destroyed'. This is confirmed by the plaster copy made by James Tassie from a mould by Giovanni Pichler in 1781–2 (one of sixty commissioned by James Byres), now in the British Museum. According to the *Gentleman's Magazine*, XVI, July-December 1786, p. 744, the vase was again 'repaired after its fracture by the Duchess of Gordon'. Since it was in Wedgwood's hands by 10 June 1786, and retained by him long after the date of this article, the second 'fracture' most probably occurred between the death of the Duchess of Portland on 17 July 1785 and 24 April 1786.

57. *The Times*, 7 and 12 February 1845; *Gentleman's Magazine*, new series, XXIII, p. 300.

58. A similarly idiotic loophole was exposed after the theft of Goya's portrait of the Duke of Wellington from the National Gallery, London, in August 1961. On that occasion, the thief could be charged only with damage to the frame from which the portrait had been removed. The portrait was returned in May 1965.

59. The most recent summary of surviving 'first edition' vases appears in Dawson, *op. cit.*, pp. 149–50. Of the total number of fifty listed, eleven are noted as 'untraced' and others are either of inferior quality or of doubtful provenance.

60. A quantity of deep blue jasper Portland vases was made in 1791, during a temporary shortage of 'Barberini black' clay at Etruria. One of these was presented to the British Museum by Josiah Wedgwood II in 1802 (see Reilly, *op cit.*, I, p. 678 and Plate C189; *ibid*, II, p. 558).

61. The outline of the Portland vase was adopted as part of Wedgwood's trademark and appears on bone china from 1878 and some earthenwares between 1878 and *c.* 1900.

62. A. Phillip to Sir Joseph Banks, 16 November 1788. Mitchell Library C213, quoted by L. Richard Smith, *The Sydney Cove Medallion*, Wedgwood Society of Australia, New South Wales Chapter, Sydney, 1978, p. 25, n. 1.

63. Josiah Wedgwood to Sir Joseph Banks, 12 March 1790, Royal Society MSS Lp. 9. 167 (printed in *Philosophical Transactions of the Royal Society of London*, 1791, LXXX, pt. II, p. 306; WMS 39–28409 Commonplace Book, 15 June 1791, p. 30.

64. *European Magazine*, 1789 and some later editions of *The Economy of Vegetation*; Rylands Library, Manchester, English MSS 1110, p. 49.

CHAPTER TWENTY-THREE
Handing Over

1. W/M 1460 3 March 1788, Josiah Wedgwood II to Josiah Wedgwood.
2. E26–19078/9 31 January 1790, Josiah Wedgwood to Lord Auckland.
3. WMS uncatalogued, printed announcement, Etruria 18 January 1790.
4. F. F. Cartwright, *A Social History of Medicine*, London, 1977, p. 103.
5. See, for example, LHP 27 August 1771; E25–18781 4 October 1777.
6. See LHP 13 August 1780, 31 August 1780, '4 or 5' September 1780, 9 September 1780, 14 September 1780, 21 September 1780.
7. WMS 2–30188 5 February 1784, John Flaxman to Josiah Wedgwood; WMS 2–30189 (draft) 20 February 1784, Josiah Wedgwood to John Flaxman. The interior of Etruria Hall was destroyed early in this century and it has not proved possible, from the slender evidence that has survived, to reconstruct Flaxman's design.
8. E26–18862 endorsed 'Rec'd Novr 21 1778'; E26–18982, List of Male Servants, horses and carriages May 1794.
9. E26–18982 May 1794.

10. E25–18806 29 December 1777, T. Bentley to Josiah Wedgwood.
11. W/M 6 10 September 1786, John Wedgwood to Josiah Wedgwood.
12. *Ibid.*, 15 November 1786, John Wedgwood to Josiah Wedgwood.
13. *Ibid.*, 3 December 1786, John Wedgwood to Josiah Wedgwood.
14. *Ibid.*, 14 December 1786, John Wedgwood to Josiah Wedgwood.
15. LHP 28 July 1789, translation by Josiah Wedgwood II.
16. W/M 6 26 April 1788, John Wedgwood (from Rome) to Josiah Wedgwood.
17. W/M 32 17 June 1793, Josiah Wedgwood to John Wedgwood (draft).
18. *Ibid.*
19. *Ibid.*
20. LHP 2 June 1790 and 7 June 1790, Josiah Wedgwood II to Josiah Wedgwood.
21. LHP 12 April 1791, Josiah Wedgwood II to Josiah Wedgwood.
22. W/M 21 postmarked 27 April 1790, Tom Wedgwood to Josiah Wedgwood II.
23. W/M 26 postmarked May 1790, Josiah Wedgwood to Tom Wedgwood.
24. 2 December 1790, Josiah Wedgwood to James Watt. Quoted by Eliza Meteyard, *A Group of Englishmen 1795–1815*, London, 1871, p. 34.
25. Quoted by Julia Wedgwood, *The Personal Life of Josiah Wedgwood*, London, 1915, pp. 360–1, Susannah Wedgwood to Josiah Wedgwood, 1787 and 3 April 1794.
26. W/M 12 7 July 1792, Tom Wedgwood to Josiah Wedgwood.
27. This banking house was identified by Eliza Meteyard (*The Life of Josiah Wedgwood*, 2 vols., London, 1865–6, II, p. 66) as the London and Middlesex Bank, Stratford Place, London (see also R. M. Hower, *The Wedgwoods: Ten Generations of Potters*, privately reprinted, New York, 1975, from the *Journal of Economic and Business History*, IV, nos. 2 and 4, February and August 1932, and others), an identification corrected by Una des Fontaines in 'The Darwin Service and the First Printed Floral Patterns at Etruria' (Wedgwood Society *Proceedings*, no. 6, 1966, p. 76 and n. 2), who pointed out that this bank was not founded until 1862.
28. W/M 32 17 June 1793, Josiah Wedgwood to John Wedgwood (draft).
29. LHP 16 April 1793, Josiah Wedgwood II to Josiah Wedgwood.
30. E25–18837 12 May 1788, Josiah Wedgwood to Josiah Wedgwood II.
31. E26–19108, Last Will and Testament of Josiah Wedgwood dated 2 November 1793. Proved July 1795.
32. E26–18993 9 May 1790, Josiah Wedgwood to Josiah Wedgwood II.
33. Quoted by Desmond King-Hele, *Erasmus Darwin*, New York, 1963, p. 26.
34. WMS 39–28410, Commonplace Book, 'Dr Darwin's prescription for Mr W Nov 20 1794: Alum 5 grains, nutmeg 10 grains, Make them into a powder, which is to be taken at XI in the forenoon & VII in the evening every day with the following draught: Decoction of Bark 14 drams, Tinct of Bark 2 drams; Mix Rhubarb half a dram, to be divided into 6 papers, one of which to be taken every night at bedtime'.
35. Meteyard, *Life*, II, p. 610.

36. This account is based on Tom Byerley's letter dated 18 January 1795 to Samuel Boardman in Liverpool (see Robin Reilly, *Wedgwood*, 2 vols., London, 1989, I, p. 142, where it is quoted at length). This flatly contradicts the account published by Barbara and Hensleigh Wedgwood (*The Wedgwood Circle 1730–1897*, London, 1980, pp. 103–4) in which it is suggested, with circumstantial detail, that Josiah's death was due to a self-administered overdose of laudanum supplied by Erasmus Darwin. This imaginative story, for which there appears to be no evidence but hearsay of the utmost unreliability, was first published by Lady Farrer (K. E. Farrer) (ed.), *Letters of Josiah Wedgwood*, 3 vols. Manchester, 1903–6, I, p. vii). It is entirely discredited by the account of Tom Byerley, who was present during the greater part of Josiah's last illness and had no reason to lie to his old friend Samuel Boardman.

CHAPTER TWENTY-FOUR
The Wedgwood Legacy

1. Cambridge University MSS. Quoted by Desmond King-Hele, *Doctor of Revolution*, London, 1977, p. 252.
2. W/M 1460 3 January 1792, Josiah Wedgwood II to Josiah Wedgwood.
3. W/M 47 14 October 1799, Josiah Wedgwood II to John Wedgwood.
4. For example, W/M 21 27 April 1790, Tom Wedgwood to Josiah Wedgwood II; LHP [n.d.] 1790, Josiah Wedgwood II to Tom Wedgwood; WMS 95–17650 February 1791, Tom Wedgwood to T. Byerley.
5. W/M 21 25 February 1802, Tom Wedgwood to Josiah Wedgwood II.
6. WMS 1–572 3 April 1802, Dr Matthew Baillie to R. W. Darwin. Copy made by Josiah Wedgwood II to send to Tom Wedgwood (the original was sent to Darwin).
7. Eliza Meteyard, *The Life of Josiah Wedgwood*, 2 vols., London, 1865–6, II, p. 585; Eliza Meteyard, *A Group of Englishmen 1795–1815*, London, 1871, pp. 156–8.
8. Meteyard, *A Group of Englishmen*, pp. 156–8.
9. W/M 21 25 February 1802, Tom Wedgwood to Josiah Wedgwood II.
10. Erasmus Darwin, *Zoonomia; or, The Loves of Organic Life*, 2 vols., London, 1794–6, II, pp. 300–50.
11. Quoted by King-Hele, *op. cit.*, p. 248, Erasmus Darwin to Tom Wedgwood, 10 August 1794.
12. W/M 21 15 May 1804, Tom Wedgwood to Josiah Wedgwood II.
13. W/M 28 28 February 1800, Josiah Wedgwood II to Tom Wedgwood.
14. WMS 96–17766 16 September 1805, Josiah Wedgwood II to Sir James Mackintosh.
15. WMS 24–18026 A Partnership Agreement 1 October 1800; Una des Fontaines, 'Wedgwood's London Showrooms', Wedgwood Society *Proceedings*, no. 8, London, 1970, p. 207.

16. See WMS 121–23467 13 February 1802, WMS 121–23480 July 1802, WMS 121–23490 1 December 1802, T. Byerley to Josiah Wedgwood II; WMS 10–1808 21 June 1804, Simon Schopp, Augsburg, to Wedgwood and Byerley; WMS 121–23467 13 February 1802, T. Byerley to Josiah Wedgwood II.

17. V. W. Bladon, 'The Potteries in the Industrial Revolution', *Economic History*, no. 1, London, 1926, p. 126.

18. WMS 96–17796 16 September 1805, Josiah Wedgwood to Sir James Mackintosh. The manuscript of this letter, quoted at length by Meteyard, *Life*, pp. 297–9, is now incomplete.

19. Mayer MS quoted by Meteyard, *A Group of Englishmen*, pp. 183–4.

20. WMS 13–12815, 'Balance Account of Josiah Wedgwood & Byerley 1810 corrected as agreed', 10 May 1814.

21. WMS 50–29940, 'List of bad debts accruing in 1807 . . . and Outstanding Debts' 29 December 1810.

22. WMS 28–20068–69 [12?] November 1811, Josiah Wedgwood to John Wedgwood (draft).

23. See Robin Reilly, *Wedgwood*, 2 vols., London, 1989, II, pp. 505 and 509.

24. WMS 27–19835 13 July 1817, Catherine Wedgwood to Josiah Wedgwood II.

25. Frances Allen to Elizabeth Wedgwood [July 1843]. Quoted by H. E. Litchfield (ed.), *Emma Darwin: A Century of Family Letters*, 2 vols., Cambridge, 1904, II, p. 83.

26. Hope Wedgwood to Julia Wedgwood, 22 September 1887. Quoted by Barbara and Hensleigh Wedgwood, *The Wedgwood Circle*, London, 1980, p. 334.

27. E25–18264 1 October 1769.

28. Sir G. Stanton, *Embassy of Lord Macartney to the Emperor of China 1792–3*, London, 1797, p. 42.

SELECT BIBLIOGRAPHY

1. MANUSCRIPT MATERIAL

The Wedgwood collection of manuscripts deposited at Keele University and held at the Wedgwood Museum, Barlaston, has provided by far the greatest part of the primary source material for this biography. This remarkable collection is still in the process of being catalogued. The principal subdivisions are:

Etruria Collection (E prefix), which includes most of the surviving letters from Josiah Wedgwood to Thomas Bentley.
Liverpool Collection (generally identified by an L prefix, which has been discarded for the notes in this volume)
Leith Hill Place Collection (LHP prefix)
Mosley Collection (W/M prefix)

Detailed references to these and to all other primary source material are given in the Notes and References.

2. PUBLISHED BOOKS

Ashton, T. S., *The Industrial Revolution*, London, 1948. *An Economic History of England: The 18th Century*, London, 1955
Auckland, Robert J., 3rd Baron, Bishop of Bath and Wells (ed.), *The Journal and Correspondence of William, Lord Auckland*, 4 vols., London, 1862
Beard, Geoffrey, *The Work of Robert Adam*, Edinburgh, 1978
Bentley, Richard, *Thomas Bentley*, London, 1927
Berg, Maxine, *The Age of Manufactures*, London, 1985
Bindman, David, *John Flaxman R.A.*, London, 1979
Boardman, James, *Bentleyana; or a Memoir of Thomas Bentley*, Liverpool, 1851
Burton, William, *Josiah Wedgwood and His Pottery*, London, 1922
Byng, Hon. John, *The Torrington Diaries*, ed. C. Bruyn Andrews, 4 vols., London, 1936
Cannon, John, *Aristocratic Century*, Cambridge, 1984

Clark, J. C. D., *English Society 1688–1832*, Cambridge, 1985
  Revolution and Rebellion, Cambridge, 1986
Clarkson, T., *History of . . . the Abolition of the African Slave Trade*, 2 vols.,
  London, 1808
Constable, W. G., *John Flaxman*, London, 1927
Cunningham, Allan, *Lives of the Most Eminent British Painters, Sculptors
  and Architects*, 2nd edn., 6 vols., London, 1830
Darwin, Charles, *Life of Erasmus Darwin*, London, 1879
Darwin, Erasmus, *The Botanic Garden*, Part I *The Economy of Vegetation*,
  London, 1791; Part II *The Loves of the Plants*, Lichfield, 1789
  Zoonomia; or the Laws of Organic Life, London, 1794–6
Day, Thomas, *The Dying Negro*, London, 1773
Deane, Phyllis, *The First Industrial Revolution*, Cambridge, 1965
Dickinson, H. W., *James Watt*, Cambridge, 1936
Edgeworth, R. L., and Edgeworth, Maria (eds.), *Memoirs of Richard
  Lovell Edgeworth*, 2 vols., 1820 (reprinted Shannon, 1969)
Falkner, Frank, *The Wood Family of Burslem*, London, 1912
Farrer, K. E. (Lady Farrer) (ed.), *Letters of Josiah Wedgwood*, 3 vols.
  Manchester, 1903–6
Fitzmaurice, Lord Edward, *Life of William, Earl of Shelburne*, 3 vols.
  London, 1875–6.
Fothergill, Brian, *Sir William Hamilton, Envoy Extraordinary*, London,
  1969
Goodison, Nicholas, *Ormolu: The Work of Matthew Boulton*, London, 1974
Granville, Mary (Mrs Delany), *Autobiography and Correspondence*, 2 vols.
  London, 1862
Gray, J. M., *James and William Tassie*, Edinburgh, 1894
Hamilton, Sir William, and d'Hancarville, P. H., *Antiquités étrusques,
  grecques et romaines*, 4 vols., Naples, 1766–7
Hankin, Christiana C., *The Life of Mary Anne Schimmelpenninck*, London,
  1860
Harris, John, *Sir William Chambers*, London, 1970
Haynes, D. E. L., *The Portland Vase*, 2nd revised edn., London, 1975
Hillier, Bevis, *Master Potters of the Industrial Revolution*, London, 1965
  Pottery and Porcelain 1700–1914, London, 1968
Honour, Hugh, *Neo-Classicism*, London, 1968
  Romanticism, London, 1978
Hower, Ralph, *The Wedgwoods: Ten Generations of Potters*, privately
  reprinted from the *Journal of Economic and Business History*, vol. IV,
  nos, 2 and 4, February and August 1932, New York, 1975
Irwin, David, *John Flaxman 1755–1826*, London, 1979

Jewitt, Llewellyn, *Life of Josiah Wedgwood*, London, 1865
The Wedgwoods, London, 1865
Jouveaux, Emile, *Histoire de trois potiers célèbres: B. Palissy, J. Wedgwood, F. Böttger*, Paris, 1874
King-Hele, Desmond, *Erasmus Darwin*, London, 1963
Doctor of Revolution: The Life and Genius of Erasmus Darwin, London, 1977
Klingender, Francis D., *Art and the Industrial Revolution*, London, 1972
Landes, D., *The Unbound Prometheus, Technological Change and Industrial Development in Western Europe from 1750 to the Present*, Cambridge, 1969
Lindsay, J., *Autobiography of Joseph Priestley*, Bath, 1970
Litchfield, H. E. (ed.) *Emma Darwin: A Century of Family Letters*, 2 vols., Cambridge, 1904
Litchfield, R. B., *Thomas Wedgwood*, London, 1903
Lyte, Charles, *Sir Joseph Banks*, Newton Abbot, 1980
McKendrick, Neil, Brewer, John, and Plumb, J. H., *The Birth of a Consumer Society: The Commercialization of Eighteenth-century England*, London, 1982
Malet, Hugh, *The Canal Duke: A Biography of Francis 3rd Duke of Bridgewater*, Newton Abbot, 1961
Malmesbury, 3rd Earl of (ed.), *Diaries and Correspondence of Sir James Harris, First Earl of Malmesbury*, 4 vols., London, 1844
Mankowitz, Wolf, *The Portland Vase and the Wedgwood Copies*, London, 1952
Mantoux, P. *The Industrial Revolution in the Eighteenth Century*, London, 1947
Marshall, Dorothy, *Eighteenth Century England*, London, 1968
English People in the Eighteenth Century, London, 1956
Mathias, Peter, *The First Industrial Nation: An Economic History of Britain 1700–1914*, 2nd edn., London, 1983
The Transformation of England, London, 1979
Maxwell, C. (ed.), *Travels in France during the Years 1787, 1788 and 1789 by Arthur Young*, Cambridge, 1950
Meteyard, Eliza, *A Group of Englishmen 1795–1815*, London, 1871
The Life of Josiah Wedgwood, 2 vols., London, 1865–6
Montfaucon, Bernard de, *Antiquité expliquée*, 5 vols. and Supplement 5 vols., Paris, 1719
Muirhead, J. P., *Life of James Watt with Selections from his Correspondence*, London, 1859
The Origins and Progress of the Mechanical Invention of James Watt, 3 vols., London, 1854

Nicolson, Benedict, *Joseph Wright of Derby*, 2 vols., London, 1968

Paget Toynbee, Mrs (ed.) *Letters of Horace Walpole*, 16 vols., London 1905

Pearson, Hesketh, *Doctor Darwin*, London, 1930

Pellew, Hon. George, *The Life and Corespondence of the Rt. Hon. Henry Addington, First Viscount Sidmouth*, 3 vols., London, 1847

Penderell-Church, J. J., *William Cookworthy 1705–80*, Truro, 1972

Porter, Roy, *English Society in the Eighteenth Century*, London, 1982

Porter, Roy and Teich, Mikulás (eds.), *The Enlightenment in National Context*, Cambridge, 1981

Price, E. Stanley, *John Sadler*, privately printed, 1948

Prideaux, J., *Relics of William Cookworthy*, Privately printed, 1853

(Priestley), *Memoirs of Dr Joseph Priestley Written by Himself to the year 1795*, 2 vols., London, 1806

Reilly, Robin, *Pitt the Younger*, London and New York, 1978
Wedgwood, 2 vols., London, 1989

Reilly, Robin, and Savage, George, *Wedgwood: The Portrait Medallions*, London, 1973
The Dictionary of Wedgwood, Woodbridge, 1980

Russell, Colin, *Science and Social Change 1700–1900*, London, 1983

Russell, Lord John (ed.), *Memorials and Correspondence of Charles James Fox*, 4 vols., London, 1853–7

Rutt, J. T. (ed.), *The Theological and Miscellaneous Works of Joseph Priestley*, 25 vols., London, 1817–31

St Fond, B. Faujas de, *Voyage en Angleterre, en Ecosse et aux Iles Hébrides*, 2 vols., Paris, 1797

Savage, George and Finer, Ann (eds.) *The Selected Letters of Josiah Wedgwood*, London, 1965

Schofield, R. E., *The Lunar Society of Birmingham*, Oxford, 1963

Seward, Anna, *Memoirs of the Life of Dr Darwin, Chiefly during his Residence at Lichfield*, London, 1804

Shaw, Simeon, *History of the Staffordshire Potteries*, Hanley, 1829

Smiles, Samuel, *Josiah Wedgwood*, London, 1894

Stanton, Sir George, *Embassy of Lord Macartney to the Emperor of China 1792–3*, London, 1797

Stone, Lawrence, *The Family, Sex and Marriage in England 1500–1800*, London, 1977

Stone, Lawrence and Stone, Jeanne C. Fawtier, *An Open Elite? England 1540–1880*, Oxford, 1984

Taylor, Basil, *Stubbs*, London, 1971

Thomas, John, *The Rise of the Staffordshire Potteries*, Bath, 1971

Towner, Donald, *Creamware*, London, 1978

Walpole, Horace, *The Last Journals*, 2 vols., London, 1910

Ward, John, *The Borough of Stoke-upon-Trent*, London, 1843

Warrilow, Ernest J. D., *History of Etruria, Staffordshire 1760–1951*, Hanley, 1962

Watkin, David, *Athenian Stuart: Pioneer of the Greek Revival*, London, 1982

C. R. Cockerell, London, 1974

Weatherill, Lorna, *The Pottery Trade and North Staffordshire 1660–1760*, Manchester, 1971

Wedgwood, Barbara and Hensleigh, *The Wedgwood Circle 1730–1897*, London, 1980

Wedgwood, Josiah (I), *Account of the Barberini, now Portland Vase. . . .* London, 1788 (?)

Wedgwood, Josiah Clement, *A History of the Wedgwood Family*, London, 1908

Wedgwood, Josiah Clement and Wedgwood, Joshua, G. E., *Wedgwood Pedigrees*, Kendal, 1925

Wedgwood, Julia, *The Personal Life of Josiah Wedgwood*, London, 1915

Williams, Basil, *The Whig Supremacy 1714–60*, Oxford, 1962

Williamson, G. C., *The Imperial Russian Dinner Service*, London, 1909

Wilson, C., *England's Apprenticeship*, London, 1965

Young, Arthur, *A Six Months' Tour through the North of England*, 4 vols., London, 1768

3. JOURNALS, PROCEEDINGS AND TRANSACTIONS

(References quoted in the text)

English Ceramic Circle *Transactions*

Northern Ceramic Society *Journal*

Royal Historical Society *Transactions*

Wedgwood Society *Proceedings*

Wedgwood International Seminar *Proceedings*

INDEX

Adam, Robert 90, 158, 163, 164, 291
Adam brothers 84, 118, 119–20, 152
Adams, William 133, 209
Adams family 29
advertising 214–17
agate 19–20, 82, 92, 109n
Ainslie, Sir Robert 222
Alders, Thomas 7, 8, 18, 20
Alembert, Jean le Rond d' 122
Alexander Severus, Emperor 316
Allen, Elizabeth ('Bessie') see Wedgwood
Allen, Louisa Jane ('Jenny') see
    Wedgwood
America: Boston Tea Party 231–2;
    'Cherokee clay' 14, 77, 79, 159–60,
    311; exports to 217, 222; taxation
    disputes 227–30; war of
    independence 232–9, 255–6, 257
Amherst, Jeffrey, 1st Baron 26
Amsterdam 220–1
Angelini, Giuseppe 296
animal figures 90
Anson, George, Baron 7
Anson, Thomas 54, 128, 211, 241
Antipuffado 215–16
Antiquarian Society 315, 325
aristocracy 202–4
Arkwright, Richard 140, 144
armorial ware 31, 211
Ashenhurst, Mrs (of the Ridgehouse
    Estate) 48, 58, 62, 66
Ashton, Hodgkinson & Co. 58
Auckland see Eden
Augustus the Strong, Elector of Saxony
    12–13, 14

Babington, Thomas 289
Bacon, Sir Francis 92, 199
Baddeley, John 209
Bagot, Sir William 54, 165, 232, 241
Baillie, Dr Matthew 343
Bakewell, James 101, 104, 130, 136
Bank House 67–8, 70–1, 93, 181
Banks, Sir Joseph: Chapel attendance
    247; JW's pyrometer 313, 315; Lunar
    Society 199, 247; Portland vase copy

showing 324–5, 328; portrait 295;
    Sydney Cove clay 329
Barbauld, Anna Laetitia 87, 174
Barberini family 317
Barlow, Stephen 143
Barrat, Joseph 103
Barrett, George senior 127
basaltes 85, see also black basaltes
bas-reliefs 87, 152, 154, 208, 294–5
Bastille medallions 277
Bateman, T. 56
Bath showrooms 210, 211n
Battersea Enamel Works 30
Bavaria, Electors of 14
Baxter, Alexander 102, 104, 124, 125, 131
Beauclerk, Lady Diana 297
Bedford, Francis Russell, 5th Duke of 203
Bell Works 29, 139
Bent, James 69, 111, 143, 340
Bent, William 143
Bentley, Hannah (née Oates) 36
Bentley, Mary (née Stamford) 36, 172,
    211n, 245–6, 250–1
Bentley, Thomas: accounts 112–13,
    115–16; advertising 215–16; advice
    on education 171, 173, 174, 176, 334;
    background 31–2; Bank House
    67–8, 70–1, 93, 181; Boulton
    relationship 83, 87; canal schemes
    50–7; care of Sukey 171–2; Chelsea
    Decorating Studio 99–101, 104, 106;
    colour trials 153; death 248–9, 251–2;
    Etruria plans 66–72; export
    marketing 219; Flaxman's work
    294–5; Franklin acquaintance 287;
    friendship with JW 31–2, 95, 98–9,
    111–12, 182, 240–1; friendship with
    Priestley 195; friendship with Sarah
    W. 245; 'Frog' service 124, 128–9;
    health 247–8; jasper trials 156; JW's
    illness 69–70; JW's letters ix, xi,
    32–3, 43, 58, 97, 243–5; London
    showrooms 94, 98–9, 119–21, 130,
    250; marriage 245–6; Octagon Prayer
    Book 52–3; politics 253–5; portrait
    163; print-and-enamel patterns 137;
    Russian orders 124; sponsorship